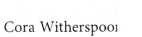Cora Witherspoon

Cora Witherspoon

A Life on Stage and Screen

AXEL NISSEN

McFarland & Company, Inc., Publishers
Jefferson, North Carolina

Unless otherwise noted, all illustrations are from the author's collection.

ISBN (print) 978-1-4766-8510-6
ISBN (ebook) 978-1-4766-4661-9

LIBRARY OF CONGRESS AND BRITISH LIBRARY
CATALOGUING DATA ARE AVAILABLE

Library of Congress Control Number 2022015514

Front cover: Cora Witherspoon by Clarence Bull,
MGM, 1938 (Photofest)

Printed in the United States of America

McFarland & Company, Inc., Publishers
Box 611, Jefferson, North Carolina 28640
www.mcfarlandpub.com

In memory of
Chester P. Sadowy
(1949–1999)

Table of Contents

Preface

"I have always been sort of a character actress."[1]

Alex Barris once described her as a "gawky tree full of birds." David Ragan observed that "her face was made for gossiping." Walter Winchell wrote at the height of her career that her "actressing on the New York stages and in the cinema studios is big time."[2] Tennessee Williams portrayed her in his *Memoirs* as the denizen of a New York hotel for women of a certain age and limited prospects where he ran the elevator at night. He also outed her as a morphine addict. Born into a prominent family in New Orleans in 1890, Cora Bell Witherspoon was an orphan by the age of ten and a professional actress by 15. She appeared on Broadway between 1910 and 1946 and in Hollywood films between 1931 and 1954. After a smattering of roles in television in the 1950s, she retired to Las Cruces, New Mexico, and died there in 1957. She never married.

Witherspoon's career spanned 50 years and six decades from the era of the Gibson Girl to that of the Sweater Girl. During her half-century on the stage and the screen, she supported a breathtaking number and variety of stars from Laura Nelson Hall in 1905 to Judy Holliday in 1954; from Henrietta Crosman, born in 1861, to Natalie Wood, born in 1938. In between, and in chronological order, she worked with stars like Amelia Bingham, Ruth Chatterton, Jessie Bonstelle, Grace George, Marie Doro, Ina Claire, Ruth Gordon, Ethel Barrymore, Fay Compton, June Walker, Tallulah Bankhead (on stage and screen), Lillian Gish, Francine Larrimore, Miriam Hopkins, Spring Byington, Myrna Loy, Ann Sothern, Madeleine Carroll, Jean Harlow, Katharine Hepburn, Gloria Stuart, Gladys George, Maureen O'Sullivan, Norma Shearer, Shirley Temple, Bette Davis, Vera Zorina, Gertrude Lawrence, Martha Scott, Mary Martin, Sylvia Sidney, ZaSu Pitts, Irene Dunne, Rosalind Russell, Jane Russell, Fay Emerson, Gene Tierney, Barbara Hale, Joan Evans, Betty Field, Nancy Kelly, Ann Harding, Miriam Hopkins, Teresa Wright, Frances Dee, Mary Astor, Nina Foch, and Arlene Dahl.

Witherspoon also supported male stars like Leo Ditrichstein (for ten years), Henry Miller, Fredric March, Glenn Hunter, Harry Ellerbe, George M. Cohan, Wheeler and Woolsey, Harry Richman, Bob Hope, Roland Young, Robert Montgomery, William Powell, Dick Powell, Robert Taylor, Harold Lloyd, Frank Morgan, Wallace Beery, Sidney Toler, W.C. Fields, Charles Coburn, John Lund, Robert Cummings, Bing Crosby, Franchot Tone, Hurd Hatfield, and Basil Rathbone. And those are just the more familiar names...

Witherspoon was first and foremost a top tier Broadway character actress. Two of my previous subjects, Beulah Bondi and Agnes Moorehead, had more spectacular screen careers, but they had nothing on her as far as their stage careers were concerned.

1

Witherspoon appeared regularly on the "Great White Way" for 25 years between 1910 and 1936 and made a comeback there in 1941, after the main phase of her film career was over. In the end, she had appeared in 36 Broadway shows and had created 31 roles. Witherspoon played characters like Sallie McBride in *Daddy Long Legs*, Josephine Trent in *The Awful Truth*, Martha Culver in *The Constant Wife*, Prudence in *Camille*, and Mrs. Grant in *The Front Page*. Only twice, *Russet Mantle* in 1936 and *Ramshackle Inn* in 1944, did she come in as a replacement.

Witherspoon trickled into films on the East Coast in the early 1930s, did two films at RKO in 1931, and then, in 1936, the trickle became a gush when MGM brought her to Hollywood for a showy role in *Piccadilly Jim*. Like many supporting actresses, her screen time was limited, but she made the most of it, whether waiting on Tallulah Bankhead in her first film, *Tarnished Lady*, or fawning over Judy Holliday in her last, *It Should Happen to You*.

Witherspoon was W.C. Fields' shrewish wife Agatha Sousé in *The Bank Dick*; Bette Davis's fair weather friend Carrie in *Dark Victory*; the frowsy maid Patty in *Quality Street*, paired off with Eric Blore; and, in one of her finest screen performances, she was the overbearing dowager Mrs. Williamson in *The Mating Season*.

Both in the theater and in films, Witherspoon portrayed a comprehensive range of stereotypes of older women: the termagant wife, the snobbish society woman, the viper-tongued gossip, the lovelorn spinster, the flibbertigibbet or a combination of these types. She was unique in her striking portrayals of libidinous older women, who by the standards of the day were *not* attractive. In the end, she became her own type.

Witherspoon appears to have been the real-life embodiment of a Helen E. Hokinson cartoon woman. In an interview with the *Brooklyn Daily Eagle* in 1935, though, she reflected on the disparity between her characters and herself:

> "Playing silly women has nothing to do with my character," she says, with the raising of the eyebrows, as they might be raised by a spoiled child who is compelled to do something she doesn't want to do…. "Because of my nose that turns up, because I have a naturally gay character and a voice that breaks, I may fit these parts," she agrees. But she is convinced that the roles she plays best are those she never plays, the dramatic roles. "The roles you play," she protests, "affect your reputation. If you play a lovely woman, off stage you are taken for a lovely woman. And if you play silly women all the time…"

As if to underscore the contrast between Witherspoon in real life and many of her characters, the interviewer remarks that "her pleasant personality immediately makes me feel less formal. She smiles. And when she smiles she smiles all over her face." Two years later, Witherspoon observed: "I like simple direct people who think clearly and are unaffected. I've been accused of affectation myself but not by anyone who knew me…. What appears to be an affectation may be natural. Only people who think clearly are capable of insight that reveals a difference."[3]

While most classic Hollywood character actresses lived quiet, uneventful, and well-regulated lives, Witherspoon was the exception to the rule. Though scant evidence remains, it is sufficient to tell us that life for her was difficult at times. During the years of her Hollywood heyday, possibly long before then, and probably long after, she was addicted to morphine, which she self-administered with a hypodermic needle. This substance abuse problem was known to some of her friends and associates and became public knowledge in September 1940, when she was charged with "possessing hypodermic equipment suitable for use in narcotic injections" and narcotics addiction. She was arrested again in July 1951 for public drunkenness, when out walking her dog. The *Los Angeles Times* carried the story on page two with a picture of a disheveled, indignant Witherspoon and an even larger picture of her dog. The Associated Press broadcast the story to the world.

Thus Witherspoon was publicly outed in 1940 as a drug addict and in 1951 as a possible alcoholic as well. Her financial insolvency was also a topic in the newspaper columns. It is painful to consider the public shaming she was subject to on several occasions; a "bad press" that has no parallel in the life story of any other character actress I can think of. Yet Witherspoon soldiered on, as if nothing had happened. Clearly, she was a functioning addict, working the hardest during the years we know for certain that she was addicted. Fortunately, this scandalous press focus did not impact negatively on her professional life; in fact, it may even have served to remind producers that she was still available at a point when her screen career was on the wane.

A *Boston Globe* staff writer observed in 1976, in connection with the publication of a book on Norma Shearer, that "if these 'Films of…' books continue someone will be coming up with the definitive book on Cora Witherspoon."[4] Well, it has taken 46 years, but that book is now in your hands. This is a full-scale biography, though, not just a "Films of" type book. It covers Witherspoon's family background and personal life but is primarily a detailed account of her entire acting career and the contribution she made to the American entertainment industry in the first half of the twentieth century. This is a book about an actress and the women she played.

When I think of the many hours of pleasure my research into Hollywood character actresses has given me, I am grateful to these women for their strength and resilience, their infinite talent, and their inspirational lives. I try to honor them by being honest and forthright about their strengths and weaknesses. I am neither a hagiographer nor a muckraker, but I do have a camp perspective on life, which I consider to be a useful quality in dealing with subjects whose importance is not universally acknowledged.

For assistance in various matters relating to this book, I would like to thank Ron Bowers, Howard Mandelbaum, Fredrick Tucker, and Amanda Woolard. I have dedicated this volume to my teacher, colleague, and friend Chester P. Sadowy, who died all too soon of a massive heart attack in 1999. He would have turned 50 that year. I remember thinking when Chester died that it would never be as fun at work again. Unfortunately, I was right. Chester supported me at a time when I did not feel supported by many colleagues. I think he rather enjoyed having an "in your face," openly gay man in the department. I will miss Chester as long as I live.

Note: The abbreviation NYPL refers to the Cora Witherspoon clipping file, Billy Rose Theatre Division, New York Public Library for the Performing Arts. Unless otherwise stated, production dates for films are taken from the AFI catalogue at aficatalogue. afi.com.

1

Cousin Cora

Early Life and Career

Miss Witherspoon is highly connected in New Orleans,
being related to the Denis, Bell and Witherspoon families.[1]

In the usual, hyped-up terms of the studio press release, Cora Witherspoon's father was once described as "a well-known lawyer" and her mother as "one of the social leaders of the picturesque Louisiana city."[2] The truth was less spectacular and more interesting. As the epigraph from 1907 indicates, Witherspoon belonged to the upper echelons of New Orleans society. It fails to mention, though, that she was a poor relation and, from the age of ten, an orphan. Her father Henry never amounted to much, and her mother Cora did not live long enough either to make much of an impact on her youngest child. Unlike nearly all their female relatives, married and single, Cora and her sister Maude worked and supported themselves their entire lives.

Henry Edgeworth Witherspoon was born in Greensboro, Alabama, on April 6, 1844, as the youngest of the four children of Daniel McCalla Witherspoon (1805–55) and Mary Jane Casey Witherspoon (1815–69). The family moved to Mobile soon after Henry's birth, where his father died when Henry was ten.[3] A slave schedule from 1860 shows that Henry's widowed mother Mary owned six slaves: five men between 40 and 70 and a woman of 26.[4] Like his two older brothers, Henry Witherspoon fought in the Civil War on the Confederate side. On May 1, 1862, when he was only 18, he was appointed aide-de-camp to General Danville Leadbetter (1811–66), a career general who had also been chief engineer of the state of Alabama. That month, Leadbetter was given command of the 1st Brigade in the District of East Tennessee. Henry resigned on July 22.[5] He moved to New Orleans in 1865, when he was 21.[6]

H.E. Witherspoon, as he was known, lived for nearly 54 years on this planet and left few traces of worldly success or other achievements. Rather than being a lawyer, "well-known" or not, I have only found evidence that he worked as railway agent and a clerk. This is how he appears in a handful of news items; in the 1880 U.S. census, the year he turned 36; and in two voter registration records from the 1890s, towards the end of his life. Judging from the modest home his surviving family members were still occupying in 1900, two years after his death, he did not leave his widow and two daughters well provided for.

One could claim that Henry's main achievement in life was to have married the daughters of two rich and powerful men. On December 16, 1868, he wed Priscilla McDowell Withers at her home in Conti Street in Mobile, Alabama. "Sylla" Withers was one of the ten children of General Jones Mitchell Withers (1814–90), a rich lawyer, cotton broker, U.S. and later Confederate army officer, newspaper editor, and one-time mayor of Mobile. Henry was 24 and Sylla was 23.[7] Several news items in New Orleans newspapers in 1869 give us some idea of Henry's interests and activities. He was involved in charitable work; was a member of the Crescent City Yacht Club and competed in regattas; and was a velocipede enthusiast, the velocipede being a forerunner of the modern bicycle.[8] All this sounds very much like the activities of a gentleman of leisure. The young couple were only married between two and three years, before Sylla died in 1871 and was laid to rest in the Withers family plot in Mobile's Magnolia Cemetery.[9]

Fast forward nine years. When the census was taken in Baltimore on June 8, 1880, we find Henry living with his widowed sister Leslie Frick, her four children, and a cook at 20 McMechen St., which was razed to make way for the Jones Falls Expressway. Henry is 35, widowed, and employed as a clerk.[10] He was not to be single much longer, though, nor was he to remain in Baltimore. On August 24, 1880, he was married to Cora S. Bell, aged 30 according to the record, in Chicago's Grace Church, which was then located on S. Wabash Ave. between 14th and 15th St., but has since been razed. The Rev. W.E. Phillips officiated.[11]

As it happened, Miss Bell was actually 34, and, furthermore, she was not a "miss." She was born Cora Slocomb Bell in New Orleans in December 1845, the daughter of a prominent merchant in the city called Samuel Bell (1800–76) and his wife Caroline Matilda Headington Bell (1816–74).[12] Cora was the couple's seventh child and fifth daughter and was named after the wife of her father's friend and business associate, the philanthropist Cora Ann Cox Slocomb (1811–84).[13] I mention this, because our Cora Witherspoon was also, indirectly, named for this woman, whom she never knew.

As it turns out, Mrs. Slocomb had a granddaughter who was also named after her: Mary Cora Urquhart. This child, born in New Orleans in 1857, grew into a major, international stage star of her day under her married name: Cora Urquhart Brown-Potter. She was one of the first American society women to become a stage actress. Having a similar background, but born 33 years later, the way for *our* Cora to be able to pursue a stage career without losing caste and burning her bridges was no doubt paved by the pioneering career of her namesake and fellow Orleanian Cora Urquhart Brown-Potter. Brown-Potter made her debut in Brighton, England, in 1887 and spent most of her career in London and on tour around the world, while New York society snubbed her on her few appearances there. She retired to Guernsey in 1912 and died in France in 1936.[14]

To return to Witherspoon's mother. Both her parents were dead by the time she married Henry Witherspoon in 1880, but she had a large extended family consisting of seven surviving siblings and their families, all living in New Orleans. Henry and Cora may well have known each other, or at least known *of* each other, for quite some time before tying the knot in 1880. One of my more interesting discoveries in researching Witherspoon's family background was that her father's older brother John married her mother's older sister Caroline in 1867, so that her Uncle John and Aunt Carrie were doubly so, both by blood and by marriage.[15] Two brothers married two sisters, in other words.

When the census was taken on June 9, 1880, "Cora S. Bell" was living with John and Carrie Witherspoon at 275 Indiana St. in Chicago.[16] In just a few months, she would be married to John's brother Henry, a marriage which was the second for both parties. Henry was widowed in 1871, as we have seen, and Cora was actually a divorced woman, having contracted an ill-conceived early marriage in 1865, when she was 19. Henry must have known of this "mésalliance," which lasted until 1877.

The man in question was Charles Vincent, who hailed from Norfolk, Virginia, "his family having been counted among the leaders of society Norfolk in years agone."[17] The young couple were married by "Rev. Mr. Beckwith" in New Orleans on August 3, 1865, the same year Henry Witherspoon moved to the Crescent City. Because Cora Bell was a minor, according to the statutes of Louisiana she had to have her father's written consent to the marriage. In a further twist, Cora's brother William A. Bell had to be a witness to the fact that was he "well acquainted" with his coming brother-in-law Charles Vincent and swear that he was "above the age of twenty-one years." Bell even had to provide a surety for Vincent's debt of one thousand dollars to the state of Louisiana, that would only be rendered null and void after two years, if "it should not appear that there existed at the time of granting such License any legal impediment to such marriage."[18]

Charles and Cora Vincent had two children, Carrie and Robert. Carrie was born in New Orleans in 1868 and her brother was born about a year later. I have discovered that Carrie Vincent died at 202 Dearborn Ave. in the Chicago "Loop" on May 15, 1881, thus about nine months after Henry and Cora married. She was 13 years old and was buried in Graceland Cemetery.[19] What happened to the boy, I do not know for certain. There is reason to believe that he died sometime between 1870 and 1880. He and his sister were living with their mother in their maternal grandparents' home in New Orleans when the census was taken on June 25, 1870. Their father was not living there. Eighteen seventy was the year the couple separated. By 1880, Cora only had her then 12-year-old daughter with her when she shared a home with John and Carrie Witherspoon in Chicago.[20] Robert would have been ten or eleven had he been alive.

By the time the Bell-Vincent marriage was over, and Charles had gone to the unusual step of divorcing Cora, they had been living apart for seven years. On January 18, 1877, an article appeared on the front page of the *National Republican* newspaper, published in Washington, D.C., lampooning the Vincents' rocky relationship under the title "She Would Not Remain: Why Did She Leave Him Alone and Forsaken." This anonymous, satirical piece explains that Charles Vincent found himself in New Orleans at the close of the Civil War. "He had long heard of the beauty of the girls of the Crescent City, and withstood all their bewitching flatteries and attractions until he met Cora Bell, and then he surrendered almost immediately." The article gives the correct date of their nuptials and even notes that they were married by "Rev. Mr. Beckwith, now bishop of Georgia." The account goes on to relate that "it was smooth sailing for five years, and in the interim one child came to brighten their lives and cement the ties existing between them." As we have seen, there were two children born during this period. Then, in 1870, the article states, when they were sojourning in Norfolk, Virginia, "a change passed over the little family, and discord put up its first milestone, many more of which were rapidly added." Cora, "who had always been a woman of impulse, suddenly resolved to deny herself Charles' company in the future, and seek the roof of her parent, Samuel Bell, who still resided in New Orleans": "she packed her baggage and went south by the next train without condescending to bid her husband good-bye or inform him of her intention of abandoning his roof and protection for all time to come." The article concluded: "Now he asks the court to grant him a divorce."[21]

Charles Vincent was granted a divorce from Cora Vincent by Judge Wylie in Washington on June 7, 1877.[22] Not only was divorce rare at this time, but it was even rarer for a husband to divorce his wife. As it happens, Charles had a motivating factor in his desire to marry again. Like Henry, he would prove to have a talent for courting and marrying the daughters of rich, powerful men, but in Charles's case the fortune-hunter tendencies were more pronounced. Now he had an even bigger fish to fry than Cora Bell. On June 16, 1877, nine days after he obtained his divorce, he married heiress Rosa Postell Steele (1847–1920) in Washington, D.C., though one newspaper claimed the couple had eloped to Baltimore.[23] Rosa was the daughter of Franklin Steele (1813–80), an immensely rich lumber baron, industrialist, and early settler of Minneapolis. Charles and Rosa Vincent had three children: Rosa C. Vincent Potter (1879–1965), Frederick Steele Vincent (1880–1916), and Maud Vincent Garnett (1883–1969). The couple was divorced in October 1884, after two rounds in court.[24] Charles Vincent died in obscurity in the nation's capital in late 1897. In his death record, he is listed as a "laborer" and "widowed." He is also listed as being 52, which means he was born in 1845. This also means he was a minor and married Cora Bell illegally back in 1865.[25]

Henry and Cora Witherspoon welcomed their first child, Maude Lillian, in Chicago on March 16, 1882, after about a year and a half of marriage.[26] In June 1884, the year he turned 40, Henry was struck by a serious illness and was described as "very ill" in the *New Orleans Times-Picayune*. He was then working as "Southern Passenger Agent of the Gulf Coast line," a railroad line. In August that same year, he is described as "Passenger and Ticket agent of the New Orleans and Washington through line" in a news item about his "entirely renovated and repaired as well as handsomely decorated" new office at 102 Canal St. Maude's 1970 obituary states that she moved to New Orleans from the city of her birth in 1886, but clearly the move happened before then.[27]

The main event, which all this has been leading up to, did not take place till January 5, 1890. On that day our subject, Cora Bell Witherspoon, entered the world in New Orleans, Louisiana. There is no question about her date of birth, which is consistent in the records.[28] Witherspoon is unusual among the actress class for never trying to make herself younger than she was. The only time I have discovered her less than accurate about her age, she made herself out to be *older*.[29]

Little Cora was in many ways a belated child. Her mother and namesake was in her

This is the earliest known photograph of Witherspoon, taken in a studio with her doll when she was about a year old. Witherspoon would remain cute as a button for quite some time, despite going through a rough patch during her teenage years, as so many of us do. She was born into a large, wealthy, and well-connected family in New Orleans in 1890, though her father appears not to have had much career success. He died in 1898 and her mother two years later. Thus Witherspoon found herself an orphan at the age of ten and was raised by her mother's unmarried sister Sophie and brother Samuel Bell (Billy Rose Theatre Division, The New York Public Library for the Performing Arts).

44th year when Cora was born, and her father was a year older. Not only that, Cora was the last-born first cousin on both sides of her family. Because she was born at a time when most of her aunts and uncles were becoming grandparents, not parents, many of her cousins were substantially older than her. In fact, Witherspoon was closer in age to their children, her first cousins once removed. She never knew any of her grandparents, who all died long before she was born; and five of her uncles and one aunt had passed on before she arrived on the scene.

Despite these losses, many remained who could claim kinship with Cora Witherspoon, the most famous, and at times the most infamous, member of the extended Bell and Witherspoon families: Aunts and uncles, first cousins, second cousins, first cousins once removed, and cousins by marriage. She had relatives coming out of her ears. What she did not have, though, for long, was what was considered a traditional, nuclear family. She was an orphan by the age of ten, though she was far from abandoned. She would always have her older sister Maude as the one constant in her life; and, until their deaths, her mother's brother Samuel and sister Sophie would act *in loco parentis*.

Witherspoon's ancestry was Southern on both sides and through several generations. The notable exception was her thrifty and industrious maternal grandfather Samuel Bell, who was born in Belfast in 1800. Samuel immigrated to the United States in 1816 and settled in Louisville, Kentucky, the year his future wife Caroline Matilda Headington was born there. The couple married in 1834, when she was 18 and he 34. Witherspoon's maternal grandparents settled in New Orleans in about 1838, where Samuel Bell built a thriving business as a merchant and later a banker. He died of cerebral embolism in 1876, two and a half years after his wife.[30]

While the descendants of Samuel and Carrie Bell were remarkably unified and stable in their tendency to live in New Orleans all their lives, the Witherspoons were more peripatetic and geographically spread. As we have seen, Cora's father Henry moved away from Alabama when he was 21 and spent the last 33 years of his life mainly in New Orleans, but also in Baltimore and Chicago. His three older siblings also spent their lives away from their native state. Henry's oldest brother, Thomas Casey Witherspoon (1836–1917), was a cotton dealer and raised his family in Natchez, Mississippi, before moving to St. Louis in 1878.[31] He and his wife Mary Ann Conner Witherspoon (1843–97) had two sons: Thomas Casey Witherspoon II (1868–1957) and William Conner Witherspoon (1872–1951). Cousin Thomas was an eminent surgeon, who spent his career in St. Louis and Butte, Montana. Cousin William worked as a salesman. His descendants still live in St. Louis. Both brothers were involved in scandalous divorces, remarried much younger women, and ended their lives in California.

Henry's other brother, John M. Witherspoon (1837–1888), who married Cora Witherspoon's maternal aunt Caroline M. Bell (1841–1925), was a banker and lived in Chicago until his death from sciatic rheumatism at 51.[32] Uncle John and Aunt Carrie had three children: Grace Witherspoon (1869–1949) was an unmarried sometime school teacher, John M. Witherspoon (1872–1928) was an unmarried architect and engineer, and Leslie Witherspoon (1876–1922) was married and worked as a salesman and was later vice president of a construction company. Grace and Leslie lived in Los Angeles, while John lived in Arizona.

Henry's only sister, Leslie Witherspoon Frick (1840–1917), spent her adult life in Baltimore, where she had married a scion of the socially prominent Frick family, William Frick, Jr., a civil engineer and machinist, in 1864.[33] He died between 1875 and 1880, leaving her with four children to raise on her own. Leslie would name the youngest of them after her brother: Henry Edgeworth Frick (1875–1960). I initially thought this aunt was an uncle! Leslie appears as a male in no less than three U.S. censuses: 1850, 1860, and 1910.[34] Leslie and her older brother Thomas died within two weeks of each other in 1917.[35]

Witherspoon's New Orleans childhood would have been dominated by her mother's large and socially prominent family, who nearly all lived either on St. Charles Ave. or at most two or three blocks north or south of that fashionable thoroughfare, in the Garden District, Touro, and the Fourteenth Ward. Cora Witherspoon, Sr., had seven siblings who lived to adulthood and a sister who died young.[36] In order of birth, the nine brothers and sisters Bell were Maria Winn Bell Norton (formerly Wisdom; 1835–99), William Alexander Bell (1836–84), Mary Ann Bell (1839–49), Caroline M. Bell Witherspoon (1841–1925), Arabella Harlan Bell Denis (c. 1843–1918), Samuel H. Bell (1844–1923), Cora Slocomb Bell Witherspoon (1845–1900), Sophie J. Bell (1847–1915), and Mary Elizabeth Bell Renshaw (1852–1941). These aunts and uncles and their spouses produced 20 cousins who lived to maturity between 1854 and 1887. In turn, these 20 first cousins only produced 15 first cousins once removed over the course of the more than half a century between 1882 and 1933.

Witherspoon was undoubtedly closest to her mother's unmarried brother Samuel and unmarried sister Sophie. Sophie moved in with her sister Cora and her daughters, probably after Henry's death in 1898. During the years between her sister's death in 1900 and her own death in 1915, Aunt Sophie was niece Cora's loyal supporter, chaperone, and friend, who made it possible for an innocent, privileged, and protected teenage girl to embark on an acting career involving extensive travel and exposure to potential dangers and risks.

Samuel H. Bell was a man of some distinction in New Orleans. "The man who did more than any individual to found and organize Metairie Cemetery," he was the cemetery's manager and guiding spirit from its inception in 1872. In his obituary, he was also described as a "swamp lands rescuer, landscape gardener and Confederate veteran."[37] Samuel spent the last 33 years of his life in a domestic partnership with a cotton merchant called Ernest Cucullu, born in New Orleans in 1835 and thus nine years his senior. They had met during the Civil War and lived for decades in a rambling Victorian house, which still stands at 1422 N. Rampart St., only a few blocks north of Witherspoon's childhood home at no. 1014.[38] Uncle Samuel, who had no children of his own, no doubt helped finance his niece's education. As we shall see, he also gave her encouragement and material assistance when she decided to become an actor.

Her sister Maude, who was 18 when their mother died and eight years older than Cora, might also have been a source of emotional support for her. Unfortunately, there is evidence that Maude was not always a positive influence in her sister's life as she was growing up. Maude looked down on her sister for being, in her opinion, physically unattractive and did not support her decision to go on the stage.[39] Fortunately, the sisters would grow closer in later life and ended up living on the same property in Las Cruces, New Mexico. This was after Maude had lost her life partner, Annie Miller.

Information about Cora Witherspoon's early life is limited but varied. What follows are a few vignettes about her and her family, that I have gleaned from the columns of New Orleans newspapers and from archival sources. They cover the first 15 years of her life, up until her professional stage debut in 1905. First of all, in a voter registration record dated August 22, 1891, we find H.E. Witherspoon, a self-employed clerk from

Still wearing her hair down and in short skirts, Witherspoon (far right) is on the cusp of womanhood in this undated family photograph. She was always a "big girl"; not overweight, but big boned, broad shouldered, and tall. I am almost certain that the woman next to her is her beloved aunt Sophie Bell, her mother's younger sister, who cared for her after her mother died in 1900 and chaperoned her during the first ten years of her acting career, until Sophie's death in 1915. Unfortunately, I have not been able to identify the three other adults and the child. My guess, though, would be that the elderly woman is another of Witherspoon's maternal aunts, while the middle-aged woman may be an older cousin with her husband and child. In a curious coincidence: Witherspoon was the youngest first cousin on both sides of her large extended family, just as my previous subject, Beulah Bondi, was (Billy Rose Theatre Division, The New York Public Library for the Performing Arts).

Alabama born in 1844, who has lived in New Orleans since 1865, residing at 238 N. Rampart St. He has lived in the Sixth Ward for seven years, which means that his daughter Cora was possibly born at this address, at the corner of Bienville Street on the edge of the French Quarter. The site is now a parking lot. The family was still living at this address in October 1896. Henry was still working as a self-employed clerk.[40]

Apart from the marriages of two older male cousins, Frank Frick for the first time at 33 and Mortimer Norton Wisdom for the third time at 44, the notable family event of 1898 was the death of Witherspoon's father. Henry Edgeworth Witherspoon expired at six o'clock in the morning of Saturday, February 26. He was 53 years old. There were no obituaries in the local papers, only the following death notice: "WITHERSPOON—On Saturday, February 26, 1898, at 6 o'clock a.m., H.E. Witherspoon, aged 53 years, a native of Greensboro, Ala. The funeral will take place from his late residence, 1014 N. Rampart St., on Sunday, Feb. 27, at 2 o'clock p.m. Interment private." Henry was the first to be laid to rest in the plot his brother-in-law Samuel Bell had secured for his and his family's use in Metairie Cemetery.[41] Cora Witherspoon would be buried there nearly 60 years later. We note that by the time of Henry Witherspoon's death, the family had moved seven and a half blocks north on Rampart St., near the corner of St. Philip St.

Mrs. H.E. Witherspoon, Cora's mother, made a rare appearance in the newspaper columns on May 27, 1899, when she was awarded a medal and first prize for "best rag dolls" at the Louisiana state fair. The author of the article noted that only three women had won awards at the fair and that all three were "New Orleans women, born and bred" and "self-made women in the same sense that we speak of the successful self-made man."[42] It is tempting to speculate that the widowed Cora Witherspoon, Sr., was augmenting the family income through the making and selling of these fine rag dolls, a ladylike activity that might bring in some needed extra cash. Two weeks earlier, Mrs. Witherspoon's eldest sister, Maria Winn Bell Norton, had died in New Orleans at the age of 64.[43] She was the first of Cora Senior's six sisters to pass away, apart from Mary Ann, who had died as a child half a century earlier.

The census enumerator James Sanchez called at the cottage at 1014 N. Rampart St. on June 1, 1900. He found ten-year-old Cora Witherspoon living there with her 54-year-old, widowed mother, her 18-year-old sister Maude, and her soon-to-be-53-year-old aunt, Sophie Bell. That is, Aunt Sophie was only admitting to 39. The census further records that Cora Witherspoon, Sr., is the mother of two children, who both are living, though we know she gave birth to four. Mrs. Witherspoon was listed as a "landlord" and Maude as being "at school."[44]

Death called at the house only a month and a half later. On the evening of Tuesday, July 17, 1900, Cora Slocomb Witherspoon passed away from uterine cancer. A death notice appeared in the *Times-Picayune* on July 19: "Mrs. Cora S. Witherspoon, 56 years, 1014 N. Rampart." Her age was given incorrectly here, but correctly in her death certificate. She was 54. On Thursday, July 19, an obituary was also printed, on page 12 of the *Times-Picayune*. There we can read that death occurred "on Tuesday evening, just as the sun was sinking to rest." Furthermore, "Mrs. Witherspoon was a noble, earnest woman, whose qualities endeared her to many" and "a loving, devoted mother, a true friend and an earnest, faithful Christian." It was noted that she was born Cora S. Bell and that she was the sister of Mr. S.H. Bell, secretary of the Metairie Cemetery Association. The article stated that she "was married early in life to Mr. H.E. Witherspoon, who preceded her some time ago to the grave." The truth was that she was 34 when she married Henry Witherspoon and he had been dead for only two and a half years. "Mrs. Witherspoon had been ill for some time, suffering from an incurable malady": "She bore her long suffering with patience and fortitude, and died, as she had lived, in loving peace with her savior. Her long illness was solaced by the tenderness and care of her brave young daughter, Miss Maud [*sic*] Witherspoon, and the love and attention of her brother, Mr. Bell." It was mentioned that Maude was working as the cashier of the Christian Woman's Exchange and there was a lengthy description of Maude's devotion and how she had lost her mother "at a time when a girl most needs her mother's care." Mrs. Witherspoon was "laid to rest in the beautiful burial plot of her brother" Wednesday morning. "The interment was private."[45]

In a comprehensive feature article from 1937, we can read that Witherspoon "was educated by private tutors at home and went to finishing school in Paris when she was 14."[46] I have been able to discover a little more than that. In 1902, Witherspoon was 12 years old and was attending the Pursell-Shields Graded School for Girls. The school had been founded by Mrs. M.E. Pursell-Shields in 1897, as the Graded School for Girls. Pupils of all ages were admitted and "given a thorough, practical education." The school specialized in preparing pupils for the high school department of H. Sophie Newcomb College and was originally located at 2829 Chestnut St. in the Garden District. It moved down the street to no. 2913 in 1901. The school year began October 1.[47]

In the *Times-Picayune* for June 17, 1902, we can read about the school's closing exercises the previous evening, where "four bright graduates" had been graduated. "The large and handsome parlors were nicely decorated with flowers and palms and potted plants." A reception committee consisting entirely of men "performed its duty in the most courteous manner, and provided the guests with seats." After an opening prayer, the pupils sang Mendelsohn's "Maybells and Flowers." Then "Cora Witherspoon recited a French selection," before "this young lady was awarded a medal for proficiency in French." Other pupils received medals for spelling, scholarship, algebra, and Latin. There were further musical numbers, one girl read the class essay, and finally the graduates were given their diplomas. "A class song concluded the exercises."[48]

In 1902 as well, Witherspoon was the secretary of the St. Anna's Society. St. Anna's Episcopal Church is still located at 1313 Esplanade Ave., not far from Witherspoon's home on N. Rampart St. The current church building is from 1952. The society had its own hall at 1315 Barracks St., a stone's throw from the church. There on February 7, 1902, they held a raglan party, where "Dancing and games of all kinds was the order of the evening": "The affair was a miniature carnival for the little folks, all of them having on masks and attired in fancy costumes." After refreshments had been served at 10 o'clock, "the children, highly delighted with their evening's entertainment, departed for their homes."[49]

On the afternoon of Monday, February 23, 1903, 13-year-old Cora attended a "musicale" in the "spacious rooms" of the Pickwick Club. She was accompanied by her aunt Sophie J. Bell. Her much older cousin, the noted New Orleans lawyer Mortimer Norton Wisdom (1854–1919), was also among the guests. The reception was "one of the most largely attended, as well as one of the most beautiful and interesting functions of the week," according to the *Times-Democrat*. The paper's society column was more concerned with listing the guests, than with relating what music was performed.[50]

H.H. Niemeyer once observed that "when a player signs a contract in the studios, it is the custom to record the biographical facts of their lives on a printed form." One of the "facts" that materialized for the first time in the press when Witherspoon arrived in Hollywood was that she had been partially educated in Paris. In a feature article at the height of her Hollywood film career by the aforementioned Niemeyer, based on the "biographical notes" Witherspoon had written on the studio's "printed form," he records that she "went to a finishing school in Paris when she was fourteen." Another article from this period noted: "When she was a youngster her family in the good old New Orleans tradition sent her to school in Paris. There she learned to speak French and German and acquired a British accent by frequent trips across the Channel." In 1941, the *Quincy Patriot Ledger* recorded that "at 14 she went to school for 18 months in France and there conceived an ambition to play on the French stage—something that she has never fulfilled." The same basic information—redolent of the press release—was used in an article on Witherspoon in the *Chicago Sun* in 1943.[51]

It seems unlikely that such a costly education would have been bestowed on an orphan girl, but Witherspoon was usually veracious in recording the facts of her life— including her age, so there is little reason to doubt that she spent time at school in Paris. Maybe her uncle Samuel, who had no children of his own, paid for her education. Maybe the extended family chipped in. Cora was considered plain, so perhaps the family thought it a good idea that she be prepared to provide for herself in the future; not that a finishing school was likely to prepare her for more than marriage.

The question remains when this Parisian sojourn took place. Witherspoon turned 14 on January 5, 1904. In Europe, the school year normally begins in August or September, so if she went over in the late summer of 1903, she would not have been back till late 1904. Indeed, there is no mention of Witherspoon in the local newspapers between February 23, 1903, and November 6, 1904. On the latter date, the *New Orleans Item* noted that she was acting as secretary of a three-day festival to be organized by her local church St. Anna's November 17–19.[52]

On the evening of Thursday, February 2, 1905, Witherspoon assisted at a "musical and dramatic entertainment for the benefit of the Maison Hospitalière," a home for elderly, impoverished women that had opened in 1893 and continued to serve the community for the next 113 years. It closed in the wake of hurricane Katrina in 2006, though the building still stands at 822 Barracks St. in the French Quarter. The benefit was held at the French Union Hall under the direction of Witherspoon's older friend and mentor Jessie E. Tharp. Since she was not listed as being part of the orchestra, the vocal quartette, or the banjo quartet, we can assume Witherspoon contributed a monologue or dramatic sketch to the program, as did her friend Jessie. The *Times-Picayune* noted that "quite a large audience was in attendance." In mid–July 1905, a group of amateurs formed a dramatic club in New Orleans to be called "The Thespians." The elected officers of the club were all men, but "among the young ladies taking part" were Witherspoon, Jessie Tharp, and Marcelle Parrat. The club planned to give its first performance in September.[53]

We know young Cora struggled with her appearance growing up, in a region, a time, and a segment of society where a young woman's physical attractiveness was subject to intense evaluation and would determine the future course of her life. So, too, it was with Witherspoon, though she would live off her looks in a way no one could have imagined. An article in the *Rochester Democrat and Chronicle* in 1932 was headlined: "'Pug-Nosed' Girl to Stage Modiste, That's Cora Witherspoon's Story." There she described herself as once a "'pug-nosed, flop eared, pie-eyed little girl.'" Article author Jean Walrath observed: "Now she is acknowledged to be one of the most smartly gowned women on the American stage and has that 'certain something' air that makes people look twice and then again. Her pale skin bears no rouge and there is no purple smear around her eyes." After conveying Witherspoon's "ideas on the 1933 fashions," we are told that she "wears only black and white, has cropped hair, and contends that good materials are three fourths of a good costume." The article continues: "The reason why Miss Witherspoon knows how to make a gown that would transform a 'mousey' little creature into an enchantress is because she practiced so many years on herself. As a child, with tears in her eyes, because people told her she was ugly, she would stand on a chair in front of a mirror trying her hair this way and that and pinning materials into all lines to make her 'look like somebody.'"[54]

The source of at least some of this emotional abuse was later revealed to have been her older sister Maude, who as late as 1939 expressed her amazement at Cora having become famous. Witherspoon elaborated on her sister's attitude in a 1942 interview with the telling title "Cora Witherspoon's Life Gives Homely Girls Hope": "As a girl, my sister used to tease me about my alligator eyes and dog ears.... My mirror discouraged me, but I worked so hard to overcome my shortcomings and to emphasize carriage, clothes and personality that I forgot all about my lack of beauty. It's a blessing not to be too pretty if you want a career. Take Bette Davis, for instance. I've often wondered if she ever felt

the way I used to and look where she is!"
Ironically, Witherspoon did not escape
having her appearance evaluated in this
interview either. Marjory Adams wrote:
"there's no dignified dowager look about
the lithe, vivacious lady who reminds
one somewhat of Ina Claire." Her eyes,
Adams added, were "as young as a debutante's and not nearly so bored."[55]

Witherspoon's background as an
unattractive child cast a long shadow.
This trauma even caused her to give
up her chance at her own movie serial,
when producer Bryan Foy at Warner
Bros. offered her the part of Mrs. Jiggs
in a projected series based on the comic
strip *Bringing Up Father.* Witherspoon
explained to John Hobart in 1939, "with
disarming candor": "'You see I've always
been plain. Since I was a little girl in New
Orleans, I've been told about my pig eyes,
my pug nose, my alligator mouth. And all
my life, I've thought about my looks, my
looks, my looks—and tried to improve
them. So I couldn't bring myself to be
identified permanently as Mrs. Jiggs,
who is a freak, a caricature; it would have
meant a wasted lifetime. Well, I probably
was a fool. Think of the money it would
have brought me, plus a steady job (they
were planning three pictures a year) and
radio engagements and world fame. But
I couldn't do it.'"[56] The idea for the series
was abandoned.

Witherspoon once said self-deprecatingly in
an interview, that the only thing she had going
for her when she first started out as an actress
was "a lot of hair." That is certainly confirmed
by this undated portrait of her as a young
woman with a Gibson Girl hairstyle, but otherwise the look of a maiden schoolteacher. The
characteristically pencil-thin eyebrows would
come later (Billy Rose Theatre Division, The
New York Public Library for the Performing
Arts).

Though the press sometimes gave that impression, Witherspoon was far from
untrained and untried by the time David Belasco cast her in her first Broadway show,
The Concert, in 1910. Her professional stage career had been underway for five years by
then. It began in her native New Orleans in 1905, when she was only 15 years old. Witherspoon summed up her five years' experience prior to Broadway in an interview in
1949: "First employment in a stock company in New Orleans—24 consecutive weeks—a
new play weekly—followed by five seasons of stock in Detroit, Buffalo, St. Louis, Denver,
New Haven and Chicago." She said further: "The stock companies of those days were
the training schools for most of the best actors—a play a week and three or four changes
of costume for each play—three matinees and seven nights weekly. We would rehearse
daily (except Thursday) from 10 a.m. to 4 p.m.—matinee days until 1 p.m. and often after
the performance at night."[57]

It turns out, though, that Witherspoon's exposure to the stage and to actors and singers began when she was a child. In an article in the *New York Herald Tribune*, we find the following rare anecdote from her childhood in New Orleans:

> There lived in the Latin quarter of New Orleans a kindly wigmaker and his buxom wife, named Variole. They catered to the opera singers who made their gallant stand at the old French Opera House. Most of them lived at the pension called La Maison Bourbon, a ramshackle, white stucco frame edifice with lacey grillwork, and at all hours of the day and night the dark mahogany corridors rang with the sounds of scales and obligati. Little Cora Witherspoon accompanied M. Variole on his professional visits to La Maison Bourbon and became so steeped in the traditions of grand opera that for a few delicious weeks she practiced her childish tremolos before her bedroom mirror in anticipation of an opera debut. A single audition, however, managed to deprive her of any such lofty ideas. So she bided her time till that fateful debut in "Janice Meredith."[58]

Indeed, the Variols (without the "e") were wigmakers in New Orleans for decades and their shop was located for many years at 220 Bourbon St. in the Latin Quarter. Michel Variol and his wife Angeline Bourgouin Variol founded the business in the 1870s and their son, Michel Charles Variol, joined the family concern and continued it into the 1930s. The elder Monsieur Variol died from blood poisoning on December 4, 1896, so Witherspoon was young indeed when she did the rounds with him.[59] When the business finally closed, it was one of only two wigmakers remaining in New Orleans.

According to an interview from 1941, Witherspoon decided to become an actress when she was 12 and "thenceforth announced it to her family." At first, it appears, "her family ... was shocked by the idea, and all her nice friends in New Orleans would step to the other side of the street when she came into view." Her sister Maude in particular "'really didn't like it.'" Yet there were exceptions. Her maternal uncle Samuel Bell told her: "'If you must go, little girl—go with a big ambition ahead of you.'" Fortunately, he was a trustee of the Grand Opera House and was able to persuade the manager, Charles Fourton, to give her an audition. The 15-year-old girl audaciously chose to portray both Elizabeth I and Mary Queen of Scots. "It was more pull than talent," she reflected modestly many years later, "that won her a place in the stock company."[60]

According to the *Times-Democrat* on the day of her debut: "Considerable interest attaches to the stage debut of Miss Witherspoon, who is a New Orleans girl and prepared for the stage under the able tutelage of that well-known and accomplished actress, Miss Emily Melville. She will be given an ingenue role, and her friends are looking forward to her appearance with pleasure." Then in her mid–50s, Emilie Melville (1851–1932) was part of the Baldwin-Melville stock company at the Lyric Theatre, the other of the two stock companies in New Orleans at this time. In her heyday in the 1870s and '80s, Melville had been an international star, who toured all over the world, including Australia. She had played Juliet to Lawrence Barrett's Romeo and Ophelia to Edwin Booth's Hamlet. She was also known for her roles in comic opera. When she died in San Francisco in 1932, the *New York Times* called her the "Doyenne of Our Stage."[61]

By this time, both the press and her social milieu had clearly determined not only to accept but to support Witherspoon's theatrical ambitions. She was described in the *New Orleans Item* as "a talented and charming girl, who is prominently connected in the social world." The paper assured its readers: "Naturally the friends of the fair Orleanian are greatly interested in her dramatic career and there will doubtless be quite a hearty welcome accorded her by her townspeople."[62]

Witherspoon made her professional stage debut at the Grand Opera House on Sunday, September 24, 1905, as Tabitha Drinker in *Janice Meredith*, an historical drama by Edward E. Rose and Paul Leicester Ford based on the latter's similarly titled novel. According to a review of the original New York production in 1900, "The play tells a story of the revolt against the British Crown, and illustrates the vicissitudes and perilous adventures that befell a Continental captain, who penetrated the Hessian lines in quest of information for General Washington and who was saved at a moment of extreme peril, by the intrepid, sagacious, and expeditious conduct of the girl that he loved." The advertisement for the play in the *Item* called it "A Fine Play of the American Revolution and the Battle of Trenton."[63]

In the New Orleans revival, the eponymous heroine was played by Frances Whitehouse. Witherspoon was cast as the ingénue Tabitha Drinker, "a part especially calculated to bring her forth favorably." On September 25, the subheading of the review in the *Times-Democrat* read "Miss Witherspoon Makes Successful Debut": "Cora Witherspoon, the local debutante, was thoroughly acceptable as Tabitha, who is something between an ingenue and a soubrette. She has beauty which is not of the conventional type, an excellent voice and rather graceful bearing, and she unquestionably possesses much more than average adaptability for the profession of her choice. She bids fair to become a pronounced local favorite."[64]

In an interview in 1944, Witherspoon recalled her debut nearly 40 years earlier: "she was instructed to 'enter hurriedly and collide with a uniformed Hessian soldier.' She kept her half of the contract but the Hessian, apparently worried about his stipend from the crown, failed to materialize. So, not finding this immovable body, Miss Witherspoon landed with irresistible force flat on her face, her hoop skirt over her head and her white starched pantalets in full view of the audience. She disentangled from the bulky crinolines, grinned sheepishly and decided to devote her life to making people laugh."[65]

Janice Meredith had been the second offering of the season. By the third week, the company's new leading lady, Laura Nelson Hall, had arrived and was to star in *A Modern Magdalen*, Haddon Chambers' adaptation from the Danish play *The Jansen Family*. Hall, who was 29, had made her stage debut eight years earlier. In 1904, her life had been struck by tragedy, when her husband, a fellow actor, shot and killed himself. She would make her Broadway debut in 1907 and died in obscurity in 1936. The reviews do not reveal what Witherspoon's role of "Lizzie" entailed, but she appeared in the supper scene and her name suggests a maid in a play where the major female characters are called Katinka, Olivia, and Evelyn.

Witherspoon was given one of her best opportunities that fall in *Mrs. Dane's Defense* by Henry Arthur Jones. The *Times-Democrat* reported on November 6, that "the character of Mrs. Bolsom-Porter was taken at very short notice yesterday morning by Miss Cora Witherspoon on account of the sudden illness of Miss Lilian Dix, but instead of stumbling through the part, as would be wholly excusable under the circumstances, the young actress made a pronounced hit in it. She was animated and vigorous in every scene and her excellent work contributed in no small degree to the success of the performance." *Mrs. Dane's Defense* deals with "the effort of a woman who has sinned to reinstate herself in society and to marry a good young man by a series of daring lies, and it ends with her defeat and humiliation." Mrs. Bolsom-Porter is Mrs. Dane's neighbor and "a malicious social regulator," who employs a detective to "ascertain the facts." She

On September 24, 1905, Witherspoon made her professional stage debut with the stock company at the Grand Opera House in *Janice Meredith* and played an entire season there. Originally built as the Varieties Theatre in 1871, this building stood on Canal Street, on the site currently occupied by the Ritz-Carlton Hotel. The theater closed in 1906 and was demolished to make way for a department store.

finally has to apologize for "groundless suspicions and unwarranted disparagement," even though her suspicions are correct. The role was created on Broadway by Ethel Hornick in 1900. According to the *Times-Picayune*: "Miss Cora Witherspoon was given the difficult role of Mrs. Bulsom-Porter [*sic*] on short notice, and she did remarkably well. With her ambition and ability she is laying the foundation for a stage career of more than ordinary fame." The *Item* noted that Witherspoon was "well received."[66]

The play of the week starting November 26 was Madeline Lucette Ryley's *An American Citizen*. Again, Witherspoon was given the opportunity to play a character role far beyond her years, as Carola Chapin is described in the stage directions as "an over-dressed lady of 50." The widowed Mrs. Chapin was typical comic relief character and exactly the type of silly, fussy, and flirtatious dowager role Witherspoon would later play on film. Witherspoon received several good notices for her performance: "Miss Cora Witherspoon had quite an important role, Mrs. Chapin, and presented it admirably. She has been doing remarkable work since her advent this season upon the stage"; "Miss Cora Witherspoon left little to be desired in her interpretation of Mrs. Chapin"; and "Miss Cora Witherspoon weeps the part of Carola Chapin with many tears, much grace and a few pocket handkerchiefs."[67]

Next Witherspoon "made the most of a small part" as Mrs. Ashton in *Hearts Aflame* by Genevieve G. Haines from 1902, "a play of social life." She also participated in the only disaster of the season, *Cinderella* performed as a Christmas play for children in a new version by the house director Charles Le Soir; and the following pantomime "Scaramouche." The *Times-Democrat* noted that "by the time 'Cinderella' had been disposed of more than half the audience had left." Maybe it was just as well, as the pantomime was deemed "one of the most risqué ever presented to a reputable audience in New Orleans": "'Scaramouche' ought not to be presented in any theatre without being labeled 'for men only,' and even men could get along very well without witnessing any such unsavory stage story, whether in dialogue or pantomime." And here a sheltered, not-yet-16-year-old daughter of the "haute bourgeoisie" was taking an active part! Not only that: as the Queen of the Azures, "Miss Witherspoon, the cigar factory girl, who married the King of Azures, could hardly have been excelled. She carried out every detail of her role and her consort, the king, Louis Morrison, kept the house in a continual uproar with the stories of their domestic troubles." While the *Times-Picayune* thought Morrison and Witherspoon should be "complimented on the drollness of their makeup," the *Times-Democrat* felt Witherspoon's make-up was "unnecessarily offensive."[68]

Witherspoon summed up a most eventful year in a Christmas greeting to the readers of the *Times-Picayune* on December 26, 1905: "I know that I was ambitious to be a figure on the stage. I know that I have managed to jump from the amateurs into good company, and I am sure I am working like a good one to please. I would rather win here in my native home than anywhere else in the world. I surely wish everyone here a merry merry Christmas and a happy new year—Cora Witherspoon."[69]

The first play of 1906, starting on New Year's Eve, was *The Gay Lord Quex* by Arthur Wing Pinero. Witherspoon was given yet another good opportunity, as Miss Moon, a manicurist, who is in and out in the scenes set in a beauty salon, getting patrons to buy things they do not need and drumming up business for the "palmist" Valma, whom she loves from afar. The *Times-Picayune* wrote that she "continues to give evidence of marked talent and made the most of a small part."[70]

The season continued with Witherspoon lending her talents to *The School for Scandal*, *Prince Karl*, *The Pride of the Jennico*, *Sowing the Wind*, *Romeo and Juliet*, and finally *Mistress Nell*. In the first of these, she was "a good Lady Sneerwell." In *Sowing the Wind*, she was "a clever Bridget." She was found "pleasing" as Lady Montague in *Romeo and Juliet*. Finally, she and a colleague "did well the little assigned to them" in *Mistress Nell*, where Witherspoon played Lady Hamilton.[71] When the season was finally over for her on February 24, 1906, she had acted in 13 different plays. The five months spent in Monsieur Fourton's company were Witherspoon's drama school. She learned on the job and gained more extensive, varied, and concentrated acting experience there in a single season, than she could have hoped for during several years spent in a traditional drama school. She said herself in 1941, that "actual practical experience received in stock companies is the best training available, for 'you learn more from an audience than from any school.'"[72]

Apart from a benefit performance of Dion Bouciault's *The Octoroon* at the Lyric Theatre on May 14, 1906, where she "supplied the leading female role and acquitted herself in a creditable manner," there were no further developments in Witherspoon's acting career until the end of the year. In mid–December, the *Times-Democrat* reported that she had "been added to the forces of the Baldwin-Melville stock company. She would be 'pleasantly remembered,'" the paper added, "for some excellent work she did in Manager Fourton's Grand Opera House Stock Company." Her engagement seems to have been of short duration. She made her debut with the company playing two roles in *On Piney Ridge* at the Baldwin Theatre on December 16. "Cora Witherspoon appeared in doubles and got a warm welcome," wrote the *Times-Picayune*. According to the *Item*: "Miss Cora Witherspoon, … who made her first appearance with the Baldwin-Melville Company, made quite a favorable impression in the dual role of Chlotilde Beverly and Mrs. Lane."[73]

We next find press reports of Witherspoon's doings in the spring of 1907, when she was 17 years of age. On May 22, she was one of the "society girls" involved in selling the 40-page special "woman's edition" of the *New Orleans Item* newspaper, which was "issued for the benefit of the Women's and Children's Dispensary and the great cause of district nursing in New Orleans." The *Item* predicted that the newsgirls would "doubtless create a condition of incipient bankruptcy among the wandering newspaper readers of the impressionable male contingent when they go into action." Witherspoon and Jennie Griswold were responsible for a stand outside Fuerst and Kraemer's confectionary store at 833 Canal St., near Dauphine. Witherspoon's 38-year-old cousin Belle Norton and her companion Sadie Griffin were also on the newsstand committee.[74]

At the organizational meeting for the "Woman's Item" on May 13, Witherspoon had "announced that a benefit would be given her on the 23rd at one of the theaters, and asked for the patronage of the ladies present, which was freely accorded the little New Orleans lady."[75] She was only 17 at the time, yet was cunning enough to recognize the publicity value of advertising her own event in such a congenial setting as a meeting of right-minded, woman-identified, and charitable women.

In Helen Pitkin's column "Women at Home and Abroad" in the *Times-Democrat* for May 19, Witherspoon was touted as "one of the most gifted young actresses that New Orleans has produced." Readers were told, that at her benefit performance she would give "an ambitious portrayal of Zaza." According to Pitkin, Witherspoon was "highly connected in New Orleans, being related to the Denis, Bell and Witherspoon families." Her readers were assured that "it is purely the love of her art which guides her footsteps in the Thespian way." Witherspoon would go to New York "immediately after the benefit performance," where she had been engaged for the following season by David Belasco.[76]

For Witherspoon, the testimonial benefit performance was the major event of 1907. It symbolized her having attained a position as an actress in her own community and, equally importantly, that she had that community's support for her unusual choice of career. Testimonial benefits were commonly given by and for established actors, who for various reasons needed the additional income. They were called benefits, because the profits of the performance were given to the beneficiary of the performance, who also starred in it. Thus they were a good way for the performer to showcase their talents, while earning some extra cash.

Witherspoon's benefit was originally scheduled for May 23, then changed to May 27, and finally took place on Saturday, June 1 at 8 p.m. at the Tulane Theatre. *Zaza* was a complex play in no less than five acts and the postponement was "found necessary in order to give an elaborate presentation." The Tulane once stood directly across from its sister theater the Crescent, on either side of a covered arcade, which ran between Baronne St. and Roosevelt Way. The theaters and the arcade were swallowed up by the extension of the Roosevelt New Orleans Hotel. Tickets to the performance cost 50 cents. The event was heavily advertised in the local papers. Among the 20 "patronesses," we find Witherspoon's aunt Arabella Denis (Mrs. Henry Denis) and Adelaide Labatt Wisdom, the wife of Witherspoon's eldest cousin Mortimer Wisdom.[77]

On June 1, 1907, Witherspoon gave a testimonial benefit performance at the Tulane Theatre, which stood directly across from its sister theater, the Crescent, on the site of the present-day Roosevelt New Orleans Hotel. She chose to play the lead in *Zaza*, which had been produced by David Belasco in 1899 with Mrs. Leslie Carter in the title role. It was an audacious choice, since Zaza was a former prostitute and the mistress of a married man. At this point, though, Witherspoon could do no wrong in the eyes of the elite of New Orleans. She had overcome any opposition to her unorthodox choice of career, and from here on out her hometown would be solidly behind her.

Zaza was an audacious choice of vehicle, since the heroine was a prostitute turned music hall entertainer and the lover of a married man. As the reviewer for the *New York Times* wrote of the first American production: "Nothing quite so glaringly vicious as the symbols of vice in 'Zaza' had ever before been put before decent American eyes."[78] The English-language adaptation from the French of Pierre Berton and Charles Simon was by Witherspoon's future mentor David Belasco, who first produced the play in Washington, D.C., in 1898 and at the Garrick Theatre in New York the following year. The title role was created by Réjane in Paris and by Mrs. Leslie Carter on Broadway, when the latter was 37. In later years, the part would be played in Hollywood films by Pauline Frederick, Gloria Swanson, and Claudette Colbert.

Zaza was a vast and ambitious undertaking for a cast consisting mostly of amateurs and had no less than 23 different players in named roles. As her married lover Bernard Dufresne, Witherspoon had Bernard Shields. Marie Westerfield played Dufresne's wife. San Remo Socola directed. On June 2, the *Item* reported that the testimonial benefit had been "a 'financial and social success.'" The theater had been "packed to the doors." Witherspoon's "ability as an actress was reflected in her clever work": "The boxes were filled with well-known people, and throughout the performance she received hearty acknowledgments. The stage settings were splendid. Some of the love scenes were comical and provoked laughter." The *Item*'s report concluded that Witherspoon's "popularity was never better illustrated than during the performance at the Tulane Theater." According to the *Times-Picayune*, "Miss Witherspoon, in the part of the frivolous high-tempered woman, elicited admiration from her auditors, who gave her frequent ovations": "the flowers and other presents sent over the footlights filled a dressing-room."[79]

When interviewed in her dressing room, Witherspoon said she had would leave New Orleans at the end of July and would start rehearsals at the Belasco Theatre in New York August 27. She did not know what part she would have but was confident she would receive a role in one of the new plays Belasco was writing for stars like David Warfield and Frances Starr. Her immediate plans were to "rest up for the next two or three weeks on the gulf coast, the guest of friends."[80]

Six days after the benefit, and before going on holiday, Witherspoon appeared again at the Tulane Theatre. The play being performed this time was *The Charity Ball* and the performers were "The Thespians," who were "filling an important place in local amateur theatricals." *The Charity Ball* had been written by David Belasco and Henry C. De Mille and had opened at the Lyceum Theatre in New York on November 19, 1889. It was the old story of "the duplicity of a man toward a girl who has surrendered herself unwisely to him." The girl was Phyllis Lee, played by Witherspoon, and the man was Dick Van Buren, portrayed by Jules Weinfurter. Phyllis in turn is loved by the righteous rector and Dick's brother, John Van Buren (St. John Perret). Witherspoon's acting teacher and friend, Jessie Tharp, played Ann Cruger, who in turn loves John Van Buren in this romantic roundabout. According to the review in the *Item*, the players "covered themselves … with glory" and Witherspoon "deserves the largest part of the praise."[81]

The summer holiday did not go as planned. In early July, Witherspoon and her aunt Sophie were staying at the fashionable Montross Hotel in Biloxi, Mississippi, about 90 miles northeast of New Orleans along the Gulf Coast. On the evening of Wednesday, July 5, they were involved in a "frightful trolley car accident" at Long Beach, between Gulfport and Pass Christian. "From the account of the accident," wrote the *Times-Picayune*, "it seems a marvel that one or both of them were not killed or maimed for life." The Gulfport and Mississippi Coast Traction Company's car became unmanageable at its final stop at Long Beach at around nine o'clock, so that the motor man lost control of it: "after reaching the end of the line it continued on until it plunged into a ravine, where it lodged at an angle of forty-five degrees, with the front end in the ravine." Witherspoon and her aunt were the only passengers at the time. They were sitting at the front of the car across the aisle from each other. In Aunt Sophie's account, "suddenly the lights went out, and then came a jar and a terrible crash." She was thrown to the floor and received a blow to the head, which stunned her and bled profusely, but did not render her unconscious. Witherspoon, through some miracle, was able to stay in her seat, and escaped with a sprained back and the shock. The injured women were assisted by the crew and taken to a local residence, before being transported back to the hotel, where they were attended by a physician.[82]

The accident and its aftermath may have impacted Witherspoon's ability to join Belasco's company in New York at the required time, though it seems unlikely that she had been engaged by him as early as 1907. Her first recorded stage appearance away from New Orleans, that I have identified, was in Buffalo, New York, on October 28, 1907. She appeared with a stock company at the Lyric Theatre, which once stood at 447 Washington St. in Buffalo and is currently a parking lot. The company had recently been assembled in New York by the theater's manager, Mr. Laughlin. He believed it to be "in every sense satisfactory" and that it "equals in collective strength and individual ability any organization of the kind ever submitted to the theatre-going public" of Buffalo.[83]

Mr. Laughlin opened his season at the Lyric with the Eleanor Merron's rural comedy drama *The Dairy Farm*, "a wholesome story of bucolic life before the Civil War." The company's leading man was Edgar Baume and Jane Wheatley the leading lady. Frances Nordstrom was the second woman, Angela McCaull the ingénue, and Henrietta Bagley the character woman. Veteran character actor James H. Wallack enacted the role of the Squire, that "he originated and made famous." Witherspoon was one of the minor members of the company along with Harry Driscole, Albert Lando, Gordon Langhorne, Frances Fraunholz, and Fred G. Hearne. "The new stock company made a very favorable impression" in their debut vehicle, which ran a week. The closest Witherspoon came to a "notice" was the following line in the *Buffalo Times*: "Miss Cora Witherspoon, Miss Frances Nordstrom and Edward Poland deserved the plaudits they received in their respective parts." The reviews do not tell us what those parts were. The Lyric had stood empty for seven weeks due to being in receivership, but this evening "every seat in the house had been sold and more than 200 standing room tickets had been issued."[84]

An article about the new company in the *Buffalo Enquirer* mentioned that "Miss Witherspoon has had excellent training under successful managers." A news item devoted to Witherspoon herself assured the readers of the *Buffalo Sunday Morning News*, that she was "a tall, graceful and charming young woman," who had had "beneficial experience in stock companies in New Orleans and in other Southern cities." There was no specific mention of an association with David Belasco. The *Illustrated Buffalo Express* carried a photo of Witherspoon in a pensive pose, bare-shouldered in a peasant blouse, on November 3, identifying her as "A member of the Lyric Theater stock company."[85] The same photo had appeared in the *Times-Picayune* on June 2 and probably shows her as Zaza.

Witherspoon's stay in Buffalo was a brief one, as the new stock company only played one more week at the Lyric Theatre.[86] Her last recorded stage appearance in 1907 was with the stock company of the newly completed Bijou Theatre in New Haven, which had opened that year at 28 Church St. and which is no longer standing. The play was the three-act comedy *Turned Up*, which opened on December 16 for a week's run. According to one review, it was "one continual scream from the time the curtain goes up at first until it rings down at the end of the last act." Witherspoon played Mrs. Pannall. Leading lady Jane Wheatley, ingénue Angela McCaull, and character man Frances "Fraunie" Fraunholz from the Lyric Theatre company were also in this production.[87]

After a brief return to the Baldwin-Melville stock company in New Orleans to play Aramantha Markham in *Ninety and Nine*, a "very lurid melodrama" suggested by Ira D. Sankey's famous hymn, it was reported in the *New Orleans Item* on March 21, 1908, that she had "left to-day on board the S.S. Antilles for New York, where she is studying the dramatic art": "Miss Witherspoon was accompanied by her aunt, Miss Sophie Bell."[88]

While in New York, Witherspoon was offered a substantial engagement with the Suburban Garden stock company in St. Louis, that would keep her busy for three months between May and August 1908. In St. Louis, Witherspoon supported guest stars Virginia Harned, Amelia Bingham, Henrietta Crosman, and James K. Hackett. The season opened on May 24 with Harned playing her signature role of Trilby O'Farrell in *Trilby*, which she had created on Broadway in 1905. Witherspoon was Mrs. Bagot and "played the mother of 'Billee' effectively." Little Billee was played by Walter B. Gilbert. Witherspoon also supported Harned as Princess Cherbatsky in *Anna Karenina* ("Miss Cora Witherspoon and James Bliss, as the Prince and Princess Cherbatsky, were funny, with their family jars"); and, possibly, in *The Second Mrs. Tanqueray*.[89]

On June 7, the *Times-Picayune* reported that the young actress was "giving a good account of herself this season" as a member of the Suburban Theatre Stock Company, "considered one of the best in the country": "She is engaged especially for character parts, and has been highly praised for her clean-cut and intelligent interpretation of her roles. It is hard work, but excellent training, and she glories in it all. She has as yet no plans for the next season, but she is sure to get her chance, and make the most of it."[90] Witherspoon had an older cousin in St. Louis, William Conner Witherspoon, the son of her father's eldest brother Thomas. Maybe she stayed with him, his wife Mary and their sons Houston and William in the capacious residence at 4538 Maryland Ave. in the "CWE," that they shared with Mary's parents, sister and brother-in-law, and three servants. This extended family circle would be broken up three years later, when William, then 40, divorced Mary and married 22-year-old Lillian Stagel Nunley.[91]

Amelia Bingham took over as leading lady at the Suburban Garden on June 14 and Witherspoon did *The Sporting Duchess*, *A Contented Woman*, *The Cowboy and the Lady*, *The School for Husbands*, and *A Modern Magdalen* with her. She got one of her best notices for *The Cowboy and the Lady*. The *St. Louis Globe-Democrat* wrote that "The 'Miss Prissims' of Miss Cora Witherspoon is one of the big hits of the play. In the dance-hall scene she swells a minor role into pretentiousness and scores heavily."[92]

Bingham passed the baton to Henrietta Crosman on July 19, and Crosman was starred in some of her most familiar vehicles: *Sweet Kitty Bellairs*, *The Sword of the King*, and *Mistress Nell*. In *Mistress Nell*, which had ended her season at the Grand Opera House in New Orleans, Witherspoon was considered "among the most effective of the secondary players."[93] Finally, she supported James K. Hackett in *The Prisoner of Zenda*, *The Crisis*, and *The Pride of Jennico*. In *The Crisis*, wrote the *St. Louis Post-Dispatch*,

"Miss Cora Witherspoon will be seen as the motherly and charming Mrs. Brice, Stephen's mother."[94] Though a couple of weeks remained of the Suburban Garden season, Witherspoon's engagement ended in late August. She and Aunt Sophie went to Biloxi, Mississippi, for a holiday. On September 16, they left for New York, "to be absent all winter."[95] Witherspoon was soon to meet the man who would mean more to her career than any other.

Leo Ditrichstein was born in 1865 in Timisoara, which is now in Romania. He was frequently referred to as being "Hungarian by birth." Unlike most young men of his class, he opted to go on the stage, rather than attend college. Ditrichstein soon achieved success in a variety of roles and theatrical genres, including musical theater, where he impressed with his fine tenor voice. He came to the United States in 1890 and made his American stage debut with Gustav Amberg's company at the Irving Place, a German-language theater, the following year. It was there he was discovered by Charles Frohman, who engaged him, though he spoke "very little English then." His break-through role in English was as Zou-Zou in *Trilby* in 1895. Ditrichstein's career as a light opera singer ended practically overnight the following year, when he lost his voice permanently. Later, he would write a play, *The Great Lover*, about an operatic singer who has a similar experience. Ditrichstein wrote his first play, *Gossip*, in collaboration with Clyde Fitch for Lily Langtry in 1895. There would be many more, mostly inspired by or directly adapted from continental European originals.[96]

Ditrichstein's heyday as a matinee idol lasted roughly until 1918, including the eight years during which Witherspoon was a small but integral part of all his major stage successes from *The Concert* to *The Matinee Hero*. She learned more from him than from any other stage professional and he undoubtedly meant more to getting her stage career off the ground than anyone else, including David Belasco. He simply believed in her and, though the parts were never large, he kept her employed longer than anyone else. She made it clear in an interview in 1922, that "it was under Ditrichstein, with whom she remained eight years, playing repertoire, that Miss Witherspoon learned, she says, everything she knows about the stage." One piece of advice from him she appears to have heeded was that "the wise, the successful actor, is he who in his preliminary years discovers his limitations, learns the sort of thing that he can do best, and thereafter does it."[97]

Though it usually escaped notice in capsule accounts of her career, Witherspoon's long collaboration with Ditrichstein pre-dated her being hired by Belasco to support the star in *The Concert* in 1910. In the fall of 1908, Ditrichstein engaged her for his stock company at the Colonial Theatre in Cleveland, which opened its eight-week season with *The Ambitious Mrs. Alcott* on November 9. The *Philadelphia Inquirer* got it partially right, when it recalled in 1943 that "Miss Witherspoon's first stage experience was in stock with Leo Ditrichstein in Cleveland in a series of Ditrichstein farces. He asked her if she could play a woman of 70, and being 17, she was certain she could. This led to her New York debut with him in 'The Concert,' produced by David Belasco."[98] This was her first stage experience in stock *with Ditrichstein*. As we have seen, she already had extensive acting experience prior to coming to Cleveland.

Ditrichstein's company was described in the press as "one of the best balanced dramatic and comedy companies yet to be seen on a local stage." It was a large one, and included actors like Charles B. Wells, Earl K. Mitchell, Newton Lindo, Forest Freeman,

Harry Andrews, Howard Hull, Edward Longman, Jack Mahoney, Anne Sutherland, Jane Gordon, Fola LaFollette, Catherine Carter, Eva Randolph, Margaret Lewis, and Natalie Jerome. The *Cleveland Plain Dealer* mentioned especially that "light comedy roles will be played by Cora Witherspoon, whom J. Gordon Edwards, one of America's leading stage directors, pronounced the coming great American comedienne." After the season had started, the paper wrote: "Mindful of the good companies that have been seen at the Colonial in the past it is no small praise to characterize the new organization as the best of them all. To see such players at any time is a treat of rare quality and when they appear at Colonial prices the incident makes dramatic history."[99]

In addition to the season opener, they played one week each of *Sham Battles*, *Before and After*, *A Superfluous Husband*, *Harriet's Honeymoon*, *The Last Appeal*, and *Vivian's Papas*, before the engagement at the Colonial came to an end on January 2, 1909. Witherspoon was seldom mentioned in the notices, but her efforts in *Before and After* led the reviewer to observe that "Miss Cora Witherspoon shows that comedy is a part of her nature and training." After *Vivian's Papas*, the *Cleveland Plain Dealer* observed that "Miss Cora Witherspoon shared the honors of the evening with Miss Grey [Jane Grey, the leading lady]. Her playing of the role of the chorus girl has a clever touch."[100]

Witherspoon had no time for a break, as Ditrichstein wanted her for his next engagement too, which was to begin immediately. So it was that Witherspoon made her first and, as far as I know, only appearance in vaudeville, when she joined Ditrichstein in his one-act farce "Button, Button, Who's Got the Button?" with senator's daughter and Ditrichstein's family friend Fola La Follette, Howard Hull, and Patrick O'Brien.[101] What was in fact a small vaudeville tour started at the Grand Opera House in Pittsburgh on January 4, 1909, the day before Witherspoon's 19th birthday; went from there to the Temple Theatre in Detroit and the Majestic Theatre in Chicago, and ended at the Columbia Theatre in St. Louis on February 6. It was only six months since she had appeared at the Suburban Garden Theatre in St. Louis. Here she was, back again, only this time in vaudeville.

The *Pittsburgh Daily Post* deemed the program currently at the Grand Opera House "one of the best vaudeville bills of the season." Ditrichstein and La Follette played an absent-minded dentist, Dr. Burton, and his jealous wife, while Cora Witherspoon and Hull played "a couple in love": "It is a laugh from the start and enacted in the only way farce should be enacted, with the utmost gravity and earnestness. The audiences took to the play yesterday with keen relish, and laughter and applause ruled once the story got underway." The *Pittsburgh Press* thought it "a clean and wholesome playlet, and altogether is one of the most delightful absurdities that Mr. Ditrichstein has yet produced." The *Chicago Daily News* wrote that "nothing could be neater and brighter."[102]

The brothers who ran the Suburban Garden Theatre, Jacob and Sol N. Oppenheimer, wanted Witherspoon back for their next season in St. Louis. This time, she would be supporting Amelia Bingham for her five-week engagement starting May 30, followed by three weeks with guest star Wilton Lackaye, three weeks with Marguerite Clark, and two weeks with Countess Venturini, before Witherspoon moved on to another engagement at the end of August. Among the plays she acted in this season were *Madame Sans-Gêne*, *Her Other Self*, *The Climbers*, *New Lamps and Old*, *Peter Pan*, *Frou-Frou*, and *Camille*. She made her greatest impact as the Queen of Naples in *Madame Sans-Gêne*, starring Amelia Bingham. Her home-town newspaper reported that she "was given five curtain calls after her great emotional scene—not bad for a mere slip of a girl, but she is made of the stuff, and before many years she will twinkle as a star at the head of her own company." The *St. Louis-Globe Democrat* wrote: "Others in the cast whose work required some skill are … Miss Cora Witherspoon."[103]

Her Other Self was a new melodrama about "the enslavement of a high-bred young woman to the drink habit," which had its world premiere in St. Louis on June 20, with author Stanislaus Stange in the audience. Both he and leading lady Amelia Bingham gave curtain speeches. Fifty-year-old Bingham played "a girl-dipsomaniac pitifully struggling against her inherited love of drink," while 19-year-old Witherspoon played her aunt! What a testament to the power of stage illusion. The *Post-Dispatch* noted that "Miss Cora Witherspoon has only a slight demand to meet as Jane Belmar, Catherine Alwyn's aunt." In Clyde Fitch's *The Climbers*, her final play with Bingham, "Miss Witherspoon was nowhere amiss in her interpretation of the character of the only conventionally gentle woman of the story."[104]

New Lamps and Old was something different, being a Romanian-Jewish drama by Ronetti Roman, translated by Oscar Leonard. Witherspoon supported Wilton Lackaye as his wife Esther. The play was panned by the *Globe-Democrat*, who called it "a novel, if to many a tiresome, experiment" and "the most monstrous thing ever set before an English-speaking audience": "The only interesting moments during the long unfoldment of the plot occur when Miss Cora Witherspoon, as a flighty wife, delivers lines which are really reflective of a certain phase of life, and acquits herself with credit, and when Mr. Lackaye is given center of the stage one, two or three too brief occasions." The *Post-Dispatch* mentions Witherspoon among the actors who "acquitted themselves with much credit."[105]

On July 25, Marguerite Clark inaugurated her part of the season with *Peter Pan*. Witherspoon was cast in the first of her only two known ethnic minority roles, as Tiger Lily, daughter of a Native American chief, a role created on Broadway by Margaret Gordon in 1905–6. Charles H. Weston reprised his Broadway role as the dog "Nana." The *Post-Dispatch* pointed out that this was a "first night of 'Peter Pan' without Maude Adams," who was entirely identified with the title role: "The friendly Indians, with James Gordon as Great Big Little Panther, and Cora Witherspoon as Tiger Lily, were good, too." The *Globe-Democrat* thought "it was enjoyable to see the dignified members of the stock company in such roles as the Indians and pirates." "This fortnight run of one play establishes a new Suburban record," they pointed out a few days later.[106] Incidentally, Marguerite Clark (1883–1940) married a New Orleans plantation owner and millionaire in 1918 and later lived in a mansion on St. Charles Ave. Like Witherspoon, she lies buried in Metairie Cemetery.

Though the Countess Venturini was not quite done with her season at the Suburban Garden, Witherspoon was and left the company after *Camille*. She briefly assisted at the opening of a new company at the Bush Temple Theatre in Chicago, where they began the season with *Zaza* on September 4, but her ultimate destination was even further west. Her final engagement of the year, and the decade, was with the Friend Players at the Shubert Theatre in Milwaukee. Managed by and named for Arthur S. Friend, this stock company had Lowell Sherman as its leading man this season, Fanny Hartz as its leading lady, and, starting in late November, Ruth Chatterton as its ingénue. Witherspoon would also recall that she worked with two other soon-to-be-famous actors in Milwaukee: Pauline Lord and Lenore Ulric.[107]

Witherspoon remained in Milwaukee till just after her 20th birthday, adding more valuable experience and many more roles to her repertoire. During 12 weeks in this provincial, midwestern stock company, she played Madge Larrabee in *Sherlock Holmes* ("did herself credit"), Agnes Powell in *St. Elmo* ("'betrayer of an honest love'"), Juanita Arguilla in *The Dictator* ("quite hot stuff—tropical—with a red gown, a dashing air and a slashing knife"), Euphemia McCreery in *Held by the Enemy*, Olivia in *Twelfth Night*, Mrs. Van Buren in *The Charity Ball*, Madame Balfontaine in *Divorçons*, and Lady de Winter in *The Three Musketeers*. She also had minor roles in *Carmen* ("Miss Witherspoon and numerous others fill in the animated scenes"), *The Pit* (had one of the "excellent parts"), and *The Amazons*.[108] The only play that season she was *not* in was *Captain Jinks of the Horse Marines*, probably because there was no role for her.

The most revealing interview Witherspoon ever gave on a purely personal level appeared in the *Milwaukee Journal* on the last day of 1909, which was a Friday. She was only days away from her 20th birthday, though she claimed to be 21; and was appearing that week as Lady de Winter in the *Three Musketeers* and rehearsing the following week's play, *The Amazons*, during the day. The eye-catching headline was "Actress Hates Men," and the subheading was no less unorthodox: "Girlish Wow Not to Marry Until 28 Leads Miss Witherspoon to Scorn the Opposite Sex."

In this extraordinary article, which consists almost entirely of a long, directly quoted statement from Witherspoon, the "talented young actress" is described as "confessedly a hater of men." The remainder of the article reads as follows:

> Her profession, naturally, demands that she mingle with them and even enact love scenes with masculine members of the company, but off the stage she prefers companions of her own sex. "It isn't because I'm priggish or believe in equal suffrage," said Miss Witherspoon, "although I believe that woman, in every way, is man's equal. Nor it isn't because I've been disappointed in love. When I was in a New Orleans convent the prefect of discipline advised us girls against marrying before we reached the age of 28. So five of us swore on graduation day to renounce the companionship of men until we reached that age and every year on Jan. 1 we write to each other renewing our allegiance to the treaty we made. It was hard at first to refuse dinner and theater invitations, but one by one all my boyfriends disappeared. Of course, that made it easier for me, but when I went on the stage I had to tolerate their company. Instead of eagerly waiting for my twenty-eighth year, so I might marry, I've just forgotten that I'm ever going to be that age and I've got so I don't like men a bit. That's why I take such interest in my part in *The Amazons* next week. It's a woman's suffrage play and we can show them on the stage that we can get along without them. If more girls would resolve on New Year's to associate only with their own sex, some conceited young men might realize how insignificant they are."

The article was accompanied by a portrait of a pensive, top-knotted, and suitably spinsterish-looking Witherspoon holding her hand to her right cheek.[109]

What a testament to the power of youthful teachings! We know, of course, that Witherspoon did not just stay true to her vow until she was 28, but indeed preferred to "get along without them" her entire life. No doubt, Aunt Sophie was on hand to ensure that her niece remained resolute in her celibacy, as Sophie herself had been all her life. After five years in stock, at 20 years of age, unencumbered by romance, with only her faithful aunt at her side, it was time for Cora Witherspoon to take the next, decisive step in her career.

2

Belasco and Beyond
The 1910s

> She is made very happy by the fact that she has always
> had excellent directors. Belasco gave her her start.[1]

With her usual modesty, Witherspoon once described herself on first coming to
New York, as "an ugly brat with nothing but a lot of hair to recommend me." Though she
hammered several times at the gates, in 1910 they finally opened. In the fall of that year,
she found herself exactly where she wanted to be, after five years of conscientious and
hard work in stock companies in the South, the East, and the Midwest. She sometimes
made it sound as if she landed at Mrs. Martin's "famous theatrical boarding house" by
chance. An interviewer in 1936, for example, describes how, "by a stroke of good fortune, she went to live at a rooming house in the roaring forties which was patronized by
many theatre people." There she met Ruth Chatterton, and Philip Merivale, who had just
come over from England. Both "were amused by the young girl's intense desire to get on
and taught her where to go and how to apply for a job."[2]

A somewhat later and more detailed account of these early New York days records
that the boarding house was on W. 45th St., and that $12.50 a week bought you three
meals a day, as well as a room. "She was chaperoned by a maiden aunt, who saw to it that
young Cora did not keep the scandalous hours of other theatrical people. 'I used to envy
Ruth Chatterton, who shared the room next to mine, with her mother…. She could sleep
as long as she liked and had her breakfast brought up on a tray.'" Philip Merivale "wore
bright yellow socks that fell over his shoes." Ina Claire and Otto Harbach also lived
there. "The great dissipation of the evening was an ice cream soda, and the girls used
to walk past the Lambs' Club [at 128 W. 44th St.], hoping that some young blade would
come out and buy them their nightly treats."[3]

What made her stay in New York in 1910 different from previous sojourns was that
she had gotten a job on Broadway. Legendary producer David Belasco had finally come
through and hired her for his latest show, *The Concert*, starring her mentor and friend
Leo Ditrichstein. Apart from Ditrichstein, no single individual meant more to the development of Witherspoon's professional acting career than Belasco. Born in San Francisco
in 1853 to Sephardic Jews who had emigrated there from London during the Gold Rush,
Belasco started as an actor and stage manager in the West, before relocating to New
York in 1882. There he built a reputation for writing, producing, and staging plays with a
level of realism that had not hitherto been seen on the American stage. He helmed more
than 100 Broadway productions and helped develop the acting careers of performers as

diverse as Mrs. Leslie Carter, David Warfield, Maude Adams, Jeanne Eagels, Ina Claire, and Barbara Stanwyck.

Witherspoon often told the story of how she had gotten her start with Belasco. The earliest version I have found is in the *Providence Evening Bulletin* for January 21, 1911, when the actress was still part of Belasco's company. According to Belasco's press agent, "'Two large, square front teeth and an infectious giggle won for Miss Cora Witherspoon the part she is now playing in 'The Concert.'" Belasco himself claimed that "'if he had searched all Christendom he could not have found such a pair of front teeth, combined with just such another giggle.'" The lesson to be learned from this, according to this news report, was that "histrionic ability is not an absolute necessity in these days": "Those who wish to go on the stage should have a choice giggle, a fine dental display, a complete outfit of whiskers, an obese frame or an attenuated one, or some other material distinction necessary to the embodiment of a 'type.' The stage manager will provide all the acting that is needed, and convey it to the beginner in twenty more or less easy lessons." In a different version of the story, Belasco was also smitten with Witherspoon's distinctive laugh. He told her, "'that is the kind of a laugh I have been looking for for a long time. There is a part in 'The Concert,' I want you to play and you won't have to study very hard for it. All you've got to do is act and laugh your own self.'" It was not all sunshine and roses, though. Witherspoon recalled in 1939, that Belasco had once thrown a plate at her, "angered because she insisted on waving her hands around on the stage."[4]

As we have seen, the truth was different from these anecdotes. The 20-year-old woman Belasco first hired to play a minor role in *The Concert* had already gained a fund of experience during her five years as a professional actress. Thus the account of Witherspoon's and Belasco's first meeting in the *Times-Picayune* for September 14, 1913, seems closer to the truth. After her benefit performance of *Zaza* in 1907, her uncle Samuel Bell took her to New York. "[O]ne afternoon after a performance of 'Rose of the Ranchos' he and his tall young niece stood at the door of Mr. Belasco's private office. Belasco came hurrying up. Mr. Bell presented his letters, and introduced Miss Witherspoon. Mr. Belasco acknowledged the introduction and read the letters. Then he looked almost regretfully at the young lady. 'I do not encourage any young lady to go on the stage,' he said. 'But,' spoke in Cora Witherspoon. I'm going, Mr. Belasco—I'm going. I've played Zaza!' It was a magic word. It brought up, no doubt, visions of a certain Titian head. The girl whipped out her press notices. Belasco did not engage her just then, but his interest had been aroused. Later, he gave her a part in 'The Concert.'"[5] *The Rose of the Rancho* closed at the Belasco Theatre on June 29, 1907, but it reopened on August 31 and ran till the end of the year. Thus it would seem that Witherspoon and her uncle had their meeting with the great man in the fall of 1907. It would be three more years till he cast her in *The Concert*.

The Concert was simply a phenomenon. Adapted by its star Leo Ditrichstein from a German original by Hermann Bahr, the reasons behind the tremendous success both of this run-of-the-mill play and its unlikely star would be difficult for modern audiences to fathom. In 1910, 45-year-old Ditrichstein was a middle-aged, portly, balding, and height-challenged actor with a distinct German accent, yet he was one of the biggest matinee idols of his day. He was about as far from younger stars like John Barrymore and Douglas Fairbanks as can imagined, yet he was able to draw large audiences to his comedies and farces for many years in the early part of the twentieth century.

In 1913, he was described as "the closest approach to the Richard Mansfield of old that the American stage can boast." A drama critic reviewing a performance of *The Concert* in Seattle towards the end of the show's long run tried to describe his appeal. According to J. Willis Sayre, Ditrichstein was "a master at a type of very high-class character comedy, comedy with the trace of a mustache and the trace of a German accent, the comedy which invests the personality of a superior individual who languidly absorbs hero-worship as his just meed and deserts. He perfectly presents the picture of the childish virtuoso who seeks feminine adoration and having found it, throws it away with blasé indifference."[6] It is hard to know if the critic is describing the actor or his character here, which only goes to show how close this star character actor often came to playing artists whose image was similar to his own.

In retrospect, *The Concert* gives the impression of being the best written of the many plays Witherspoon did with Ditrichstein in the teens. It had its world premiere at the Nixon Theatre in Pittsburgh on September 19, 1910. On September 13, the *Pittsburgh Daily Post* had reported that all performances at the Nixon were

The legendary producer David Belasco played a large role in taking Witherspoon's stage career to another level. In 1910, after they had been in contact for three years, he finally cast her in *The Concert*, which was her first bow on Broadway and which would keep her continuously employed for three years, in New York and on tour.

"under the personal supervision of David Belasco himself," who was to arrive "with his chiefs of staff next Saturday." After the premiere, "the wizard had to make a speech of thanks before the audience would be satisfied." The *Washington Post* felt this production marked a change of course for Belasco from melodrama to comedy: "Once the apostle of 'the thur-ill,' he has ceased to cast thrills and is bent on lightening the burden of life with laughter."[7] No one could have known that night, that *The Concert* would keep its star, company, and crew continuously employed for nearly three years.

The summary of the plot of *The Concert* in the *Pittsburgh Press* has the advantage of brevity: "The comedy has to do with [a] piano virtuoso, whose foolish women pupils are all in love with him. He takes all the adulation as his due and finally goes to a bungalow with one of his pupils only to be followed by his wife, and the husband of his companion, both of whom have been advised of the trip by another jealous pupil. The couples take two acts to straighten out the tangle, and each go home happy." In the original cast, Ditrichstein took the central role of the star musician Gabriel Arany; Janet Beecher played his wife, Helen Arany; Jane Grey played the erring wife, Stella Dallas; and William Morris was her husband, Dr. Dallas. Witherspoon was cast in a minor but named role as Edith Gordon, one of the "geese," which is the master's none too flattering nickname for his women music students. As Miss Gordon, Witherspoon only appeared in the first act, which was set in the reception room of the Arany residence, "indeed an aviary, the gay-plumaged things pecking and screaming about him, each hungry for a crumb of his speech."[8] Among the more showy supporting roles were the caretaker couple at the bungalow in the Catskills, Mr. and Mrs. McGinnis, created on Broadway by John W. Cope and Belle Theodore; and Arany's secretary Miss Merk, originally played by Catherine Proctor. More of Miss Merk shortly.

After the week's trial in Pittsburgh, *The Concert* moved for another week-long try-out at Ford's Theatre in Baltimore, before opening at the Belasco Theatre on Tuesday, October 4, 1910. Belasco had a tradition of always opening his New York shows on a Tuesday evening. Thus five years after becoming a professional actress, Cora Witherspoon made her Broadway debut at the age of 20 in the play that would remain the biggest hit of her theatrical career. According to the New York papers, *The Concert* "scored a distinct success, a success that may well be measured by the over a score of curtain calls at the close of the second act." The *Brooklyn Daily Eagle* noted in April the following year, that the play "continues to break box office records" and had been "playing to capacity audiences for nearly nine months": "it might run all summer were it not for David Belasco's invariable rule of giving his players a period of rest during the hot weather." Thus Belasco scheduled to close the play for the summer on June 3. "Owing to the fact that Leo Ditrichstein is indisposed as a result of the hard work incident to the exacting and arduous role of Gabor Arany in 'The Concert,'" Belasco decided to end the original New York run of the play a week early, and quite neatly and appropriately after its 300th performance on May 27, 1911.[9]

Witherspoon's involvement with the play was far from over, but it was time for a well-deserved holiday. She visited family in New Orleans and vacationed in Biloxi, Mississippi.[10] Maude had been certified as a pharmacist in February 1910 and would take the final exam and be qualified by the Louisiana State Board of Pharmacy in November 1911.[11] By the time the U.S. census was taken in April 1910, she had moved in with an older women, Annie Miller, and her 22-year-old son at 4515 Freret St., where the two women would live for the next ten years. Annie was born Anna Mathilda Venables in New Orleans on June 1, 1866, but she was raised in Tangipahoa parish as one of the eight children of a bookkeeper and later a store clerk. She married in 1887, at age 20, but her husband Warren H. Miller died of consumption in December 1889. She had also lost a child. Annie had worked as a telegraph operator for many years.[12]

During the summer of 1911, Witherspoon stayed with Maude and Annie at Freret St. and with her cousin Belle Norton and Belle's partner Sadie Griffin in their fashionable boarding house at 3206 St. Charles Ave. Belle and Sadie were also together for decades, until Belle's death in 1933. The vacation was over on September 2, when Witherspoon and Sophie Bell boarded the *Comus* bound for New York.[13] The same basic pattern of visits to family in New Orleans and a sojourn in Biloxi was repeated during the summer of 1912.[14]

Because *The Concert* had not yet exhausted the demand for tickets in New York, the show returned to the Belasco Theatre on September 14 for a month.[15] The first, lengthy tour, which would last the entire 1911–1912 theatrical season, began at the Blackstone

Theatre in Chicago on October 16. Witherspoon was still playing Edith Gordon and the major cast was unchanged. From there, the show moved to the Grand Theatre in Cincinnati; the Lyceum in Rochester, New York; and finally to Boston and an historic opening night at the Hollis Street Theatre on December 25, 1911; historic specifically in our context, because that was the first time Witherspoon played Miss Merk, the first defining role of her career. As previously mentioned, Arany's personal secretary had hitherto been played by Catherine Proctor, who had been "well received in the role."[16] Proctor left the cast at this point, making it possible for Witherspoon to be "promoted" to the better opportunity Miss Merk represented. She would play Miss Merk until *The Concert* ended its long career in 1913. My guess would be that, apart from the Ditrichstein, Witherspoon was the only actor who was in every performance of *The Concert* from start to finish. Clearly, Ditrichstein valued loyalty of this kind. In the coming years, it would be rewarded.

Like Edith Gordon, Miss Merk only appeared in the first act. The character of the role and, indirectly, its visibility is suggested by the many descriptions of Miss Merk in the reviews, where she was variously termed "the lovesick secretary," "a plain, unattractive and angular female," the "sentimental secretary," "the emotional Miss Merk," the "sobful housemaid," "an anaemic and ardent secretary to the virtuoso," "the simple-minded secretary," and "the pianist's unattractive but susceptible secretary." As the *Los Angeles Times* analyzed the play: "The folly of that peculiar kind of emotional interest in musicians and actors is cleverly presented in all its absurdity, especially in the role of Miss Merk, the old maid and be-spectacled secretary very well given by Cora Witherspoon."[17] As one of the quoted descriptions shows, Miss Merk was sometimes mistaken for a maid.

The three-week run in Boston ended on January 13, 1912, with Witherspoon having received her first notices for her efforts in *The Concert*, including this from Philip Hale of the *Boston Herald*: "The other members of the company acted capitally. If Mr. Kearney was conspicuous [as McGinnis] ... and Miss Witherspoon by her portrayal of the lovesick secretary, it was because the dramatist gave them fuller opportunity."[18] From Boston, the tour continued to Springfield, Hartford, Montauk, Washington, D.C., Philadelphia, Brooklyn, Baltimore, Pittsburgh, Buffalo, Detroit, Columbus, Louisville, Dayton, Cleveland, Akron, Canton, East Liverpool, Wheeling, Altoona, Harrisburg, Reading, and Plainfield, before going on hiatus in late May 1912. The 1912–13 tour started at the Hyperion Theatre in New Haven on September 14, 1912, before returning to the Belasco Theatre for two weeks, ending there September 28. Then came stops in Binghamton, Elmira, Wilkes-Barre, and Scranton; a week at the Grand Opera House in New York City; back to Reading and Harrisburg; Pottsville; back to Plainfield, Hartford, and Boston; Bangor; back to Springfield; Rochester; back to Buffalo, Chicago, and Louisville; Indianapolis; back to Dayton, Columbus, and Cleveland; Cincinnati, St. Louis, Kansas City, St. Joseph, Omaha, Denver, Salt Lake City, Los Angeles, San Diego, Riverside, Santa Barbara, Bakersfield, Fresno, San Francisco, Oakland, San Jose, Sacramento, Salem, Tacoma, Victoria, Vancouver, Portland, Seattle, Spokane, Missoula, Butte, Helena, Grand Forks, Winnipeg, Minneapolis, Winona, Lacrosse, and Madison, before the tour came to its irrevocable end back in New York City on May 24, 1913.

Naturally, there were many changes in cast along the way. The more important were that Lily Cahill was promoted from playing a minor role to playing Stella Dallas in January 1912 and that Isabel Irving took over for Janet Beecher as Helen Arany in September

"MISS MERK"

CORA WITHERSPOON

LEO DITRICHSTEIN—
"GABOR ARANY" "THE CONCERT"
THE GRAND—

ISABEL IRVING
"HELEN ARANY"

the apparent satisfaction of his wife and the husband. These two, simulating mutual affection, propose an exchange en familie. The subsequent developments proved to the satisfaction of each of the guilty pair that the old love is better than the new. And so they are reconciled.

As Arany's wife, Miss Irving presents a serious and convincing character portrayal.

The same may be said, in a

This drawing appeared in the *Kentucky Post* on January 21, 1913. It shows Witherspoon as the secretary Miss Merk in *The Concert*, which was being performed that week at the Grand Theatre in Cincinnati. Witherspoon had made her Broadway debut in another, minor role in *The Concert* in 1910. Leo Ditrichstein was both the author and star of what would prove the biggest hit of Witherspoon's stage career. In addition to the play's producer David Belasco, Austrian-born Ditrichstein had the most significant impact on Witherspoon's career by keeping her employed the better part of a decade. At this point, Isabel Irving played Ditrichstein's long-suffering wife in the play, a role originated by Janet Beecher.

that same year. In February 1912, Witherspoon was first featured in the advertisements, together with Beecher, Morris, James Kearney and Belle Theodore. By the time they returned to Boston in November 1912, Nye Chart was playing Dr. Dallas and the versatile Catherine Proctor had returned to the cast to play Stella Dallas. Madge West was the final Mrs. Dallas. In mid–March 1913, the *San Francisco Examiner* claimed they had played *The Concert* "more than a thousand times."[19]

The Concert was unquestionably both a commercial and a critical success. Many of the reviewers pulled out all the stops, using phrases with superlatives like "one of the best comedies that have been performed in Boston for the last 20 years," "one of the most rarely delightful comedy productions of recent seasons," "the most effervescent comedy that has struck Washington in many a day," "the greatest comedy success of recent years," "the supreme delight of the present theatrical year," "far and away the best thing in high-class comedy to be seen in St. Louis in a decade," and "the finest comedy that has been produced in the last twenty years." *The Concert* was deemed "a genuine Belasco triumph," "as joyous fun as is ever to be had in a theater with anything above rambunctious farce," "a delicious comedy ... so well acted that its deftness is much enhanced in the performance," "truly remarkable," "altogether a brilliant success," "rich in a cast of unusual merit," and "the comedy gem of the season."[20]

Obviously, there were a few dissenting voices and naysayers. After the world premiere in Pittsburgh, the *Press* described *The Concert* as "thin as air, almost" and "more farce than comedy." The *Post-Gazette* in the same city objected to "a first act that is distinctly thin and sadly marred by two coarse and unnecessary violations of the laws of good taste and good sense in the lines put into the mouths of two of the characters." The *Daily Post* wrote: "the cast is in the main unprecedented for trifles of this kind." Indeed, all was not well in Pittsburgh, where fault was found even with Ditrichstein's "facial make-up": "It is too sallow and needlessly aged. Arany is only 45 and it would strengthen the visual value of the role if he were to enhance the facial and physical charms of the man." Clearly, they thought Ditrichstein needed all the help he could get in the looks department.... The *New York Tribune* found it a major fault in the main character, that he had no redeeming qualities. "He may be a 'master,' but he is unquestionably a cad," this observer averred and, furthermore, "he is a tiresome and depressing person to have about the house. In the play you have him for about three hours."[21] These harsh words were a drop in the bucket, though, compared with the many raves.

As far as I can tell, Witherspoon was not "noticed" as Edith Gordon. Once she was cast as Miss Merk, she was noticed nearly every time and in positive terms. Unfortunately, I have to deal with this avalanche of accolades selectively and with brutal brevity. The critics deemed her performance "a gem in its way," "A clever bit of character work," "exceptionally good," "a clever accomplishment and elicits well-deserved applause," and "a little bit which she makes a gem of comedy." They also thought that her "comedy hit as Miss Merks [*sic*] adds greatly to the pleasure of watching 'The Concert'"; that she "contributes a liberal share of comedy as the angular secretary who also is smitten by her master's charms"; that she "handled this exaggerated role in a manner that left doubt as to whether it might have been portrayed more capably"; and also that "Cora Witherspoon, as Miss Merk the secretary, was another weepy person. She splashed, she splattered, she waded in woe.... [She] wrung all the moisture of humor out of an ungracious part and brought down the house."[22]

Finally, there was this lengthier assessment in the *Salem Statesman Journal*: "Miss

Merk, Arany's private secretary (who just couldn't help loving him) was the only real comedy role in the play and was handled masterfully by Miss Witherspoon. Her hysterical nervousness really made us nervous and her declaration of love suited well her upturned nose, tight Psyche knot of hair and slovenly make-up. She made one devoutly grateful that providence had not made us all private secretaries to a genius."[23]

The sole negative review of her performance I have found was in the *Sacramento Bee*, where E.S. Carroll wrote: "The only apparent point on which any adverse criticism might be based would be in the character of Miss Merk, Arany's secretary, as played by Cora Witherspoon. Her interpretation was so much the extreme in burlesque that it approached buffoonery, jarring somewhat as compared with the high comedy of the other parts and the excellent humor of the piece." The competing *Sacramento Star*, though, disagreed with Carroll's assessment of the same performance, writing: "Especially effective was Cora Witherspoon as an anaemic and ardent secretary to the virtuoso."[24] *The Concert* set a pattern for Witherspoon's appearances on Broadway for the next 35 years. While her parts were usually fairly limited in scope, and she typically appeared only in one or two acts of a three-act play, Witherspoon would stand out among the supporting players in the show and be singled out in the reviews.

When *The Concert* closed in New York in May 1913, Witherspoon only had one last hurrah to go as Miss Merk. Yet Ditrichstein had no intention of leaving his talented and loyal young protégée at liberty. During the summer of 1913, he starred in a six-week season of plays at the historic Alcazar Theatre in San Francisco with leading lady Isabel Irving, second lead Madge West, and Witherspoon in support. As usual, this engagement was somewhat "inflated" when reported by the *New Orleans Times-Picayune*, always eager to play up Witherspoon's successes. Under the heading "Brilliant Engagement for Miss Cora Witherspoon," her hometown newspaper reported on April 6 that Witherspoon had received "a most flattering offer" from Fred Belasco, brother of David, and manager of the Alcazar Theatre in San Francisco: "He has engaged Leo Ditrichstein for a six week's season to appear in all his successes, opening in 'The Concert.' Miss Witherspoon has been offered the position of leading woman, playing opposite the star." The news item concluded: "This is a very brilliant opportunity for the young actress.... She will now be a full-fledged leading woman."[25]

Unfortunately, this was not strictly speaking true. Ditrichstein was indeed taking Irving, West, and Witherspoon (and Anne Livingston) with him from the "Concert" touring company. As the *San Francisco Chronicle* made clear, though, in his "stock-starring engagement at the Alcazar.... With him, as his leading woman, is Isabel Irving." Witherspoon was granted featured player status, though, as a longtime member of Ditrichstein's company. In the ads, Irving's, Witherspoon's, and West's names were all featured below the name of the star, with Irving's name in all capital letters.[26]

Even before the season started at the Alcazar on June 9, 1913, the *San Francisco Chronicle* wrote that it "promises to be the most notable event in the history of that theater." The six-week season included four plays with which Ditrichstein was intimately associated as author and star. The first, predictably, was *The Concert*, which was given for two weeks with the four veterans reprising their roles. The remaining players were taken from the stock company at the Alcazar, including Louis Bennison (Dr. Dallas), Burt Wesner (McGinnis), and Anna McNaughton (Mrs. McGinnis). The *San Francisco Examiner* noted that "society, prevented in large measure from greeting Ditrichstein's former visit on account of the grand opera season and the Lenten restrictions [in March

1913], was at the Alcazar in force last night." The run was extended to a second week "to accommodate the crowds." These two weeks at the Alcazar were Witherspoon's final appearance as Miss Merk, hands down the role she played most often in her career. The critic for the *Examiner* gave her a fitting farewell: "Miss Witherspoon's acting as his secretary is genuine art."[27]

As his second offering, Ditrichstein had a new play to try out called *Such Is Life*, based on a French original called *Pour Vivre Heureux* by André Rivoire and Yves Mirande. The *San Francisco Chronicle* reported: "If [*Such Is Life*] fulfills the expectations of Ditrichstein and his stage associates … it will be his starring vehicle next season at the Belasco Theatre, New York." *Such Is Life* differed from *The Concert* in that Ditrichstein would be playing a good husband, and Irving a bad wife, the star explained to a journalist from the *San Francisco Examiner* during a break in a rehearsal at the Alcazar. He added: "And there is another point of difference. Miss Cora Witherspoon is going to be given a chance to look pretty." The *San Francisco Chronicle* reported some weeks later that "Miss Witherspoon's natural graces are to be given more ample scope for display than they received in her portrayal of his lovelorn secretary."[28]

I will have more to say of the play when we get to the New York production. In San Francisco, it "made an emphatic hit" and was "far and away the best legitimate production in town." Witherspoon and Anne Livingstone were "natural in their work." Another paper wrote: "Madge West and Cora Witherspoon, illuminants of any cast, are allowed but the slenderest parts, although Miss Witherspoon, in her little role, was by far the most natural feminine player last night." Neill Wilson of the *San Francisco Examiner* quipped that "Isabel Irving … is about as much at home as the sporty wife of an artist as a duchess in a steam laundry." He disliked the title and predicted, correctly as it turned out, that the play would "face the theatrical season next September under a title made of sterner stuff."[29]

The two final offerings of this special limited season were the Ditrichstein farces *Before and After* from 1905 and the more familiar *Are You a Mason?* from 1901. In the former, Witherspoon played a "shoddy adventuress." The play did not meet with the critics' approval, who felt it was currently below Ditrichstein's level and represented a step back from *The Concert* and *Such Is Life*. *Are You a Mason?*, on the other hand, was welcomed as "one of the minor standards of the stage, a comic classic, a perennial." It was the eleventh time this farce was revived at the Alcazar. Witherspoon played Eva Perry, the wife of Frank Perry (Kernan Cripps), a young husband who pretends to be a mason and "is responsible for most of the developments of the farce." The *San Francisco Chronicle* wrote of her efforts, that "Miss Witherspoon's pleasant face gives vivacity to any part she may essay."[30] Ditrichstein did not act in *Are You a Mason?* His season at the Alcazar closed a week earlier than planned, on July 12, 1913. Witherspoon and Aunt Sophie returned to New Orleans for a brief stay with Maude and Annie, before boarding the *Comus* on July 23 bound for New York.[31] It was time to try *Such Is Life* before a Broadway audience.

After a brief trial run at the Lyceum Theatre in Rochester, New York, *Such Is Life* opened at the Belasco Theatre in New York on September 4, 1913. That is, producer Belasco had heeded the critic's call to change the title, and *Such Is Life* was now *The Temperamental Journey*. It still dealt with a talented yet impoverished artist, Jacques Dupont, who is thought dead and returns home to discover that his ostensible widow is about to marry her lover and that his whole family life has been a sham. The unfaithful wife was still being played by Isabel Irving.

From the positive notices she received in the New York papers, we can learn more about what Witherspoon's supporting role entailed. She played Fanny Lamont, the girl-friend and later the wife of Jacques's faithful friend, the musician Billy Shepherd (Richie Ling). Fanny is first encountered with Billy in the dead artist's studio at the opening of the second act, where she has "stolen … from a forbidding father" and "tries to arouse him [Billy] from his depression." This scene was "performed cleverly," according to the *Rochester Democrat and Chronicle*. The *New York Tribune* described Fanny as "the incarnation of feminine common sense, the kind of wholesome young woman who is a true helpmeet, and a tower of strength in hours of sorrow." Thus, she clearly functioned as a foil to the duplicitous Mrs. Dupont. The final act was set in the drawing room of the composer and his wife, "in which prosperity has overtaken them." The *Brooklyn Daily Eagle* thought Witherspoon gave an excellent character sketch as "Billy Shepherd's common sense fiancée" and the *New York Sun* concurred that she "gave a capital sketch of a matter-of-fact young woman who always kept her head." It was also said of her that she "scores without overplaying as the wife" and was "clever as Fanny Lamont." As for the play in its entirety, the critics could not agree whether or not it was "mounted to perfection," "capital entertainment," "thin, superficial and utterly unreal," or "one of the most pronounced successes of the season."[32]

On September 29, after three weeks at the Belasco, *The Temperamental Journey* made way for David Warfield in *The Auctioneer* and moved to the Theatre Republic for the remainder of its run. It closed there on December 20, after a respectable 124 performances, and moved to the Broadway Theatre in Brooklyn for a week. Unlike previous Belasco-Dietrichson ventures, the show was not taken on tour and closed permanently on December 27, 1913.[33]

Stories of older men grooming much younger girls and women for marriage (with themselves) and playing the role of father-figure and potential lover at once will hopefully never regain the popularity they held in the nineteenth and early twentieth century. *Daddy Long Legs* is such a story, which began in 1912 as successful serial novel written in epistolary form and originally published in the *Ladies Home Journal* by Jean Webster ("a niece of the late Mark Twain"[34]), was subsequently dramatized by the author herself, and finally was adapted for the screen several times.

Described as "a modern Cinderella story" about "a most winsome little maid and her middle-aged lover," in one of those curious career coincidences, the role of the "little maid" Jerusha "Judy" Abbott was played by Witherspoon's former neighbor in the theatrical boarding house in New York, Ruth Chatterton. *Daddy Long Legs* was 20-year-old Chatterton's third show in New York, where she had made her debut in *The Great Name* in 1911, but it was significant in that it "served to introduce her as a star to Broadway." Witherspoon was cast as Sallie McBride, Judy's college roommate and sister of Judy's coeval would-be seducer, the "unspeakable cad" James McBride (Charles Trowbridge).[35] Sallie is a typical friend and sidekick role, so it is hardly surprising that in the first sound film version from 1931, which starred Janet Gaynor, Sallie was played by the best friend and sidekick of all time, Una Merkel. If it seems unlikely that Witherspoon and Merkel should ever have been cast in the same role, you have to recall that Witherspoon had just turned 24 when she assumed the role of Sallie. Merkel was 28 when she played it in the Fox production directed by Alfred Santell.

From the overarching perspective of Witherspoon's career, *Daddy Long Legs* was her first Broadway show that was not produced by David Belasco and that did not star Leo Ditrichstein. Its guiding spirit was yet another major player in the world of early twentieth-century American theater: Henry Miller. Witherspoon worked for many major producers down through the years, but Miller was the only one who could rival Belasco in importance to her career. In an interview in 1925, she acknowledged that "the direction of David Belasco and Henry Miller had contributed greatly to her development as an actress."[36]

Daddy Long Legs had an unusually long pre–Broadway tour, starting at the National Theatre in Washington, D.C., on February 23, 1914; moving from there to the Lyceum Theatre in Rochester, New York; English's Opera House in Indianapolis; Powers' Theatre in Chicago, where it played for 25 weeks and over 200 performances; before finally reaching the Gaiety Theatre in New York on September 28, 1914. Witherspoon received a few notices for her performance, which was termed "effective" (*Washington Herald*), "likable" (*Rochester Democrat and Chronicle*), "realistic" (*Indianapolis News*), and "charming and youthful" (*New York Times*). *Daddy Long Legs* finally came to an end at the Gaiety Theatre on May 15, 1915, after 264 performances.[37] From start to finish, Witherspoon had spent a year and a half doing this play in which she only appeared in the second act.

All through the summer of 1914, Witherspoon had been performing in *Daddy Long Legs* in Chicago and had not been able to return home for her annual summer holiday. The following year, though, she was back in New Orleans and staying with Maude and Annie in their home in Freret St. She arrived sometime in June and stayed till mid–August. It was especially important to be home at this time, as her beloved Aunt Sophie was in failing health. When Witherspoon finally sailed for New York on August 14, it was without her faithful aunt at her side. Instead, she was accompanied by her friend Alice Graveley.[38] Three weeks later, on September 7, Sophie Bell died in New Orleans at the age of 68, probably in the home of her youngest sister at 5342 Coliseum St. She was laid to rest the next day in the Bell-Witherspoon plot in Metairie Cemetery, with her sister Cora and brother-in-law Henry.[39]

I have no doubt Witherspoon felt the loss of Aunt Sophie more keenly than any other person in her life. Sophie had made a home for her in New York and wherever else they went for the last 15 years and had been an integral part of her career success during the past decade. In 1913, the *Times-Picayune* described Sophie as her "constant companion and with whom she makes her home in a charming apartment in New York."[40] From here on out, Witherspoon was on her own. With only one known exception, she never shared a home with anyone again.

After proving with *Daddy Long Legs* that she could stand on her own feet and get hired by other producers than Belasco and support other stars than Ditrichstein, Witherspoon returned to the Ditrichstein fold in the fall of 1915. *The Great Lover* was "a whimsical expose of the grand opera world"[41] in three acts, an adaptation from the Italian by Ditrichstein himself in collaboration with Chicago journalists and playwrights Frederic and Fanny Hatton, known for *Years of Discretion*. The play had been four years in the making. Ditrichstein had the original idea and, after some years without making much progress, he hired the Hattons to help him carry it out. Ditrichstein had moved on from Belasco and was now being managed by producers George M. Cohan and Sam H. Harris. It looks as if Witherspoon had followed him there, as she worked for Cohan and Harris not just in *The Great Lover*, but also in *The King*, *The Winning of Ma*, *Three Faces East*, and *The Matinee Hero*, her final play with Ditrichstein.

Ditrichstein's character this time was Jean Plaurel, an operatic star with a magnetic power of attraction, particularly over the female segment of his audience. We encounter him at a critical time of life, when he loses his voice and is forced to recognize his limitations both as a man and as an artist. "On the stage," wrote the *New York Times* of Plaurel, "he is the greatest Don Giovanni of his time, and off the stage he is a very passable Don Juan." According to Ditrichstein, the appearance of the hero was inspired by seeing a performance with Maurice Renand, "the famous baritone"; otherwise, Plaurel was a "composite character, not based on Enrico Caruso or any other one operatic star." The three acts were laid consecutively in the office of the manager of the Gotham Opera House, in the star's dressing room at the Gotham Opera House, and in the apartment of the great singer.[42]

"At the end [Plaurel] is left alone with his fading love letters and is giving himself over to the melancholy of declining years when the telephone rings and the little brown-haired divorcee who had called in his dressing room the other day is there to arrange for their first tête-à-téte." Witherspoon played this divorcée, Mrs. Peter Van Ness, "a society woman who is not immune to the attractions of the great lover."[43] This minor character only appears in person in the first act; though, as the summary above indicates, she makes a reappearance on the other end of the phone, just as the final curtain is about to come down. It was a testament to Witherspoon's loyalty, if nothing else, that she spent two years of her life playing such a modest role in this unimportant play.

Having been originally called *Jean Plaurel* in the planning stages, the show had its world premiere as *$2,000 a Night* at the Empire Theatre in Syracuse, New York, on October 11, 1915, played Rochester, New York and Detroit, before being retitled *The Great Lover* for the opening at Ford's Theatre in Baltimore November 1.[44] Witherspoon stayed with her cousin John W. Frick and his wife May at their home on University Parkway and May hosted a tea for her at the Baltimore Country Club.[45] *The Great Lover* ran for a respectable 245 performances at the Longacre Theatre in New York between November 10, 1915, and June 10, 1916. It reopened at the newly renamed Cohan and Harris Theatre in New York on September 4, 1916, and ran for a further three weeks, before being taken on an extensive, seventh-month tour starting at the Detroit Opera House September 25, which included Chicago, Boston, Philadelphia, Washington, Pittsburgh, Akron, Dayton, Cincinnati, Columbus, Indianapolis, St. Louis, Cleveland, Buffalo, Newark; back to New York City; and Springfield, before coming to a close in Stamford, Connecticut, in early May 1917.[46]

Witherspoon's efforts in this play rarely rated a mention in reviews, but the *New York Sun* wrote after the Broadway premiere, that "Julian Little gave distinction and humor to the role of the secretary and proved how rare is the possession of breeding and the good tone on the stage. Cora Witherspoon did something of the same kind with the episodic part of a woman of the world." After her appearance at the National Theatre in Washington, D.C., she was alluded to in one review as "the big blonde." In St. Louis, she was "the divorcee with the big, flashing eyes."[47]

Not many days would have passed between the end of *The Great Lover* in Stamford and her next engagement with Jessie Bonstelle's celebrated stock company. In addition to Bonstelle herself, the members of the company this season included Florence Sheffield, Marie Curtis, Arthur Allen, Adams Rice, Corliss Giles, Hugh Dillman, W.A. Wilkes, William Pringle, Franklin Pangborn, J. Harry Irvine, Seymour D. Parker, Frank Howson, Maude Snyder, Marian McMichael, and Herbert Robertson. Rice also acted as the stage manager. Bonstelle's company normally played Buffalo first, followed by

Leo Ditrichstein in a pose from the final moments of *The Great Lover*, a comedy he wrote about an operatic star who loses his voice, as Ditrichstein himself had done. Witherspoon had a modest role as an amorous lady with a keen interest in the singer. She only appears in person in the first act, but in the play's finale it is her the hero is speaking to over the phone.

Detroit, but this year she reversed the usual order.[48] So on May 14, 1917, Witherspoon found herself at the Garrick Theatre in Detroit, where the Bonstelle Company's eighth season in that city was being inaugurated with a week-long production of Hulbert Foot-ner's recent drama *Shirley Kaye*. Bonstelle herself played the title role, created by Elsie Ferguson on Broadway during the 1916–17 season.

In order of presentation, the 11-week season in Detroit also saw productions of *The Professor's Love Story*, *Hit-the-Trail Holliday*, *The Cinderella Man*, *It Pays to Advertise*, *A Thousand Years Ago*, *The Great Divide*, *Our Mrs. McChesney*, *His Majesty Bunker Bean*, *The New Henrietta*, and *Divorçons* (with *The Tenth Point* as a curtain raiser). Witherspoon appears to have had a part to play in most of these week-long shows. I can only mention a few of her more important roles. *The Professor's Love Story* by James M. Barrie had first been produced on Broadway in 1892, and there had been five subsequent revivals. The *Detroit Times* wrote that "Miss Cora Witherspoon makes a convincing dowager Lady Gilding."[49] Ethel Dane had played the role in the most recent New York revival earlier that year.

It Pays to Advertise had been a big hit and ran for a year in 1914–15. In Detroit, Witherspoon got some of her best reviews in the role that had been created by Louise Drew: "The Comtesse de Beaurien of Miss Cora Witherspoon shone like the traditional 'rich jewel in an Ethiop's ear.' She has complete command of Parisian French, and she delivered her lines with astonishing fluency and characteristic verve"; "Cora Witherspoon was admirable as the alleged French countess and her voluble French was as [illegible word] as it was excited. In this role Miss Witherspoon had her best chance of the Bonstelle season up to date." I would also have liked to have seen her in *A Thousand Years Ago*, a kind of fantasy romance of the Orient by Percy Mackaye from 1914, where she played the slave girl Zelima.[50]

The Great Divide by William Vaughan Moody was a rare drama in this season's Bonstelle repertoire, which consisted almost entirely of then popular, now entirely forgotten, comedies. It first opened in the 1906–7 season and had been frequently revived, most recently in 1917. Witherspoon played the role created by Laura Hope Crews of "jolly Polly Jordan." In *His Majesty Bunker Bean*, a 1916 comedy by Lee Wilson Dodd, Witherspoon played a "putative Countess" and "'seeress' who puts one over on Bunker, with her crystal gazing."[51]

The final performance of the season at the Garrick Theatre in Detroit was on Saturday, July 28 and on Monday, July 30, Bonstelle and her company opened their 12th season at the Star Theatre in Buffalo with *It Pays to Advertise*. In Buffalo, the company included Corliss Giles, William Pringle, Adam Rice, Arthur Allen, Hugh Dillman, Marie Curtis, Flora Sheffield, Franklin Pangborn, J. Henry Irvine, and Frank Howson. Seymour Parker was the "scenic artist," and Witherspoon had the rare experience of being directed by a woman, Williamene F. Wilkes. She reprised her role as the Countess in *It Pays to Advertise* and was described as "most capable" and "one of the dominant figures." The season opener was followed by a week each of *His Majesty Bunker Bean*; *Good Morning, Rosamond*; *Hit-the-Trail Holliday*, and *The Cinderella Man*, with the sixth and final week divided between *The Professor's Love Story* and *Divorçons*. Her "psychic Countess" in *His Majesty Bunker Bean* was found to be "clever" (twice) and "quite up to the mark."[52]

August 13 saw the world premiere of a new comedy by Constance Lindsay Skinner called *Good Morning, Rosamond*, based on her novel of the same title. The author was in attendance at the premiere. Witherspoon was paired with Franklin Pangborn, who had also been in Detroit, "as Mabel, hopelessly in love with Wilton Howard, who is too poor to marry her." The play was produced at the 48th Street Theatre on Broadway by the Shuberts and Jessie Bonstelle in December 1917, but only lasted 8 performances. Witherspoon was not in it, being busy in her new show with Leo Ditrichstein.

In Buffalo, Witherspoon was also praised for her Mrs. Temple in *Hit-the-Trail Holliday*: "Cora Witherspoon as the gushing young widow could not have been improved upon. She looked the part, and acted it to perfection"; "Cora Witherspoon as Mrs. Temple, suffrage and temperance worker, [and another actor] carry their portions of the comedy excellently."[53] The company disbanded after the final performance on September 8.

Between its world premiere at the Euclid Avenue Opera House in Cleveland on November 5, 1917, and the closing of its post–Broadway tour in Chicago on May 19, 1918,[54] Witherspoon lent her talents to Leo Ditrichstein's latest venture, entitled *The King*. Since *The Great Lover*, Ditrichstein had had a failure in Chicago with an adaptation of a play by Calderón called *The Judge of Zalamea*.[55] *The King* would be far from a failure, but it would be equally far from the smashing success of *The Concert*. Once again, Ditrichstein had adapted a European play, this time of French origin. From impersonating musicians, artists, and singers, he had now moved on to royalty. The *New York Times* explained that "Mr. Ditrichstein's rôle is that of the monarch of a mythical Slavic kingdom, and it is his amorous adventures in Paris with which the piece is concerned." The play, according to *Brooklyn Daily Eagle*, was "a satirical burlesque of kingly conventions and the snobbishness of democracy."[56] The producers were Cohan and Harris.

Once again, Witherspoon's opportunities were limited, as she played the minor role of Mademoiselle Georgette Delaunay, described in one of her few notices as "a modish incarnation of a Paris stage favorite." After Cleveland, the show went to Hartford, before it opened at George M. Cohan's Theatre in New York on November 20, 1917. Witherspoon's friend Miriam Doyle played Sousette Bourdier, while future film star William Powell made his Broadway debut in the role of Rivolet. *The King* closed in New York on March 9, 1918, after 127 performances. "Supported by his New York company intact,"[57] Ditrichstein took his play post–Broadway to Newark, Baltimore, Boston, and Chicago.

The reviews this time were decidedly mixed. The *New York Times* wrote that "the wit of the play sparkles incessantly, and the laughable detail with which it is embroidered seems marvelously fresh and spontaneous," but found "much of the production was exceedingly crude." The *New York Tribune* concurred that "the play is quite the most vulgar of the Broadway stage of now, and proves how delightful vulgarity can be when it is rich enough and honest." The *Brooklyn Times Union* thought that "the play is funny— really and hilariously funny—and it may even now be written down as a big, smashing hit." The *Brooklyn Times Union* panned it, observing that "not since 'The Phantom Rival' has Leo Ditrichstein appeared to such poor advantage.... [I]n this newest theatrical nightmare in three acts Mr. Ditrichstein has to carry most of the play on his own shoulders—and he is incapable of supporting the load." According to the *New York Sun*, "Mr. Ditrichstein had trained his entire company to be worthy of surrounding his own skillful and engaging performance."[58]

The *Boston Globe* found that "as refined satire it is among the best seen here within recent seasons." The review in the *Boston Herald* compared the English adaptation to the French original to the detriment of the former. A news item on Witherspoon in the *Boston Globe* on April 7, 1918, noted that she "has been associated with Leo Ditrichstein for seven years, having made her first appearance with him in 'The Concert.' Then followed 'The Temperamental Journey,' 'The Phantom Rival' and last season 'The Great Lover.'"[59] She had in fact been associated with Ditrichstein since 1908 and was not in *The Phantom Rival*, being fully occupied at the time with *Daddy Long Legs*.

This lovely portrait dates from around 1915 and appears to have been taken in a hotel or theater. At first glance, I thought Witherspoon was holding a scruffy dog in her arms (that would have been like her), but on closer inspection it is an ostrich fan. Notice her peachy skin, her wistful yet hopeful expression, and her button nose. A life of hard knocks would change her irrevocably into a deeply lined and empty-eyed travesty of her former self (courtesy Fredrick Tucker).

On July 8, 1918, Witherspoon opened in a new four-act comedy by Isaac and Michael L. Landman called *The Winning of Ma* at the Apollo Theatre in Atlantic City, New Jersey, which played for a week. It was based on Bessie R. Hoover's "Ma Flickinger" stories. The reviewer for the *Philadelphia Inquirer* felt that the "young and ambitious producing managers" George M. Cohan and Sam H. Harris had "found a success in it" and described the play as "a quiet comedy of bucolic life in a Michigan precinct, with the sort of characters which are to be found in the wilds of any State": it "revolves around the love affair of the youngest girl of the Flickinger household, little Opal [Marion Coakley], and the winning over of Ma Flickinger [Zelda Sears], who has been a severe ruler of the household up to this time." Witherspoon "gave a fine characterization of Jules Peebles, the married daughter who had her domestic trials and tribulations and aided in bringing about a change in Ma's conduct."[60]

While this Cohan and Harris production did not make it to Broadway, their next one with Witherspoon in the cast did. No sooner had the thumbs been turned down on *The Winning of Ma*, the producers cast Witherspoon in their next theatrical outing, *Three Faces East*, which opened at the National Theatre in Washington, D.C., on August 5, 1918. This "Secret Service war play" marked the dramatic debut of screenwriter Anthony Paul Kelly and was a big hit at the Cohan and Harris Theatre in New York, when it opened there on August 13.

Three Faces East starred Emmett Corrigan and Violet Heming as the spies Valdar and Helene. Set in Berlin and London, the show was described in one early review as "a play of the secret service in which the work of a band of spies is circumvented by the keener wit and skill of a 'master' detective." It was well received by the critics, as "one of the most thrilling melodramas that has been presented on a Washington stage" and "quite the best mystery play of several seasons."[61]

It is not possible to glean from the reviews what Witherspoon's role as Miss Risdon entailed, but it was no doubt a modest part. So modest, in fact, that Witherspoon jumped ship long before *Three Faces East* had ended its successful run of 335 performances. Nearly one month to the day after the show opened in New York, Witherspoon opened in another Cohan and Harris play called *The Matinee Hero* at Parsons' Theatre in Hartford, Connecticut, where *The Concert* and *The King* had also played, in 1912 and 1917, respectively.

This would be the last time Witherspoon supported Leo Ditrichstein, who, as the play's title indicates, was now portraying a type of character more like himself than ever. As the *Hartford Courant* noted: "He has played the great and popular pianist; the great and popular singer; the not at all great but interesting and amusing monarch; and in the present play he acts the actor—the darling of all the matinee-goers of all the land."[62] Ditrichstein portrayed Richard Leroy, who has built a successful career in the commercial theater with the able assistance of his practical and devoted wife, but who longs to play Hamlet and other great, classic roles. Witherspoon was cast as the reporter Miss Hopkins.

Ditrichstein had written the play with veteran dramatist A.E. Thomas. On September 16, after four performances in Hartford, *The Matinee Hero* moved to the Tremont Theatre in Boston for three weeks, then played two performances at the Collingwood Theatre in Poughkeepsie on October 5, before opening at the Vanderbilt Theatre in New York on October 7, as the first production of that theater's fall and winter season.[63]

There were several changes of cast before the New York opening. The Broadway cast included Catherine Proctor as the sagacious and forgiving Mrs. Leroy; Vivian Rushmore as the "other woman," Blanche Langlais, who tempts Leroy to stray from the narrow path, but also encourages him to develop his talent in new directions; Robert McWade as the theater manager Sam McNaughton; and Brandon Tynan as Frank Fairchild, a playwright and Leroy's friend and advisor, who just happens to have "intimate knowledge" of Miss Langlais. Miss Rushmore, who had replaced Margaret Dale by the time the play opened in New York, was so bad as the temptress, she was rapidly replaced by Mary Boland.[64]

Overall, the play was not well received. Unlike his previous stage successes, noted the *Hartford Courant*, "there is not an abundance of humor." The *New York Tribune* was frankly hostile: "The pity is that this really fine theme of the sincere conflict of the artist in choosing between the work that brings easy success and his aspirations should have been expressed in a play of such crudeness and tastelessness.... It represents a curious jumble of ideas." The *Brooklyn Daily Eagle* could not resist a jab: "There was a great deal of talk last night about paltry plays, and it must have made Leo Ditrichstein, who was performing in one of the kind, blush under his greasepaint while he denounced them." According to the *New York Evening World*, *The Matinee Hero* "offered little, even to the limited intelligence of confirmed theatre-goers."[65]

While the reviews for the play were mixed at best, Witherspoon was frequently singled out for praise, making this another breakthrough role for her with the critics. "Cora Witherspoon was sincere and good as the newspaper woman," wrote the *Hartford Courant*. "A word is due to Miss Witherspoon for her excellent scene with Leroy," wrote the *Boston Herald*. According to the *Boston Globe*, "Cora Witherspoon's impersonation of the newspaper woman is welcome because of its lack of conventional exaggeration." According to the *New York Herald*: "Cora Witherspoon played the part of a reporter with a degree of intelligence and distinction that would have been of great service in other places on the distaff side of the cast." Finally, *Brooklyn Life* added its need of praise: "Cora Witherspoon in the small part of a newspaper woman is especially pleasing."[66]

From a purely pecuniary perspective, though, this change of role did not pay off. *The Matinee Hero* lasted a modest 64 performances and closed in December, while *Three Faces East* ran well into 1919. As it happens, Witherspoon did not stay in this show either, despite the praise that had been heaped on her. On November 16, she opened in a revival of *Daddy Long Legs* at Henry Miller's Theater in her original role as Sallie McBride. Ruth Chatterton reprised her starring role as the orphaned Judy Abbott and Henry Miller himself took Charles Waldron's old role as Judy's mature benefactor Jervis "Daddy Long Legs" Pendleton.

Critical opinion on the success of and need for the revival was divided. The *New York Times* was ecstatic, writing that "the late Jean Webster's humor and sentiment, and her instinct of salient, delicious character, exerted a sway upon its audience the like of which has not been felt for several seasons." This encomium notwithstanding, and an assurance from *Brooklyn Life* that "there is no reason why the piece cannot run for a long period to big business," the *Daddy Long Legs* revival lasted less than a month.[67]

For her final show of 1918, Witherspoon was teamed yet again with Zelda Sears from *The Winning of Ma* company. The leading role this time was played by Grace George, a major Broadway star at the time and wife of veteran producer William A. Brady, who produced all her plays. The new comedy was called *The Widow's Might* and was written by the Englishmen Leonard Huskinson and Christopher Sandeman. It was described as "a delightful comedy of New York life," centering on the well-to-do widow of the title, Eileen Carstairs (George), "a brilliant bit of femininity." She sounds like an upper-class, wasp Dolly Levi, only her matchmaking is more a case of "unmatchmaking," as she has to save a friend married to a much older man from the dire consequences of an indiscretion. Witherspoon was cast as Poppy Maynford, "a wheedling wife in good color" and Mayne Lynton played her "silly ass husband very pleasingly indeed." The *Washington Herald* thought she "made an excellent Poppy Maynford."[68]

The play had its world premiere at the Stamford Theatre in Stamford, Connecticut December 16, 1918, before being staged briefly at the Court Square Theatre in Springfield, Massachusetts (December 19), Parsons' Theatre in Hartford, Connecticut (December 21), and finally the Shubert-Belasco Theatre in Washington, D.C. (December 24–28). The *Washington Evening Star* thought there was "cause to question the longevity of this production."[69] Indeed, "the widow's might" proved insufficient to propel her to Broadway.

As it happened, Witherspoon's affiliation with Grace George was not yet over. In early March 1919, it became clear that she was to support the 39-year-old star yet again in "a new comedy of contemporary life" by Mark Reed about "the socially elect of a certain progressive American city whose pet and particular hobby is their Country club's golf course." First-time author Reed had finished his play and mailed it off to George 15 months earlier, before joining the army and seeing active service in France. The war soon being over, the author was able to be on hand both in Detroit and Cleveland to supervise the production of his first work for the stage.[70] Reed would later be known for *Petticoat Fever* and *Yes, My Darling Daughter.*

Alexander Woollcott summed up the paper-thin plot of Reed's debut play in his review for the *New York Times*: "it relates the tempest in a teapot when Francis Nesmith [George] makes a bad stroke at the eighth green, loses her temper, ploughs up the turf with her mashie, and is suspended from the club for sixty days. That would mean she couldn't go to the dance, nor exhibit her Pekingese at the dog show—an outrage, and unthinkable calamity. So she turns the town upside down in her campaign for reinstatement, invades the church, agitates the bar, messes the politics, and unleashes scandal. She flirts, cajoles, threatens. She plots. She woos one man with glances and another with liquor. She begs and bribes and lies. Oh, it is a most devastating extravagance on the feminine mind in politics and great will be the wrath of the Suffragists thereat."[71] Witherspoon's role in all this was to play George's loyal friend and supporter Elsie Goward.

The producer of *She Would and She Did* was George's husband William A. Brady and the director was 31-year-old John Cromwell, who would have a long career as an actor and director on Broadway between 1912 and 1971 and become the father of James Cromwell in 1940. Cromwell also played Witherspoon's "easygoing husband" in the play. The *New York Daily News* thought "Mr. Cromwell's resigned Frank Goward is one of the funniest bits in a very good comedy."[72]

She Would and She Did had a relatively long gestation period and did not open in New York till September 11, 1919. In March, the play was tried out for a week in Detroit and a week in Cleveland, where George had not been seen in a decade. One reviewer wrote that the play had "more bright lines than have been heard on the local stage in a like period in a long, long time." Another found "it is too full of lines" altogether. Critics were quick to stress that George, who was nearing the critical age of 40, was "as youthful and charming as ever" and "as youthful and charming as she has been for—well, for several years."[73]

Witherspoon, too, was warmly welcomed back in Detroit. The *Detroit Free Press* wrote: "Lending aid of impeccable character [is] Cora Witherspoon, well remembered for her good work as a member of the Bonstelle company, and whose portrayal of the loyal henchman to the spirited heroine is a well limned effort." According to the *Detroit*

Times: "Miss Cora Witherspoon is well known in Detroit having been a member of the Bonstelle company. She has developed into a clever and thoroughly capable actress, and was warmly welcomed by her friends."[74] It was nearly two years since she had acted with Jessie Bonstelle's company.

After Cleveland, the production took a lengthy "time out" over the spring and summer. According to the *New York Herald*: "Grace George will return to the stage here, but in order to work public enthusiasm gradually to a climax, her resurgence will not take place until next season." She wanted to make another attempt to start a repertory company.[75] The revamped production was tried out August 4–6 at the Savoy Theatre in Asbury Park, New Jersey, and August 7–9 at the Broadway Theatre in Long Branch, New Jersey, before it finally reached Broadway and the Vanderbilt Theatre in mid–September.

She Would and She Did is chiefly notable in Witherspoon's career as the occasion for her being skewered by the poison pen of the legendary Alexander Woollcott, whose review we have already sampled. He loved, nay, *raved* over George's performance and liked the play, but abhorred the production. "It was," he wrote, "a comedy as light as thistledown ... the work of a highly promising newcomer named Mark Reed." According to Woollcott, producer Brady "has taken a comedy as thin as an eggshell and allowed it to be kicked around the stage as though it were a football." He found the performance "abominable": "Cora Witherspoon, May Collins, John Adair, Jr., ... are awkward, strident and heavy-handed, and most of the rest are only less so. 'I hear loud voices,' cries Miss Witherspoon as Mrs. Goward. We should think she did."[76] Let us hope Woollcott's scathing review did not have a role to play in Witherspoon's subsequent breakdown.

From Witherspoon's perspective, the news about the play was not all bad. The *New York Herald* found that "[Grace George] and Cora Witherspoon as her ally in her struggle for reinstatement were charmingly womanly and unreasonable in all their tactics. In these two characters centered all the interest the piece contained. There was scarcely an endurable or plausible person among the others." The *Brooklyn Citizen* wrote: "Of the rest of the cast the best work was done by Cora Witherspoon, John Cromwell, Ned Burton, John Stokes and Edward Arnold." *Brooklyn Life* thought Mrs. Goward was "played very well by Cora Witherspoon." Finally, the *Springfield Republican* also differed with Woollcott's thumbs down, writing that "Cora Witherspoon deserves highest commendation for her work in a role obviously designed as a foil." *She Would and She Did* closed after only 36 performances on October 11, 1919. Witherspoon attributed its rapid demise to the Actors Equity Association strike of 1919, which "stopped everything."[77] It was her final play of the decade.

In November, Witherspoon went on a much-needed vacation to her native city and stayed with Maude and Annie on Freret St. for what may have been the last time, as they moved to Las Cruces, New Mexico, the following year. At the age of 37, Maude was still working as a pharmacist. Now 53, Anna had quit her job with the Western Union Telegraph Co. after 26 years. Her son Warren had married in 1917, with both Annie and Maude in attendance. He was a successful lawyer and, as the first president of the New Orleans Mid-Winter Sports Association, would go on to become a co-founder of the Sugar Bowl in 1934, before his death in 1947.[78]

Witherspoon was slated to remain with her sister and Annie till December 1. On December 7, Cynthia St. Charles described the actress in her society column in the *New Orleans States* as "a lovely-looking, charming and very talented New Orleans girl who is now a real New York actress." Miss St. Charles wasted no time in mentioning that

Witherspoon "has been in New Orleans resting after a breakdown": "When the theatrical strike in New York stopped everything she was in Grace George's company. She says she feels quite fit, after a month of rest and quiet in New Orleans, and now she has gone back to New York to get ready for her next engagement." Nothing more is known about Witherspoon's collapse at this time, but it indicates her frail condition both mentally and physically and may have been due to overwork. Despite what St. Charles reported, she did not go into Henry Miller's next show, "playing at his own beautiful theater."[79] That would have been *The Famous Mrs. Fair*, which opened at Henry Miller's Theatre on December 22. Two years would pass before Witherspoon was seen on Broadway again.

3

"The Best Dressed Woman on the American Stage"
The 1920s

She has often been termed the best dressed
woman on the American stage.[1]

Though the 1920s got off to a slow start professionally, this decade was arguably Witherspoon's most satisfying time on the stage. She only appeared in seven productions on Broadway during this ten-year period, but that was because three of them were major hits and—touring included—would take up roughly four and a half years of her life. These hit shows were *The Awful Truth* (1922–23) and *Grounds for Divorce* (1924–25), both starring Ina Claire; and *The Constant Wife* (1926–2), starring Ethel Barrymore.

In contrast, between 1930 and decamping to Hollywood in 1936, Witherspoon appeared in 15 shows on Broadway, but that was only because none of them were big hits, few of them ran more than a couple of months, and several of them were outright flops. In the 1920s, her roles—including her three hits—were not so very large, but they paid the bills. Typically, she would appear in only one or two acts of a three-act play. In the 1930s, the parts got somewhat better, but the plays got worse. She was able to perfect the sophisticated society woman type that she would also play on the screen, but she never played these characters for long. Since it is impossible for a character actress to rise above the level of the play she is in, Witherspoon ended up going down with several shows that proved not to be seaworthy.

This decade saw the sundering of her last close family ties with the city of her birth, when her sister Maude moved to Las Cruces, New Mexico, in 1920 "for reasons of health"[2] and her beloved uncle, Samuel Bell, died in 1923. She still had a large extended family of cousins in New Orleans, though, and would return for holidays, though less frequently than before. She had made her home in New York City for some time. In 1920, she was living alone in an apartment at 77 E. 56th St. in Midtown and conveniently close to the theater district. This would be her home for several years; at least until 1925. Early that year, a New Orleans society columnist wrote: "Cora has an attractive apartment in 56th street, just off Park Avenue, where she has established herself amid pleasantness of bright cretonnes, reposeful chairs, silken cushions, and nice rugs and pictures, which is a delightful vantage point from which to start hard work on a dramatic career, as she does." The following year, the same writer referred to how New Orleans "habitues of New York ... have had the treat of cozy tea-table talks in her [Witherspoon's] apartment

50

in Fifty-sixth street."[3] No. 77 was located on the north side of 56th Street between Madison and Park. There were five units in the building, indicating it was probably a small brownstone. Among her neighbors were the married actor couple Arthur Albertson and Esther Howard. Witherspoon had worked with Howard in *She Would and She Did* and with both of them in a production of Jesse Lynch Williams's Pulitzer Prize-winning play *Why Marry?* for Melville's Burke's stock company in Northampton, Massachusetts, in May 1919.[4] She would work with Albertson in *The Fall of Eve* in 1925. Both sides of this block are unrecognizable from Witherspoon's day. The tiny sliver of a brownstone at no. 58 is all that remains among the looming, modernist office buildings one block east of Trump Tower.

Witherspoon shared this apartment for a time with another woman, a fellow actress called Miriam Doyle. Miriam Adele Doyle was born in Maywood, a suburb of Chicago, on February 17, 1894, as the second to last of the seven children of Austin J. Doyle and Pauline A. Weishaar Doyle. Her father was the longtime manager of the Brewers' Association, and Miriam grew up in Maywood and later in Englewood, Illinois. She made her Broadway debut as Florence Hardin in Bayard Veiller's melodrama *Back Home*, based on Irvin S. Cobb's "Judge Priest" stories, in November 1915. Several Broadway shows followed until 1927, after which she became a stage director with several Broadway credits, a ballsy move for any woman at this time. She was associated with Rowland Stebbins as a director and co-producer. Doyle served overseas with the Red Cross during World War II. By the late 1940s, she was working as a production assistant for Howard Lindsay and Russell Crouse.[5]

Witherspoon and Doyle may first have met in the cast of *The King* in November 1917, where Doyle played Sousette Bourdier, the daughter of the Socialist MP played by Robert McWade. They were also in *The Outrageous Mrs. Palmer* together in Boston in 1920, where Miriam had the ingénue role. By 1922, they were living together in Witherspoon's E. 56th St. apartment. Witherspoon was 32 and Doyle 28. I do not know exactly why, but my gut feeling tells me there was something more to this than just two friends sharing an apartment. As far as I know, Miriam Doyle is the only person Witherspoon ever shared a home with. By 1929, Doyle was living at 222 E. 61st St. In later life, she lived in Wilton in "a very old cottage in Connecticut that had a beautiful rose garden." She died there on November 17, 1962, aged 68.[6] Like Witherspoon, Doyle never married.

To return to our story. If you recall, Witherspoon had some kind of nervous breakdown at the end of 1919. She expected to go into Henry Miller's new show *The Famous Mrs. Fair*, but that did not happen. Maybe she was not sufficiently recovered. The play opened at Henry Miller's Theatre on December 22 without her. Thus her first show of the new decade was a play with a similar title. *The Outrageous Mrs. Palmer* was a new comedy by Harry Wagstaff Gribble. It starred Mary Young and was produced by her husband John Craig, who also took one of the supporting roles. Born in 1879, Young had first appeared on Broadway in 1899 and made a hit with John Barrymore in *Believe Me, Xantippe* in 1913. She became a film and television actress in later life, including a cameo with Witherspoon in the latter's final film *It Should Happen to You*, 34 years after their play together in Boston.

The Outrageous Mrs. Palmer dealt with a self-absorbed leading lady, "a typical spoiled darling of the footlights," whose only son is reported to have been killed fighting in World War I, after she has lied to his young fiancée and said he is illegitimate to try and get rid of her. As the *Boston Herald* described it in advance, the leading role was "a striking impersonation of the wayward actress whose only son goes off to war and so brings her lurid life to a dramatic crisis."[7] Mary Young's eldest son had been killed fighting in Europe at the age of 22. Her stage son Philip, who turns out not to be dead at all, was played by 29-year-old Charles Bickford. Witherspoon played Young's married daughter, Rowena Herrick. Miriam Doyle was also in the cast as Philip's fiancée Natalie Thompson.

Rehearsals started in Boston on January 12, 1920, and *The Outrageous Mrs. Palmer* opened at the Arlington Theatre in Boston on February 2. The show lasted 12 weeks in Boston, a very healthy run there, and closed April 24. The *Boston Globe* thought it "an unusual and highly interesting play," that "affords Miss Young one of the best roles of her entire career" and "a tremendous personal triumph": "Cora Witherspoon, a new-comer to the stage of the Arlington, did some very clever work as Rowena Herrick, Mrs. Palmer's married daughter." The *Boston Herald* was in agreement, writing that "except-ing for its too great length, Mr. Gribble's play is very interesting": "Miss Witherspoon and Mr. Bickford, as the daughter and son respectively, gave an excellent performance as sensible, unaffected young American people." A week into the run, the *Boston Herald* went all out and characterized the play as "the most brilliant dramatic performance" in the history of the Arlington Theatre.[8] By the time *The Outrageous Mrs. Palmer* opened at the 39th Street Theatre in New York on October 12, 1920, Witherspoon was no longer in the cast. Her role was created on Broadway by Miriam Elliott. Bickford and Doyle had also been replaced by other actors by this time.

It was at the tail end of 1920, that Witherspoon embarked on a second career, that would capture the imagination of press agents and journalists alike and be mentioned in more news items once she got to Hollywood than all her other interests, hobbies, and talents combined. She started working as a theatrical costume designer, primarily for producer Henry Miller, who had suggested she give it a try. It can be documented that she designed for two of Miller's shows: *Just Suppose* starring Patricia Collinge, which opened at Henry Miller's Theatre on November 1, 1920; and *Mary Rose* starring her friend Ruth Chatterton, which opened at the Empire Theatre on December 22. Wither-spoon may also have done Ina Claire's costumes in *Grounds for Divorce*, which she also performed in, some four years later. She ultimately gave up this sideline, because it was too stressful. An article from 1927 also claims that she was "a designer of clothes for one of the biggest and best known Fifth Ave. dress makers" for two years, and another, from 1936, that "for a whole season she was head designer in the theatrical department of the famous couturier, Harry Collins."[9]

After a slow start to the decade, Witherspoon finally got a new engagement on Broadway, where she had not been seen since supporting Grace George in *She Would and She Did*. When William J. Hurlbut's *Lilies of the Field* opened at the Klaw Theatre at 251 W. 45th St., it was exactly two years since Witherspoon last stood on a New York stage, the longest break in her Broadway career since her debut there in 1910. *Lilies of the Field* was the beginning of 15 years of continuous employment on the "Great White Way," which lasted until she went to Hollywood in 1936.

One could have wished for a more auspicious vehicle for what was practically a comeback for Witherspoon in the fall of 1921. For the star of the play, Marie Doro, it was a genuine comeback. Born Marie Katherine Stewart in Duncannon, Pennsylvania, in 1882, Doro had a dark-eyed, dark-haired, doll-like beauty. She was only five foot two inches tall; small enough to have been able to play Oliver Twist convincingly when she was 30. Now she was 39. She had spent the years since her mentor Charles Frohman's 1915 death aboard the *Lusitania* in Hollywood, though most of her films have been lost. *Lilies of the Field* would prove her final show on Broadway. She lived abroad for many years and died a recluse in New York in 1956.[10]

In *Lilies of the Field*, Doro portrayed Mildred Harker, a devoted and virtuous wife and mother, who is divorced from her philandering husband on specious grounds and loses custody of her child. Somewhat later, believing her child dead, and under the influence of a dubious female friend, Maisie Lee (Josephine Drake), and her "fast" milieu, Mildred allows herself to be tempted into a "liaison" with a tremendously rich and sympathetic man, Lewis Willing (Norman Trevor). All ends well, when Mr. Willing finally makes an honest woman of her and motivates her ex-husband monetarily to return the child, who is not dead after all, to her care.

The clue to Witherspoon's character Gertrude Ainlee is given in one review: "Cora Witherspoon, Alison Skipworth and Florence Flynn figured conspicuously and cleverly among the golddiggers shamelessly paraded in a play fairly reeking of vicious atmosphere." Their costumes were by Hattie Carnegie. After tryouts at the Park Theatre in Bridgeport, Connecticut, and the Stamford Theatre in Stamford, Connecticut, *Lilies of the Field* opened in New York on October 4, 1921. Witherspoon's old mentor David Belasco attended the Bridgeport opening of the show, which was produced by Garrick Productions.[11]

According to the legendary Alexander Woollcott: "For the greater part of the evening, 'Lilies of the Field' consists of an assortment of gaudy courtesans sitting around loose and chatting over their lives in a humorous and philosophical manner that is enormously entertaining." The trouble with the play, according to Woollcott was the plot, "as uningenious, ungainly and generally incredible as any that a playwright has ventured to proffer to Broadway in many months." As the "bounteous Maisie," Woollcott thought Josephine Drake was the "bright particular star of the entertainment," rather than Doro, whose "sole concern is with the twists and turns of the aforesaid plot." Woollcott devoted an entire paragraph to praise of the veteran British character actress Alison Skipworth, but unfortunately made no mention of Witherspoon in his review for the *New York Times*.[12]

Of the "kept women" the title alluded to, the *New York Herald* wrote: "They may not usually toil nor spin, yet most of them worked hard last night to be witty. Never was the strain after the laugh catcher more evident. They all succeeded in being unspeakably vulgar." Words of praise were vouchsafed only two actors in this review: "Miss Alison Skipworth supplied most of the good acting among the guests that haunted the flat and Miss Cora Witherspoon had most of the distinction."[13]

Most of the reviews were "mixed" at best. We find telling descriptions such as "one grand slam of furnished apartments and unwedded bliss," "a somewhat incoherent dramatization of a feminine mob," "a case of a lady lost among the ladies" (Doro, that is), and "intensely funny in spots." "Why we should be asked to consider the subject [of 'lilies of the field'] is not clear," opined the *New York Tribune*. "The play is only dialogue—for the most part stale and cheap and vulgar." Witherspoon herself said in an interview with her hometown newspaper the *Times-Picayune*, that the play was "'a success, but really very shocking.'"[14]

On February 13, 1922, an item appeared in the *New York Evening World* to the effect that "Cora Witherspoon of 'Lilies of the Field'" had "gone back to work after being ill."

The nature of the illness was not specified. *Lilies of the Field* closed on February 25, after a highly respectable 169 performances. The New York company of *Lilies of the Field* went on tour, but Witherspoon did not join the traveling band. Her part was taken by Ethel Wilson. Instead, it was announced that she would be part of Henry Miller's company at the Columbia Theatre in San Francisco beginning May 1. Three new plays would be performed during this five-week summer season.[15] They were *Her Friend the King* for the first two weeks, followed by *The Awful Truth* in the third and fourth weeks, and *La Tendresse* in the fifth. Witherspoon was not in the season-opener by A.E. Thomas and Harrison Rhodes. The second play, though, would turn out to be one of the more significant successes of her stage career.

Before I discuss *The Awful Truth* at length, let me deal briefly with *La Tendresse*. Both these plays starred Ruth Chatterton. *La Tendresse* was an adaptation of a French original by Henri Bataille, who had died only two months previously. Witherspoon played Mademoiselle Tigraine. One critic wrote that "Miss Chatterton proved herself one of the best actresses of the present generation" in the leading role in this play. When she had to decide to open in *La Tendresse* or *The Awful Truth* on Broadway in the fall, Chatterton chose the former.[16] Witherspoon, on the other hand, went into *The Awful Truth*, which probably offered her the better opportunity. Her role in *La Tendresse* was created on the New York stage by Mary Fowler.

The Awful Truth, which was author Arthur Richman's only hit on Broadway, is remembered today for giving Irene Dunne and Cary Grant their best screen opportunity. My impression is that the stage play was not so different from the 1937 film adaptation, directed by Leo McCarey at Columbia based on a screenplay by Viña Delmar. Witherspoon's character in the play, Josephine Trent, corresponds roughly to Aunt Patsy, played by Cecil Cunningham, in the film. One significant difference is that Josephine is equipped with a husband, Eustace Trent. Not counting the two weeks trial in San Francisco, Witherspoon devoted almost a year and a half of her life to *The Awful Truth* between August 1922 and December 1923. This was far from her best comedy, but it was even further from being the worst. The part was small, but then there are no small parts....

Here is Heywood Broun's succinct summary of the plot: "Richman's story concerns a young woman who gets a divorce from her husband through a misunderstanding. He suspects her of an affair and she becomes too annoyed to deny it. At the beginning we find her about to marry a self-made man who has made millions. He tells her of the open spaces and is a fearful bore, but the match seems necessary. However, the new fiancé, and more particularly his aunt, are worried about the rumors they have heard about Lucy's misconduct. The first husband is called in to set the rumors at rest. He lies, as he believes, like a gentleman. Once he is back upon the scene Lucy realizes she loves him and, by means of a trick, removes his suspicions and abandons her millionaire for the old love."[17]

Ina Claire took over for Ruth Chatterton as Lucy Warriner on Broadway, because Chatterton was going into *La Tendresse*. Bruce McRae was cast as her ex-husband Norman Satterley. He had previously starred with Claire in *The Gold Diggers*. McRae was a remarkably long-lived leading man, who was born in India in 1867 and had supported Ethel Barrymore for many years. Thus he was 55 years old when he played Norman Satterley and 26 years older than Claire, who turned 29 during the New York run of the play. Paul Harvey, who played the "other man," Oklahoma oil millionaire Daniel Leeson, was 40. His suspicious aunt was played by Louise MacKintosh.

The director was Henry Miller's son Gilbert. Several reviewers, including Alexander Woollcott, gave him the credit for the play's successful staging. Henry Miller was evidently proud of his offspring. In short curtain speech at end of second act in San Francisco, he said: "In all my years on the stage I have never seen a premiere performance like this one." Another San Francisco newspaper reported him as calling the world premiere of *The Awful Truth* "The finest first performance I have ever seen on the stage."[18]

By early August 1922, it was clear Witherspoon would reprise her role in the New York production. Rehearsals began the week of August 20. In addition to the two-week trial in San Francisco, it was deemed necessary to spend one week at Ford's Theatre in Baltimore directly prior to the New York opening at Henry Miller's Theatre on September 18, 1922. At this point, George K. Barraud took over for Geoffrey Kerr as Josephine's husband Eustace Trent. The play ran in New York for 144 performances, closing on January 20, 1923. The remainder of the year would be taken up with a two-part, cross-country tour of the play, where Arthur W. Metcalfe took over for George K. Barraud as Eustace Trent.[19] The tour started at the Montauk Theatre in Brooklyn only two days after the end of the Broadway run. From there, the play went to St. Louis, Chicago, Omaha, Grand Junction, Salt Lake City, Los Angeles, back to San Francisco, Medford, Salem, Portland, Seattle, Spokane, Helena, and Bozeman, before taking a break over the summer.

Witherspoon was not idle during the play's summer hiatus. On July 22, she opened in a new comedy by Avery Hopwood called *The Alarm Clock* at the Belasco Theatre in the nation's capital. It was an adaptation from *La Sonnette d'Alarme* by Maurice Hennequin and Romain Coolus, where the action had been reduced from five to three acts and moved to New York City. Witherspoon portrayed an "over-solicitous married lady, wife of an absent congressman," Mrs. Dunmore. She instigates the action by suggesting to wealthy, gouty bachelor banker Bobby Brandon, played by her *Awful Truth* co-star Bruce McRae, that it would improve his quality of life (and rid him of what she deems a couple of undesirable acquaintances), if he transported his nephew, Homer Wickham (John Daly Murphy), the nephew's sweetheart Mary Kent (Marion Coakley), and her mother, Susie Kent (Blanche Ring), from his and their native Kam's Corners to New York. The *Washington Evening Star* wrote that "the cast is excellent in every respect." McRae was adjudged a "finished farceur" and Blanche Ring was "incomparable" and "the center of the stage and the spotlight." Witherspoon was deemed "adequate." *The Alarm Clock* was a hit in Washington and extended to a second week.[20] When Hopwood's play opened in New York on Christmas Eve 1923, Witherspoon was no longer in the cast and Gail Kane was playing her role. It did not run.

Witherspoon was not at liberty to do *The Alarm Clock* on Broadway, because she was committed to doing the fall tour of *The Awful Truth*. It began on October 1 at the Garrick Theatre in Philadelphia, where they spent two weeks, followed by Washington, Pittsburgh, Boston, back to Brooklyn, ending in Newark, New Jersey, on December 8. In general, reviewers were more impressed with the production than with the play, with more than a suggestion that a talented cast and crew were being wasted on unworthy material. Alexander Woollcott was the chief exponent of this view. In his review for the *New York Times*, he called *The Awful Truth* "a bright diverting little piece": "Mr. Richman's piece is perfectly cast, graciously mounted and acted as delicately and suavely as he could possibly have asked." He could not resist adding: "It makes one weep inwardly to think how many American plays ranging from three to four times as good as this trifle by Arthur Richman, have fairly ached for the distinction his producer has imparted to 'The Awful Truth.'" According to the *Pittsburgh Daily Post*: "Arthur Richman's fragile offering runs to good-enough talk with humorous deftness, but limps toward anything in the direction of an effective situation. It is tolerable mainly for the skill of the cast selected by Henry Miller." Robert Benchley summed it up well: "in the hands of an almost perfect cast, ... it seems much better than it probably is."[21]

Yet there were some raves as well, such as the review of the world premiere in the *San Francisco Chronicle*, where George C. Warren described *The Awful Truth* as "a comedy that lashed the mind with its brilliant lines, acting that made the blood tingle through sheer delight at its perfection and a performance as smooth as a summer sky." He found the second act "as fine a bit of high comedy writing as we have had since Oscar Wilde wrote his brittle and immortal bits of life." The third act, though, was not so good. Warren even came back and wrote a second review of the sets![22]

After the Baltimore try-out in mid–September, the *Sun* was not impressed, calling the play a "not a very attractive comedy on the whole. Make-believe most of the time. Clever speeches here and there." The critic complained of audibility problems, because the theater was larger than suited the play. There were "lapses in diction," too. After the New York premiere, the *Brooklyn Times Union* wrote: "one goes away with the impression that one has been masticating roseate air.... The awful truth is that the play, in spite of the genuine wit and skill which went into the writing of it, is really flimsy in structure and somewhat lacking as to substance.... [T]he action of the characters is often improbable and ... there really isn't enough to the play to stretch the full three acts."[23]

According to the *Brooklyn Daily Eagle*: "Mr. Richman can write bright lines, but he cannot quite place them end to end in such a manner that they constitute a bright comedy."

The *Brooklyn Standard Union* assured its readers that, despite the title, "there is nothing at all vulgar in the play." One critic thought Ina Claire was "doing the best work of her career" and another that she had "scored a distinct personal hit." The *Daily Eagle*, though, criticized her for not speaking loudly enough. Finally, The *Chicago Tribune* dismissed the play as "a quite preposterous little fabrication ... of no importance whatsoever."[24]

Witherspoon received some brief commendations for her efforts as Josephine Trent: "is breezy as Lucy's friend" (*San Francisco Chronicle*); "looks like Irene Bordoni" [a Corsican-American actress and singer] (*Baltimore American*); "particularly delightful" (*Baltimore Evening Sun*); "acted with distinction" (*New York Herald*); "did gallantly" (*St. Louis Post-Dispatch*); and "is pleasing as a mutual friend" (*Spokane Spokesman-Review*). She got a whole sentence in the *Salt Lake Telegram*: "Cora Witherspoon as Josephine Trent, bosom friend of Miss Warriner, who knows the 'awful truth' and still does not mistrust, played well her part." And in the *Washington Evening Star*: "The supporting cast, especially Arthur W. Metcalfe and Cora Witherspoon, as a happily married but prosaic couple, yet with good sound common sense, contributed to an enjoyable performance."[25] Witherspoon performed her role for the last time at the Shubert Theatre in Newark on December 8, 1923.

Eight days after *The Awful Truth* tour ended, Witherspoon's closest remaining relative besides her sister, Uncle Samuel, passed away in New Orleans at the age of 79. She was fortunate to have had him in her life for so long; eight years longer than Aunt Sophie. Samuel Bell died of a heart attack. This was symbolic, since he was mourning the death of his longtime companion Ernest Cucullu, who had died four months earlier at the age of 88. Under the heading "Pals Not Divided in Death," the *New Orleans States* carried a feature article on December 23, 1923, about the two men's unique relationship. The article made a point of the fact that Ernest had wanted to be buried with Samuel, rather than in his own family's traditional burial ground. In Metairie, Ernest's name is not on the headstone with the Bells and the Witherspoons but is found on the coping of the low stone border surrounding the plot. Samuel's obituary in the *New Orleans Item* concluded with the words: "Mr. Bell died a bachelor, and followed to the grave Captain Ernest Cucullu, who died recently. The two men were both civil war veterans, and had made their home together since the sixties."[26]

The Awful Truth tour was no sooner ended in December 1923, than Henry Miller wanted Witherspoon for Ina Claire's new play *Grounds for Divorce*. The elder Miller was directing this one, and his son Gilbert Miller, who was now general manager of the Charles Frohman Co., was producing.[27] Thus their roles had switched from *The Awful Truth*. All of 1924 and the first three months of 1925 would be taken up with this play, but there was also time for a three-month trip to Europe during the summer hiatus.

Grounds for Divorce was a continuation of the genre and thematics of *The Awful Truth* under a different title. Like Witherspoon's last show, it was a sophisticated, cosmopolitan, upper-class comedy of remarriage starring her effervescent friend Ina Claire. Bruce McRae had even been cast as her leading man, clearly with an eye to continuing their fruitful collaboration from *The Gold Diggers* and *The Awful Truth*.[28] From Witherspoon's perspective, though, there was an important difference. This time she got to play both the heroine's best friend *and* the "other woman."

According to the summary in *The Best Plays of 1924–25*, "Denise Sorbier [Claire] is much in love with her husband, Maurice [McRae], the handsomest and most successful divorce lawyer in Paris. But she rebels at his neglect of her and when her temper boils over, throws an inkwell at him, misses and leaves. Later she takes the advice he has given other clients and applies for a divorce. A year later Maurice is about to marry Marianne [Witherspoon]. Denise, hearing this, literally flies back from Rome, reawakens Maurice's desire for her and reëstablishes her romance." The plot summary in the *Washington Evening Star* was even more succinct: "A wife, neglected by her husband-lawyer specializing on divorce cases, divorces the man himself for his inattention to her and wins him back just in the nick of time—in fact, just fifteen minutes before he is going to marry Marianne."[29]

What these summaries do not mention is that Marianne is Denise's "catty best friend" and is responsible for sowing dissatisfaction with her husband in Denise's heart. Once Marianne realizes Maurice is returning to his ex-wife, she throws an inkwell at him too, this time with red rather than black ink. Witherspoon recalled in 1926: "Henry Miller, who directed the comedy, had two ink bottles on the table in case of emergency. One night I threw the bottle and it didn't break. I threw the second one and it remained firm. The curtain came down in dead silence. The whole act was ruined. The next day we found that Mr. Miller had been practicing with the bottles and had worn a hole in the canvas wall. It was just my luck to throw both bottles so they hit that spot and there was nothing behind them to cause them to break."[30]

The author of this concoction was the popular and prolific playwright Guy Bolton. He is primarily known for writing the book for numerous Broadway musical comedies, most famously *Anything Goes* in 1934. This time he had adapted a straight play by

Hungarian Ernest Vajda called *The Lady of the Divorces* in which Lili Darvas had starred in Budapest and which had been "little less than a theatrical sensation on the continent."[31]

The plan was for quite an extensive pre–Broadway tour in the spring to build up interest, leading up to a Broadway premiere early in the fall, followed by a post–Broadway tour. Thus *Grounds for Divorce* had its world premiere at Nixon's Apollo Theatre in Atlantic City, New Jersey, on February 25, 1924, but did not open in New York till September 23.[32] From Atlantic City, the show went to the Shubert-Belasco Theatre in Washington, the Pitt Theatre in Pittsburgh, and the Garrick Theatre in Detroit, before spending 20 weeks at the Princess Theatre in Chicago. The pre–Broadway tour ended on May 31, 1924, after a final week at the Shubert Theatre in Cincinnati.

Five days after the *Grounds for Divorce* spring tour ended, Witherspoon applied for a passport, which was issued in Washington the following day. Her passport application described her as being five feet, six inches tall with a high forehead, gray eyes, straight nose, medium mouth, oval chin, auburn hair, fair complexion, and an oval face. She had no distinguishing marks. She was still living at 77 E. 56th St. in New York. On June 7, she sailed for Europe aboard the *Orbita* to visit the British Isles, France, Italy, and Switzerland.[33] As far as I can tell, she travelled alone. She may have met up with Ina Claire, who was also vacationing in Europe and rumored to be seeking a divorce from her husband James Whittaker.

Witherspoon arrived home in New York aboard the *La Savoie* from Le Havre on September 2, having been away almost three months.[34] She came back with a lot of new opinions about Europe, which she shared with Nanette Kutner in the *New York Graphic* in late October. Witherspoon noted with approval that "over there the wives are not jealous and narrow-minded, for they allow their husbands to dance with other women, and the husbands don't make a fuss if their wives dance with other men." "That is as it should be!" commented the now 34-year-old bachelorette. Witherspoon also felt that "dancing has led to many a divorce": "Everyone knows that it is very monotonous to always dance with the same partner, therefore foxtrotting with one's husband becomes a great bore." Never having been married herself, clearly did not stop her from having theories about marriage. Witherspoon also related that she had learned a "very peculiar dance," that they did at the "French watering places": "it is called the Java. It is done very quickly and is a sort of hop, toddle and jig combined."[35] I imagine that Witherspoon was "javaing" with the best of them that summer.

Two weeks after her return from Europe, *Grounds for Divorce* opened at the Auditorium in Baltimore, where it stayed a week. The play finally reached New York and the Empire Theatre on September 23, 1924, and closed there on January 10, 1925, after 127 performances. Then followed a post–Broadway tour between January 19 and March 21, 1925, to Newark, Boston, Philadelphia, Springfield, Hartford, and Brooklyn. Between Cincinnati and Baltimore, that is, during the summer hiatus and before the show opened again in the fall, the decision was made to replace leading man McRae with Witherspoon's friend from her earliest days in New York, Philip Merivale. McRae had gotten bad notices in the spring; one reviewer remarked that he "sometimes stuttered and became confused over his lines" and another that he "never did enunciate with entire clarity." Merivale had been appearing on Broadway since 1910, just like Witherspoon, and was coming from another Frohman production, *The Swan*.[36]

The critics were mostly indulgent towards this rather *recherché* trifle. In a representative response, the *Chicago Tribune* wrote: "The play is a gay and pagan little fandango, just long enough for its kind, and planned and plotted with theatrical tidiness. I do not know how far Mr. Bolton has taken it from the Hungarian; and I chance a guess that the distance is considerable." Burns Mantle dismissed it as "A pleasant but unimportant incident of the theater season." Yet the acting was "pretty nearly perfect" and the cast "incomparable" and "perfection to the point of self-negation," whatever that means.[37]

Witherspoon was frequently singled out for her efforts as Marianne. Detroit had not forgotten that she had appeared there with Jessie Bonstelle's company in 1917: "Among the ladies Detroiters will recognize a former Bonstelle favorite in Cora Witherspoon who gains much credit here for being just catty and bad-tempered enough to be very funny." The *Cincinnati Enquirer* wrote: "Cora Wither-

This photograph of Witherspoon at age 34 was included with her 1924 passport application. Her trip to Europe in June, July, and August 1924, when she visited England, France, Italy, and Switzerland, is her only documented foreign journey as an adult. She had spent about a year and a half at school in Paris 20 years earlier.

spoon is sufficiently 'catty' in the role of Marianne Regnault to cause every observer of the play to be glad that Maurice escapes her at the very altar." The *Boston Herald* thought "Miss Witherspoon was pleasing to the eye; the part demanded of her only insinuations and high temper." Other notices said she "hits off the catty Marianne with fine effect," "would be pleasant if the authors had not made her a cat," and "deserves favorable mention." Interestingly, the *Columbus Dispatch* felt that "Cora Witherspoon is a good actress, but not the type for Marianne."[38] *Grounds for Divorce* was Witherspoon's last play with her friend Ina Claire, who would go on to several other hits on Broadway, like *The Last of Mrs. Cheyney, Our Betters, Biography,* and *End of Summer.* Though she was only three years Witherspoon's junior, she survived her by many years and died in 1985.

The rolling out of Witherspoon's next Broadway show followed the same pattern as *Grounds for Divorce*: tryouts "out of town" in the spring and then a Broadway opening early in the fall. The show was *The Fall of Eve*, originally called *Aren't Men Brutes*, co-authored by husband-and-wife writing team John Emerson and Anita Loos and produced and directed by Emerson as well. It was only their second stage play; the first had been the recent *The Whole Town's Talking*, but they had written quite a few screenplays together.

The star of the show was that diminutive dynamo Ruth Gordon in her fifth Broadway outing at age 28. What Gordon lacked in stature and conventional beauty, she more than made up for in talent, charisma, and drive. This time she was playing a priggish, controlling, and judgmental young wife, Eva Hutton, who must reassess her values and responses when she ends up in a compromising situation herself. Her husband Ted Hutton, a lawyer, was played by Witherspoon's neighbor at 77 E. 56th St., Arthur Albertson. Witherspoon was the heroine's harmful friend yet again, called Amy Parker this time. Amy's role was to sow the seeds of doubt in Eva's mind about Ted's fidelity: "A misanthropic neighbor, who is carefully read on the psychology of the new immorality, and in consequence is described as physically pure, takes advantage of the wife's jealousy to convince her that all men are beasts.... The Freud served her by Amy ... feeds the flames of Eve's jealousy until it becomes an uncontrollable monster."[39] Eva refuses to attend the play opening of her husband's actress client, whom Amy has convinced her is having an affair with Ted. Eva ends up drunk and falls asleep on the sofa of one of a pair of confirmed bachelor friends of her husband's and, for a while, is convinced it is her duty to divorce Ted and marry the friend.

The *Stamford Daily Advocate* wrote after the world premiere at the Stamford Theatre in Stamford, Connecticut, on May 8, 1925: "The play is really a triumph for Miss Gordon, though all of the supporting cast is very satisfactory." In Washington, D.C., the show met with the same approval: "Ruth Gordon's genius for comedy finally has met a play that gives it rather a comprehensive test": "Cora Witherspoon is a perfect Amy." When the play returned to the Stamford Theatre for three performances August 21–22, the local critic saw "a marked improvement in the piece." In Asbury Park, New Jersey, on August 24, the co-authors were in attendance, having come from Hollywood expressly for that purpose.[40]

The Fall of Eve premiered at the Booth Theatre on August 31, 1925. The opening paragraph of the detailed review in the *New York Times* credited Witherspoon's Amy with creating the entire plot of the play, calling her "a foul-minded spinster, a 'speaking cat,' a harridan and harpy, who believed too eagerly in the inevitability of appearance where men and women are concerned; who considered men 'beasts,' while all the real facts proved quite the contrary, and who poisoned the mind of one who listened to her evil tongue." If that was not enough, the anonymous critic also referred to her as "this creature, this vixen, this hussy." Clearly, Amy had gotten his goat. He, one assumes it was a man, goes on to admit that "in the play itself the confidante had only a minor part. She was merely the spring to the action."[41]

The *Brooklyn Times Union* observed that the supporting players "are given no more opportunity than to play shadows in the background." The critic added that Witherspoon "comes nearer than the others to a three-dimensional role, and she plays it well." The *Brooklyn Citizen* also commended her for her efforts: "Cora Witherspoon, as the catty Amy, plays one of the meaner parts we have seen in many a day and she does it well too"; as did the *Brooklyn Standard Union*: "Cora Witherspoon was excellent as a trouble-making, sporty spinster." Arthur Pollock of the *Brooklyn Daily Eagle* disliked the play intensely, writing that it was a farce "inaccurately labelled a comedy" and "provided only the lamest excuses for laughter": it was "not only dull but often downright stupid." He admitted, though, that "Ruth Gordon is the saving of it": "The rest of the cast have little to do but walk in and out and feed her." Brett Page harkened all the way back to 1910, when he observed that Witherspoon was "as acidulous and excellent as she was in 'The Concert' with Leo Ditrichstein." *The Fall of Eve* closed in New York on October 10, 1925, after only six weeks and 48 performances. During the run of the play, Witherspoon "signed contracts for twenty-four designs of gowns and coats."[42]

In her quirky memoir *Myself Among Others*, published in 1971, long after Witherspoon's death, Gordon recalled how the legendary Jeanne Eagels had suggested she play

Eva's early scene with Amy. Eagels told her that "'your part can be awfully unsympathetic, but it needn't be. The key is to *listen*. Listen to Cora Witherspoon tell you what to do. Listen hard. Let *her* be the unsympathetic one and you blindly follow her instructions.'" When Gordon responded that she thought she *was* listening to her, Eagels expanded on her advice: "'You do, but the way *you're* doing it, you listen and make it *your* idea. That makes you as big a cheat as Cora.'" Instead, Eagels suggested Gordon "'do it as though you're *pretty*. Not a battle-ax like Cora. Act as if you're *terribly* pretty and trying to remember what homely *Cora* said. And after she says it, don't be too sure what she meant. The audience will laugh and adore you.'"[43] Judging from the critics' response, Gordon followed Eagels' instructions to the letter.

When *The Fall of Eve* was not followed by a post–Broadway tour, Witherspoon found herself at liberty for the first time in a while. She had found a new engagement by February 1926, when the melodrama *Hush Money* (aka *No Questions Asked*) opened at the Park Theatre in Bridgeport, Connecticut, on the 22nd of that month. Both the co-author Alfred "Al" G. Jackson and cast member Richard Gordon were from Bridgeport, so the play was assured a warmer reception there than it would receive in New York. Lead actress Justine Johnstone came from the musical comedy field, and this was her first straight role. Between Bridgeport and New York, Frederick Burton replaced Walter Walker as the judge and Kenneth Thomson replaced Walter Gilbert as the hero Harry Bentley. An ad in the *Bridgeport Telegram* assured potential patrons that this was "A Clean Wholesome Play." *Hush Money* was labeled "a melodrama of today."[44]

Hush Money opened at the 49th Street Theatre in New York on March 15. This story of criminal complications among con men, gigolos, and cougars in a rarified, upper-class atmosphere by Jackson and Mann Page seems to have reflected well on no one involved, be it onstage or backstage. Thus it must have felt like slumming for Witherspoon, after her years spent in the capable hands of the Millers *père et fils*. All the sadder and more poignant, too, that her long-term mentor Henry Miller died during the run of this mediocre play, on April 9. He was 67. The producer of *Hush Money* was Charles K. Gordon; and the director, William B. Friedlander, was also new to her.

The New York critics were not impressed. The *New York Times* wrote that "it is a crook comedy built around a 'frame-up,' and it is concerned at considerable length with a diamond necklace…. The play is of complicated structure not too well knit." Most of the cast save the leads were "pretty bad." The *Brooklyn Standard Union* described the play as "the story of idle wives of rich men who are tempted to indiscretions by attractive men of the underworld, who have all the social graces, and who trail such women for the opportunity to rob them of their jewels." It will surprise no one that Witherspoon played one of these idle women, Mrs. Rudolph Wurzman. According to the *Brooklyn Times Union*, *Hush Money* was "the sort of a crook play in which everyone double crosses one another so much that you sort of lose track of who is crooked and who is straight…. [I]t would make a fine movie … because the cast looks better than it acts." *Hush Money* lasted 56 performances and closed May 1, 1926.[45]

On April 27, the *Denver Post* had revealed that Witherspoon would be performing at the Elitch Gardens Theatre during the summer season. Originally, the centerpiece of the first zoo west of Chicago, Elitch Gardens had been the first professional theater in Denver when it opened in 1890 and became the first summer stock theater in the country in 1893. One of its two founders, Mary Elitch Long, was still alive at 70, though she had sold the property in 1916 to John Mulvihill, who remained as manager and proprietor until his death in 1930. The summer of 1926, the stock company was headed by Fredric March and Florence Eldridge, who would marry the following year, and also included returning players Beulah Bondi, Edward Butler, and Moffat Johnston; juvenile lead Earle Larimore, ingénue Marion Swayne, Douglass Dumbrille, L'Estrange Millman, Gavin Muir, Winifred Durie, and Frank McDonald. Melville Burke was returning as director. Twelve plays were to be presented, two more than the previous year.[46] They ended up playing 11.

The *Post* described Witherspoon prior to her arrival as "one of those actresses who is looked upon as absolutely reliable by theater managers and is always in demand." According to the *Post*, she was also "reputed to be one of the best dressed women on the stage." Upon arrival, she was described as having "a gorgeous sense of humor" and being "tall, Titian-haired and slender." Talk about a build-up! Denver audiences had their first chance to see her live in Ferenc Molnár's *The Swan*, which opened the season on Saturday, June 12. The *Post* recorded: "Cora Witherspoon as Princess Maria Dominica won the sympathy and affection of her audience with her initial performance in Denver." The role of the princess had been created on Broadway by Alison Skipworth in 1923. In the raucous George Abbott comedy *Love 'Em and Leave 'Em*, which had just ended its run on Broadway, "Cora Witherspoon as the 'spotter' for the Ginsburg stores draws a character that is at once true to life and excruciatingly funny."[47] The role of Miss Streeter was played by Eda Heinemann in New York and by Edna May Oliver in the 1929 film version entitled *The Saturday Night Kid*, starring Clara Bow and Jean Arthur.

Witherspoon got an even better opportunity in the third week, when she played Ethel Westcourt in *Dancing Mothers*, "the ultramodern drama of the jazz age in which Cora Witherspoon is distinguishing herself ... this week": "Witherspoon is the mother—Mrs. Hugh Westcourt—and she does as fine a piece of characterization as has been seen in Denver, adapting herself to the part so widely different from anything she yet has played here, in a manner that is astonishing." The role had been originated on Broadway by Witherspoon's *Outrageous Mrs. Palmer* co-star Mary Young in 1924. In *The Music Master* by Charles Klein, she and fellow character actress Winifred Durie found themselves "cast in relatively unimportant parts," but nevertheless "added their bits to the perfection of 'The Music Master.'"[48]

The triumph of Witherspoon's season of summer stock in Denver, though, came on July 11, when she opened in the lead role in George Kelly's hit comedy *Craig's Wife* with Douglass Dumbrille as her beleaguered husband Walter and Beulah Bondi as the housekeeper Mrs. Harold. Witherspoon was given star billing above Eldridge and March. The play was in its tenth month on Broadway at the time. On the day of the opening, the *Post* noted that "Miss Witherspoon will have what she declares the finest acting role in her professional career." Afterwards, the verdict of the same paper was that she had "added to her laurels, and a more perfect characterization seldom has been seen here. She didn't merely ACT her role—she WAS 'Craig's Wife,' letter perfect."[49]

Burns Mantle devoted his syndicated column July 25 to Elitch Gardens and his return to "the scene of my theater beginnings." They were playing *Craig's Wife* the week he was there, with "Cora Witherspoon giving a particularly sharp and interesting performance in the Chrystal Herne role." He called it "the biggest financial success the Gardens theater has had in years." In summing up the season at Elitch Gardens, the *Post* wrote in mid–September 1926, that Witherspoon's performance "will not soon be forgotten here." Years later, she described it as "one of my favorite roles."[50]

The second half of the season consisted of *Icebound, Not Herbert, Liliom; Easy Come, Easy Go; Hell Bent Fer Heaven*, and *These Charming People*. Witherspoon had some part to play in all of these save *Hell Bent Fer Heaven* and *Liliom*. In the former, there was no role for her, and she got some time off instead. The week prior to the opening of *Liliom* on August 8, Witherspoon was "taken suddenly ill, and unable to appear." She was replaced by Mary Morris (1895–1970).[51] Morris had created the role of Nina in the first, 1916 New York production of Chekov's *The Seagull* and Abbie Putnam in O'Neill's *Desire Under the Elms* among her several Broadway credits. So Witherspoon never played Mrs. Muskat, the libidinous owner of the amusement park where the eponymous hero works and plays. Nearly 30 years later, though, *Liliom* would be Witherspoon's final show, when she played Mother Hollunder in stock at the Sombrero Playhouse in Phoenix.

In Owen Davis's drama *Icebound*, where Witherspoon played Sadie Fellows, the *Post* found that "every member of the excellent cast is playing his role for everything that is in it." In the brand new "mystery comedy" *Not Herbert*, "Cora Witherspoon as Mrs. Blaine does convincing work as the society matron whose home is being guarded by a force of detectives to prevent the theft of her emeralds." The farce *Easy Come, Easy Go* was also of recent vintage, written by the versatile and prolific Owen Davis. Witherspoon played nurse Molly Costigan, a role created on Broadway by Nan Sunderland. The show had closed there in April, after 180 performances. Finally, the Elitch Gardens stock company rounded off its 1926 summer season the week of August 29 with Michael Arlen's *These Charming People*. Witherspoon played Julia Berridge and she and Moffat Johnston were said to "carry away the honors in this comedy built about the lives of ultramoderns of Great Britain."[52] On September 6, the actress was again "between engagements."

For Witherspoon, her season at Elitch Gardens must have been a heady experience, as "her appearance in leading roles called forth 'bravos' from the audience." She was rumored to be coming back the following season and "casting sheep's eyes in the direction of Denver,"[53] but she never returned to the stock company. She was about to embark on one of the longest runs of her Broadway career.

On September 17, 1926, the *New York Times* announced that Ethel Barrymore was returning to Charles Frohman, Inc., which would "mark Miss Barrymore's return to the management with which she was first identified." Rehearsals for her new play were to begin "in about two weeks." The play was *The Constant Wife* by W. Somerset Maugham and would give her "one of the best roles of her career."[54] Barrymore had starred in Maugham's *Lady Frederick* on Broadway back in 1908, when she was 29. Now she was 47.

The starting point in *The Constant Wife* is that Constance Middleton (Barrymore) and her husband John (C. Aubrey Smith), an eminent doctor, have been married for 15 years and have a 14-year-old daughter. John is having an affair with Constance's friend Marie-Louise (Verree Teasdale), which Constance silently condones, because she is no longer in love with her husband. The trouble only begins when Constance's younger sister, Martha Culver (Witherspoon), is determined to bring it all out into the open, despite the adamant opposition of her and Constance's mother, Mrs. Culver (Mabel Terry-Lewis). To make matters worse, Marie-Louise's husband Mortimer Durham (Walter Kingsford) discovers John's cigarette case in their marital bed. To add more fuel to the fire, an old flame from Constance's youth, Bernard Kersal (Frank Conroy), makes a reappearance on the scene after many years abroad.

Witherspoon, then, was cast as Barrymore's younger sister and appears, albeit briefly, in all three acts. In Maugham's stage directions, Martha Culver is described simply as "*a fine young woman.*" She is 32 and lives with her mother. Mrs. Culver considers herself and Constance to be "the brains of the family," unlike Martha and the late Mr. Culver.[55] In their unconscious, mother-daughter comedy act in the opening scene, Mrs. Culver is the comedian and Martha is the "feed." That means that Mrs. Culver gets all the good lines.

It is Constance Middleton, though, who speaks the most meaningful phrases of the play, lines that reveal its cynical and modern spirit. Constance says things like "When all is said and done, the modern wife is nothing but a parasite"; "Now that women have broken down the walls of the harem they must take the rough-and-tumble of the street"; and what many have seen as the theme of the play: "It seems rather hard that what is sauce for the gander shouldn't also be sauce for the goose." Finally, and equally famously, Constance says: "I may be unfaithful, but I am constant." The play is still a striking and amusing indictment of the sexual double standard and has been revived on Broadway three times. The *Milwaukee Journal* called it "an exceedingly deft argument in behalf of the notion that wives have as much right to step about as have husbands."[56]

Martha Culver was not the showiest supporting role in the play, but it was a perfect fit for Witherspoon. She is more or less cordially disliked by all the other characters, including her own mother. Martha is the voice of conventional morality, of righteous indignation. There is so little going on in her own life, that she wants to arrange everyone else's. In the first act, she is chomping at the bit to tell Constance about John's affair. In the second act, when it all comes out, she urges Constance to get a divorce. Even in her brief appearance in the beginning of the third act, Martha is itching to tell her sister something Constance already knows, namely that Marie-Louise has just returned from a long trip abroad. This just at the time Constance is poised to make a trip on the Continent herself, apparently in company with Bernard Kersal.

The critics would describe Martha Culver in much more unflattering terms than the author himself, as "a disagreeably caustic sister," a "slightly acidulated spinster sister," "the cattish lady who delighted at telling all the truth at the wrong time and place," and as Constance's "sufficiently nosy and opinionated younger sister." Next to "younger," the most neutral descriptive term used about her was "unmarried." Though her character was not popular with her stage family, the critics, or the audience, Witherspoon had the consolation of being as elegant as ever in the role. According to one newspaper following the premiere: "Cora Witherspoon's two sport outfits; a two-toned striped effect in gray, and a vivid green and black affair, quite knocked out the right eye of every woman in the house."[57]

Of all places, *The Constant Wife* had its world premiere at the Ohio Theatre in Cleveland on November 1, 1926. The eminent British author was in attendance and "there was a stir of excitement throughout the house all evening; possibly because the trim figure of Mr. Maugham, with a white carnation on the lapel of his English-cut overcoat, had been sighted in the lobby." As the local newspaper explained: "It is not often that Cleveland audiences witness premieres of such plays as this; and it is rare, too, that a distinguished author sits in the audience, rubbing shoulders with us." It was "a gala occasion, if ever there was one." The only disappointment was that Maugham "could not be induced to give a curtain speech, nor even to present himself on the stage, so that everyone might take a good look at him."[58]

After a week in Cleveland, they spent a week each at the New Detroit Theatre, the Nixon Theatre in Pittsburgh, and the National Theatre in Washington, D.C., before finally coming into New York and Maxine Elliott's Theatre on November 19. The play was well received on its pre–Broadway tour. In Detroit, one could read that Maugham's characters were "so glib, so pert, so saucy—they just say the darndest things." The support provided for Barrymore was "very fine indeed": "they make the author's lines their own and are perfectly at home with Miss Barrymore." More specifically: "Cora Witherspoon makes the meddlesome sister sufficiently irritating." The *Pittsburgh Daily Post* pointed out that "the casting doesn't appear to have been with an eye to Apollos." The *Pittsburgh Press* concurred that "the supporting players ... were not cast for beauty," but added that "that is neither here nor there.... A finer cast could not have been gathered." Barrymore had "contributed a work of art to stage history" and "the other players were superbly cast and gave a finished performance." "Mabel Terry-Lewis as her mother is another excellent characterization, no less than Cora Witherspoon as the other daughter, and C. Aubrey Smith as the husband." The *Washington Evening Star* deemed it "the most unmoral and the most refined play of the season."[59]

The New York critics were no less impressed. Brooks Atkinson led the pack: "It is a deft and sparkling comedy of no overwhelming importance, and its central role is so well suited to Miss Barrymore that it might have been written for her. In fact, it probably was." He felt that the author was "just about at his best" and his play "a light comedy of a high order": "It is the best play of its kind that has come from England in a long time." The *Brooklyn Times Union* called it "a production of rare distinction. Supporting the star is a cast that is at all times noteworthy with every role in capable hands. In short it is gorgeous entertainment for anyone who likes subtlety and wit in the theatre": "[A]s the sister who had 'come out and gone in again,' Cora Witherspoon had her moments." The *Constant Wife* was also called "the season's finest pleasure." "Such affectionate infidelity has probably never been seen before in the theater," wrote Arthur Pollock.[60]

That was exactly the problem, according to Barrett H. Clark, who was one of the few critics to object to the play on moral grounds. He described it as "dreadfully immoral" "sociologically speaking": "The dramatist has so little regard for the accepted laws of morality that he shows us a woman who dares to live in sin with a man, and defend herself on the ground that she has paid her husband for board and lodging! And the husband actually wants her back after her six weeks' jaunt!" Clark was jumping to conclusions here. The ending is much more open with regard to the true nature of Constance's relationship with Bernard and the character of the trip they are taking together; indeed, it is not even certain that they *are* going together. As the *Milwaukee Journal* described it, "The most potent of the play's charms is the deftly contrived doubt as to just how far the heroine is going in her fling at independence."[61]

There were a few other dissenting voices in this chorus of approval. The headline of the review in the *Camden Courier-Post* read: "Comedy Almost Talks Self to Death: Only Ethel Barrymore's Artistry Saves 'The Constant Wife' from Boredom." Pierre de Rohan felt that "only a confirmed bachelor like Mr. Maugham could have evolved the silly solution which constitutes the third act." The *Constant Wife* was "not really a play, but merely a sparkling, artificial talk-fest."[62]

For Witherspoon, the year 1927 was entirely taken up with playing *The Constant Wife* in New York and on tour. In early August, it was the fifth longest running straight play on Broadway, after *Abie's Irish Rose*, *Broadway*, *The Ladder*, and *The Squall*. On

August 13, the original New York production of *The Constant Wife* closed after 295 performances, making it Witherspoon's second longest run on Broadway.[63] She was far from done with the play, though, and stuck with Barrymore till the not so bitter end. The post–Broadway tour lasted nine months and took them to Stamford, Brooklyn, Camden, Wilmington, Springfield, Hartford, Boston, Chicago, Milwaukee, St. Louis, Kansas City, Denver, Grand Junction, Salt Lake City, Los Angeles, and San Francisco.

The stage manager on the tour was a young, up-and-coming man of the theater called George Cukor, who some years later would induce Witherspoon to make her film debut in what was his own solo directorial debut, *The Tarnished Lady*.[64] Cukor was the only film director whom Witherspoon worked for three times: in her first film, in her last, and in one in between called *The Women*. It was not as exciting as it sounds. The parts he offered her were little more than walk-ons.

As for *The Constant Wife*, on tour the news continued to be good and the supporting cast continued to be praised by the critics as "faultless," "extremely good," and "thoroughly good." As Martha Culver, Witherspoon was said to have "her effective moments" and to do "some shrewd bits of work." Her accolades were brief this time; she had to be content with words like "more than satisfying," "well played," "charming," "delightful," and "amusing." In Denver at the end of April 1928, they still remembered her fondly from her time at Elitch Gardens in the summer of '26. She got an ovation on her initial appearance on the stage, and "her subsequent performance more than justified it." Her friend Virginia Whitehead hosted a luncheon in her honor on May 3. Only Kenneth Hunter, who had taken over for C. Aubrey Smith as John Middleton, and Frank Conroy were present from the cast. The final verdict on her performance, as the show entered its last, month-long stretch at the Curran Theatre in San Francisco, was that "Cora Witherspoon does the catty sister nicely and looks very well," and that she "adds a biting impersonation of the disappointed, catty woman."[65] It was all over on June 23, 1928. Five days later, Leo Ditrichstein died of heart disease in Vienna, where he had gone to seek medical treatment. Ditrichstein had retired four years earlier and gone to live in Florence. He was 63.[66]

Witherspoon's next Broadway outing, *Olympia*, had been adapted by Sidney Howard from an original by the ubiquitous Hungarian dramatist Ferenc Molnár. It had a small cast consisting of only seven players: Fay Compton, Laura Hope Crews, Ian Hunter, Arnold Korff, Richie Ling, Grant Stewart, and Witherspoon. The British actress Fay Compton was in the title role of a haughty princess, who gets taught a lesson. Compton had only acted in New York once previously, in a musical revue in 1914, so this was her "debut in America … as a dramatic star." *Olympia* also constituted the Broadway bow of another British actor, who would have a more extensive career in America, Ian Hunter, who played a dashing army captain who is not the mercenary adventurer he is made out to be.[67] After a week's trial at the Shubert Belasco Theatre in Washington, *Olympia* opened at the historic Empire Theatre in New York on October 16, 1928.

The play did not meet with universal approval. Atkinson of the *Times* was unimpressed, observing that "possibly Mr. Molnar enjoys himself rather more than his guests" and that "'Olympia' is high comedy beaten thin." Rowland Field opined that "as entertainment, the play can hardly be said to have come up to expectations." Burns Mantle thought that at least "the casting is perfect." Donald Mulhern described *Olympia* as "nothing less than Humpty Dumpty dressed up in girl's clothes and a coronet" and said it had "a heavy foot on the pun pedal." Arthur Pollock concluded that it was "by no means Molnar's best": "All but a few minutes of the final act is padding." Finally, Robert

Sisk called it "a failure": "this excellent cast fails to make a soggy and sodden play snap into life."[68]

Despite the disapproval of the play as a whole, Laura Hope Crews scored a personal hit in the role of Olympia's meddlesome and snooty mama. Atkinson wrote: "it is Miss Crews as the dominating mother who keeps the piece sparkling." Other reviewers described her as "superbly amusing" and "difficult competition" and noted that "hers is a beautiful performance." Two years earlier, Crews had played the role of her career, as the manipulative mother of all time, Mrs. Phelps, in Howard's 1926 drama *The Silver Cord*, which lent its name to an entire range of dysfunctional relationships between mothers and their offspring. Witherspoon also was praised, for her Countess Lina, "a waspish gossip," who discovers that Olympia has been "compromised." Atkinson had a good word for her too: "As the astringent Countess Lina, the inevitable acid tale-bearer of a social comedy Cora Witherspoon does Molnar the honor of giving a thoroughly disagreeable—and skillful—performance." Donald Mulhern described her as "dangerous as a court gossip."[69]

The public was no more thrilled by *Olympia* than the critics, and the show closed on November 16, 1928, after only 39 performances. Witherspoon quickly got a new engagement and was in rehearsal with her new play the following month. *Precious* was a new "farcical comedy" by James Forbes, best known for *The Famous Mrs. Fair* and *The Show Shop*, and it was originally called *Final Fling*. It was staged by Melville Burke, who had directed Witherspoon at Elitch Gardens; and produced by Rosalie Stewart, "the foremost woman producer in America,"[70] who had produced George Kelly's *The Torch Bearers*, *Harriet Craig*, and *Daisy Mayme* and the stage version of *The Enchanted April*. *Precious* would be Stewart's last production on Broadway.

After two weeks of tryouts in a theater in New Rochelle, New York, and at Werba's Theatre in Flatbush, starting on New Year's Eve 1928, the play opened at the Royale Theatre in New York on January 14, 1929. According to *The Best Plays of 1928–29*, *Precious* dealt with a familiar comic situation: "Fighting the laws of nature and the advice of his best friends, Andrew Hoyt [John Cumberland] marries Eva Mills [Dorothy Hall], young enough to be his daughter. Realizing a month later that he has been duped by Eva and her designing sister, Stella [Witherspoon], Andrew schemes to force Eva to elope with a young and handsome architect, Oliver Denton [Edward Leiter]."[71]

By and large, critics were not impressed by what had been publicized as "an ingenious comedy of 20th century marriage." One review was subheaded: "Expert Cast Draws Laughs from Brittle Script." According to this reviewer, "The players help magnificently," but they were playing "paper figures in a paper play." The *Brooklyn Daily Eagle* begged to differ, calling *Precious* "one of the most delightful comedies that has appeared this season." Burns Mantle observed that, of the four leads, "only Miss Witherspoon is deft at make-believe, and she is easily tempted into overplaying." Rather a left-handed compliment, one thinks. Rowland Field called *Precious* "an unimportant farce": "The players do their best to instill the lines with a zest that the playwright has, unfortunately, left out." He thought Witherspoon was "giving a good performance as Stella Peck, sister of the bride and chief complicator of the plot." The female lead Dorothy Hall received most of the sparse accolades that were accorded the show. "She is the sole justification for the play," wrote the *New York Times*.[72]

Lasting only three weeks and 24 performances, *Precious* was the first flop of Witherspoon's stage career. She had been a professional actress for almost 25 years, so it was a long time coming. *Precious* was adapted for the screen in 1932 and released as *Bachelor's Affairs* starring Adolphe Menjou and Joan Marsh with Minna Gombell in Witherspoon's role.

After *Precious*, Witherspoon hit a dry spell. She may have worked in radio during this time, as her name appears in a long list of "well known actors who now are appearing in radio productions or who are to be used in the near future."[73] She finally got an engagement at the start of the fall season in a new play produced, written, and staged by Myron C. Fagan called *Nancy's Private Affair*. The show starred Fagan's then girlfriend Minna Gombell and the cast also included veteran British character actress Alison Skipworth. In this conventional, if not classic, comedy of remarriage, where a reluctantly divorced wife, Nancy Gibson (Gombell), goes through an extreme makeover to regain the love of her wayward playwright husband, Witherspoon portrayed Nancy's sister-in-law and confidante Sally Lee, who orchestrates the scheme to get Nancy's man back. The "heavy" this time, the mother of the young woman who has displaced Nancy in her husband's affections, was played by Skipworth.

The plan was for *Nancy's Private Affair* to be tried out for a week by Chamberlain Brown's stock company in Greenwich, Connecticut, starting September 9, 1929, and two weeks in Boston, before a Broadway opening September 30.[74] The play was deemed a success by local newspapers in Connecticut, but Fagan felt it was not yet ready for Boston or New York. By the time the play finally opened on Broadway in mid–January 1930, neither Witherspoon nor Skipworth were part of the cast.

4

On Stage and Screen
1930–1935

"Curiously enough I've never longed to play
romantic or tragic parts…. I've always been content
to play a part that had a touch of high comedy
although one of my favorite roles is that of Mrs. Craig
in George Kelly's fine play 'Craig's Wife.'"[1]

Cora Witherspoon embarked on her forties just as the world was entering the 1930s. The outlook for her personally was considerably brighter than for the average run of humanity at this difficult Great Depression time. The big 4–0 held no terrors for a character actress. She was one of the most respected, popular, and frequently employed players on Broadway. During the next five years, the end of the major phase of her Broadway career, she appeared in 15 productions on the "Great White Way." The first half of the 1930s also saw her screen debut in the East and her brief first sojourn in Hollywood.

Despite Witherspoon's continued career success during her final years in New York, the year of 1930 turned out to be an unsettled one. That year she was cast in no less than five Broadway-bound stage productions. None of them lasted long. Only one of them made it to Broadway *with* Witherspoon. Robert E. Sherwood's *Waterloo Bridge* gave her one of the best roles of her stage career.

To the extent that *Waterloo Bridge* remains in the cultural memory today, it is through the slick, sanitized, 1940 film version starring Vivien Leigh and Robert Taylor. Like so many Hollywood films, though, *Waterloo Bridge* was originally a play, which opened at the Fulton Theatre in New York on January 6, 1930, the day after Witherspoon's 40th birthday. Rehearsals had begun in early November 1929, only a few days after the stock market crashed.[2] I imagine Witherspoon was little effected by the crash. She was earning a solid, steady salary and, given her customary lack of economy, probably had few savings to lose. The play was tried out in Boston and Hartford, before the New York opening.

Waterloo Bridge starred June Walker and Glenn Hunter as the star-crossed lovers Myra Deauville and Roy Cronin. Walker had a long career on Broadway and is maybe best remembered for creating the role of Lorelei Lee in the original production of *Gentlemen Prefer Blondes* in 1926. Hunter was a popular leading man of the 1920s both on stage and screen. Veteran director Winchell Smith "came out of temporary retirement to bestow his unusual gifts as director on the new production." One critic gave him credit for the play's "forthright action."[3]

That action hinges somewhat incredibly on the fact that Roy, the soldier-hero, is too naïve and inexperienced to recognize that Myra, the fellow American he has met by chance on London's Waterloo Bridge during World War I, is a prostitute. Roy has enlisted in the Canadian army early in the war to help the Allies fight "the Hun" and is on leave in London for the first time, while Myra is an ex-chorus girl, stranded in London, who finds herself forced from lack of other opportunities to engage in the world's oldest profession.

Witherspoon played Myra's colorful Cockney friend and colleague Kitty. She is found on stage when the curtain goes up, "seated on [a] bench, eating an apple." Kitty is described in no uncertain terms in the stage directions as "a blatant London tart, profoundly pessimistic but meticulously cheerful, about thirty-five, heavily painted, and conveying only occasional suggestions of the charm she might once have possessed."[4]

Kitty's big scene comes at the beginning of Act II, when she discovers Roy alone in Myra's shabby room. Sherwood writes in the stage directions that "Kitty is not particularly interested in this guest of MYRA's, but is trying hard to be sociable.... Later she begins to see the possibilities and to exploit them." In a monologue that is a miracle of manipulation ("she's such a little thing," "It's a constant struggle," "She's so *lonely*," "She 'asn't a living soul to take care of 'er"), Kitty voices her wish that "some day, some nice young man would come along—and appreciate Myra.... And marry 'er and give 'er a' ome and protect 'er," planting the seeds of the idea that Roy might be that man. She clinches it when she exclaims: "'Er condition is desperate—desperate, I tell you! An' if the young man I've been 'oping for don't pop up soon, 'e'll be *too late*! That's what 'e'll be."[5] Clearly, the suggestions of *"too late"* are too much for soft-hearted and gullible Roy, and he is putty in Kitty's hands. In her defense, she is doing this from unselfish motives and to give her friend some hope for the future. Myra's situation *is* desperate, and she does need to be saved.

It is finally the sanctimonious and self-pitying housekeeper Mrs. Hobley, played by long-time Broadway character actress Florence Edney (1879–1950), who lets Roy know that Myra is not all that he thinks she is. He does not thank her for it, though, telling her famously to "shut your God-damned face."[6] In the final scene back on the bridge where they first met, the lovers are forced to part, as Roy must return to the front, but only after he has arranged that Myra will be provided for even if he should die. Thus *Waterloo Bridge* combines a familiar "fallen woman redeemed by the love of a good man" plotline with a "brief encounter" timeline and a wartime London setting in November 1917. The play offers no certain knowledge in the end about the couple's fate, together or apart.

Despite the play's merits and a fine cast, the reviews were mixed. After the world premiere at the Tremont Theatre on November 21, 1929, the *Boston Globe* deemed *Waterloo Bridge* "one of the most fascinating little plays yet written about the romance of wartime days in London." It went down well in Hartford too, as "a story admirably staged, simply told, honestly ended in no 'ending' at all in a theatrical sense. And most effectively acted." In New York, though, it met with a less warm welcome. "It is a tedious journey in a voluble play," "lacking in event and structure," and "rather sophomoric in its point of view" wrote Brooks Atkinson in the *New York Times*. Burns Mantle concluded: "try as I would, 'Waterloo Bridge,' save for scattered moments, left me cold." According to Arthur Pollock, "It is about as threadbare a situation as can be found in the theater." His fellow Brooklyn critic Rowland Field wrote that "the dramatist [was] giving great gobs of time to characters scarcely interesting enough to deserve it," yet "altogether, it is an affecting little adventure, beautifully written and filled with fine acting."[7]

Witherspoon's individual efforts were universally praised and garnered her some of the best reviews of her career. Here is a bouquet of accolades: "A capital character sketch is contributed by Cora Witherspoon as a big-hearted woman of loose morals"; "Kitty is as real a person as Myra"; "Miss Witherspoon has about all the lightness of the play and manages well with lines that at best must frequently be somewhat offensive to good taste"; "Cora Witherspoon is excellent as a good-natured sister in sin, vulgar in speech and attitude, quick with the defenses of her kind"; "Cora Witherspoon is a help to 'Waterloo Bridge,' playing with gusto and a surprisingly acceptable cockney accent, a street friend of the heroine's"; and finally, "As the cockney slavey, hers was the most impressive performance of its kind since Eleanor Robson was seen in 'Salomy Jane.'"[8]

Waterloo Bridge closed on March 1, 1930, after 64 performances.[9] While this play was more successful than her last two outings on Broadway—*Olympia* and *Precious*—it was a while since Witherspoon had been in a hit. She would have longer to wait. When the U.S. census was taken in April, she was living at 25 E. 55th St., a stone's throw from her old apartment on E. 56th St. and just a few doors down from the Friars' Club. Long since gone, this building stood close to the northeast corner of Madison Ave. and had only three units. Witherspoon paid $125 a month rent.[10]

Witherspoon's next production started rehearsals Monday, June 30, 1930.[11] *Reunion* was written by S.K. Lauren and produced by Bela Blau, as his first venture on his own. Lauren's play *Those We Love*, co-written with George Abbott, had ended a respectable run of 77 performances at the John Golden Theatre in April. Abbott had also acted in the play and directed it. This new venture was without Abbott's participation and was to be directed by Blau. Somewhat surprisingly, Witherspoon was to have a leading role this time; and *Reunion* was a drama, rather than a comedy. Her leading man was Charles D. Brown, who turned 43 on July 1 and whose many Broadway credits extended back to 1911.

The new play "showed what befell, from one afternoon through the following morning, during the 25th reunion of 'the good old class of naughty five' at Eric university, a purely fictional institution and a co-ed one at that." A college instructor, Will Halliday (Brown), has not had the career in science he hoped for, because he married and had to provide for his family, which includes sons Jack (Billy Quinn) and Peter (Alan Ward). His wife Bertha (Witherspoon) has had a challenging life, too, having to "make ends meet out of a salary that no self-respecting business would pay a sales manager."[12]

After two weeks of rehearsals, *Reunion* was tried out at the Brighton Theatre in Brighton Beach, New York, starting July 14, and at the Savoy Theatre in Asbury Park, New Jersey, starting July 21. It was expected to open on Broadway before the end of the month, as the first play of the new season.[13] It never made it there.

In Brighton Beach, one critic found that "the acting is good or very good, and it will be better when the players have learned their lines." Arthur Pollock thought it was "gentle, pretty and quite unimportant" and "nothing more dramatic than a series of understatements, pale and faint": "Like its hero, the play is self-effacing, and before the evening is over it has succeeded in effacing itself almost completely." He summed it up as "a weak watercolor." Charles Hastings, on the other hand, wanted to "see this play proceed to Broadway for a long run." In Asbury Park, Max Davidson found that "several of the leading roles need strengthening." He specifically commended four of the actors, but not Witherspoon.[14]

She came in for praise from others, though, for this new departure. The critic from the *Brooklyn Standard Union* thought she was "worthy of honorable mention"; Roland Holt remarked that "Cora Witherspoon, who will not be in the New York cast, was

convincing as the harassed mother"; and Hastings observed that "Miss Witherspoon cap-
tured high honors, as 'Mrs. Halliday.' Here is a superb actress, as you know." Hastings
felt further that her latest performance would "add greatly to her previous record." "An
enthusiastic audience brought Mr. Brown and Miss Witherspoon before the curtain several times following the last curtain," he told the readers of the *Brooklyn Times Union*.[15]

Surprisingly, even before *Reunion* opened in Brighton Beach, it was announced
that Witherspoon would be joining the cast of Bayard Veiller's new melodrama *Jane
Doe*. Apparently, she had only agreed to do *Reunion* for the two weeks out of town. *Jane
Doe* was being produced by Charles Dillingham, a major Broadway producer, who had
presented *Waterloo Bridge*. Rehearsals were to begin about August 1, under the direction
of Lester Lonergan.[16]

The title of the play was changed to *That's the Woman* before it opened at the Broad
Street Theatre in Newark, New Jersey, on August 25 for a one-week tryout prior to its
Broadway premiere the following week. It was another suspenseful court room drama
from the author of *Within the Law* and *The Trial of Mary Dugan*. The show starred
Phoebe Foster as the "femme" to be "cherchez'd," with Gavin Muir as the defendant
Richard Norris, accused of murdering his best friend, and A.E. Anson in an important
supporting role as counsel for the defense.

According to the critic for the *Jersey Journal*, "Fine work is also done by Cora Witherspoon, the young man's mother."[17] Yet this engagement proved even more limited than
the last. By the time *That's the Woman* opened at the Fulton Theatre in New York on September 3, Witherspoon was no longer in the cast. Her role was played by veteran character actress Effie Shannon, 23 years her senior. The play did not last a month on Broadway
and was veteran playwright Bayard Veiller's last.

By mid–September 1930, Witherspoon was in rehearsal with yet another show. *Oh,
Promise Me* was a new farce by Howard Lindsay and Bertrand Robinson, produced by
Sam H. Harris and staged by the authors themselves. The play was described in a press
release as "a more or less preposterous comedy dealing with an attempt to 'shake-down'
a millionaire 'sugar daddy' for a quarter of a million dollars." The *Jersey Journal* elaborated: "It's a sort of May–December affair, the girl in the case being young and innocent
and the man being old and wise in love-making. The young girl enters into the scheme
of things in the hope of winning a great amount of publicity for the young and aspiring
lawyer, whom she loves. Of course the case gets to the court, and after much back-biting
and general mixups the trial ends to the satisfaction of all."[18]

Like *That's the Woman*, *Oh, Promise Me* had its world premiere at the Broad Street
Theatre in Newark, on October 6, 1930. After a week, the play transferred to the Boulevard Theatre in Jackson Heights, New York. It was to have opened in New York City
the week of October 20, but according to the *Newark Ledger* was "not a finished prod-
uct" and had "yet to be welded into one, speedy, straightforward comedy." The *Brooklyn Times Union* was gladly prepared to bet "any surplus of dollars" that *Oh, Promise Me*
would "never reach Broadway in the shoddy coat it wore at its premiere last evening."
The reviewer particularly objected to all the foul language and found "little use in parad-
ing the unsavoury story in this brief review." Furthermore, "if the show should find its
way to Broadway, … several important changes in cast will be necessary." The *Jersey
Journal*, on the other hand, predicted that the play was "another 'smash hit' headed for
Broadway" and the *Brooklyn Standard Union* described it as "the funniest, most succu-
lent entertainment to hit the downtrodden stage in many a year."[19]

Witherspoon left the cast between the initial tryouts in Newark and Jackson Heights and the second round of tryouts in Brooklyn and Atlantic City, before the November 24 opening at the Morosco Theatre in New York. Mary Philips, who had been with Witherspoon in *Lilies of the Field* and would be with her again in *A Touch of Brimstone*, took over her role of Elsie Carpenter, a "back-biter." In the first tryouts, Witherspoon had been commended for "splendid work," for appearing "to advantage" as "a snappy wench with an eye on the boys," and for fitting her role admirably.[20] Unlike *Reunion* and *That's the Woman*, *Oh, Promise Me* was a success and ran until March 1931.

After all the false starts and dead ends following *Waterloo Bridge*, Witherspoon was finally able to get back on a Broadway stage in January 1931. The vehicle for her return was *Philip Goes Forth*, a comedy by the critically acclaimed and popular playwright George Kelly, who had been absent from the stage for "several seasons." Kelly was best known for *The Torch-Bearers* and *The Show-Off* and had won a Pulitzer Prize for *Craig's Wife* in 1925. Though Kelly kept writing plays until the mid–1940s, he was already past his prime. It was frankly stated by reviewers that *Philip Goes Forth* "may not take rank among the author's best works," that "George Kelly has written better," and that when Kelly "offered his first new comedy in two years ... we were disappointed."[21] The play was staged by the author himself and opened at the Biltmore Theatre (now the Samuel J. Friedman) on January 12, 1931, after tryouts in Baltimore; Lancaster, Pennsylvania; and Washington, D.C.

One critic described the play as "a slyly satiric lecture on the futility of amateurs aspiring to become playwrights." The would-be playwright in this case is the titular hero Philip Eldridge, who is 23 and claims he has wanted to write a play for four years.[22] He rebels against his practical, autocratic father and goes to New York in a huff, rather than pursue the path that has been laid out for him in the family business. Ultimately and somewhat predictably, Philip turns out to have a more natural bent for business than stage drama and finally returns happily to the family fold and business. Philip was played by 30-year-old, Atlanta-born Harry Ellerbe in his Broadway stage debut.

Kelly was known for his strong women characters, but *Philip Goes Forth* is unusual even for him in having four good roles for older women. For Witherspoon, the contrast of her latest part with the Cockney streetwalker Kitty could not have been greater and illustrates the variety in her stage roles at this time. Florence "Florrie" Oliver is a rich, elegant, recently widowed woman with a grown daughter, Cynthia (Madge Evans), and appears in the first and the last of the play's three acts.

On her first appearance, Mrs. Oliver is described in the stage directions as "a tall, graceful woman, and enormously chic—rather a study in black chiffon, with a small, modish black hat, and a magnificent black fur neck-piece. She wears a choker of small pearls, pearl earrings, and a quite fabulous-looking diamond bracelet on her left wrist." Witherspoon probably had a hand in her own costuming. In one of her two scenes, she wore a "black and white flecked tweed outfit" with a "short cape bordered in platinum fox. Black accessories emphasize the ensemble theme." This outfit by the French designer Madeleine Vionnet, "Queen of the bias cut," was so notable, that it was drawn and described in the fashion columns of the day.[23]

In the opening scene, it is Mrs. Oliver who urges Philip to "go forth," based on somewhat dubious reasoning: "I think the very fact the one *thinks* he can write a play, is proof that he can do it.... Simply go forth,—and do it.... I shall be watching you, dear boy, from afar." It appears that she once wanted to write a play herself and hopes "you will have more courage than I did." It becomes clear, though, from the following conversation with her friend and Philip's aunt, Mrs. Randolph (Thais Lawton), that she is not really in sympathy with "the damn fools" who want to do things: "isn't it too dreadful. Why can't they keep still, or, at least, go on doing what they *are* doing."[24]

In her first scene, Mrs. Oliver keeps saying that she absolutely *has* to go, but does not. She is sailing for Europe the following day. When she returns in the third act, six months have passed, during which time our hero Philip has been trying his hand at playwriting in New York and living at Mrs. Ferris's pleasant boarding house with his old college chum, sometime collaborator, and chief encourager, Mr. Shronk (Harry Gresham); and some genuinely artistic types, including the unsuccessful pianist Mr. Haines (Harold Webster) and the ethereal, eccentric poet Miss Krail (Dorothy Stickney). It turns out that Philip's wise and charismatic, middle-aged landlady Mrs. Ferris (Marion Barney) was the leading lady Estelle Mace in younger days. Mrs. Oliver, in her younger days as a "matinee girl," was one of Mace's biggest fans.

While the play itself met with a mixed reception, for Witherspoon it constituted a personal triumph. On the positive side, *Philip Goes Forth* was described as "the best of the new plays that we have met this season," as "a sitting-room comedy, faultlessly cast and tidily performed," as "one of the season's most entertaining works," and as "one of the most interesting exhibits of the season." One reviewer remarked that "it would be difficult to assemble a cast more perfectly fitted for the parts portrayed."[25]

On the critical side, reviewers found that "the acting and the frequent delicious lines, indeed, cloak a theme somewhat lacking in weight," that the play was "an inconsequential comedy, loosely put together, avoiding all intensity," and that it had "a good idea, and founded in essential truth, but not well handled here." Brooks Atkinson thought "Mr. Kelly is looking down from a great height" and described the play scathingly as "a potpourri of drab social comedy, buffoonery and homiletics."[26]

It was suggested that the audience was more interested in "the unusually fine characterizations of Cora Witherspoon as Mrs. Oliver, a volatile widow who encourages Philip to go forth," than in the hero himself. Indeed, reading the reviews one gets the impression Witherspoon was the saving of the show. The *Baltimore Sun* regretted that "space is lacking in which to tell of the exquisite marriage of the comedienne and high-comedy role found in the case of Cora Witherspoon and Mrs. Oliver." According to Burns Mantle: "'Philip Goes Forth' is at its best … in those scenes in which Cora Witherspoon plays a smart and superficial widow full of amusing gab." A reviewer at the Lancaster tryout wrote: "The laughs of the play go to Cora Witherspoon, an ultra-bored and dilletanteish lady." According to a New York critic "honors go to the ever-swell Cora Witherspoon. The play is worth seeing for her acting alone."[27]

As if that was not enough: Witherspoon was "delightful," "superb," "steadily amusing," "delightfully amusing," "irresistibly comic," "amusingly naïve and cynical at one and the same time," "nicely manipulating the comic role of the mother of the girl he loves," and "provided excellent comedy." The play's New York run ended on April 4, 1931, after 97 performances, and was followed by two weeks at the Broad Street Theatre in Philadelphia.[28]

Witherspoon's film debut in 1931 was so modest that no one noticed it. On the face of things, starting out in a movie directed by George Cukor with a screenplay by Donald Ogden Stewart, which also had the distinction of being Tallulah Bankhead's first sound film, would seem an auspicious beginning. Yet it was anything but, for reasons that had nothing to do with Witherspoon.

Like their star, scenarist Stewart and director Cukor were both new to sound films; indeed, this was Cukor's first solo directorial effort. As Bankhead recalled: "All three of us were having our first fling on the talking screen, pioneers in a garrulous new medium." According to Brendan Gill, Stewart, "who had made his name as a humorous writer ... found little to be humorous about in the dreary story on which his script was based." Yet the story was his own.[29] Stewart, then, was not at his best. Neither—as it turned out—was Bankhead. And then there was the fact that Witherspoon's part was so small you might miss it with an ill-timed trip to the bathroom. Given that the film flopped, maybe it was just as well.

Tarnished Lady was Witherspoon's first encounter with Bankhead, who had been living and working in London throughout most of the 1920s. Their stage work together in *Forsaking All Others* and *Jezebel* was still in the future. Bankhead had contracted to do five films for Paramount and was being paid $5,000 a week for her ten weeks' work on this film, a total of $50,000.[30] In *Tarnished Lady*, she portrayed an impoverished New York socialite trying to keep up a brave front and support her mother in the manner to which she had grown accustomed. Witherspoon played a frazzled saleslady in the second scene of the film, who has to refuse Bankhead credit for a new winter coat in the department store owned by Bankhead's friend Osgood Perkins. Bankhead goes straight to complain to Perkins, who lets her have the coat. She wants to have Witherspoon fired for her ostensible rudeness, but later relents. This scene foreshadows Bankhead having to become a saleslady herself in the same store. The heroine says of herself: "I have a genius for not doing what I'm supposed to do."

Bankhead has a distinctly British accent and is "beddy, beddy unhippy" throughout the film. Perkins is the early 1930s version of the gay best friend and appears to have no designs on her himself. There is nothing distinctive about this saleslady role or Witherspoon's performance. She is dressed in a basically black ensemble and has her usual curly, permed hairstyle of the period. She gets no close-ups, of course. Vernon Duke's score for this weeper is hilariously soap operatic.

Production began at Paramount-Publix New York Studios in Astoria, Long Island in January 1931. Witherspoon's uncredited bit part can have taken little more than a day to shoot, either right before or during the run of *Philip Goes Forth*. Her fledgling efforts in films went "unnoticed." Edwin Schallert rendered the most succinct verdict on the film, when he wrote in the *Los Angeles Times* that "'Tarnished Lady' is very tarnished indeed." Bankhead recalled 20 years later that, "Though it had a fine director, a first-rate writer, and a luminous, er, star, it was a fizzle."[31]

An event of greater importance to Witherspoon than her film debut took place while she was playing in *Philip Goes Forth*. She met and adopted one of the great loves of her life: her dog "Lucky." In the earliest and most plausible version of the story, she got him at the "Bide-a-Wee Home for Dogs and Cats" on Houston Street in New York's Greenwich Village, where "for a $2 fee and assurance of a good home," animal lovers could "take away their choice of the strays." In a different version, she found him "at the corner of Madison avenue and Eighty-Sixth street": "'He came running up to me at the street-corner, in a dying condition—half-starved, and with three welts the size of that on his back.'"[32]

Witherspoon described Lucky as "a cross between a Shetland pony and a doormat." As far as his breed background was concerned, he was "variously described as a Maltese terrier, a wire-haired fox, a Tibetan terrier and a spaniel of sorts." His proud owner

would often insist he was "the most
famous dog in the world." Witherspoon also insisted that she
belonged to Lucky, rather than the
other way around and that he was
"the better known of the two."[33]

Mel Washburn devoted his
entire "Spotlight" column to a
story about Lucky in mid–July
1937, under the subheading "Pooch
Loses to Fan." It appeared that
Lucky had "investigated a new
electric fan in his owner's hotel
apartment." When the blades
grazed his muzzle, Lucky "coun-
tered with a left hook" and suffered
an injury to his paw. Witherspoon's
maid Virginia, in trying to rescue
the dog and stop the fan, got her
hair caught in it. Her cries brought
Witherspoon on the scene. She
could not locate the switch and
ended up throwing the fan across
the room, short-circuiting the
hotel's lighting system.[34]

Under the title "The Hound of
the Witherspoon," Lucky was the
subject of a feature article by John
Hobart in the *San Francisco Chronicle* in late July 1939. The darling
dog with the dark, soulful eyes is
pictured looking into the camera,
while Witherspoon regards him
with undisguised affection. Lucky
was even the subject of a UP news
bulletin, which among its scin-
tillating contents mentioned that
the dog was known for his collection of autographed photos from
such notables of the day as David
Belasco and Tallulah Bankhead.[35]

Witherspoon was a one-dog
woman, that is, one dog at a time.
"I'm not a dog-collector," she said
in 1939, "like Alice Brady. Why,
Alice has 20 of them; they're all
over the place, under sofas, on

Witherspoon admitted in an interview with veteran drama critic Elliott Norton in 1941, that she had
"gone Hollywood" during her first years there and
hired both a maid and a chauffeur. The maid (left) is
said to have come from New Orleans, and her name
was Virginia. The delightful dog in her arms is Witherspoon's beloved "Lucky," whom she had adopted
from an animal shelter in New York in 1931. Lucky
was the subject of numerous news articles, had his
own collection of autographed photographs from
celebrities like David Belasco and Tallulah Bankhead, and was one of the best friends Witherspoon
ever had. This snapshot is probably from 1936 and
may have been taken on the roof of the Hollywood
Roosevelt Hotel, where Witherspoon stayed on
arrival in Los Angeles that year. Lucky lived a long
life and died sometime after 1944. The other dog has
not been identified (Billy Rose Theatre Division, The
New York Public Library for the Performing Arts).

tables and in your hair. Lucky is enough for me."[36] Incidentally, Brady died of cancer only three months after having her canine collecting tendencies critically exposed by Witherspoon.

Dogs played a significant role in Witherspoon's life. Lucky was only the most famous and long-lived of them. She would take her dog everywhere. *San Francisco Chronicle* columnist Mildred Brown Robbins describes meeting Lucky at a party in 1939, "an affectionate and lively youngster despite his 12 years in this vale of tears." He was still alive in 1941, when he posed for a photographer from the *Quincy Patriot Ledger*, and was last heard from three years later, when the cast of *Ramshackle Inn* almost had to go to Chicago without Witherspoon. She refused to budge from New York, if the hotel would not accommodate Lucky.[37]

In early May 1931, *Tarnished Lady* was released and on May 14 Witherspoon's mentor, David Belasco, died at age 77. On June 1 that year, she opened in Congreve's *The Way of the World* at the Guild Theatre. It was produced by the Players Club of New York, as the tenth in a row of their week-long classic revivals; was directed by B. Iden Payne; and had a cast full of stage notables like Fay Bainter, Ernest Cossart, Walter Hampden, Moffat Johnston, Eugene and Kathleen Lockhart, Selena Royle, and Dorothy Stickney. Witherspoon played Mrs. Marwood, who is conducting a secret affair with Fainall (William S. Rainey), her best friend's husband, but is also secretly in love with Mirabell (Hampden).

Again, Witherspoon's performance was better received than the production as a whole. Brooks Atkinson felt "this loosely-strung revival touches only the surface of a closely-entangled play." Surprisingly with such experienced players, diction and audibility was a problem, and he commended Witherspoon for speaking with a clarity that pulled her scenes up. According to Burns Mantle, "The players last night were not doing their best by the text. Being nervous, they were hurried, and they slurred many speeches. Those not familiar with the text missed much of it…. [T]he result was rather disastrous." Even so, "Cora Witherspoon flashed a brilliant line or two as Mrs. Marwood and these were effectively parried by Selena Royle, playing Mrs. Fainall."[38]

The production was "lavishly costumed and much of it heavily played." Witherspoon's dress was described in detail by Irene Veil in her fashion column, as "a cream lace and orange combination with black gloves, fine black lace being posed to form a border for the petticoat, the balance of which was fashioned of three tiers of cream lace." In his summary of the season, Mantle noted that "the public did not rise to Congreve and the Players were glad to get a $5,000 profit out of it, which is the least they have made since first they started resurrecting classics."[39]

Magnolia is a village on the North Shore of Massachusetts, which was once the site of the massive and magnificent Oceanside Hotel. For a time, the Oceanside had its own theater. It was here that Witherspoon appeared with the Magnolia Players for a week in mid–August 1931. The presentation was *Notorious Lady*, a new play by 26-year-old John Entenza. Pauline Fredericks had been slated to star in this play at the Pasadena Playhouse in 1930, but nothing came of it.[40]

Witherspoon played the leading role of Julia Farr, "a sophisticated ex-patriate who returns to battle with an American milieu." According to the *Boston Herald*, this was "another sophisticated drawing-room comedy of daring dialogue and small happenings." Yet the paper found that "Cora Witherspoon as Julia was superb, the essence of femininity": "As an extremely silly woman who always got her way and was adored, she was bewilderingly convincing. With what variety of color she spoke her lines, and how untheatrical and hackneyed [sic] her gestures. Hers was the only major part, the others all fell in behind."[41]

There was no question, then, that Witherspoon could carry a play. As a vehicle, though, *Notorious Lady* could not carry her anywhere else. As for the fate of the Oceanside: the 440-room hotel at the juncture of Hesperus and Lexington avenues was reduced to rubble in the course of 60 minutes by a massive fire in December 1958.[42]

Though Witherspoon's Hollywood film career did not begin in earnest until 1936, she made two films at RKO in September, October, and November 1931. The first of these was the slightly more than an hour-long Wheeler and Woolsey comedy *Peach O'Reno*, "a travesty on the Reno divorce mill."[43] This B movie was directed by William A. Seiter, who would later direct Witherspoon in *On the Avenue.*

As her screen husband, she had the veteran stage comedian Joseph Cawthorn, 22 years her senior. The two portrayed Joe and Aggie Bruno and the film begins with the celebration of the Brunos' silver wedding anniversary, which ends disastrously with the couple headed for Reno and a divorce. It is an odd experience watching Witherspoon as a frumpy, middle-aged, middle-class housewife and mother of two grown daughters, played by Dorothy Lee and Zelma O'Neal. The most unusual thing is her hair, which is piled on the top of her head and has a distinctive white streak in it. Witherspoon's characteristic profile is just about the only thing that is recognizable. Typically, too, she shows up in a bare-shouldered and bare-backed evening gown for a long scene in a Reno night club and casino. Hardly the thing homely Aggie Bruno would wear.

The humor in *Peach O'Reno* has not aged well. As if the Brunos' marital squabbles and the zany antics of the divorce lawyers played by Wheeler and Woolsey were not enough, the film develops into a full-fledged variety show. Bert Wheeler spends about half the film in drag as Miss Bunny Hanover—Cawthorn calls her "Miss Hangover"—and "how that boy can impersonate"! "The folks at the Mayfair yesterday seemed to enjoy Wheeler's female impersonation more than anything else," wrote Irene Thirer in the *New York Daily News.*

The verdict on the film ranged from "the funniest Wheeler-Woolsey comedy to date" to "funny in spots, but spotty in others."[44]

Witherspoon had the satisfaction of being billed sixth for her efforts and was frequently mentioned in reviews, usually in tandem with Cawthorn. According to the *Houston Chronicle*, the couple "steal a lot of the better comedy moments from the featured comedians." The *San Francisco Chronicle* wrote that "veterans Cawthorn and Miss Witherspoon are richly comic as the couple seeking divorce." The *Altoona Tribune* thought they did "exceptionally well." The *South Bend Tribune* wrote that Witherspoon "does herself proud, no less, and how she ever gets her hats perched at their precarious angles is nothing short of miraculous." A columnist in the *Knoxville Journal* described her as "a tall and sensitive lady who might pass for Miss Edna Mae [sic] Oliver."[45]

As fate would have it, Witherspoon's second film at RKO starred the selfsame Edna May Oliver, who was six years her senior and had arrived in Hollywood in 1930. In RKO films like *Half Shot at Sunrise, Cimarron,* and *Fanny Foley Herself,* Oliver was fast finding her type as the upright, imperious but not unsympathetic widow or spinster with the signature sniff. Her only film with Witherspoon, *Ladies of the Jury,* provided her with a breakout role as the upper-class dowager and amateur detective Mrs. Livingston Baldwin Crane.

The film was directed by Lowell Sherman. He and Witherspoon had acted together in a stock company in Milwaukee in 1909, when she was just starting out. *Ladies of the Jury* was an adaptation of a moderately successful, 1929 Broadway comedy of the same title by Fred Ballar. It unfolds mainly in a jury room, where 12 jurors—five women and seven men—have to determine whether a French ex-chorus girl played by Jill Esmond has killed her wealthy husband. The best part of the film is the opening segment at the trial, where Oliver antagonizes classic angry old man actor Robert McWade, here seen as a judge, by applying her upper-class rules of etiquette to his court room, as if it were her drawing room. It was more than a dozen years since McWade and Witherspoon had supported Leo Ditrichstein in *The King* and *The Matinee Hero*.

Witherspoon portrays one of the jurors, Miss Lily Pratt, who is described in one review as a "reform worker."[46] Miss Pratt is unremittingly sour-faced and suspicious and, with the male jury foreman, a holdout vote for a guilty verdict, while Mrs. Crane is convinced of the woman's innocence. The most interesting thing about Miss Pratt is her mode of dress: a mannish, tweedy two-piece suit worn with a tie and a man's slouch hat pushed so far down on her head, that Witherspoon is almost unrecognizable.

The *Boston Globe* went all out, calling *Ladies of the Jury* "the year's funniest, most thoroughly enjoyable comedy." Oliver got rave reviews, while Witherspoon garnered less praise and attention than for *Peach O'Reno*, though she was billed sixth here too. The *Washington Evening Star* critic E. de S. Melcher, who was always in her corner, found her "specially amusing." The *Baltimore Evening Sun* thought the picture better than the play, "for the very simple reason that a capable cast has been assembled to animate the smaller roles." The paper noted that "some skilled members of Equity appear in the cast. One of them is Miss Cora Witherspoon." The *Brooklyn Daily Eagle* concurred, writing that the film had "perhaps the best rounded cast of the season." "All are especially selected 'types' and all do unusually good work," noted the *Cleveland Plain Dealer*.[47] In retrospect, both *Peach O'Reno* and *Ladies of the Jury* show that Hollywood had no idea what to do with Witherspoon at this point or what types of roles she was known for on the stage.

Witherspoon went directly from the set of *Ladies for the Jury*, where production ended in late November, to rehearsals for a new play, *The Tadpole*, which was to open at the John Golden Theatre in New York on December 29, 1931. The authors were Winchell Smith and Wilmarth Lewis. Smith had not written a play since *Lightnin'*, but had worked as a director, including of *Waterloo Bridge*. He was also to direct *The Tadpole*. The cast was headed by Harry Ellerbe from *Philip Goes Forth* and also included Natalie Schafer, Harry Davenport, Frank Monroe, Jane Wyatt, Porter Hall, H.C. Potter, and Ina Claire's brother Allen Fagan. Witherspoon played Mrs. Lawrence, variously described in the reviews as "a delightful semi-invalid," "the vague-minded mother of the groom-to-be," and "that indolent, fuss-budget woman so well played by Cora Witherspoon."[48]

Prior to the Broadway opening, there were tryouts at Brandt's Boulevard Theatre in Jackson Heights, New York, and Parsons' Theatre in Hartford. Both authors hailed from Hartford, which seems to have assured the play an unduly cordial reception. The *Brooklyn Daily Eagle* described *The Tadpole* as "an oversubtle and unbelievable medley of sentimentality," but also noted that "it would not be easy to improve on the fine performances of Harry Davenport, or Frank Monroe, or Cora Witherspoon." Obviously straining to be positive, the *Hartford Courant* found the play "something in the nature of a singularly pleasant and attractive one-act play stretched into three." Witherspoon had "some admirable lines to deliver, which she gets over the footlights most skillfully."

According to the *Springfield Republican*, *The Tadpole* "came forth from the wings as a pleasant creation of no definite category or destination." Louise Mace found Witherspoon "an apt purveyor of the Mary Boland type of comedy."[49]

As early as the first week of the *Tadpole* tryouts in Jackson Heights, it was announced that Witherspoon was jumping ship and going into a new show called *Jewel Robbery*.[50] She probably realized that the good ship "Tadpole" was not going to reach the port of Broadway and, indeed, it never did. It foundered and sank in Hartford.

In *Jewel Robbery* by Bertram Bloch, based on a Hungarian play by Lazlo Fodor, Mary Ellis and Basil Sydney were co-starring for the tenth time. They had been married since 1929 and were returning to Broadway after a "highly successful engagement" in London in *Strange Interlude*. According to the plot summary in the *Jersey Journal*: "The story deals with a jewel thief, who is gallant, cultured and attractive. His manners are so charming that he persuades the wife of one of his victims to permit him to get away after a jewel store robbery and then she spends a week-end with him on the Riviera." Sydney played the jewel thief and Ellis the errant wife. Witherspoon's role was limited to the first act, where she played the heroine's best friend Marianne, a wife "who talks incessantly on unfaithfulness in wives" and who "is content only when a new man is in the wind."[51]

Though the reviews were devastating, Witherspoon was praised for her individual performance. The settings and costumes were also admired, Brooks Atkinson remarking that "the production is lustrous. Aline Bernstein's settings have a neat, alluring splendor. The costumes are sinfully luxurious." The entertainment value of the play, he found "only tepid after all." The critic for the *Washington Evening Star* preferred a culinary metaphor: "Patrons of the theater who like their theatrical meals well cooked will find this slightly cold around the edges." Burns Mantle thought *Jewel Robbery* "nothing much for Mary Ellis and Basil Sydney to have waited all these months for." "Such a lot of brickmakers and no straws," he added. The *Brooklyn Standard Union* wrote that the play was "something less than mildly diverting and something more than soporific fodder": "It makes a great deal of noise without saying anything, expends a lot of energy without going anywhere and takes a moderate amount of time without offering any return." Witherspoon was "amusing as a full-bloom Hungarian Juliet whose Romeos are constantly coming and going" and did "splendid work." After tryouts in Washington, D.C., and Newark, New Jersey, *Jewel Robbery* opened at the Booth Theatre January 13, 1932. It closed February 27, 1932, after 54 performances, and Witherspoon was once more at liberty.[52]

If you ever wanted to explain what "casting against type" is, you might point to Lillian Gish in *Camille*. It is hard to imagine any leading lady physically and mentally less suited to portraying a jaded, worldly, Parisian courtesan, than the ethereal, ageless, and spinsterish Gish. Indeed, the entire 1932 production of a new stage version of Alexandre Dumas's famous novel was a kind of curiosity, a museum piece. It came about in an unorthodox fashion, because a band of wealthy and civic-minded Denverites, including Delos Chappell and his actress wife Edna James, had saved and restored the historic Grand Opera House in Central City, Colorado, 35 miles west of Denver. They needed a suitable entertainment as the focal point for the theater's grand reopening in mid–July 1932. Gish was invited to star in a production that would recreate both the spirit and the letter of 1878, the year the opera house originally opened, down to the scalloped footlights on the stage's edge.[53] The "Central" was once the finest opera house between the Mississippi and the Pacific coast and had closed in 1927.

Camille was directed and designed by Robert Edmond Jones. Jones also co-produced and collaborated on the new stage adaptation of the Dumas novel with the Chappells. The special musical arrangements were by Macklin Marrow, who also conducted the orchestra. Raymond Hackett, a former Broadway child actor, who scored a major hit as an adult in *The Cradle Snatchers* and was now 30 years old, was cast as Armand Duval. Witherspoon played Marguerite Gautier's confidante Prudence Duvernoy. Edna James Chappell played Anaïs. Lillian Bronson, Helen Freeman, Moffat Johnston, and Ian Wolfe were also in the large cast.

For the grand gala reopening on Saturday, July 16, 1932, the 700-person audience attended in costumes of the period and arrived in horse-driven coaches. Tickets to the premiere cost an exorbitant $100 a seat. The performance was followed by a ball at the Teller House hotel next door. After playing a week in Central City, the company disbanded. Lillian Gish went to "take the cure" in Bad Neuheim, Germany, for several weeks. Witherspoon also appears to have been on hiatus.

In the fall, the original company reunited for a tour that started at Parsons' Theatre in Hartford, Connecticut, on October 14, 1932, and included stops in Springfield, Albany, Utica, Rochester, and Newark, before coming into New York City for a two-week engagement at the Morosco Theatre November 1–12. Gish biographer Charles Affron writes that "*Camille* had a pathetically short New York run of fifteen performances." Based on the review in the *Brooklyn Citizen* and Burns Mantle's summary of the season, though, my impression is that the New York run of *Camille* was never intended to be more than a two-week, limited engagement. The show opened on a Tuesday; hence it lasted 15 rather than 16 performances.[54]

Brooks Atkinson gave a telling description of Gish and the play in the *New York Times*: "She is as detached from worldly turmoils as a vagrant wisp of cloud." "Even in a part to which she is unsuited," he continued, "she can silence a first-night audience." He found that "her company is of no great assistance" and concluded: "What with one thing and another it is frankly hard to discover why any one should want to revive this outmoded play." The *New York Daily News* critic felt that "Lillian Gish ... can no more suggest the Camille of tradition, or the Camille of fact, than she could suggest a popular conception of Cleopatra, or the Du Barry, or Catherine of Russia." In fairness, the critic for the *Brooklyn Citizen* was wildly enthusiastic. Gish was "truly superb as the lady of the camelias" and "the best 'Camille' the stage has offered in recent years."[55]

As the fluttery, prattling Prudence, Witherspoon was "amusing," "appeared to excellent advantage," and "got every bit of humor from the part and also offered one or two serious moments, proving her ability does not end with comedy." On the more negative side, it was felt that she "sacrifices, evidently by direction, all the rowdy comedy of the vulgar one." On the whole, opinions were divided on whether Gish's *Camille* was "a dramatic feast fit for the gods" or "a none-too-successful experiment."[56]

Witherspoon did not often appear in the gossip columns, but no less a figure than Walter Winchell thought it worth mentioning in late November 1932, that she had "renounced the stage over the holidays to become a professional buyer." Mark Barron provided further information in his column: "The decline of the theater has sent many an actress into business.... Cora Witherspoon, who gave such a splendid performance in 'Waterloo Bridge,' is now a professional buyer."[57] It was ironic that Witherspoon should appear to be struggling to find work on the stage when, in fact, the first half of the 1930s was one of the busiest times of her career. After *Camille* closed on November 12, she was off the stage only about two months. In 1933 she would land directly in the path of one of the most tempestuous thespian tornados of the twentieth century.

On January 6, 1933, the *New York Times* announced that Tallulah Bankhead would star in *Forsaking All Others*, a play she had acquired after producer Arthur Hopkins had relinquished his option. She had selected Arch Selwyn to produce the play and rehearsals would begin the following week under the direction of Henry Wagstaff Gribble. According to Bankhead herself, she was not up to the "dickering with scene designers, directors, actors, theater managers and booking agents," that being a producer entailed. She engaged her "old acquaintance" Selwyn "to be my proxy in fiscal and professional matters": "I didn't want this to leak out. The enemy would say Tallulah must be desperate indeed to produce her own play." Industry insiders were not fooled, Rowland Field writing: "it is more than hinted that Miss Bankhead is the actual producer." Jean Dalrymple, who acted as press agent for the show, recalled many years later that the production department was "a department of utter confusion and chaos…. Everybody had something to say."[58]

Forsaking All Others marked Bankhead's return to Broadway after an absence of ten years; years spent as a rising star in London and as a star who failed to rise in Hollywood. According to biographer Lee Israel, Bankhead "had a tendency to hire friends, but they were talented friends who did no disservice to the play." As her leading man, she selected Fred Keating, "an eminent magician who specialized in making birds vanish." She had heard he was down on his luck. It was his first dramatic role.[59]

After several changes of cast, the male second lead was to be played by Anderson Lawlor, "Tallulah's then 'official' young man" and one of her legion of concurrent and consecutive "caddies." A caddy, according to Brendan Gill, was "a gentleman of pleasing appearance and deportment," who must "be beside her at all times to open doors, order food and drink, pay (with money given him beforehand) the bills presented in restaurants and bars, hail cabs, and see her safely home. In her youth, these companions were usually heterosexual or bisexual; as she grew older, they tended to be much younger than she and to be homosexual." Lawlor was predominantly gay and had the advantage of being a fellow Alabamian.[60]

Ilka Chase would play the heroine's confidante and bridesmaid, described by Bankhead as "a venomous witch full of suspicion and speakeasy brandy—the bridesmaid, not Ilka." Witherspoon had been cast as an older friend of the heroine by January 11. When her casting was announced, she was in Detroit replacing Jessie Busley, an actress more than 20 her senior, in a production of the Jessie Bonstelle stock company called *Bridal Wise*. In the *Forsaking All Others* cast list, we also find familiar names like Barbara O'Neil, who was promoted from a maid to a named role between the tryouts and New York; and Henry Fonda as "A Gentleman."[61]

Casting was complete and rehearsals had begun by January 15. Bankhead liked director Henry Wagstaff Gribble and was particularly amused by his name, but Gribble was ill and only lasted two weeks. Arthur J. Beckhard took over as director January 25. His withdrawal was announced February 14, after the tryout in Washington. Thomas Mitchell, "called in at the last moment to rewrite and direct the piece, accomplished wonders in a few days at clarifying and motivating what hitherto had been a formless concoction."[62] Mitchell stayed the course.

Originally entitled *There Was I, Forsaking All Others* was written by Edward Roberts and Frank Cavett; the latter had been a cameraman on Bankhead's film *The Devil and the Deep* at Paramount. The plot was summarized as follows in *The Best Plays of 1931-32*: "On the eve of Mary Clay's [Bankhead's] marriage to Dillon Todd [Lawlor] Constance Barnes [Millicent Hanley], who had done the continent with Dillon the season before, returns and figuratively files a prior claim on the groom. Dillon in a weak moment marries Constance and sends Mary word that he will not be able to keep his appointment at the altar. Next day Dillon is sorry and would renew his engagement. Mary is open minded about it and willing to forget until she suddenly realizes that it is Jefferson Tingle [Keating] she has really loved all the time. She takes Jeff and Dillon is left waiting." Bankhead's friend Robert Benchley dubbed the play "The Bounder's Bride." Witherspoon's character, Paula La Salle, "functioned as a surrogate mother to Mary Clay," who wants her to sue Dillon for breach of promise.[63]

The play had a "stormy pre–Broadway tour" to Wilmington, Washington, and Boston. In Washington, Bankhead's father the congressman "helped paper the house with eminences." In Boston, the "Gallery Girls" in the balcony drowned out even the orchestra with their boisterous support of their beloved Bankhead and equally vocal disapproval of her stage adversaries. "Thanks to the frantic rewriting and redirecting it had undergone on the road," the production "had already a certain reputation as an embodiment of bedlam" before it reached New York. The play opened at the Times Square Theatre on March 1, 1933, the day "the banks closed with a bang that rocked Herbert Hoover to the basement." They had to accept checks at the box office or by mail.[64]

Overall, the performers were better received than the play. The *Washington Evening Star* thought *Forsaking All Others* "far from a plum," with "a cast which is far more expert than the play." The *Boston Herald* opined: "It is a pity that Miss Bankhead for her first appearance in Boston was not provided with a better play. She and company deserved one. This play is not only without dramatic interest, its dialogue consists chiefly of dull lines that are to be taken by the charitably disposed as witty." Others found the play was "made almost continually amusing by gay badinage and spirited playing," "a bit rawboned," "an aimless three acts of chitter-chatter," and "an over-dressed wraith."[65]

Brooks Atkinson described the play in his inimitable fashion, as "a cheerful little earful of bright retorts and verbal fencing numbers" and a "smart comedy with tremor of brave emotion." "For burlesque there is Cora Witherspoon." Among the "noble cast" supporting Bankhead, the *Wilmington Mornings News* thought Witherspoon most worthy of mention, "the dear, ex-Gibson girl and friend of the heroine's mother," and the *Boston Globe* found her "deserving of praise." According to Burns Mantle, "Cora Witherspoon offers herself brightly as a slightly cartooned lady of the near past."[66]

Bankhead kept the play alive through artificial respiration for 14 weeks, before finally letting it die a natural death. *Forsaking All Others* closed June 3, 1933, after 110 performances. Bankhead claimed to have lost $40,000 on the production,[67] but no doubt recouped her losses when she sold the film rights to MGM. The film version starred Joan Crawford, with Billie Burke in Witherspoon's role.

The tense and thought-provoking crime and suspense drama *Midnight* (aka *Call It Murder*) was the most worthy and well-crafted of Witherspoon's four East coast films. The film was in production at Eastern Services Studios in Astoria, Long Island from mid–May to mid–June 1933, at the end of Witherspoon's run in *Forsaking All Others* and just before she opened in *Shooting Star*. It was Chester Erskine's directorial debut. He only directed eight films over the course of 38 years, including *Frankie and Johnny* with Witherspoon in 1934 and most famously *The Egg and I* in 1947.

Midnight was based on a play of the same title by Claire and Paul Sifton, which had had a short run on Broadway in 1930–31 with Maud Allan in Witherspoon's role. The plot is rather ingenious and shows how the law does not always mete out the same justice to all. Two women commit the same crime of passion, yet their outcomes are different due to politics. Helen Flint goes to the electric chair, while Sidney Fox gets off scot free the night of Flint's execution, partly because she is the daughter of the jury foreman at Flint's trial, played by O.P. Heggie. There is some doubt cast at the end, though, about whether Fox actually fired the fatal shots.

In the midst of the mayhem, we find Witherspoon in the guise of middle-class matron and Fox's aunt, Elizabeth McGrath. This pettish, insensitive, and silly woman, who wants to play bridge to pass the time while they are waiting for Flint to go to the chair at midnight, has several of the traits that would dominate Witherspoon's later screen image. "Well, that's that. Oh, come on, let's play bridge" is her laconic comment, when Heggie refuses the defense lawyer's plea to go to the governor and ask for a stay of the sentence of execution. The fine cast also included (in order of billing) Henry Hull as a journalist who is instrumental in saving Fox from being charged with murder, Margaret Wycherly as Fox's mother and Heggie's wife, Lynne Overman as Heggie's ne'er-do-well son-in-law, Humphrey Bogart as Fox's shady boyfriend and the murder victim, Granville Bates as Witherspoon's husband, and Moffat Johnston, who had been with her recently in *The Way of the World* and *Camille*, as the district attorney who has prosecuted Flint.

Wanda Hale of the *New York Daily News* gave the film three stars and noted that "the entire cast, made up for the most part of artists from the stage, completes a group performance with a capability that leaves room for no possible improvement." According to the *New Orleans Times-Picayune* "a cast made up largely of stage veterans has made of 'Midnight' ... a breath-taking play instead of the cheap melodrama it might have been in less capable hands." Witherspoon was singled out in several reviews: "Cora Witherspoon and Lynn Overman relieve the necessary grimness with moments of genuine comedy"; "Especially clever are Overman, as a slow-witted in-law, and Miss Witherspoon as a silly card-playing matron"; and "Cora Witherspoon handles her minor part skillfully."[68]

Shooting Star, which opened at the Selwyn Theatre in New York only nine days after *Forsaking All Others* closed, was the second flop of Witherspoon's career. She had been acting on Broadway since 1910, so that is a pretty good record. This unhappy play was written by Noel Pierce and Bernard C. Schoenfeld and directed by Bela Blau, who had directed and produced *Reunion* with Witherspoon in 1930. While the heroine was called Julie Leander, *Shooting Star* was described in advance as "the play about Jeanne Eagels." According to the *New York Times*: "there have been official denials that the career of the late Jeanne Eagels gave the authors their idea."[69] The lead was played by Francine Larrimore, with Witherspoon enacting a character named Edna Judd. Henry O'Neill, Lee Patrick, and Beverly Sitgreaves were among the other more familiar names in the large cast.

The critic from the *New York Times* wrote: "The main difficulties through which 'Shooting Star' strolled were its slowness and its tendency to yell. It was too hot for this latter." Some further critical observations included that it was "a scattered play and never particularly interesting"; that the play lasted "very close to midnight" and "at least a half hour less of it would have made 'Shooting Star' seem much better"; and that it was "an elaborate episodic play" consisting of no less than 11 scenes. On the positive side, it was noted that "there were many curtain calls last night and the forecast seems to be a successful season on Forty-second street"; that it "looks like the summer's hit, thanks to the genius of one actress in interpreting the soul of another"; and that is was "a personal triumph for Miss Larrimore." As for the supporting cast of no less than 33 individuals, "there is little worth while for any of them to do." *Shooting Star* came to an abrupt end on June 24, after only 16 performances.[70]

On July 31, 1933, Witherspoon opened in a production of *Present Laughter* at the Westport Country Playhouse. Not to be confused with a later play by Noël Coward of the same title, this new comedy was written by Charles Brackett, starred Roger Pryor and Rose Hobart, and was directed by Antoinette Perry. According to the *Stamford Advocate*, the supporting cast "reads like a 'who's who in drawing room comedy on the Broadway stage.'" Witherspoon was joined in the cast by two fellow members of the *Forsaking All Others Company*, Ilka Chase and Nancy Ryan. Of Witherspoon's contribution to the proceedings, we only know that she gave "real assistance" to Hobart, Pryor, and Chase in their efforts to "give the new comedy a punch and make of it something more than just another one of those things." According to a local reviewer, "Considerable trimming will no doubt be done to the comedy before it is ready for New York." Trimmed or not, *Present Laughter* never made it there.[71] Author and future producer Brackett became a friend and would help Witherspoon to take her film career to another level in 1936.

On August 17, 1933, the *New York Daily News* could relate that "Guthrie McClintic has engaged Witherspoon to support Tallulah Bankhead in Owen Davis' 'Jezebel.'" Witherspoon was putting herself in the path of the human hurricane yet again. Trouble was not long in coming. On August 26, Bankhead checked into Doctors Hospital with abdominal pains. As she recalled in her 1952 memoirs, her stomach was "swollen up like a basketball." On September 13, McClintic announced that Bankhead would not be appearing in *Jezebel* after all. According to a news item in the *New York Times*: "Miss Bankhead has been ill and her physicians have insisted that she give up all thought of acting for several weeks." It was hoped that another actress might be found and that the play might still open in New York September 25.[72]

On September 18, McClintic "definitely suspended" the production: "Mr. McClintic dismissed the cast by paying each member two weeks' salary, according to the Equity regulation, and ordered the scenery and costumes stored." There was still some hope, though, that Bankhead would recover sufficiently to be able to appear in the *Jezebel* "later in the season." McClintic "besought the members of the company not to commit themselves definitely elsewhere until it is quite apparent whether Miss Bankhead will recover within sufficient time to resume preparations."[73]

On November 3, Bankhead underwent a five-hour radical hysterectomy. She spoke of the incident in vague terms in her memoirs: "What they found in my abdominal cavities and adjacent areas was hair-raising. There was a technical name for the contortions of my innards, but I can't remember it. My trunk lines were matted, meshed and fouled up." The "technical name" was gonorrhea. Biographer Israel Lee gets more specific: "The gonococci had invaded her uterine cavity, ascended up into the tubes and ovaries, and finally into the membrane lining of her abdominal cavity. Her body was ravaged with pus by the time of the operation; she was down to seventy pounds. Only by removing all her reproductive organs were the doctors able to save her life."[74] Bankhead was only 31 years old.

There was no question of Bankhead doing the play. Miriam Hopkins was flown in from Hollywood to take over the leading role. She arrived in New York on November 16 and rehearsals began the next day. There were further changes of cast. On December 12, the *New York Times* reported that Reed Brown, Jr., had taken over the male leading role from Robert Wallsten. Ultimately, *Jezebel* did not open on Broadway until December 19, after a three-day engagement at the Shubert Theatre in New Haven starting December 14.[75]

The plot of Owen Davis's *Jezebel* will be familiar to many based on the film version starring Bette Davis. Let me nevertheless share Bankhead's own succinct summary: "Julie [Kendrick] was a Louisiana hothead who had been helling about Europe for three years in an attempt to forget a quarrel with her cousin, Preston. On her return, dripping repentance, she was knocked for a loop on learning her kinsman was sealed to another. Julie was a jealous rip. To avenge Preston's perfidy she prodded him into a duel with the crack shot of the county. Preston was about to join his ancestors when his brother volunteered to substitute for him. This brother, a second Daniel Boone, drilled his opponent deftly. Then a yellow fever epidemic raged through Louisiana. This flattened Preston. But when he was hauled off to the pesthouse Julie went with him, while his wife took off for the Nawth. Quite a plot, brother!"[76]

Witherspoon's part in all this was playing Julie Kendrick's concerned and sometimes censorious aunt, Miss Sally, the role taken by Fay Bainter in the Warner Bros. film version from 1938. Several critics pointed out that "it is her aunt who brands her as a Jezebel." Once again, Witherspoon scored a personal hit in a play that was met mostly with derision. Brooks Atkinson thought that she was "in top form." The play was "a gorgeous affair," but "beneath the surface you can hear those old melodramatic bogeymen rumbling." Rowland Field thought Witherspoon was "very fine as Julie's aunt, Miss Sally." As for the rest, "it is a splendid cast that Mr. McClintic has gathered together for this decorative melodrama of the Southland. One can only wish that the play could have been a more exhilarating experience." Overall, Field found the play "old-fashioned and somewhat commonplace." Arthur Pollock thought Witherspoon made for "a sweet aunt," while "the play is a piece of clever carpentry, painted with the phrases of a conventional dramatist, smooth and pat and devoid of genuine emotion. Mr. McClintic has never produced a worse." Edgar Price wrote that "Cora Witherspoon, who can always be depended upon to give a fine performance, makes much of the role of Miss Sally, Julie's aunt": "As a play, 'Jezebel' is disappointing in more ways than one." Bushnell Dimond "liked immensely Cora Witherspoon as Jezebel's aunt—a delicate and sure-footed bit of acting, this." The play was another matter: "Listening to Mr. Davis's wooden dialogue, watching the gyrations of his pitiful marionettes, I was nonplussed to account for Mr. McClintic's selection of such a script." UP drama critic Jack Gaver thought the play "no great shakes." He wrote that Witherspoon gave her role "good treatment." *Jezebel* closed on January 13, 1934, after only 32 performances.[77] Witherspoon's departure from the cast was announced before it was decided to close the show. Only than ten days after *Jezebel* ended, Witherspoon opened in a new drama by John Haggart called *Mackerel Skies* at the Playhouse Theatre in New York. Besides Witherspoon, the "superb cast" included Florence Edney from *Waterloo Bridge*, Violet Kemble-Cooper, John Griggs, Tom Powers, and

Fred Stone's daughter Carol. Kemble-Cooper played a wealthy woman who actively tries to prevent her talented daughter, played by Carol Stone, from having the operatic singing career she herself had once unsuccessfully sought. A happy ending is achieved nevertheless, when Stone's Austrian-peasant-turned-wealthy-Chicago-wheat-broker father (Powers) suddenly turns up to enable her to reach her goals and marry the man she loves (Griggs). Witherspoon played Sophie (surname unknown), variously described as "a society matron," "a family friend," and "a comic character irrelevant to the proceedings." We can read in the reviews, that Witherspoon "proved that she is an actress by doing well in the small role"; and that she "played valiantly through the handicap of a severe cold."[78]

Alas, the critics disliked this one too. "Nothing really bad came of the evening, and nothing really good," wrote the critic for the *New York Times*. "The play ... lacked spirit. It ambled along from one thing to another, just as its plot ambled from Vienna to New York." The *Brooklyn Daily Eagle* observed that *Mackerel Skies* "would have been considered a 'good, powerful, strong drama' just before the beginning of the century." Now it simply seemed old-fashioned. The *Brooklyn Citizen* found that the play "had the substance and reality of the darkly flecked clouds of a clumsy scene-painter's brush and forecast an emotional storm of similar unbelief." An exception to this chorus of disapproval was the *Brooklyn Times Union*, which described *Mackerel Skies* as "A distinguished play, with an wholesome international flavor": "The play itself is no less pleasurable than the splendid acting of a superb cast." It was "one of the biggest things of the year." The public did not recognize its greatness, and *Mackerel Skies* closed even more quickly than *Jezebel*. On February 10 it was all over after 23 performances.[79] Witherspoon had racked up yet another flop.

Her character's name is all I have been able to uncover about Witherspoon's participation in the film *Frankie and Johnny*. It was Mrs. Lumpy Thornton. The only comment her performance elicited is not enlightening: "Cora Witherspoon, whom your writer has also seen on the New York stage, handled the small role of Lumpy." *Frankie and Johnnie* was "a new, sentimentalized version of the old Mississippi legend which grew out of America's most famous love song from which the picture takes its title." Helen Morgan and Chester Morris starred in the title roles, with Lilyan Tashman as Nellie Bly and Florence Reed, Walter Kingsford, William Harrigan, and Witherspoon among the "well known stage names" in the supporting cast. This was Tashman's final film, as she died of cancer on March 21, 1934, causing delays in the production.[80]

The film was helmed by *Midnight* director Chester Erskine, based on a scenario by Jack Kirkland of *Tobacco Road* fame and a screenplay by Moss Hart. According to the *Pittsburgh Press*, production was only to take three and a half weeks due to a new, innovative use of a "'floor plan' on Bristol board, on which are indicated the position of lights, camera, microphone and players." The cameras started rolling February 13, 1934, at Biograph Studios on E. 175th St. in the Bronx, "cradle of the American motion picture," which had recently reopened "completely rejuvenated and modernized for sound," "after sound pictures sterilized New York progenitors for four years." The release of *Frankie and Johnnie* was delayed two years, "because of severe censorship problems." The musicologist Sigmund Spaeth, who played an orchestra leader, referred to film as a "ill-fated" when he recollected it many years later.[81]

The *New York Times* devoted only one paragraph to *Frankie and Johnnie*, describing it as "slightly more lachrymose and off-key than a whiskey tenor": "Two years have passed since the picture was filmed in the Bronx and those two years have seen the censors grow mighty in power and authority. What they have done to the picture is more than we can imagine. Even without their scissoring, however, it still must have been pretty bad. It does us wrong." Wanda Hale of the *New York Daily News* wrote scathingly: "The late Lilyan Tashman's portrayal of the nefarious Nellie Bly, the cause of Frankie's unhappiness and Johnnie's premature ending, is, without a doubt, the only performance deserving of commendation." She gave the film one and a half stars.[82]

In March 1934, while she was "between plays," Witherspoon was included in a two-page syndicated feature article in the *San Francisco Chronicle*, which was widely reprinted. The headline read: "How Feminine Stars of Broadway and Hollywood Dive into the 'Bankruptcy Bath' to Dodge Huge Debts of Folly and Extravagance." As the title makes clear, the article was an unflattering "exposé" of the financial irresponsibility and extravagance of certain "feminine stars." Among the actors mentioned beyond Witherspoon, we find Mary Nolan, Nita Naldi, Nell Kelly, Janet Beecher, Kay Strozzi, and Mary Carr, and also a few men.

The article observed that "one of the costliest 'fads' indulged in is—illness! Of course, a lot of this sickness is genuine. But also much of it is sheer nerves, hypochondria." Furthermore, "doctors' bills generally play an important role in bankruptcy proceedings." In this connection, the anonymous author wrote, "The case of Cora Witherspoon, noted actress, is worthy of study": "Miss Witherspoon, who has had a long and distinguished career on the stage, found herself sunk to the tune of $6,678. There were no assets, except a measly $150. Cora listed among her creditors 17 doctors!" Clearly, at some time previous to this, Witherspoon had found herself forced to file for bankruptcy. The double spread included a portrait of the actress in a soulful pose.[83]

Witherspoon's long string of personal successes in unsuccessful plays continued with *Jigsaw* by best-selling novelist Dawn Powell. It opened at the Ethel Barrymore Theatre in New York on April 30, after a week's trial at the National Theatre in Washington, D.C. *Jigsaw* had the added prestige of being a Theatre Guild production: the last and the least successful show of the Guild's highly successful 1933–34 season. According to Burns Mantle, "It was so unexpectedly good a season for the Guild that even its directors were surprised."[84]

Jigsaw was "a light piece … concerned with the love adventures of one of our less attractive penthouse sets." The *Brooklyn Citizen* provided this succinct summary of the play's plot: "The divorced Mrs. Brunell's convent-graduated daughter arrives for a visit just as the mother has become infatuated with a young man with whom the daughter has already fallen in love. There is the mothers' lover of 15 years' standing to complicate matters and assorted neighbors of the chatter and cheat set. The unsophisticated but determined daughter won't take 'no' for an answer and the young man finds himself being dragged to the altar while mother goes back to her lover."[85]

Spring Byington starred as the cougar Claire Brunell, with Ernest Truex as her married, live-in lover. Gertrude Flynn played her daughter and Eliot Cabot the "young man" of mutual interest to mother and daughter. Witherspoon played Mrs. Letty Walters, "a hardened young sinner, who dotes on cocktails, on visiting her husband and children twice a year, and on soaking herself hourly in other people's apartments waiting for the unexpected, or expected, to happen." According to Arthur Pollock, "Spring Byington and Cora Witherspoon play a pair of cynical, loose ladies swapping witticisms as the play begins. Miss Byington, who can delight the world when not being asked to be too artificial, is asked to be too artificial. Miss Witherspoon is also, and loves it."[86]

Washington Evening Star stage and screen critic E. de S. Melcher waxed eloquently about our subject's contribution to this "bubble blown from a cocktail glass": "Cora Witherspoon—well, it's too bad she isn't on the stage every minute, but that's probably because Miss Witherspoon has always been one of our weaknesses. The first act is hers, however—body and soul—with the emphasis scarcely on the latter." According to the *Springfield Republican*, "As the friend of the ménage, Cora Witherspoon (who was seen in Springfield in the Gish-company) is exceptionally good and sometimes seems on the point of running away with the show."[87]

Jigsaw closed in New York on Saturday, June 9. Starting June 14, the Broadway cast spent a week at the Ridgeway Theatre in White Plains, New York, referred to in one news item as "Truex's Summer theatre" and the home of the Ernest Truex Players. At the close of the season, E. de S. Melcher included a list of the "Season's Best" in his column for May 6. Among the many things he liked that season, we find: "Cora Witherspoon in anything (particularly 'Jig Saw')."[88]

A new comedy called *Her Master's Voice* by Clare Kummer about a wealthy maiden aunt who rules her family with an iron hand in a silk glove had ended its successful run at the Plymouth Theatre on April 28, 1934, after 224 performances. Laura Hope Crews had one of the biggest successes of her career in the role of Aunt Min, who stands in the way of the marital happiness of her niece Queena Farrar and the latter's husband Ned, while her sister and Queena's mother Mrs. Martin wrings her hands. Witherspoon spent two weeks in July 1934 playing Aunt Min in summer stock productions at the Ridgeway Theatre in White Plains, New York, and the Newport Casino in Newport, Rhode Island. According to the *Newport Mercury*, "Miss Witherspoon's performance as Aunt Min … left nothing to be desired": "She carried the part of the rich aunt perfectly, with her imperious manner, her taking everything for granted so far as poor relations were concerned, and her mistaking of the husband as the hired man to whom she later gave work. Miss Witherspoon fairly won the heavy applause given her."[89] In White Plains, she had as her male co-star Bert Lytell and in Newport Harold Vermilyea.

In late August 1934, Witherspoon returned to Eastern Services Studios to contribute to a film called *Gambling*, directed by Rowland V. Lee, which would be her last to be produced on the East coast in the 1930s. It was based on a 1929 hit play written by and starring the legendary entertainer and composer George M. Cohan, who would also star in the film as a casino owner determined to find the real killer of his adopted daughter. Cohan had composed a new song, "My Little Girl," especially for the screen version. He had not been happy in Hollywood and returned to New York after making only one film there, *The Phantom President*, in 1932.[90] Now he was trying his luck closer to home. Witherspoon knew Cohan best, of course, as the producer of several of her Broadway shows with his partner Sam H. Harris in the 1910s.

In *Gambling*, Witherspoon played a character called Mrs. Edna Seeley. There was no such person in the stage version, nor is Mrs. Seeley mentioned in the AFI synopsis or the reviews of this hard-to-find film. Even fans of Cohan had to make an effort to like *Gambling*, damning it with faint praise like "the film is not bad, in fact it is quite entertaining." The same critic thought that Cohan was "not at his best." "Narrated in an inexpert succession of medium and close-up 'shots,'" the *New York Times* observed, "it qualifies as a photographed stage play rather than a brilliant example of camera technique." The *Brooklyn Daily Eagle* concurred: "it suffers from a certain visual monotony which neither the development of the plot nor Mr. Cohan's own excellent performance manages to overcome." According to the *Chicago Tribune, Gambling* was "a one man show with the great George dominant."[91] It proved the final film of Cohan's truncated screen career. The great man passed away in 1942, ten days before Witherspoon's *Midnight* co-star Sidney Fox died from an overdose of sleeping pills.

On August 26, about the time she started work on *Gambling*, the *New York Herald Tribune* announced that Witherspoon was to be "one of the principals" in a new musical comedy called *Say When* with music by Ray Henderson, book by Jack McGowan, and lyrics by Red Koehler. The paper reminded its readers that this would be "the actress's first performance in a song and dance entertainment." The *Brooklyn Times Union* noted that Witherspoon was to have "a part particularly suited to her histrionic talents." Then, in mid–October, it was announced that she was to support Tallulah Bankhead in *Dark Victory*. As we know, Witherspoon would later do the film, but was not in the stage production, which opened on Broadway the day before *Say When*.[92]

Linda Watkins and Dennie Moore were also making their debuts in musical comedy in *Say When*, coming like Witherspoon from "the legitimate."[93] Harry Richman, Bob Hope, Betty Dell, Charles Taylor, and Michael Romanoff (playing himself) also had named roles in the large cast, which was described as "the most important for a musical show in several years." Rehearsals began September 24, just as production on *Gambling* was ending, and the show opened at the Imperial Theatre in New York on November 8, after two weeks at the Shubert Theatre in Boston.[94]

Burns Mantle summarized the plot: "Bob Breese [Richman] and Jimmy Blake [Hope], crossing on a transatlantic liner with their jazz orchestra, meet Jane and Betty Palmer [Watkins and Dell], daughters of Banker Palmer [Taylor]. The boys follow the girls to the Palmer estate on Long Island and are eventually able to overcome the objections of Papa Palmer by discovering his affair with Aimee Bates [Moore]. When he gives them an assignment to broadcast a thrift program from the vaults of the Palmer Trust Company everything is practically as good as settled." Witherspoon played Myra Palmer, wife of Banker Palmer and mother of Jane and Betty. She did not have any songs of her own but was described as being "among the charming ladies who gratified with their presence, their comedy, their singing and their dancing."[95]

Say When received solid, if not rave reviews. In Boston, it was greeted as "a mighty good show in the making": "Scenically and sartorially it is stunningly outstanding, even in this era of splendid stage spectacles." Witherspoon was said to make "a good deal" of her role. According to Arthur Pollack, "No better musical comedy has been seen around in a long time." Burns Mantle gave the show three stars, the highest rating.[96]

Brooks Atkinson deigned to consider it, writing: "Although 'Say When' displays no more taste than you need to select a glass of water, it seems to this observer to be a lively show, made to order for the itinerant trade of the Great White Way." In addition to Dennie Moore, he found "Linda Watkins and Cora Witherspoon are also entertaining in the song arcades." Rowland Field noted that Witherspoon "plays Mrs. Palmer, the harassed Long Island hostess, with skill." Witherspoon's finest accolade came from Bushnell Dimond, who wrote that she and her stage husband Charles Taylor "give an agreeable account of themselves and are teamed in a number of highly amusing scenes.... Miss Witherspoon, turning from the mauve gravities of 'Camille' and 'Jezebel,' shows anew that there is no more diverting comedienne in her not too heavily populated field."[97]

During the run of the show, Witherspoon was spotted by drama critic and columnist Rowland Field "gazing admiringly at puppies in the window of an East 47th Street dog-shop." She was then in her fourth year of living with her dog Lucky. Though *Say When* was "starting to threaten the supremacy of 'Life Begins at 8:40,'" was "drawing capacity audiences" and was described as "definitely a success" and "one of the brightest spots of the current season," it closed on January 12, 1935, after 76 performances.[98]

Starting in February, the musical comedy was bound on a post–Broadway tour to Philadelphia, Cleveland, Detroit, and Chicago, but Witherspoon opted not to go along. When the show closed in New York, she had been in rehearsal with a new play for five days. *It's You I Want* was a British farce by Maurice Braddell, adapted by George Bradshaw, and staged by Forrest C. Haring and Joshua Logan. The plot as summarized by *The Best Plays of 1934–35* was as follows: "Sheridan Delaney [Earle Larimore] is tired of the women who tire him and about to leave for Scotland for the fishing and a rest. Sheridan rents his London apartment to Otto Gilbert [Taylor Holmes] whose wife, Constance [Witherspoon], is one of the reasons Sheridan is leaving town. Mr. Gilbert installs Melisande Montgomery [Leona Maricle], his mistress, in the apartment. Then Sheridan, intrigued by the pursuit of Anne Vernon [Helen Chandler], does not go to Scotland and everybody tries to hide from everybody else in his apartment. He accepts Anne in the end."[99] One assumes it was a capacious apartment.

It's You I Want was yet another flop and lasted only 15 performances at the Cort Theatre, starting Tuesday, February 5, 1935. The subheading of the review in the *Brooklyn Citizen* read: "First-Rate Players, Wasted in a Fourth-Rate Play." The main text followed up with telling terms like "rancid delicatessen," "little-ado-about-nothing," and "very badly motivated even for farce." Burns Mantle of the *New York Daily News* echoed the low opinion of his colleague at the *Brooklyn Citizen* but added that "because the producers … had the good sense to cast it with exceptional players it does produce a scene or two that prove lightly amusing." One of these players was Witherspoon, "who has the bounce of a perfectly trained quarter-miler and is ever eager to run." A picture of the actress in a black, short-sleeved dress with a white clown collar accompanied the review.[100]

The headline of Arthur Pollock's review for the *Brooklyn Daily Eagle* was "If This Were 1913 'It's You I Want' Would Be the Most Skillful Farce of the Season." Pollock thought the play "unmistakably a valuable contribution to the theater art of this season," but was doubtful whether "people want that sort of thing at this minute"; "that sort of thing" being "the French farce of a good many years ago." They "have become accustomed to realism in the theater," he continued, "and like their fun best when it is to some degree believable." He found Witherspoon and her stage husband Taylor Holmes "adept in farce's artificialities": "You laugh at them without ever looking upon them as real." Brooks Atkinson differed with Pollock and felt that, unlike veteran farceur Holmes, Helen Chandler, Cora Witherspoon and Leora Maricle "are not withered enough for this sort of mummery yet." Rowland Field of the *Brooklyn Times Union* was adamant that "times have changed in the theater and a feverish comedy of this old-fashioned type is great fun no longer."[101]

Witherspoon knew a sinking ship when she saw one. She promptly accepted a role in a new show that opened at the Shubert Theatre in Boston only three days after *It's You I Want* came to its peremptory end in New York. Unfortunately, she leaped from one leaky craft to another. *De Luxe*, by fashionable novelist Louis Bromfield and his collaborator John Gearon, was a drama rather than a farce and was set in Paris rather than London, but it dealt with the same "smart," "fast" cosmopolitan set; their various romantic relationships were similarly complicated, and the suggestions of dissolution and decadence equally evident.

Fanny Altenus, the middle-aged, amorous lady Witherspoon depicted here, was not far different from Constance Gilbert in *It's You I Want*, only Fanny was forced to pay for her pleasures herself, including her younger lover Pat Dantry, played by the supremely suave Melvyn Douglas. In the words of one reviewer, she was "the woman who lavishes her wealth on an unappreciative male."[102] The large, talented cast also included Ann Andrews, Florence Edney, Violet Heming, Blanche Ring, Beverly Sitgreaves, and gossip columnist and professional hostess Elsa Maxwell, making her Broadway stage debut basically playing herself.

Unfortunately, *De Luxe* turned out to be as big a flop as *It's You I Want* and lasted not a performance longer at the Booth Theater in New York, where it opened on March 5, after its two-week out-of-town tryout in Boston. The play inspired some of the most devastatingly negative reviews of Witherspoon's career, though fortunately she and her fellow unfortunates on the stage were never blamed for the play's many faults.

A sprinkling of choice quotations will give you an idea of how the production was received in Boston and New York during its brief existence there: "Having created their libertines and gilded trollops, the authors devote the whole evening to listening with rapt attention to their sleazy patter and watching them floating in their cups" (Brooks Atkinson); "a rather pointless saga of the slimy side of cosmopolitan society … divided up into a series of detached incidents in the lives of complete rotters of both sexes" (Rowland Field); "Neither Mr. Bromfield nor his collaborator know how to write plays, being still of the opinion that drama is something in which people talk a long evening away and find at the end that they have said nothing" (Arthur Pollock).[103]

Atkinson quipped in the *New York Times*: "it is the authors' contention that the iniquitous demi-monde of dissolute Paris is staggering under the weight of its last bottle of champagne…. To some of us who were crumpling under the authors' barrage of shop-worn phrases and stock ideas the end of the demi-monde seemed a good deal closer than the end of the play." Field went so far as to claim that this was "the most unpleasant cast of characters ever set upon a single stage."[104]

Nearly every reviewer noted that the players was infinitely superior to the vehicle and, indeed, were being wasted. "Good actors … every one of them and nicely fitted into his or her groove," wrote Burns Mantle, including "the stalwart Douglas as a tired gigolo; the fluttery Witherspoon as the cause of his weariness." Jo Mielziner's sets were universally praised. The *Brooklyn Times Union* deemed it "a production of unusual beauty in the matter of scenery." The final verdict on the *De Luxe* opening was given by syndicated drama critic Paul Harrison: "It turned out an audience in more ermine and plop-hats than you could muster for an O'Neill first night. And it flopped, with a dull, sickening round of coldly polite applause into the category of dull drama."[105]

Putting a brave face on things, Elsa Maxwell threw a party for her fellow cast members at one of her favorite haunts, the Casino de Paree. In a news photo from the party, Witherspoon in a mink stole is pictured grinning widely at one table between her stage lover Melvyn Douglas and Claudia Morgan.[106] The play closed only days later, and Witherspoon was again out of a job.

After a fallow period in the spring and early summer of 1935, Witherspoon got an engagement to spend a few summer weeks at the Cape Playhouse in Dennis, Massachusetts. This was her first sojourn with the fabled stock company on Cape Cod, which had first opened its doors on July 4, 1927, and which is in operation to this very day. It calls itself "America's Most Famous Summer Theater" with some justification.[107]

The Playhouse was trying out "a new comedy of theatrical life" that summer by Leonora Kaghan and Anita Philips entitled *All Bow Down*, which was headed for Broadway. The title was later changed to *A Touch of Brimstone*. It starred Roland Young as the egocentric, philandering, and thoroughly unsympathetic theater producer Mark Faber, with Mary Philips, who was at the time married to Humphrey Bogart, as his long-suffering wife Janet. Witherspoon had been cast and rehearsals were under way in New York by July 24 and the play opened in Dennis on August 5 for one week.[108]

Witherspoon stayed on at the Cape to take up her old role supporting Ethel Barrymore in *The Constant Wife* for the week starting August 19. It was Barrymore's first engagement at the Cape Playhouse and rehearsals began soon after her arrival on August 14. Witherspoon was invited to a summer tea on Sunday, August 18 in honor of Barrymore, Jane Cowl, and Ruth Gordon. Gordon had spent the week following *All Bow Down* starring in *Saturday's Children* and Cowl would have her turn starring in Edward Sheldon's *Romance* starting August 26. Critics found the mini-revival of *The Constant Wife* "a distinct personal triumph" for Barrymore and thought that Witherspoon "played her role with an amusing touch." On the back of this success, Barrymore decided to go on a "farewell tour" with *The Constant Wife* across America. Witherspoon agreed to accompany her in the role she had created on Broadway nearly nine years earlier. Ultimately, though, she decided to join the New York cast of *A Touch of Brimstone*. Rehearsals began September 2 under the direction of Frank Craven, who had returned to New York after three and a half years in Hollywood.[109]

After a week-long tryout at the Boulevard Theatre in Jackson Heights, *A Touch of Brimstone* had the distinction of being the first play on Broadway to open on a Sunday. This historic event took place at the John Golden (now the Bernard B. Jacobs) Theatre on September 22, 1935. This was an expensive proposition, as Equity required cast and crew to be paid double on Sundays. Brooks Atkinson feared it might turn out to be "the most distinctive thing" about the play.[110]

The reviews for *A Touch of Brimstone* were more benign than Witherspoon's two previous outings on Broadway that year, but they were decidedly mixed. Atkinson wrote that "a malicious egotist makes poisonous company unless the author of a play about him endows him with significance." Arthur Pollock quipped: "All of the characters ... are rather on the exhausting side. They [the authors] can think of a great many things for their people to say, but most of the things they think of for them to do are unbelievable."[111]

Burns Mantle, on the other hand, thought the play "a fine drama ... for its exceptionally clever and skillful treatment of its subject." He suggested that Young was miscast in the leading role, but was impressed by the acting skills of the entire company: "I discovered no single false note in any of them," he wrote, including Witherspoon "reveling in the type of catty foil which is her happiest metier." Her character, named Isabel Cobb, and Isabel's husband Wally (Richard Sterling), are part of the crowd of hangers-on and sycophants producer Mark Faber surrounds himself with to his wife's disgust. True to form, Witherspoon's shoulders were covered only by the thinnest of spaghetti straps in the black evening gown she wore in one scene.[112]

A Boston critic at the Dennis opening, which was attended by a capacity audience of 700, thought Young "miscast to a degree that must surprise even him." On the other hand, she felt that Witherspoon "plays a poisonous, gossiping woman to perfection." Somewhat surprisingly, given its unsavory content, Rowland Field thought the play "a pleasant, if unimportant, entertainment." He wrote that Witherspoon "has some fine moments as the catty Mrs. Cobb, wife of Mark's backer." At the end of the season, Mantle summed up the play as "a comedy that was intelligently done and filled with interesting character studies of essentially unattractive people."[113]

On October 1, Witherspoon and fellow *Touch of Brimstone* cast member Robert Burton appeared in the first of a series of photo comic strips in the *New York Daily News*. The strips satirized the "battle between the sexes" and lasted into the new year. *A Touch of Brimstone* did not. It closed at the John Golden Theatre on December 16, after 98 performances. The post–Broadway tour, which was to have begun at the Forrest Theatre in Philadelphia on Christmas Day and lasted until May, was cancelled.[114]

5

"The Most 'Borrowed' Hollywood Actress"
1936–1939

She of the bubbling society manner.[1]

When you appear in 15 Broadway productions in six years, chances are most of them did not have a long run. If Witherspoon took stock at the beginning of 1936, she would have noted that there were no genuine hits among these 15 shows and several out and out flops. The longest runs were achieved by *Philip Goes Forth* (97 performances), *A Touch of Brimstone* (98 performances), and by *Forsaking All Others*, which Tallulah Bankhead had kept going despite heavy losses for 110 performances. As far as quality was concerned, Witherspoon had not been in a good, solid, well-made play since *Waterloo Bridge* and *Philip Goes Forth* in 1930 and 1931. She had made her first trip to Hollywood in 1931, because "she became discouraged by the number of plays in which she appeared which were unsuccessful."[2] Witherspoon's continuously discouraging experience on the New York stage in the first half of the 1930s would have predisposed her to consider other options. Little did she know that the next few years would be her glory days in films.

First, though, she had one more New York show to go before she headed west. Ironically, *Russet Mantle* was one of the better plays she did on Broadway, and the part of "the lady from Louisville" would have been a sterling opportunity for any character actress. According to her own account, during the summer of 1935 she had been offered and accepted the role of Effie Rowley in *Russet Mantle*, but the production had to be postponed. When it was finally ready for Broadway, she was busy in *A Touch of Brimstone*. "Her play closed and she attended performances of *Russet Mantle* frequently, envious of the actress who had the role." Then the actress in question, who was called Margaret Douglass, had to leave "for private reasons." Witherspoon was offered the role again, which she gratefully accepted. The play was in its eleventh week when she took over on Tuesday, March 31, 1936.[3]

A veteran on Broadway, Margaret Douglass would go on to create the role of the Countess de Lage in *The Women* later that year. Had Witherspoon not been in Hollywood, she might have been in the running for the plum part of the countess, which was created in the well-known 1939 film version by Mary Boland. Speaking of Boland: In early 1936, Witherspoon had also been in the running to replace her, in the Cole Porter-Moss Hart musical comedy *Jubilee*. Boland was leaving the show February 16 to return to movie making at Paramount. The role of the Queen ultimately went to Laura Hope Crews, but *Jubilee* only lasted three more weeks.[4]

Lynn Riggs (1899–1954), author of *Russet Mantle*, was dubbed "the Oklahoma poet who writes folk plays" by Brooks Atkinson.[5] Riggs was best known for *Green Grow the Lilacs* from 1931, which years later formed the basis for the hit musical *Oklahoma!* Riggs had an interesting background. He was 1/16 Cherokee and he was gay. He worked intermittently as a screenwriter in Hollywood in the 1930s and '40s, writing scripts for films like *Stingaree* and *The Garden of Allah*. Among his other feats was being friends with Bette Davis and Joan Crawford at the same time.

Riggs, who lived intermittently in Santa Fe in the 1920s and '30s, had set his latest play on a ranch in New Mexico. Incidentally, this was a state Witherspoon knew better than most of her kind, since her sister Maude had lived there for 15 years. Burns Mantle summarized the plot of *Russet Mantle* as follows: "John Galt [John Beal], a young poet tramping the West, applies at the New Mexico farm of Horace Kincaid [Jay Fasset] for work. Kincaid takes him on provisionally. Kay Rowley [Martha Sleeper], visiting niece of the Kincaids and something of a social rebel, is attracted to Galt and he to her. Their youthful disgust with the failures of the older generation lead them into an expression of their own freedom which results in the usual biological consequences. John is ready to face the world an unmarried father. Kay hesitates about giving up her luxuries as the daughter of a Louisville banker, but goes finally with John."[6]

Witherspoon played the rebellious, troubled heroine's mother, Effie (Mrs. Waldo Rowley). The author's stage directions on her first entrance capture the character vividly: "A radiant picture of the most languid and svelte beauty, MRS. WALDO ROWLEY, SUSANNA'S sister, comes out the front door. She has on an organdie dress, a picture hat. Her name is EFFIE. The scene lifts at her mindless cheerfulness." Effie herself says that compared with her "rough-neck" sister, "Always potterin' around," she is "more the willowy type."[7]

Witherspoon said she had based her characterization on "women of the languid, insouciant type, cheerfully devoid of any maternal responsibility," that she had known growing up in New Orleans. "'It doesn't matter which part of the south you come from,'" she explained in an interview, "'Fashionable mothers down there are all the same.'"[8] Incidentally, Witherspoon's maternal grandmother, Caroline Headington Bell, who died long before she was born, grew up in Louisville. The excellent cast also included Evelyn Varden as Horace's wife and Effie's sister, Susanna Kincaid; Clare Woodbury as an earthy local farmer's wife, Mrs. Fawcett; and Helen Craig, John Beal's wife, making her Broadway debut as the Hispanic maid Manuelita.

In a rare moment of unbridled enthusiasm, Brooks Atkinson of the *New York Times* wrote the most positive review of any play Witherspoon had done in the 1930s, only she was not yet in the show. *Russet Mantle* was "gorgeously acted last evening at the Masque, where it ought to hang its hat for a long time if New Yorkers relish original work," Atkinson wrote. He thought it the best thing Riggs had done. Associated Press Staff Correspondent Willard Keefe referred to "'the willowy Mrs. Rowley of Louisville'" as an inspired comedy creation in his "Baedeker of short stops" for the Pulitzer Prize committee's consideration. This was just before Witherspoon took over the role. Rowland Field went out of his way to catch Witherspoon's interpretation of the part and reported in his column in the *Brooklyn Times Union*: "'Russet Mantle' is 100 performances old at the Masque and Cora Witherspoon is giving a highly amusing portrayal as Effie from

Louisville." In his retrospect of the season, Burns Mantle thought the play "wavered a little unsteadily between an exhibit of character comedy and the dramatist's natural liking for social drama." "It met with fair success," he added. *Russet Mantle* finished on April 25 after 117 performances, of which Witherspoon had done 31.[9] It was a satisfactory ending to the main phase of her Broadway career.

Fatefully, on April 28, 1936, Charles Brackett noted in diary in that he had seen Bob Leonard, the director of the picture he was currently writing the screenplay for, and "suggested Cora Witherspoon for a role in the picture." This suggestion alone qualifies Brackett for inclusion in the pantheon of Witherspoon's staunchest allies and supporters, as it would have huge and positive consequences for her acting career. On June 2, the *Los Angeles Times* announced that Cora Witherspoon, "the New York actress," had been signed to play Madge Evans's aunt in the Metro-Goldwyn-Mayer film *Piccadilly Jim*: "She is known for character work, and impersonated Miss Evans's mother in the stage play 'Philip Goes Forth.' She was recently in 'A Touch of Brimstone' with Roland Young." According to the *Brooklyn Times Union*, MGM had signed her at the same time as playwrights John Van Druten and Richard Boleslawski. On June 8, which was Brackett's final day working on the film at MGM, he had lunch with Van Druten and Witherspoon in the studio commissary: "Cora in a haze of excitement at being here, and of gratitude toward me. (Always an agreeable emotion to invoke.)"[10]

Production on the film began the following day, under the direction of Robert Z. Leonard, who was celebrating "his 30th anniversary in the film capital."[11] Witherspoon could not have known how long she would stay this time, nor that she would be a film actress off and on for the remainder of her career.

With her casting as Nesta Pett, the major antagonist of the young lovers in *Piccadilly Jim*, and an obstacle as well to the happiness of her sister Eugenia, Witherspoon was returning to Hollywood in the best possible way: to play an important featured role in a major motion picture at the most prestigious studio in Hollywood. It was as if the half-dozen films she had already done did not exist, and she was getting a fresh start swimming in the waters in which she had previously only dipped her toe. Few character actors were vouchsafed this type of "relaunch." It was only possible, I think, because Witherspoon's roles so far had been so small, innocuous, or unrecognizable, that few people would have realized it was her or remembered her in those films.

Nesta Pett, then, is a classic "heavy" role and her function in the film is to oppose the love matches of both her sister Eugenia Willis (Billie Burke) and her niece Ann Chester (Madge Evans). As it happens, their significant others are father and son. Her objection to the father, James Crocker, Sr. (Frank Morgan), is "on the grounds of my profession," according to Mr. Crocker. He is an out-of-work actor and, according to Nesta, a "shopworn Lothario." Her objection to the son, James "Piccadilly Jim" Crocker, Jr. (Robert Montgomery), is on similarly snobbish grounds: that he is a cartoonist and not a true artist (i.e., "Your son is nothing but a newspaper hack"). Witherspoon gets to deliver deathless lines like "I cannot afford at such a time to have my sister marry into a family of mountebanks," "Don't you speak to me, you fortune hunter!" and "Never try to think, Eugenia."

A major twist in the plot involves Piccadilly Jim being inspired by Nesta, her milksop husband Herbert Pett (Grant Mitchell), and spoilt son Ogden (Tommy Bupp) to create a comic strip called "From Rags to Riches" (the Pett fortune was built on rags) about a newly rich American family, the Richwitches. After Jim makes the cartoon

Classic comedienne Billie Burke (left) was not often upstaged by a fellow character actress, but in her debut film *Piccadilly Jim* (MGM, 1936) Witherspoon dominated every scene she was in, as this still shows. Actually, *Piccadilly Jim* was not Witherspoon's film debut by any means—she already had half a dozen films under her belt, but most of them were produced on the East coast. Her participation in any of them seems to have been forgotten by the time she was brought to Hollywood to lend her talents to the screen version of P.G. Wodehouse's classic comic novel about Americans in Great Britain and vice versa. Burke and Witherspoon played sisters, while Frank Morgan (right) was Burke's love interest in the film. With this film, Witherspoon embarked on the major phase of her film career, which lasted until her arrest for narcotics offenses during work on *The Bank Dick* in 1940 (Photofest/MGM).

characters more sympathetic to please Ann, Nesta finds that she rather enjoys the attention and celebrity associated with being the model for Mrs. Richwitch ("I do believe I have become the best known woman in the United States").

The film version is somewhat different from P.G. Wodehouse's novel from 1917. In the novel, Piccadilly Jim's father has already married the rich widow Eugenia, who is determined to conquer London. She is her sister Nesta's equal and rival in society, where they are in competition for social prominence. In this film adaptation, classic dizzy dame Billie Burke for once found herself completely overshadowed in her only film with Witherspoon.

For some inexplicable reason, given that they had all the resources of the MGM hair and make-up department at their disposal, Burke and Evans are having one long bad hair day, and look unusually frumpy. Witherspoon, on the other hand, is resplendent in a series of fancy outfits, ranging from a negligee to a bare-shouldered evening gown with extravagant jewels. In her opening scene, Witherspoon appears to be wearing seersucker, but then, it is summer, while Burke looks ridiculous in an explosion of tulle. It is a rare film where Witherspoon does not manage at least one appearance in a nightie or décolleté evening dress, and this is no exception. Most of her outfits are black and white, her favorite combination, including an original polka-dotted ensemble. She is equipped with a lorgnette in her first scene, which we do not see again.

Production ended July 16 and the press reported that Witherspoon had "survived her first picture without 'blowing up in her lines,' walking in front of the camera or being late." As we know, it was far from being her first picture. Though she played her role without any mishap before the cameras, Witherspoon had to contend with "a spider bite that caused her left foot to swell twice its natural size." According to one report, her foot had to be packed in ice "every minute she isn't before the camera."[12]

For her efforts in her ostensible film debut, Witherspoon was heaped with laurels. The *Detroit Free Press* wrote: "Cora Witherspoon, stage actress relatively unknown to screen audiences, is impressively humorous as Nesta, the wife who wears the trousers in the Pett household." According to her hometown rag, the *Times-Picayune*, Witherspoon "does an exceedingly funny characterization of a domineering matron." The *New York Times* thought "there are pleasant contributing performances by Cora Witherspoon, Grant Mitchell and Tommy Bupp as the obnoxious Petts." Veteran critic Rowland Field, who had reviewed so many of Witherspoon's stage performances, thought she was "excellent as Mrs. Pett." The *Honolulu Advertiser* observed: "You may not think so much of Miss Witherspoon at first, but she proves a riot at the last." The *Schenectady Daily Gazette* wrote: "we can't close our review without a word of praise for the insufferable Nesta Pett. Cora Witherspoon scored a real hit in her portrayal of this part, and we shall look for future pictures that include her name." Her new hometown newspaper, the *Los Angeles Times*, wrote: "there is a sharp-faced newcomer, who manages to be as irritating as Nesta Pett would be in real life—something of an achievement."[13]

According to other critics, Witherspoon "provides the film with some lively bits of shrewish comedy," "does well as a social climber who opposes Montgomery and his father, Frank Morgan," "contributes effective comedy," and "does an exceptionally good job as the prospective aunt-in-law." She was described as "worth seeing alone," "the villain of the piece" and "the devastating Aunt Nesta," "a wealthy woman with no sense" and "tyrannical rages," "one of those managing females who manage to mismanage the affairs of an entire family," "the new-rich Mrs. Pett, crude, domineering; a termagant, greatly impressed by a title," "an imperious menace," "excellent" as the "tartar of the wealthy American family," and "awfully amusing."[14]

Finally, the *Decatur Daily Review* wrote in connection with the second run of the film in December 1936: "Special note is to be taken of the work in this film of Cora Witherspoon, the aunt who is the center of the cartoon. She's a screen newcomer and did such a good job that she's much in demand now for character work." Then there was this interesting news item in a New Orleans paper: "Trust Warren V. Miller to spot a New Orleans face. Although he saw only a preview of Piccadilly Jim, ... he at once recognized Clara Witherspoon."[15] Miller may have been particularly well positioned to recognize Witherspoon, since his mother had been living with her sister for the last 30 years or so.

Piccadilly Jim was better received than the studio expected. A modern source suggests that MGM "had little faith in the picture and refused to promote it." The *New York Times* found the film "an engaging bit of nonsense": "it provides an uncommonly diverting hour or so of picture-watching." The *Brooklyn Times Union* thought it was "one of the outstanding film comedies of the year." Many reviews stressed the excellence of the ensemble cast, which was described as "one of the best casts of the season," "the season's pleasantest cast," and "nearly flawless." "Every role is played by an expert," wrote the *Salt Lake Tribune*. According to the *Deseret News*, the cast "comes as close to 100 per cent perfection—that is, each character being 100 per cent suited to his role—as anything that has been seen here in many months."[16]

After all this, Witherspoon's next film must have seemed like an anticlimax. *Libeled Lady* began shooting just as *Piccadilly Jim* ended. According to an Associate Press bulletin, "With two days between pictures," Witherspoon, "flew east and spent exactly five hours in New York—long enough to turn down a stage offer." The play was probably *Tovarich*, being produced by Gilbert Miller, as Rowland Field wrote that Witherspoon was "mentioned for the cast." It opened October 15 and was a big hit. This time, though, Witherspoon did not opt for a swift return to Broadway. An AP bulletin dated August 18, 1936, read: "Cora Witherspoon, New York stage actress, signed a long-term contract with Metro-Goldwyn-Mayer today. She played in 'Piccadilly Jim' as her first film." It is strange then, that Brackett noted in his diary nine days previously that "Cora Witherspoon and her companion came to luncheon": "Cora charming and entertaining until she got to her food, where upon she burst into tears and confessed that her option had not been picked up by MGM, despite all sorts of praise and promises from everyone."[17] No matter what the nature of her contract, it was frequently renegotiated, but she kept on working for MGM for several years. I wonder, too, who the unnamed "companion" was.

Libeled Lady was directed "at breakneck speed" by Jack Conway and finished production September 1. Witherspoon's gawky, gossipy, and simpering society woman character here, Mrs. Burns-Norvell, was more typical of the parts she would play on the screen than the "virago"[18] Nesta Pett, both with regard to the nature and size of the role. In this outing, Witherspoon came equipped with a grown, marriageable daughter, though one with a strangely childlike air. "Babs" was played by Bunny Beatty (aka Lauri Beatty aka Hinemoa Gerome Lauri), who happened to be the daughter of the raucous, New Zealand–born character actress May Beatty. They both had bit parts in *The Women*, where Witherspoon would also show up, but then what actress in Hollywood did not?

In *Libeled Lady*, nearly Witherspoon's entire performance is given on board a ship from England to New York, between 30 and 40 minutes into the film. The running joke is that Myrna Loy's Connie Allenbury and her millionaire industrialist father, played by Walter Connolly, are forever trying to avoid the boring mother-daughter pair on their transatlantic crossing. On a ship, that is not easy to do, but the undercover journalist played by William Powell, Bill Chandler, is able to help them out, only to have the Burns-Norvells start pursuing *him* instead. Towards the end of the film, mother and daughter reappear briefly at a charity ball at Connie's home and give her father the crucial information that Connie's now fiancé Bill is already married.

Witherspoon has no scenes with the other pair of stars in the film: Jean Harlow and Spencer Tracy. She would work with Harlow soon, though, in *Personal Property*. It is interesting to observe, that Witherspoon towers over all her co-stars and especially her doll-like daughter, who bears no resemblance to her. Again, Witherspoon is wearing mostly black or white, though who can tell for sure in a black and white film.

Libeled Lady was nominated for Best Picture and was one of the top 20 box-office successes of 1937. Given the modest size of the role, the critics' response this time was

Witherspoon's characteristic profile is in evidence in this still from *Libeled Lady* (MGM, 1936), one of her first films during her relatively few but productive years spent as a contract player at Metro-Goldwyn-Mayer. However modest and marginal to the main storyline of the film, Mrs. Burns-Norvell is still a classic Witherspoon role and contributed to her dominant screen image as an actress specializing in fashionable, fluttery, and fawning females from the upper classes. Myrna Loy (left) was one of four stars in the film, Walter Connolly (second from left) played her father, and Lauri Beatty (aka Bunny Beatty; second from right) played Witherspoon's daughter Babs. Beatty was the daughter of New Zealand–born character actress May Beatty (Photofest/MGM).

less emphatic. Witherspoon mostly had to content herself with brief mentions or listings at the tail-end of the reviews. Thus in the *Los Angeles Times*, she was listed among those contributing "other outstanding, if briefer, roles." The *Louisville Courier-Journal* wrote that "Walter Connolly, Charley Grapewin and Cora Witherspoon never give slouchy performances." The *Tampa Times* observed: "It's interesting to realize that viewers have begun to appreciate the art of such players as E.E. Clive, Charley Grapewin and Cora Witherspoon, the latter quite new to motion pictures." The *Grand Rapids Press* went all out and devoted two whole sentences to Witherspoon's performance: "Cora Witherspoon gives a clever performance as the boresome Mrs. Burns-Norvelle [*sic*] who, with her equally boresome daughter, is constantly on the trail of the heiress. When they learn that Connie Allenbury's fiancé is married they are the first to spread the news." Other, briefer mentions referred to her "excellent support," to the "excellent performance" she turned in as "a doting dowager," and referred to her character as "Public Bore No. 1 ... with Lauri Beatty, as her daughter, running her a close second."[19]

On September 22, 1936, RKO succeeded in borrowing Witherspoon for their upcoming film *Quality Street*, based on the play of the same title by James Barrie from 1901. It was her first loan out from MGM, but it would not be the last. Indeed, the following year Witherspoon was described as "the most 'borrowed' Hollywood actress."[20] The production began September 26 under the direction of George Stevens and lasted two months.

On the face of things, this was a good opportunity, playing the Cockney maid Patty, which would showcase her versatility. Equally on the plus side: Witherspoon was teamed with Eric Blore, playing a perpetually winking recruiting officer in this film set during the Napoleonic Wars. It was a comic pairing that had started in *Piccadilly Jim*, where Blore played Montgomery's valet Bayliss and was at daggers drawn with Nesta Pett. In *Quality Street*, Patty has her own storyline and romantic interest in Blore's unnamed sergeant. Patty is also integral to the main plot and is very much a co-conspirator with her employers, the maiden Throssel sisters, in trying to get Phoebe Throssel (Katharine Hepburn) hitched with dashing Dr. Valentine Brown (Franchot Tone).

Witherspoon looks particularly beady-eyed, plain, and scrubbed down here with a "natural" look, which borders on "too much information." I am thinking particularly of

One of the few romantic storylines of her own was vouchsafed in RKO's *Quality Street* in 1937, where Witherspoon was paired with quirky comedian Eric Blore. Blore had also been with her in *Piccadilly Jim*, where their characters cordially hated each other, but in *Quality Street* it was a different story. Blore had an almost maniacal and unsettling screen presence, which made him unlikely boyfriend material. His peppy recruiting sergeant and Witherspoon's folksy maid of all work nevertheless have quite the romance in a film far too much taken up with Katharine Hepburn's tiresome Hepburnisms.

the way her large breasts are hanging noticeably low, suggesting that she is not wearing a bra. Beyond that, her cotton cap is on the verge of wearing her, rather than the other way around. Patty is given to singing while working and has not given up the hope, even at 40, that she can still find love. Thus, she forms a contrast to the overly genteel Throssel sisters, with all their effete refinement and stultifying pride.

If you know anything about Witherspoon, you will recognize that Patty in *Quality Street* is one of her more uncharacteristic film roles. The *Miami News* observed: "Cora Witherspoon departs from her usual fluttery and loquacious self and portrays a character comedy part."[21]

Even though the role is significant, and her performance is more than adequate, including her Cockney accent, this is not really how we want to see Cora Witherspoon on the big screen. This is a testament to the power of typecasting, for better or for worse.

As we begin to see in *Libeled Lady*, Witherspoon did not just play types established by others, but actually became a type unto herself: personifying the fashionable, frivolous, flighty, and fawning society woman, often with a thinly veiled amativeness or threatening inquisitiveness. This was her forte to such an extent that any divergence from the upper-crust social background and the flibbertigibbet persona seems an irrelevance and an anticlimax. Many character actresses could play Cockney maids, but no one else could play Cora Witherspoon's particular brand of what a less politically correct age would have called "damn fool women." We can enjoy those performances even today, because she convinces us that there indeed are such women in the world, just as there are foolish men, and they are entertaining to watch on film, especially if they are being played by Cora Witherspoon.

Once again, Witherspoon's performance was well received, and she was often praised in tandem with Blore. We can read that "Eric Blore is magnificent as the flirtatious recruiting sergeant, and Cora Witherspoon is equally good as the ever hopeful Patty, who has waited for 15 years for a suitor to appear around the corner, and hasn't lost a bit of her anticipatory interest." Furthermore, Blore and Witherspoon "rate high when the script gives them a chance," "give their usual effective performances," and "provide some light-hearted fun in the parts of menials." Individually, Witherspoon "contributes importantly to the proceedings," "is good as the buxom cook," "spoons some zip into the housekeeper role," "is amusing as the romantic servant," and "brightens every one of her too brief scenes."[22]

Witherspoon was billed fifth in this film, which was high for her in an A feature from a major studio. In *Piccadilly Jim*, she had been billed eighth, despite her significant role as the chief antagonist; and in *Libeled Lady* seventh, which was impressive for such a limited role. At this point, MGM was clearly showcasing her talent by featuring her in every way and probably negotiating the same type of billing when she was loaned out. I have noted that in one advertisement for *Quality Street* her name was placed over that of Fay Bainter (as Hepburn's sister Susan Throssel) and Estelle Winwood (as an inquisitive neighbor), though after Blore. Witherspoon's picture was also included in the ad. In another advertisement, only Hepburn, Tone, Blore, and Witherspoon were mentioned by name.[23]

Quality Street turned out to be a dud and lost a quarter of a million dollars. My favorite comment on the film is the following from Eddie Cohen in the *Miami News*: "'Quality Street' is a delightful, quaint and charming picture—which slightly bored us."[24] At least we can be grateful it did not establish Witherspoon in folksy servant roles. In fact, she never played a servant on film again.

Witherspoon's role as zany Aunt Fritz in the Irving Berlin musical *On the Avenue* was arguably the best screen opportunity she ever got and is certainly among her half-dozen best roles, together with Nesta Pett in *Piccadilly Jim*, Patty in *Quality Street*, Mrs. Burns in *Personal Property*, Agatha Sousé in *The Bank Dick*, and Mrs. Williamson in *The Mating Season*. Aunt Fritz is the sister of the multi-millionaire played by George Barbier and the aunt and confidante of the heroine played by Madeleine Carroll. Her function is to sympathize with song and dance man Dick Powell's pursuit of Carroll; and finally to orchestrate her niece's "kidnapping" in the final scene, so she can marry Powell at city hall, rather than get hitched to explorer Alan Mowbray in her own home, as she is supposed to. Aunt Fritz's final line is to the cab driver: "The city hall and don't spare the horses!" This character is unique in being Witherspoon's only sympathetic role in nearly 50 films. Here she was playing a fairy godmother for once, rather than a wicked witch, and it suited her surprisingly well.

Aunt Fritz suited her so well, because the part showcased the brand of dizzy dame comedy that would be her trademark in films, though the comedy was more physical here than usual. This did not go unnoticed by observant critics. Edna B. Lawson wrote in the *Honolulu Advertiser*: "Miss Witherspoon has a special flair for this type of thing. She abandons herself to slapstick and makes a hit."[25]

This type of comic second lead in 1930s musicals is one we particularly associate with Helen Broderick, who was Witherspoon's contemporary and burst onto the screen in *Top Hat* in 1935. Unlike Witherspoon, Broderick's Broadway stage career had been entirely in musical comedy. The two actresses shared a sartorial elegance masking a degree of physical plainness, yet the difference in their comedy is striking. While Broderick always spoke sense in her roles as the heroine's best friend and confidante, Witherspoon usually made no sense at all.

On the Avenue provided Witherspoon with one of her best entrances ever on film, when she emerges at 18 minutes among the luxurious trappings of the home she shares with her brother and niece in a Russian-inspired Cossack outfit. She has enthusiastically taken up the Russian ballet as a hobby and is constantly practicing and prancing around, until she sees herself parodied in a musical revue number and gives up "all things Russian." Unlike her relatives, Aunt Fritz enjoys being parodied and is a good sport.

Again, Witherspoon's costumes are superb, even beyond the two Cossack outfits. She goes them one better, when she appears in an incredible black, spangled top and matching tights to learn the art of the trapeze from a Ringling Bros. trapeze artist. In the initial close-up, it looks as if she is wearing an elegant, low-cut evening gown and then the camera pulls back to reveal her surprisingly form-fitting attire. The costume leaves little to the imagination, but then Witherspoon was never averse to putting it all out there, even at 47 years of age. She was long-limbed and statuesque and liked her costumes to emphasize her fine shoulders and ample bosom.

Opposite: **Having been retouched to within an inch of her life, 46-year-old Witherspoon looks preternaturally youthful in this portrait from *On the Avenue*, a 1937 Fox musical starring Dick Powell and Madeleine Carroll. Witherspoon did no singing in the film, but she did just about everything else, as Aunt Fritz, Carroll's eccentric, faddist, live-in aunt, who goes from an infatuation with all things Russian to learning the tricks of the trade from a trapeze artist. Her spangled black tights in the trapeze scene have to be seen to be believed. Witherspoon no doubt welcomed the opportunity to show off her long legs.**

This was Witherspoon's second loan-out and the studio this time was Twentieth Century–Fox. The cameras started rolling on November 9, 1936, with director Roy Del Ruth calling the shots. Four days later, it became known that MGM had signed a new contract with the actress, whatever that entailed. She seems not to have had a standard seven-year contract, or these renegotiations would not have been necessary. At this point in her career, she was being referred to as a "character star."[26]

For her efforts this time, Witherspoon was billed seventh. The critics' response to her performance was overwhelmingly positive, proving that she could also win their approval in likable roles. As she was mentioned in nearly all the reviews, I will share only the choicest morsels here. Kate Cameron in the *New York Daily News*: "add[s] to the gaiety of the piece by contributing excellent bits of comedy to the continuity." Mildred Martin in the *Philadelphia Inquirer*: "numerous amusing encounters with Cora Witherspoon as Miss Carroll's aunt who finds more fun in fads than marrying again." Edith Lindeman in the *Richmond Times Dispatch*: "garners more laughs than the Ritz Brothers." Diggory Venn in the *San Francisco Chronicle*: "funnier than ever." Louise Mace in the *Springfield Republican*: "really promotes the most solid characterization." The *Boston Globe*: "the dizziest society woman yet lampooned by the talkies." The *Dayton Daily News*: "gives a grand performance and has moments that are about the funniest we have seen in many a day, or should we say film." The *New Orleans States*: "Cora Witherspoon's comedy is worth going a long way to see." The *Chattanooga News*: "a high spot of the show."[27]

The *Los Angeles Times* included her in the list of "Best Performances in Current Pictures": "Cora Witherspoon in 'On the Avenue.' Rip-roaring success with limited opportunities. Excellent comedienne." Kaspar Monahan took a step back in the *Pittsburgh Press*: "Cora Witherspoon in a farcical role reveals that Hollywood has been overlooking a good comedienne for many years. This veteran actress is a decided asset to any cast, particularly if she's in a comic role." The *St. Joseph Gazette* succinctly summed up her character: "Cora Witherspoon, as Miss Carroll's faddist aunt, who changes from a penchant for everything Russian to a taste for circus acrobatics and a porky trapezist, is in her customary fine mettle."[28]

Back at MGM in December 1936, Witherspoon finally got a taste of the workaday world of the American movie industry. Even glamorous studios like Metro made a large number of perfectly ordinary and usually quite mediocre films, whether they were outright B movies or simply starred actors of a lower wattage and lesser renown. *Dangerous Number* starred Robert Young and Ann Sothern and featured Reginald Owen and Witherspoon, which meant her highest billing yet: fourth place. So it would be for the remainder of her career: Small parts in big films or big parts in small films.

The *Baltimore Sun* described this minor comedy as "a running cat-and-dog fight between Ann Sothern and Robert Young, with time out for wisecracks by Reginald Owen": "Elinor has a blatant, addlepated mamma, raucously portrayed by Cora Witherspoon." The conflict and the comedy, such as it is, inheres in the contrast between Young's stodgy upper-class background and Sothern's arty, stage background. Naturally, true love prevails, and they ultimately manage to bridge the cultural divide, but only after multiple plot twists and turns that defy brief summary. Marla Shelton, who was on a short-term contract at MGM just like Witherspoon, was also in this, as performer Vera Montana, who takes Young on a tour of the big city's underworld night life and "recalls Theda Bara at her best."[29] She who would play Witherspoon's daughter in their next MGM outing, *Personal Property*.

During her career, Witherspoon was known as one of the best-dressed women both on the stage and the screen. Her customary elegance is apparent from this still from *Dangerous Number*, directed by Richard Thorpe at MGM and released in 1937. The film starred Robert Young and Ann Sothern (left) as an unusually combative couple from different social backgrounds, while Witherspoon played Sothern's ex-vaudevillian mother. Witherspoon was partial to wearing black or black and white. She often designed her own clothes and even had a stint as a costume designer on Broadway, when acting roles were scarce in the early 1920s (Photofest/MGM).

Witherspoon looked slim and trim in a black tailored suit and plumed black cap, as Sothern's "chirrupy" former vaudevillian mother Gypsy Breen, "who pops in at all hours."

"[F]luttery and loquacious," she and Owen were said to be "especially good in their roles" and to "contribute generously to the success of the comedy." Unfortunately, that success was not great. The critic for the *New York Times* was merciless: "Ann Sothern, … though she works overtime bailing out all the dialogue and superfluous business that swamps the picture shortly after it is launched, can do no more than go down with the vessel, her pretty marcel gallantly flying." He concluded in his postage stamp of a review with: "On the whole, the film seems beyond hope of improvement except possibly in the matter of the title, which should have been 'Wrong Number.'"[30] I guess they were asking for that one. Witherspoon, thankfully, was not mentioned here.

Granted, the *Salt Lake Tribune* took a more generous view, writing: "There are plenty of laughs, many of them going to Cora Witherspoon, who had fans in stitches in 'On the Avenue' and evidently intends to keep them that way." The *New Orleans Times-Picayune* agreed that "the fun she adds to the film is plenty." She was accused of "a choice bit of scene-stealing" by the *Indianapolis News*. Similarly, the *Philadelphia Inquirer* thought she "stole every scene she was in." A less approving view of her performance was taken by the *New York Daily News*, who gave the film two stars and wrote: "Cora Witherspoon, as a stage mother, burlesques a role that might have been funny as straight comedy." The *Jersey Journal* thought she was "in the top of her form."[31]

Dangerous Number was a brief shoot, taking up the last three weeks of the year, under the direction of Richard Thorpe. He was Witherspoon's fifth director in as many films. She seldom worked with the same director twice, and her friend George Cukor was the only one she worked with three times.

The year of 1936 drew to a close with one film released to thundering applause for Witherspoon's efforts, three films "in the can," and *On the Avenue* nearly done. These first seven months in Hollywood must have been a heady experience. Sadly, with a couple of exceptions, Witherspoon's best screen opportunities were already behind her. In the coming years, there would be few, if any, roles to compare with Nesta Pett, Aunt Fritz, and Patty. Unfortunately, this was a common experience, especially among supporting players who were brought to Hollywood specifically for a high-profile role in a major film. It was nearly always downhill from there. The "decline," if you can call it that, might be slow and you might stave it off for a time, but sooner or later the parts got smaller or fewer or both and your name crept down the credit list. With films like *Piccadilly Jim*, *On the Avenue*, and *Quality Street*, Witherspoon was launched on a stratospheric level that few could maintain. Her more modest part in *Libeled Lady*, and her part in a more modest film, *Dangerous Number*, were harbingers of things to come; indicators of the types of low-key roles, or low-key films, that would be the meat and potatoes of her film career.

Nineteen thirty-seven, her first full year in Hollywood, proved even busier than 1936 had been. She acted in seven movies that year, from *Personal Property* to *Professor Beware*, and saw eight of her films released. She was also more frequently mentioned in the press than any year before or since. Several of these media reports stressed her popularity and the unique position she had achieved in the industry in a brief period of time.

In late January 1937, she received the ultimate sign that she had "arrived," when she was the subject of an item in Walter Winchell's coveted gossip column for the second time. The item dealt with her preference for hotel living over having her own home: "Recently to celebrate her new MGM contract, she took a house in Beverly Hills.... Cora nearly broke her neck trying to get it ready for New Year's—and a party for her intimates.... It all came off on schedule, too, and was a nice affair.... Three days after the big doings, however, the star moved back to the hotel.... Too lonesome" Winchell wrote further that Witherspoon's "actressing on the New York stages and in the cinema studios is big time." Columnist Guy Fowler carried the following comment from the actress herself: "'No home for me.... I'm too accustomed to the night sounds of Broadway. These night-singing mocking birds and tree toads give me the creeps.'" She added in an interview with United Press correspondent Alexander Kahn: "'As the night wore on, my ears longed for the sounds of taxicabs squeaking to a stop, the rumble of the subway, police sirens—anything except those birds.'" "In the morning, Miss Witherspoon returned to her hotel with her maid and dog," Kahn reported. The previous year, she had told a reporter from the *Brooklyn Daily Eagle*, that "she loves the city. After 24 hours in the country, she has to rush back to the city. The country depresses her. She needs speed, action, confusion."[32]

The hotel in question was the Hollywood Roosevelt at 7000 Hollywood Boulevard, also home to character actresses like Elizabeth Patterson and Zeffie Tilbury. It was at the Roosevelt, that an incident occurred involving two Mexican bob cats her sister Maude had brought from New Mexico, thinking "the critters made nice, gentle pets." Not too surprisingly, they were too wild to have in a hotel apartment, and Witherspoon ended up gifting them to the California Zoological Society.[33] Later, when she could no longer afford the hotel apartment, she lived modestly in a regular apartment building in Hollywood.

At this time, then, Witherspoon's name was frequently in the papers. Another syndicated columnist, the "Hollywood Reporter" Grace Wilcox, admitted to having "a Cora Witherspoon complex" in her column for May 30, 1937: "Just let me see her name in a cast and I'm off, even if I have to go to a neighboring town to see a preview." There were rumors of a preview of Witherspoon's most recent film, *Escape from Love* (aka *The Lady Escapes*) the following week, 65 miles away in San Bernardino: "so this page may be blank next week." Diggory Venn was another columnist and Witherspoon fan. He thought *The Big Shot* was "worth seeing for her alone," adding: "She is one of this department's favorite comediennes."[34]

On April 2, 1937, H.H. Niemeyer published one of the most comprehensive feature articles ever written on Witherspoon in the *St. Louis Post-Dispatch* under the title "Any Role, Any Studio." The subheading read: "Cora Witherspoon's Ability Whether Cast as Slavey or Dowager, Has Made Her the Most 'Borrowed' Hollywood Actress in Less Than a Year's Time." "Coming out here practically unheralded and unsung," Niemeyer began, "for Hollywood knows little and cares less about dramatic reputations—Miss Witherspoon has jumped, in the short space of less than a year, to be in greater demand by directors than any other player in the films." He assured his readers, that "she is kept busy working before the cameras, day and night practically all of the time."

Niemeyer was quick to point out that she was "still on the sunny side of 45," which indeed she was not, "and looks a whole lot younger." He stressed her versatility, before going back to his earliest memory of her in *Daddy Long Legs* with Ruth Chatterton: "She hasn't been idle since." He then launched into the obligatory sketch of her life to date, based on a printed form Witherspoon herself had filled in in connection with signing her studio contract. Clearly, her dog Lucky played a prominent role in this form and, as I mentioned in the previous chapter, so he does in this article. The biographical information provided here is remarkably accurate. Her credits are listed extensively. Niemeyer even recalls that she had been in film called "Peacherino [sic]." Her stint as a costume designer is mentioned, before her personality is analyzed, including the observations that she is "cosmopolitan almost to the point of crispness," whatever that means, and "deliberate, unhurried, and a creature of charming poise." She is allowed to defend herself against suggestions of affectation in her nature, before revealing her biggest fear: "to be dependent on others in old age." Her "likes" are detailed, including fried chicken, fried bananas, watermelon, yellow roses, and the scent of honeysuckle. The article concludes with her views on the stage versus the screen and is illustrated with three recent photographs of its subject, including one with Lucky.[35]

A week after the New York premiere of *On the Avenue* on February 4, 1937, syndicated columnist Harold W. Cohen reported that Metro-Goldwyn-Mayer had renewed her contract for another year. As a featured player at a major studio, she was important enough to have her own stand-in on the set. In her case, it was Naomi Childers, who had been a $3,000-a-week star in 1920. There was even talk of her writing her memoirs for a New York publisher. The *New York Journal American* reported in late June, that she was traveling to New York for only the second time in two years "seeking data for her memoirs."[36] Nothing came of the book.

With her next film, *Personal Property*, Witherspoon was again back on the MGM "A list," but not for long. Filming started on her 47th birthday with W.S. "Woody" Van Dyke at the helm, who would also direct her in *Marie Antoinette* the following year. The film was based on a play by H.M. Harwood called *The Man in Possession*, which had been a moderate success for Isabel Jeans and Leslie Banks on Broadway during the 1930–31 season. *Personal Property*, a remake of MGM's original 1931 adaptation of Harwood's play, was Jean Harlow's penultimate film, the last she completed, and the last to be released while she was still alive. As her co-star, Harlow had Robert Taylor for the first and only time. The *New York Times* gives an apt summary of the film's plot: "The black sheep of the English Dabneys, Mr. Taylor insinuates himself into the financially tottering household of the interesting American widow, Miss Harlow, on the pretense of being a sheriff's officer representing her creditors and, while posing as her butler in a social emergency, contrives to prevent her marriage with his elder brother."[37]

Witherspoon's character Mrs. Burns is rather similar to Mrs. Burns-Norvell in *Libeled Lady*, which is pointed up by the similarity in their names. Witherspoon is given more play here, though. Mrs. Burns has a libidinous quality, that Mrs. Burns-Norvell did not have; she has more of an edge. The same goes for her daughter Catherine, played by Marla Shelton in what proved her best screen opportunity, as a young woman with a keen interest in the opposite sex. Like mother, like daughter. The two have a much more combative mother-daughter relationship than Witherspoon had with Bunny Beatty in *Libeled Lady*.

Witherspoon's big scene is the dinner party at Harlow's London home about 50 minutes into the film. She sweeps in with her daughter in tow and is just as taken with the new butler—Taylor as a bailiff in the disguise of domestic service—as Harlow has predicted she would be. "His profile is positively classic," she purrs. In a brilliant line reading, Witherspoon pronounces "profile" in mock French as "pro-FEEL." In *Personal Property*, Harlow was finally able to showcase her talent for doing imitations. Prior to the Burnses arrival on the scene, Harlow has done an imitation of both of them, which is spot on.[38]

Witherspoon was still getting the reviewers' attention, even in relatively small parts.

"You can't overlook" Cora Witherspoon, wrote the *New York Times* gratifyingly. "Cora Witherspoon's presence as a chattering English matron guarantees a bright moment or two," wrote the *San Francisco Chronicle*. "Cora Witherspoon and Marla Shelton also win laughs in this rough and tumble comedy," wrote the *Madison Capital Times*. Ida Hermann in the *Camden Courier-Post* went them one better: "Cora Witherspoon, in a minor supporting role, steals the limelight whenever she appears."[39] Indeed, she does. Mrs. Burns may well be the quintessential Cora Witherspoon character, as she embodies so many of the characteristics that would be Witherspoon's trademark in films.

After the top-notch production of *Personal Property*, the realities of being a Hollywood character actress set in pretty quickly. With *The Lady Escapes*, Witherspoon was back in the Bs, and there she would stay for the remainder of 1937, at her home studio

MGM and on loan-out to Twentieth Century–Fox, RKO, Warner Bros., and the Harold Lloyd Corporation. Witherspoon played three typical mother and mother-in-law roles this year, in *The Lady Escapes*, *He Couldn't Say No*, and *Beg, Borrow or Steal*. Her role in *The Big Shot* was more important by virtue of being larger, even if the film was "small"; and her role in *Madame X* was at least a new departure and allowed her to play a character from her native New Orleans, albeit a woman far removed from the elevated social circles Witherspoon had grown up in. Her final film of 1937 was her only full-length feature that year besides *Personal Property*. *Professor Beware* starred Harold Lloyd, returning to the screen after an absence of two years, and was directed by Elliott Nugent for Lloyd's own production company. Nugent would also direct one of Witherspoon's final films, *Just for You*, and she would pair with his father, J.C. Nugent, in *George Washington Slept Here* on the stage and *Follies Girl* on the screen in the early 1940s.

In *The Lady Escapes* (aka *Escape from Love*), Witherspoon was Fanny Ryan Worthington, heroine Gloria Stuart's thrice-divorced mother and mother-in-law to Michael Whalen. She is seen in the opening, when Stuart and Whalen marry by mistake during one of the rehearsals for their elaborate wedding, and Witherspoon faints from mortification. The big wedding had been her idea. Before the close, she ends up marrying

Fanny Worthington in *The Lady Escapes* (Twentieth Century–Fox, 1937) was another of Witherspoon's overdressed dowager and mother-in-law roles. Her daughter this time was Gloria Stuart (left), her son-in-law Michael Whalen (second from right), and the other man is Whalen's monocled sidekick Gerald Oliver Smith. What was different this time was that Witherspoon, thrice married already in the film, ends up married for the fourth time by the end of it. Before you get too excited: Her new hubby is Smith's 95-year-old screen uncle, played by Tom Ricketts, who was 84 at the time (Photofest/Twentieth Century–Fox).

herself, which was not a common development in Witherspoon's screen characters. Her fourth husband was played by Tom Ricketts, the aged uncle of Whalen's friend and side-kick Gerald Oliver Smith. Ricketts was an extremely prolific British character actor, who was 84 when he played Witherspoon's 95-year-old romantic interest in *The Lady Escapes*. He died in 1939.

The film was produced between March 22 and late April 1937 and was directed by Eugene Forde. The *Indianapolis News* noted that Witherspoon was being borrowed a second time by Twentieth Century–Fox; *On the Avenue* being the first. The fashion designer Herschel made for her "a charming gown of sapphire blue lace over orchid crepe.... The dress is made princess style, fastening high at the neck in back and leaving an open triangular decolletage." It turns out the dress received more press coverage than the performance. The *Detroit Free Press* thought Witherspoon was "all but wasted in her role."[40] Her only consolation was that she was billed fourth.

In early May 1937, Witherspoon was loaned out to RKO again, as was Guy Kibbee.[41] *The Big Shot*, directed by Edward Killy, was the kind of B movie in which character actors might star and that is what Kibbee and Witherspoon did. The real star of the picture, though, was Kibbee, who had been longer in Hollywood, had done more films, and had already starred in some of them, like *Big Hearted Herbert* and *Babbitt*. His name was above the title in the onscreen credits. In the ads, Kibbee's name was sometimes above the title with Witherspoon's below, sometimes both were above the title, and sometimes both were below. At any rate, *The Big Shot* was the only film in which Witherspoon received top billing.

The starting point of the film is that Kibbee is a small-town veterinarian from Wabesha, Bertram Simms, popularly known as "Doc" or "Simmy," and Witherspoon is his socially ambitious wife, Elizabeth. This homely couple has a fair daughter, Peggy, played by Dorothy Moore. The inciting incident is a telegram telling Simms that he has received a large inheritance from his Uncle Ferdinand. Mrs. Simms is so thunderstruck by this news that she cannot talk, to which her husband responds laconically: "I've been waiting for that to happen for twenty years." Mrs. Simms is determined that she and her family will now finally be able to take the place in society they were destined for, telling her daughter: "I've waited twenty years for this opportunity and I'm not going to let you throw it away." She tells her husband that "our Peggy has a social destiny to fulfill."

What the Simmses do not know is that by inheriting his uncle's fortune, Doc Simms has become the head of a gang of racketeers. The basic comedy of the film inheres in the various complications that ensue from the innocent and gullible veterinarian being put in this unexpected and untoward position. He buys a newspaper to use it to unmask corruption in the city, without realizing that the "rogues gallery" of local crooks he promises to publish there will contain his own portrait at the top.

To capitalize on Witherspoon's screen image, Mrs. Simms is a bit of a dizzy dame and Mrs. Malaprop, who says things like: "Oh, if that isn't just like you. Discounting your chickens before they're hatched"; "If we all put our heads to the grindstone"; "You're going to be a regular business typhoon dealing only with the most important people"; and "You can't pull the wool over my ears." More unexpectedly, she has a "thing" for their crooked lawyer, Martin Drake (Russell Hicks), and manages to suggest a lot in the way she verbally caresses his first name. At her daughter's coming out party, she is wearing a tiara and has just about the biggest ostrich fan you ever saw. This character is interesting for combining nearly all the various traits of Witherspoon's trademark roles:

termagant wife, social climber, snob, nou-veau riche, and sexual older woman.

The film's critical reception was mixed, and for the first time Witherspoon got nega-tive reviews for her efforts. Some of the crit-ics clearly had seen enough of her, while others remained enthusiastic. Diggory Venn was an admirer and could usually be counted on for words of praise. This time, he outdid himself: "The social wife is Cora Witherspoon and the picture is worth see-ing for her alone. She is one of this depart-ment's favorite comediennes." As for the film, he found it "an unpretentious business" and "an amusing parody of American life." The reviewer for the *New York Daily News* went in the opposite direction, though: "In this instance he [Kibbee] is husbanded and henpecked by Cora Witherspoon in a role so feeble it could hardly be called a supporting one; more like the blind leading the blind."[42] The film got two stars.

While the *North Adams Transcript* felt that "Kibbee and Miss Witherspoon seize the opportunity in this picture to con-firm their rating as two of the best come-dians on the screen," the *Oakland Tribune* wrote: "Kibbee's work is colorless, but the material's to blame. Cora Witherspoon, as the overbearing wife, is no help, either; and neither is a mediocre and languid support-

This regal portrait shows Witherspoon in her role as the social-climbing wife of small-town veterinarian Guy Kibbee in her only starring vehicle, *The Big Shot* (RKO, 1937). When Kibbee inherits a for-tune from his uncle, Witherspoon finally sees her chance to take the role in society she has been yearning for and to engineer an advantageous marriage for her daugh-ter Dorothy Moore. What she does not know is that their inheritance comes from ill-gotten gains and that her husband has become the nominal head of a crime ring (Photofest/RKO Radio Pictures).

ing cast." According to the *Miami Tribune*, "Cora Witherspoon is the only outstand-ing name in the support cast and she overplays her socially ambitious mother role with her usual loud exaggerations." The *Dayton Herald* felt that this was "the best vehicle in which Kibbee's name has ever topped the starring list," but added: "Cora Witherspoon, as the 'big shot's' windy, socially ambitious wife, was a bit tiring, but that didn't bother the patrons." The *Montreal Gazette* wrote that "the hen-pecking side of the Kibbee life is done by Cora Witherspoon, with some very tiresome over-playing that helps to keep all one's sympathies with the henpecked husband." To end on a positive note: The *Mis-soulian* felt that "Miss Witherspoon proves to be an excellent foil."[43] Clearly, being a star and carrying a film was a risky business. The studios never took a chance on Wither-spoon again.

Back at MGM in mid–July, the studio was finding few suitable roles for their con-tract player. Witherspoon had one scene in the remake of the ultimate weepie of all time, *Madame X*, which started production in mid–July and finished August 19. This version, directed by Sam Wood, starred Gladys George in one of the finest performances of her career. Witherspoon went from second to thirteenth place on the credit list, but at least she got screen credit. Her single scene was not a bad one and the part was different in being one of her few roles in a screen drama. The press noted that Witherspoon had been cast in a "straight" part and a "hard-boiled" role for the first time.[44]

In *Madame X*, Witherspoon appears at 28 minutes as Nora, a dealer in second-hand clothing out of "The Imperial Gown Shoppe" in New Orleans. Looking unusually frumpy and frowzy in a plain cotton dress and a dark wig, she is almost unrecognizable. Newly arrived in the city, George as Jacqueline Fleuriot does not have the fare for the taxi that brought her to the store to hock her designer dresses, which we are supposed to believe she has dragged half-way around the world in a trunk. Even after ten years away from home, they are still the latest Paris fashions…. Nora has a better idea than buying the dresses herself, which would be wasted on her working-class customers, and takes Jacqueline next door to meet Scipio (Luis Alberni), the temperamental, Latin proprietor of "Scipio's," "the best worst café in the whole world" in his own estimation. Scipio checks Jacqueline out and buys her and her dresses for $300. Lest we think Nora is doing this out of the kindness of her heart, she takes half the money for negotiating the deal.

A couple of times during her stint as a contract player, MGM threw Witherspoon into a drama and gave her a "straight" role. Both times they also put her into an unsightly black wig, which is wearing her as much as the other way around. Both roles, too, were as "women of the people," a far cry from her usual social echelon in films and, indeed, as she was growing up on the fringes of New Orleans high society. In *Madame X* (1937), a major film for Gladys George (second from right), Witherspoon had one scene set in the city of her birth, where she played Nora, a cunning but not unsympathetic dealer in second-hand clothes, who gets George a much needed job singing in a local dive owned by Luis Alberni (second from left). The cab driver on the far right (Henry Taylor) is waiting for his fare.

We do not see her again after that, as Jacqueline goes from bad to worse as an increasingly drunken "canary" at Scipio's dive, frequented by sailors and other working men. In Nora's estimation, Jacqueline may have a hangover, but she also has class.

In August, the papers reported that Witherspoon had signed a new contract with MGM "following her work in 'Madame X.'" She was back high on the credits list in her next venture, which was her first film at Warner Bros., being billed right after the stars Frank McHugh and Jane Wyman. *He Couldn't Say No*, originally called *Larger Than Life*, was written especially for the comedian and Warner's stock company mainstay McHugh and was his first starring vehicle. It was a classic "in-law" comedy, where Witherspoon played Wyman's mother, Mrs. Coney, and McHugh's potential "mother-in-law from hell." In the film, Wyman is a colleague of McHugh's at an advertising firm and the engagement is engineered by her mother, after McHugh gets a raise. Her dearly held and well laid plans are foiled, however, by a series of intricate events involving a senator, a senator's daughter, a statue of the daughter, and a bunch of gangsters—"Everything but the bloodhounds snappin' at her rear end," to quote Birdie in *All About Eve*. McHugh finally marries the girl of his dreams, who turns out not to be Wyman, but the senator's daughter played by Diana Lewis. Witherspoon at least got a lot of play in this

Witherspoon and a 20-year-old Jane Wyman played mother and daughter in Lewis Seiler's *He Couldn't Say No* (1938), Witherspoon's first of three films at Warner Bros. She played a typically conniving mother and potential mother-in-law from hell, who wants nothing more than for hero and star Frank McHugh to marry her daughter, his co-worker at an advertising agency. McHugh evades her. Wyman and Witherspoon shared the same birthday, January 5, but were born 27 years apart.

one. Dorothy Masters gave the film two and a half stars and wrote: "Cora Witherspoon and Jane Wyman are excellently cast as nagging mother and daughter in pursuit of a defenseless male."[45] The director was Lewis Seiler.

Witherspoon was back at MGM in mid–October 1937 for *Beg, Borrow or Steal*, directed by Wilhelm Thiele and starring Frank Morgan, Florence Rice, and John Beal, who had been in *Russet Mantle* with her right before she came to Hollywood. This was a variant of the familiar story of a con man, Morgan, who has to temporarily "go straight" to host his daughter's wedding and the tangled web that is woven from practicing to deceive. Witherspoon played Mrs. Elizabeth Miller, the social climbing wife of millionaire Harlan Briggs and mother of Tom Rutherford, the man Rice is slated to marry at the French chateau Morgan is pretending to own. The Millers decamp after discovering their daughter's potential father-in-law is an imposter. Their son ultimately does not get the girl. John Beal does.

On the set of *Beg, Borrow or Steal*, Witherspoon was reunited with Janet Beecher, who had been Leo Ditrichstein's leading lady in *The Concert* on Broadway and toured with her in the same play for years afterwards. Beecher was now 53, divorced for the second time, and had been working as a character actress in Hollywood since *Gallant Lady* in 1933. In *Beg, Borrow or Steal*, Beecher was billed fourth as Frank Morgan's abandoned wife, while Witherspoon had to see herself relegated to an ignominious tenth place in the cast list. To add insult to injury, Edna B. Lawson was one of the few critics who noticed her in this tiny part, writing: "Cora Witherspoon as Rutherford's voluble mother is mated to Harlan Briggs who never has a chance to get a word in edgewise."[46] Janet Beecher died in 1955.

While she played a Southerner in *Madame X* and had just made her first film for Warner Bros., Witherspoon missed out on the big opportunity that year to play one of her own kind in Warner's adaptation of Owen Davis's play *Jezebel*. Though she tended not to dwell on things, it must have been a disappointment when the role of Bette Davis's stern yet supportive aunt went to Fay Bainter. After all, Witherspoon had created the role of Miss Sally (Aunt Belle in the film) on Broadway in 1933. She was at the height of her film career, too, but the producers wanted to go in a different direction. They told her she was "too British."[47] To make matters worse, Bainter, a former Broadway star with a broader range and a more benign, nurturing screen persona, won an Academy Award for Best Actress in a Supporting Role for her performance. Bainter and Witherspoon had been together in *The Way of the World* on Broadway and, of course, in *Quality Street*.

By early December 1937, it was clear her next film would be *Madelon*, starring Luise Rainer and Wallace Beery, a filmatization of a stage play called *Fanny* by Marcel Pagnol. Fellow MGM stalwarts Frank Morgan and Jessie Ralph were also thrown into the mix at this time. Production began in late December, under the direction of now legendary James Whale. What Whale biographer James Curtis has described as "the most expensive 'B' picture of the season" was released as *Port of Seven Seas* and ultimately starred Maureen O'Sullivan as Madelon, with Beery and Morgan at the top of the bill. Witherspoon was credited in sixth place this time, as Claudine, a family friend of the heroine and her mother Honorine (Ralph). Her part was not significant enough to rate a mention in the AFI summary of the film, nor in any of the reviews I have read. Witherspoon was mentioned in a column, though, in connection with this production. "Because she travelled the road as an actress most of her life," A.D. Mackie related, she had never learned to cook and had to be shown how to shell peas for a scene in the film.[48] I have a

You would never know it, but the closed-eyed, unrecognizable woman on the right with the ill-fitting, dark wig is actually Witherspoon in an unlikely working-class "friend of the family" role in the MGM melodrama *Port of Seven Seas* (1938). Maybe her home studio had hoped she and Wallace Beery (center) would recreate some of his old magic with Marie Dressler four years after her death, but that hardly happened. The film was originally entitled *Madelon* and was to have starred Luise Rainer, but Maureen O'Sullivan (left) finally played the lead role. Bending over O'Sullivan is her screen mother, veteran character actress Jessie Ralph, who would go on to play Witherspoon's mother in *The Bank Dick* in 1940.

still of Witherspoon from *Port of Seven Seas*, where she is unrecognizable in a dark wig, which is wearing her rather than the other way around. In fact, she looks not unlike Nora in *Madame X*. The only explanation for this innocuous role is that she was under contract and MGM had to use her in something.

While being cast against type in the forgettable *Port of Seven Seas*, Witherspoon had considerably bigger fish to fry at her home studio. By mid–December, she had also been cast as the Countess de Noailles, lady-in-waiting to Marie Antoinette (Norma Shearer) on her arrival in France to become the wife of the future Louis XVI (Robert Morley).[49] Initiated by Irving Thalberg as his final project before his untimely death in 1936, directed by W.S. Van Dyke, *Marie Antoinette* was a very big deal indeed, and Witherspoon's role was the most promising she had been given since *On the Avenue*.

Marie Antoinette was a new departure for her in being her first period costume drama (not counting *Quality Street*), and what costumes! Adrian went all out on this one, so that our impression of fashion in late eighteenth-century France will never be the same. He designed 500 costumes for the cast of 152 players.[50] Witherspoon looks picture perfect in a series of portraits taken in her various elaborate and elegant, yet delightfully whimsical Rococo frocks. How she must have loved them! The last time she wore anything period was in Congreve's *The Way of the World* in the spring of 1931. Her Broadway plays had nearly all had contemporary settings, just like her films. She was perceived by producers as a quintessentially modern type. In many ways, she was.

What we see on the screen, unfortunately, is disappointing, not because the costumes do not move well or Witherspoon botches her performance, but because there is hardly anything left of her part. The fancy portraits would never have been taken unless the role was originally much more substantial. Indeed, Witherspoon revealed in a 1939 interview, that most of it had been cut. She thought it was a shame, as the part was "a nice one" as "a sort of Emily Post of the French court." It was the major cutting room casualty of her career. While Beulah Bondi would have been resentful about this till the end of her days (as she was in losing the part of Ma Joad in *The Grapes of Wrath* to Jane Darwell), Witherspoon was not one to dwell on past mishaps or perceived slights. She was actually quite funny about it all, saying in one interview: "'The shadow you see behind Norma—that's me!'"[51] It is in small, humorous moments like this, that Witherspoon really comes alive to me as an individual.

Left: Unfortunately, you can get a much clearer idea of how Witherspoon looked in her role as Marie Antoinette's lady-in-waiting in MGM's 1938 biopic about the tragically fated queen from this and other photographs, than you can from watching the film. She revealed in an interview that most of her part ended up on the cutting room floor, making it the major casualty of her film career. As far as I know, none of her roles were deleted entirely. *Right:* Witherspoon did relatively few period costume dramas in Hollywood, but the eighteenth-century rococo extravagance of *Marie Antoinette* suited her down to the gown. The 500 costumes were created by legendary MGM designer Adrian, who was more concerned with visual impact than authenticity.

The sad remains of the Countess de Noailles is little more than a walk-on, her few lines being almost unintelligible, and consisting mostly of hissed admonitions; for example, one line to Marie Antoinette to approach the King at their first meeting at Versailles ("Proceed, Madame!") and later one to the Princesse de Lamballe (Anita Louise) to remind her that they must withdraw from the royal bedchamber and leave the newlywed couple to themselves. By this point, the countess has been supplanted in Marie Antoinette's affections by the princess, though she continues to hover in the background in a few later scenes. This is literally a supporting role, where Witherspoon is always three feet behind Shearer or three feet behind Louise. As far as our current subject is concerned, you will get more out of studying her portraits from *Marie Antoinette* than the film itself, and thus I reproduce two of them here.

Despite the fleeting nature of her role, she was billed in ninth place among the film's large and powerful cast of seasoned industry veterans, again revealing that the role was scripted to be larger than it ended up being in the final edit. The long production period was over on May 25, 1938, about the same time as Witherspoon's next film, *Just Around the Corner*, at Twentieth Century–Fox. It was reported that she would go on holiday to New Orleans after production ended on *Marie Antoinette*.[52]

Witherspoon was probably done with her scenes from *Marie Antoinette* by the time she was added to the cast of *Just Around the Corner* in early May.[53] This is a "riches to rags" story about an idealistic, widowed architect, Jeff Hale (Charles Farrell), and his precocious daughter Penny (Shirley Temple) and their struggles to maintain their dignity in the fancy apartment building where they have once occupied the penthouse and where they have now been relegated to the janitor's basement flat. The current residents of the penthouse are haughty Julia Ramsby, played by Witherspoon, and her family.

This is another talkative, airheaded, unpleasant, and libidinous upper-class dowager role in the Nesta Pett, Mrs. Burns-Norvell, and Mrs. Burns tradition. Mrs. Ramsby is more insidious, though, in acting the "heavy" and making life unpleasant for cute little Penny Hale. Like Nesta Pett, she has a young, spoiled son, here called Milton. He is played by Benny Bartlett and initially has curls, that his mother loves twirling, and "fancy pants." It is Penny's task to make a "real" boy out of Milton and rid him of what she perceives as his girlish ways. She is Delilah to his Samson and cuts off all his curls. Witherspoon's big scene comes at 35 minutes, when her son shows up at a bridge party she is giving with no curls, no fancy pants, and a black eye. She has a fainting fit as a result.

Mrs. Ramsby's airheadedness is suggested by her inability to remember Jeff Hale's surname. She chatters on all the time and is very much the doting mother. She also has an attractive, grown daughter, Lola (Amanda Duff), who becomes Hale's love interest; and a much older, cantankerous, Scrooge-like brother, Samuel G. Henshaw, who would have been played by Lionel Barrymore at MGM, but is incarnated here by Claude Gillingwater.

The other "heavy" in *Just Around the Corner* is the building manager Mr. Waters (Franklin Pangborn), who has to suffer being pushed into the pool by Penny and Milton and being shoved down the laundry chute by Hale's ex-chauffeur Gus (Bert Lahr). Pangborn is in typical harassed, uptight manager mode, with his forelock characteristically awry at every stressful moment and a sheen of sweat on his brow. Pangborn and Witherspoon went way back to their work for Jessie Bonstelle's stock company in Detroit in the summer of 1917. When they were reunited on the set of *Just Around the Corner*,

Witherspoon had known Franklin Pangborn for more than 20 years by the time they did *Just Around the Corner* (Twentieth Century–Fox, 1938) together, where they were teamed up to great effect as "heavies" who are mean to Shirley Temple. Witherspoon occupied the penthouse apartment with her family, that Temple and her widowed father had once lived in, and Pangborn played the uptight building manager in the fey way only he could. He and Witherspoon had four common credits, but unfortunately this was the only film in which they had any significant on-screen interaction. Back in 1917, they had both been part of Jessie Bonstelle's celebrated stock company. Pangborn was a year older than Witherspoon and died the year after her (Photofest/Twentieth Century–Fox).

Pangborn was 48, a year older than Witherspoon, and the veteran of dozens of films since his 1926 screen debut. The two old friends had four common screen credits, but *Just Around the Corner* was the only film in which they had any significant screen time together. The semi-flirtatious, conspiratorial interaction between these two pros is one of the delights of the film. Pangborn died the year after Witherspoon, at age 69.

Karl Krug of the *Pittsburgh Sun-Telegraph* found "there are moments when Franklin Pangborn, Cora Witherspoon and Bennie Bartlett are something of an assistance" to director Irving Cummings. These same three, and Claude Gillingwater, had "the embarrassing tasks of trying to appear funny when their material is far from comic," according to Kate Cameron of the *New York Daily News*. Frank S. Nugent had nothing to say about Witherspoon's efforts, but plenty to say about the film, including this: "Certainly nothing so aggravating as this has come along before—nothing so arch, so dripping with treacle, so palpably an affront to the good taste or intelligence of the unwary beholder."[54]

Witherspoon played her fair share of mothers of girls who did not get the guy, and her Mrs. Herford in *Three Loves Has Nancy* was one of them. Her daughter in the film is not the Nancy of the title, played with customary wide-eyed innocence and country comfort by Janet Gaynor, but rather a girl called Vivian; a horse of quite a different color, portrayed by Claire Dodd. Dodd was about as believable playing hard as nails, jaded, and calculating, as Gaynor was playing the opposite. As the film opens, Vivian, who is an actress with an eye for the main chance, is on track to marry the dashing celebrity author Malcolm Niles, played by Robert Montgomery.

Witherspoon is vividly present in the opening segment of the film. Malcolm has planned a romantic dinner for two with his girlfriend Vivian, that goes sadly wrong when Mrs. Herford crashes it. Reginald Owen, as Malcolm's butler William, also does his fair share to bungle the proceedings by misunderstanding nearly all his employer's instructions. Malcolm is appalled to see Mrs. Herford charging through the door in a very large fox fur coat which, when doffed, reveals that she is insistently bare shouldered in a slinky black gown with spaghetti straps, courtesy of Adrian. Her daughter looks positively frumpy in comparison. Dodd looks hard-bitten and tired, too, and, as such, is perfect casting for this role as a marriage-ready, no-longer-quite-so-young woman. Mrs. Herford appropriates her daughter's camellia corsage, sits down to dinner with the greatest of ease, and dominates the scene entirely by talking non-stop. According to her, Malcolm and her daughter are to all intents and purposes engaged and "Papa" has been called back from London to lend his approval and attend the forthcoming wedding. Vivian is a wry observer of the battle royal between her mother and boyfriend across the well-appointed dinner table.

This dinner scene with Mrs. Herford is the instigating incident of the film, that sends Malcolm off on a lecture and book signing tour to avoid the inevitable, where he meets the real heroine of the piece, Southern homebody Nancy Briggs (Gaynor). It is only when his publisher and friend, Bob Hanson (Franchot Tone), sends a telegram that all is clear, because Vivian is going on a lengthy tour with her play, that he returns (with Nancy in tow). The tour turns out to be an elaborate ruse engineered by Mrs. Herford to lure him back and allow her daughter to get her paws on him yet again ("baiting the trap"). This plan ultimately fails, when Malcolm pretends to be engaged to Nancy. Vivian gets the message and instantly contacts another beau over the phone, before clearing out of Malcolm's apartment and his life forever. This unfortunately means that we do not see any more of the delightful Mrs. Herford.

Production on the film took place at MGM between June 29 and August 4, 1938, though Witherspoon would only have been needed for a couple of days at most. The lavish premiere of *Marie Antoinette* was held at the Cathay Circle Theatre on July 8. The director of *Three Loves Has Nancy* was Richard Thorpe, who had helmed *Dangerous Number* at MGM the previous year. Witherspoon was billed seventh in the opening and closing credits, which was pretty good considering she only has one scene. Witherspoon's name was listed with the leads and Guy Kibbee in some of the ads.[55] The reviewers, though, did not have a word for her this time.

At this time, Witherspoon was rumored to be getting a "leading character part" in *Listen, Darling*, starring Freddie Bartholomew and Judy Garland, and to be paired with Wallace Beery in *Stablemates*, both at MGM. Mary Astor ultimately got the third-billed role in *Listen, Darling* as the mother of Garland and Scotty Beckett, who has her own love interest in Walter Pidgeon. Witherspoon, as we know, never played the sympathetic mother of any child on film and seldom had attractive, leading men as "beaus." In *Stablemates*, the *Los Angeles Times* reported that it was hoped that Beery and Witherspoon could recapture

This inept still from *Three Loves Has Nancy* (MGM, 1938) manages to capture all its subjects with their heads turned away from the camera. Witherspoon portrayed Mrs. Herford, another of her matrimonially motivated mothers, that is, on her daughter Vivian's
behalf. Vivian was played by Claire Dodd (right), while the object of both their affections,
best-selling author Malcolm "Mal" Niles, was played by Robert Montgomery (center) in his
second of two films with Witherspoon. Veteran British actor Reginald Owen played Montgomery's befuddled butler, who manages to misinterpret all his employer's instructions in
this opening scene from the film, where Witherspoon crashes an intimate dinner Montgomery has planned for himself and Dodd. Her black evening gown with its spaghetti straps is
typical Witherspoon, who loved anything décolleté.

the chemistry he had had on screen with the late Marie Dressler. Columnist Erskine Johnson observed that "Wallace Beery will play a genuine love scene for the first time in 20 years
in Metro's 'Stablemates.' He will make love to Cora Witherspoon." Marjorie Gateson ended
up playing Mrs. Shepherd, the rich widow and stable owner "to whom Beery is attentive."[56]
Gateson was a major portrayer of regal, elegant, upper-class women, but she was more physically attractive than Witherspoon and less funny because of it.

    During the summer of 1938, Witherspoon was visited in Hollywood by her old
New Orleans friend and acting teacher Jessie Tharp, who was traveling with her niece
Janet Dupuy. Witherspoon gave them a tour of MGM studios and introduced them to
stars like Jeanette McDonald and Judy Garland. In early September, Hedda Hopper held
up Witherspoon, Mary Boland, Billie Burke, and Alice Brady as models for "you older
women" to copy in fall fashions.[57]

    Witherspoon was on a roll, and her next part was also one that capitalized on what
she did best. Marital status and surname unknown, Carrie is in the "fair weather friend"

category; in other words, the type of friend you should not trust any further than you can throw her. The recipient of Carrie's dubious attentions is Bette Davis as Judith Tra-herne, the hard-tried heroine of the classic woman's film *Dark Victory*. Unfortunately, this was Witherspoon's only film with Davis. The two were well suited to each other on the screen, and Davis was one to recognize the importance of good support. Wither-spoon admired Davis, calling her in a 1939 interview "one of the most serious and con-scientious actresses in Hollywood."[58]

Beyond her on-again-off-again friendship with the terminally ill Judith, Carrie has an intriguing relationship with the young, perpetually inebriated playboy and poten-tial toyboy Alec, played by Ronald Reagan, who was 21 years Witherspoon's junior. It is well worth noting whatever she is doing in the background in this film! In her first, open air scene at Judith's Long Island estate, she toys lovingly with the future president's hair, while he leans up against her in an intimate way. This comes after Alec has said to Judith, that her horse trainer, Michael O'Leary (Humphrey Bogart), will give him a commission if he can sell Judith's colt to Carrie.

Unfortunately, this subtle and intriguing storyline is not developed, though Alec and Carrie often show up in the same place at the same time. Alec remains soused through most of the film and later tells Judith's love interest, Dr. Frederick Steele (George Brent), that he has been in love with her. Carrie is also seen with an older man, Colonel Mantle, played by Charles Richman, though nothing definite is said about their relationship either. Richman had been with Witherspoon in *Jigsaw* on Broadway in 1934.

Carrie flits in and out of *Dark Victory*. During her sudden appearance in the cli-mactic restaurant scene, she says to Dr. Steele: "Judy says you're frightfully good. You must look me over sometime." Very Mae West, that line. Alec, it turns out, is at the restaurant bar, drunk yet again. In her final appearance at the Jockey Club, after Judith has run amuck and been sleeping around, Carrie calls herself one of Judith's best friends and tries to give her some advice but is rudely cut off. So Carrie becomes yet another one among the group large enough to fill the Yale Bowl, who are "sore at you," as she feels compelled to tell Judith. Last, we see her perched next to Alec at the bar, the evening after Judith has won the silver cup for riding. She tries to toast her former friend but is ignored and looks miffed.

Witherspoon is dressed to the nines throughout, including at various times a large mink stole, a large fox stole, and two larges diamond "clips" on her evening gown in her final scene. There were some fleeting mentions of her in the reviews this time, in list-ings of supporting players who "do their share," need "to be mentioned in any summary of cast excellence," and "add notable performances to a notable film play." The *Houston Chronicle* took a different tack, claiming that Witherspoon was playing a maid....[59]

Dark Victory was part of a two-picture loan-out deal MGM had negotiated with Warner Bros. The second picture was the classic Western *Dodge City* starring Errol Flynn and Olivia de Havilland.[60] The cameras started rolling on *Dark Victory* in early October 1938 and filming was not complete until late November, which means it over-lapped with *Dodge City* for about a month. Witherspoon's part in *Dodge City*, though, was not so large that it would have occasioned any major scheduling conflicts. The direc-tor on *Dark Victory* was Edmund Goulding, while Michael Curtiz directed *Dodge City*, which has the distinction of being Witherspoon's first Technicolor film and her only Western. It was also one of her few historical films. In hue, genre, and period, then, we see a different Witherspoon in this film, though we do not see much of her.

Though her home studio was MGM during her Hollywood heyday, several of her best opportunities were on loan-out to other studios. In *Dark Victory* (Warner Bros., 1939), she played heroine Judith Traherne's sophisticated, fair weather friend Carrie. She is seen with (from left) bartender Sidney Bracey; her "toyboy" in the film, Ronald Reagan (yes, you read correctly); and star Bette Davis, among others.

In *Dodge City*, Witherspoon plays the president of a temperance society, the Pure Prairie League of Dodge City, whose all-female Ladies Social Circle meeting Alan Hale stumbles upon next door to the saloon, after he has promised Flynn he will stay out of trouble. He is welcomed by two elderly ladies (Flora Finch and Vera Lewis), who introduce him to their beloved president, Mrs. McCoy (Witherspoon). She comes forward to greet him in her customary dizzy dame manner (including forgetting people's names), wearing a bonnet and an ugly, shit-brown fringed cape in the style of the 1870s. Mrs. McCoy offers him tea, which is served by another lady, and then, while seated on the podium, listens with rapt attention to his testimony, which is increasingly disrupted by noise from a fight that has broken out in the Gay Lady Saloon next door between Southern and Northern sympathizers. Hale cannot resist getting involved once the fight spreads to the neighboring building, where the temperance meeting is taking place. The women are routed, and we do not see Witherspoon again.

It is interesting that as soon as Witherspoon moves away from her trademark roles as society women of varying degrees of sense and concupiscence, one feels that her true talents are not being put to good use. In other words, while she can convince as any kind of woman on the screen, we inevitably ask ourselves why producers felt they needed exactly *Cora Witherspoon* for these mundane and generic roles. Any number of character women at MGM could have played Nora in *Madame X* or Claudine in *Port of the Seven Seas*, and any number of character women at Warner's could have played Mrs. McCoy in *Dodge City*.

Witherspoon's final film of the eight she worked on in 1938 was *Woman Doctor*, which was produced rapidly between December 7 and 22. It was her first of two films for Republic and her only one for director Sidney Salkow. Frieda Inescort starred as a talented surgeon torn between the demands of her career and trying to be a good wife and mother.

This is an example of Witherspoon's sideline in incompetent and harassed governesses, which includes Mrs. Angevine in *Just for You*. In her first scene as Fanny, Witherspoon has one of her characteristic fits when her unruly charge, played by Sybil Jason, overturns her dinner plate. It turns out this bad behavior is a bid for her mother's attention, as Jason is hoping her governess with follow through on her threat to call her mother and tell her how badly she is behaving. Later, Witherspoon is appalled at husband and father Henry Wilcoxon countermanding Inescort's orders that Jason eat the cereal for dinner that she refused to eat for breakfast, by taking her out to dinner with the woman he is having an adulterous affair with, Claire Dodd (recently seen as Witherspoon's daughter in *Three Loves Has Nancy*).

The film cannot seem to decide whether Fanny the frustrated governess is there for comic relief or to serve as the heroine's best friend and confidante. After two brief appearances where she deals ineffectually with her demanding charge, we next find her dispensing sage advice about child rearing to a conflicted Inescort. Her advice to her employer is pretty radical. In her place, Witherspoon says, she would "take a scalpel and cut that man's throat from ear to ear!"

In her final scene, we see Witherspoon supervising a play date with another girl at their home. The two young girls trick her into singing "Then You'll Remember Me" to her own accompaniment, while they sneak out onto the terrace. There Jason comes dangerously close to death, as she leans over the parapet to try to awaken their downstairs neighbor with an alarm clock on a string. This is how Wilcoxon finds her, after which he summarily fires the governess. She reminds him that he cannot do that, because he is not her employer. He does take his daughter away to Long Island, though, and we do not see Fanny again after that. Presumably, she must be sacrificed when domestic bliss is reestablished in the household by the end of the film.

The assumptions of *Woman Doctor* would be ridiculous, if they were not simply chauvinist. While the daughter turns a blind eye to her father's adultery and idolizes his mistress, who was once her mother's friend; the mother is despised for devoting herself to her patients as a highly skilled surgeon and not being able to operate on her daughter's puppy Maxie at the hospital, after he is run over by a car. While the daughter is disappointed by her mother not being able to attend her recital, the father gets off scot free. He is not there either, after all, though he does have more time to spend with her, including taking her on entirely inappropriate dates with his new girlfriend. Inescort does have the support of her colleagues at the hospital, though, including the chief of staff. The ending of the film is highly ambiguous. Inescort is allowed by her magnanimous husband to keep on working as a kind of reward for saving their daughter's life in a spectacular airborne operation, but the basic problems occasioned by her busy schedule as a surgeon have not been resolved.

In this film, we get a rare glimpse of Witherspoon wearing glasses as she does needlepoint during the play date scene and singing as well, albeit completely off key. The *Los Angeles Times* liked the film, while the *New York Times* did not. The former felt that "Cora Witherspoon scores as the nurse."[61]

Witherspoon looks uncharacteristically benign in this still from *Woman Doctor* (Republic, 1939), where she played an increasingly harassed governess to enfant terrible Sybil Jason (right). Witherspoon wears glasses in keeping with her spinsterish role, which was rare, though she sported a lorgnette in her first scene in *Piccadilly Jim*. *Woman Doctor* starred British Frieda Inescort as a talented surgeon and is a vivid illustration of the sexual double standard (Photofest/Republic Pictures).

The times were changing, as Witherspoon neared the end of the major phase of her film career in early 1939. Suddenly, it was as if everything came to a grinding halt, and she only worked on two films that year. The first of them was *For Love or Money*, probably the stupidest, most inconsequential film she ever did. It was her first film at Universal and directed by Albert S. Rogell between March 9 and 25. Witherspoon played Mrs. Sweringen, a rich, spoilt, thoroughly unpleasant woman. Heroine June Lang is her put-upon secretary and companion in much the same way as Joan Fontaine is to Florence Bates in *Rebecca* and Ida Lupino to Mary Boland in *In Our Time*.

Witherspoon first appears ten minutes into the film, when a letter mistakenly arrives for her containing $50,000. She does not want it, not realizing what it contains. Lang urges her to open it, before she takes it herself. Realizing her good fortune, Lang proceeds to give her employer a piece of her mind and quits on the spot. Actually, she literally throws in the towel—or more specifically, she throws it in Witherspoon's face. In her next scene, at 18 minutes, Witherspoon is having her fortune told by a turbaned fortune-teller, when hero Robert Kent arrives to find out what she did with the missing money. She directs him to Lang and the main part of this pointless film begins. Witherspoon puts in an appearance at the end of the film, too, in a long scene in a restaurant, as a kind of *Deus ex machina*. Naturally, she is in negligee for her first two scenes and evening wear for her last. She has a kind of bandage around her chin while having breakfast in bed and is smoking in her scene with the swami, something she seldom did in films.

The Women would prove Witherspoon's last hurrah at MGM, though she still had 15 years left to spend off and on in the movies. Metro had meant a lot to her, but now they were cutting her lose. Witherspoon is actually the first woman we see in the film, playing Mrs. Van Adams, whose scruffy Yorkshire terrier type dog "Lillikins," with a large ribbon around her scrawny neck, gets involved in a fracas with another small dog on the sidewalk outside Sydney's Park Avenue Salon. Mrs. Van Adams comforts her with baby talk. She then enters the beauty parlor and leaves her dog with dog sitter Olive (Theresa Harris). When she gives her the dog's "special drinking water" in a glass bottle, Olive tells her the dog never wants to drink it. Mrs. Van Adams responds that you never know when she might want it. That is the extent of her participation in the film.

As fate would have it, her friend George Cukor directed her first and her last films and, in between, he directed her in this. He must have been perfectly aware of Witherspoon's love of dogs. She is dressed in basic black, as she had been in their first film together, *Tarnished Lady*, and looks elegant and distinguished. Depending on when her scene was filmed, it would be six to nine months till she worked on a film again; an eternity to someone used to doing seven or eight films a year.

When a Hollywood character actress returns to the stage, it is never a good sign. It means she has time on her hands. After her brief participation in *The Women* and in the middle of summer, Witherspoon did a stage play for the first time in more than three years. She admitted to being "pretty nervous": "The theater seemed like a huge tooth that needed filling."[62] Sutton Vane's "mystical-fantasy" play *Outward Bound* had been a moderate hit on Broadway in the spring of 1924, after success in London's West End. The drama succeeded even better, though, in a 1938–39 revival starring Laurette Taylor, which lasted 255 performances at the Playhouse Theatre in New York. The West coast production opened in Santa Barbara on July 20, 1939, two days after the New York revival closed. It was then nine years since the release of the original 1930 Warner Bros. film version, starring Leslie Howard, Douglas Fairbanks, Jr., Beryl Mercer, and Dudley Digges.

The West coast production opened at the Curran Theatre in San Francisco on July 24 and spent two weeks there, before moving to Los Angeles and the Biltmore Theatre on August 14. The mini-tour ended there on August 26. Besides Witherspoon, the cast included well-known stage and screen players like Cecilia Loftus (Mrs. Midget), Reginald Denny (Tom Prior), Richard Cromwell (Henry), and Dorothy Jordan (Ann). Edward Cooper (Mr. Lingley), Philip Winter (the Rev. William Duke), Evan Thomas (the Rev. Frank Thompson), and Colin Campbell (Scrubby) completed the cast. The play was staged by Auriol Lee and the sets were by Kate Drain Lawson.[63]

In this spiritual drama "concerned with the flight of the human soul after death,"[64] an ocean liner is used as a microcosm of the world. But this is no ordinary ship. As the journey progresses, the passengers realize that they are all dead. They find themselves in limbo between life and the everlasting; their ultimate destination and fate, which is not a conventional heaven or hell, will not be determined until they have made a reckoning of their lives before "the Examiner," the Rev. Frank Thompson.

Witherspoon played the haughty and hyphenated Mrs. Cliveden-Banks, "a withered old harridan of fifty odd—probably once beautiful."[65] A thoroughly unpleasant and trivial woman, she manipulated her husband into marrying her and then henpecked him into a premature death. Her punishment is to have to be a good wife to him for all eternity. Mrs. Cliveden-Banks was one of the classic dowager roles of the 1920s. She had been created on Broadway by Charlotte Granville and by the even more illustrious British character actress Alison Skipworth in the 1930 film version. Isobel Elsom played the role in the 1944 remake *Between Two Worlds*.

The play's somber theme was brought even closer to home, when the production's veteran property man, Max D. Hamburger, died suddenly on the day of the San Francisco premiere. He died of a heart ailment at the age of 56 in his Geary St. hotel room, directly across from the theater.[66]

The production received decidedly mixed reviews. The *San Francisco Examiner* thought it "a noble effort," but opined that "the first and second acts were slow" on the opening night. The reviewer blamed the direction and the lighting for the production's lack of pace and effectiveness. The *Oakland Tribune* found the first night "dull" and thought director Lee "eminently unsuccessful at the premiere in recreating the old spirit of excitement and alarm that the play should occasion." The critic added: "It was really a strange first night for the players didn't seem nervous as much as bewildered."[67]

Apparently, the production had not greatly improved by the time it reached the Biltmore Theatre. The *Los Angeles Times* thought the first act "lagged," the second "gained sharpness," and the third "amassed that cumulative eeriness which is at once the secret of the work's longevity and a tribute to the undiminished power of what we call the 'theater.'" The *Hollywood Citizen-News* found the production "completely professional" and "stocked with familiar faces." Witherspoon was "top-notch as Mrs. Cliveden-Banks, the hoity-toity society damsel who decides she must be dead because her corsets never felt so comfortable." The *Los Angeles Daily News* felt "a cast of New York and Hollywood names … enacted the piece efficiently," but "fails to give the play the smooth ensemble performance it demands." The halting tempo was still a problem. Witherspoon was among those who nevertheless provided "excellent acting" and "makes her comedy lines crackle."[68]

According to the *Los Angeles Times*, Witherspoon was "responsible for no small number of the laughs" in the production. She was not just noticed for her performance. *Oakland Tribune* drama critic Wood Soanes recorded that, when greeted by an enthusiastic audience on her first entrance at the San Francisco premiere, "she waved to the first nighters." Soanes was not impressed by the show and added sardonically: "had it only been a wave of farewell!" The *Los Angeles Times* carried an item about Witherspoon's contretemps with assistant director Russell Lewis, who did not want her to wear her new silver foxes in a play set during a warm summer aboard ship. According to the *Times*, "The actress bade her maid carry the furs with her to the wings lest they be stolen from her dressing-room; then, as she made her entrance, she snatched the furs, threw them around her neck, and with a defiant gesture in 'Russ's' direction, made a majestic entrance."[69] I can hardly imagine Beulah Bondi pulling a stunt like that!

An event of seemingly only passing significance, but with likely long-term negative effects, occurred during the run of *Outward Bound* on the coast. Witherspoon was not often the subject of AP news bulletins. When she was, the news was seldom good. The bulletin dated Los Angeles August 25 and widely reprinted in local papers across America read: "Tripped by her dog's leash in her hotel apartment, Cora Witherspoon, Broadway actress appearing in a stage version of 'Outward Bound,' was in a hospital Thursday with a fractured knee. Her physician said she would be laid up for six weeks or longer. Her part in the play was taken by Patricia O'Callaghan, her understudy and the assistant manager for the company. The dog's name, by the way, is 'Lucky.'"[70]

The caption accompanying a photograph of Witherspoon, probably dressed for *Outward Bound*, in the *Los Angeles Daily News*, gives additional details. The fall and subsequent broken knee had occurred Wednesday night, August 23. Witherspoon was taken to the Wilshire Hospital. She would only miss three performances, as the run was ending with the matinee on Saturday, August 26. She probably also missed the gala premiere of *The Women* at Grauman's Chinese Theatre on August 31. The police estimated that "there were more than 15,000 jamming the boulevard to watch the parade of stars into the theater."[71]

Less than a month before the accident, Witherspoon and her dog Lucky had been the subject of a long feature article in the *San Francisco Chronicle*. According to the writer John Hobart, "In the same breath with which she says 'How do you do?' she will tell you about her dog." According to Hobart, Lucky was "fabulous, if uncertainly pedigreed"; he "stares at you from under a shaggy matting of white eye-fringe, his tongue dangling from his mouth in a friendly fashion, his tail wagging jauntily."[72] In addition to her sister, Lucky was Witherspoon's closest friend. She was never alone, as long as she had her dog.

Fortunately, Maude Witherspoon was visiting her younger sister in Los Angeles at the time of the accident. As part of her surprise visit, she had been present at the *Outward Bound* opening on August 14. Some days prior, Maude gave an interview to the *Hollywood Citizen-News*, where she made it clear that she had not originally approved of her sister's decision to go on the stage. Maude also expressed her amazement that her "'pie-eyed, pug-nosed, alligator mouthed, dog-eared little sister'" sister had become famous. Cora, in turn, referred to Maude as "the 'brains of the family.'" The sisters were staying together at the Biltmore Hotel, which was adjacent to the theater and which still stands at 506 S. Grand Ave. in downtown Los Angeles, while the theater was razed in 1964.[73] An extension to the hotel was later built on the site.

Maude did not return to Las Cruces until mid–October, after a three-month absence from home. With her knee on the mend, her sister Cora headed east for a well deserved holiday in New York City. On September 15, her friend Charles Brackett had received a request for a loan from her per letter "to get her back to New York." And then comes the clincher: "she's been refused by the M.P.R. [Motion Picture Relief Fund] because she refuses to take a cure for her drug habit...." This brief, laconic statement is significant for being the first surviving evidence of Witherspoon's drug addiction, which would have such serious consequences for her exactly one year later. It was not the last time "poor Cora Witherspoon" put a "touch" on Brackett.[74]

Clearly, Witherspoon got her loan, either from Brackett or someone else. On her way to New York, she stopped over in Chicago. In a contemporary feature article on John Barrymore, we can read that Witherspoon visited him in his dressing room at the Selwyn Theatre after a performance of *My Dear Children* and gave him half of the cast from her leg! The other half, she had him autograph for her. She was later forced to ask for the gifted half back: "Doctors had found her leg not quite mended and she needed the cast again."[75]

Witherspoon's last "gig" of the year and the decade was the role of Mrs. Orcutt, the house matron of the Footlights Club, a boarding house for young women with thespian ambitions and careers, in George S. Kaufman and Edna Ferber's *Stage Door*. She played this role not on the stage or the big screen, but, indeed, on the small screen; in fact, it constituted her television debut and was probably taped in New York. The hour-long teleplay aired on NBC on December 17, 1939, and starred Margaret Curtis as Terry Randall and Michael Whalen as her love interest. The television cast also included six members of the original 1936–37 Broadway production at the Music Box Theatre: Frances Fuller (Kaye Hamilton), Janet Fox (Bernice Niemeyer), Lee Patrick (Judith Canfield), Edmund Dorsay (Lou Milhauser), Richard Kendrick (Keith Burgess), and Ralph Locke (Adolph Gretzl).[76]

Mrs. Orcutt is described in the play's stage directions as "a woman of about forty-six. In her manner and dress you detect the flavor of a theatrical past. Her dress is likely to have too many ruffles, her coiffure too many curls." A former actress who left the stage for marriage, Mrs. Orcutt is seen briefly throughout the play, showing prospective residents around the club and supporting her young female residents. The role was created by Leona Roberts on Broadway, by Elizabeth Dunne in the 1937 RKO film version starring Katharine Hepburn and was played by Elsa Lanchester in the 1955 television adaptation directed by Sidney Lumet and starring Diana Lynn. A reviewer for the *New York Daily News* remarked that "television really comes into its own with its airing of Broadway stage fare. This was one of the best of the air theatre's offerings, from the angles of acting, direction and technical camera work."[77]

6

Witherspoon's War
The 1940s

> "I'm a prosaic person…, and nothing ever happens to me. I go on
> season after season playing on Broadway with stars and I never have fights
> with the luminaries, never hate an engagement, never do the thousand
> and one temperamental things which I suppose are expected."[1]

As a new decade commenced, Witherspoon was nearing the end of the major phase of her film career, though she could not have known it. There would be time for four final films in 1940, before disaster struck and she felt compelled to move back to the East coast. On January 5, she turned 50. The papers reported that her hair had turned "completely white" after her leg injury eight months earlier.[2]

By early January 1940, Witherspoon was probably already working on her first film of the forties.[3] *I Was an Adventuress* was a well acted and well written, middle-grade feature from Fox in the crime and adventure vein about a lady con woman and burglar, played by Vera Zorina, who is trying to go straight and live happily ever after with Richard Greene, while her former cronies Erich von Stroheim and Peter Lorre are unwilling to let her go. Witherspoon played Cecile, Greene's spoilt and pettish aunt, and the mother of Anthony Kemble Cooper, whom she keeps on a short leash. She does not show up until 54 minutes into the film, by which time the action has moved to Greene's family estate outside Paris. Posing as Zorina's cousin and his friend, Lorre and Von Stroheim crash the weekend party and are invited to stay.

For me, Witherspoon's scene with sinister, soft-spoken, and ambiguously accented Lorre is the highpoint of the film. After hostess Zorina says she wants to put all their valuables in the safe, because there have been burglaries in the neighborhood, Lorre wastes no time in going around to collect the jewelry for his "cousin" Zorina. He takes Witherspoon's bracelets, necklace, and ring, but tells her to leave the large diamond brooch, which is worthless. "Ah well, so was the man who gave it to me," Witherspoon responds. "Oh, Nicholas, I feel so safe with you in the house." As the columnists reported, Witherspoon's hair is indeed quite white at this time. Predictably, she wears a dress with spaghetti straps, but has a short, see-through, bolero jacket with spangled stripes over it. The jewels used in the film were real.[4]

Opinions were divided on the success of the venture, which was Zorina's first dramatic role and marked Erich von Stroheim's return to the screen. According to the *Los Angeles Times*, "Winsome jewel thieves in swanky hostelries are nothing new to our movies." Witherspoon was among those listed as "seen and heard." The *New York Times* wrote that "despite the coterie of talents mentioned in the screen credits, the film is a spiritless little offering." The *Chicago Daily News* found it "one of the superlative delights of the movie year," while the *San Francisco Examiner* thought "Sig Ruman, Cora Witherspoon and Fritz Feld do well by their roles."[5]

After doing *I Was an Adventuress* at Fox, Witherspoon also lent her talents to an entry in the "Charlie Chan" series at the same studio. Witherspoon and Don Beddoe had been added to the cast by February 25, 1940.[6] *Charlie Chan's Murder Cruise* came exactly halfway in the massive series, being film number 24 out of 47. It was a remake of *Charlie Chan Carries On* from 1931, based on Earl Derr Biggers's story of the same title. Director Eugene Forde was a mainstay of Fox's B movie unit between 1932 and 1947 and directed several Charlie Chan films. Forde had previously directed Witherspoon in *The Lady Escapes* (1937) at Fox. In addition to Sidney Toler in the title role and Beddoe, the film was well cast with industry veterans such as Lionel Atwill, Leo G. Carroll, Harlan Briggs, Claire Du Brey, and James Burke.

The main focus of the film is on the father-son relationship between Mr. Chan and "Son Number Two," Jimmy Chan (Victor Sen Yung). Witherspoon's character Susie Watson is one of the sharpest and most vivid delineations of the type of "damn fool woman" character she so often played on film. She even gets to fawn over Mr. Chan, when she discovers she is in the presence of the famous detective. Susie finds his being there reassuring and good advertising for Hawaii. "Scream once and Charlie Chan is on the job," she quips.

Within the first minute and a half of the film, Susie has screamed her head off, been slapped by police inspector Wilkie (Burke), and slapped him right back. Susie has an ambiguous love interest in, or just a palsy relationship with, fey Frederick Ross (Beddoe), who ends up dead. She has some of her funniest exchanges with Du Brey's sepulchral Mrs. Watson, telling her in the latter's first scene: "Listen, Mrs. Watson, you'd better put that crystal ball of yours away before someone hits you with it." In the final scene at the San Francisco morgue, Witherspoon says to her: "Why don't you move in? You'd love it here." Though she is fairly visible (and very audible) in the film, Susie Watson has no real plot function. She is never a suspect nor an intended murder victim and seems mainly to be there for comic relief, which this unintentionally comic film does not need.

I would suggest most of the film's (low) budget has gone into Witherspoon's outward trappings, if it were not for the fact that character actors often provided their own costumes. Any shortages in Witherspoon's own copious wardrobe were no doubt made up for by Helen A. Myron, who was responsible for the costumes here during the final year of her five-year contract with Fox. Witherspoon capers through the film in a series of fancy, low-cut peignoirs and gowns with a lot of fur trim and even sports a small, conical Asian rice hat in the party scene. She is surprisingly trim and buxom at 50 years of age. Her signature pencil-thin eyebrows are in place and her hair still looks whiter than usual, as in *I Was an Adventuress*.

Witherspoon received a gratifying amount of attention for her efforts in this programmer. Here is a bouquet of quotes from the critics: "just another trip around the old circuit, brightened up a little bit by the presence of Cora Witherspoon, Don Beddoe and Leo Carroll in the company"; "Cora Witherspoon is also on hand to stir up laughter, as a relief to the suspense of the manhunt"; "Lionel Atwill and Cora Witherspoon are also good in their roles.... Miss Witherspoon as the flighty wealthy woman who was always seeing faces that she could not describe." James L. Neibaur wrote in 2018, that

"Ms. Witherspoon's comic performance as an amusingly edgy type exhibits her versatility as a fun character actress who specialized in comedy.... Witherspoon's performance is a good example of comic relief that serves the narrative as opposed to overwhelming or distracting from it." The *Times-Picayune* concluded: "It is not a Grade A Chan, but it affords one or two moments that suggest the epigrammatic sleuth at his best."[7]

When the U.S. census was taken in April 1940, Witherspoon was living alone at 1311 N. Formosa Ave. in Hollywood. Her rent was $50. Her age was accurately given as 50, but she was enumerated as a widow. She had two years of high school. According to the record, she only worked 5 weeks in 1939 and earned $1,300. She is listed with an independent source of income apart from her wages.[8]

In mid–June, Witherspoon was mentioned in Grace Wilcox's feature article on Hollywood character actresses, which was headed "Hollywood's Most Interesting Women." According to Wilcox, "An entire volume is not sufficient for the high lights in the lives of Marjorie Rambeau, Charlotte Greenwood, Lucile Watson, Blanche Yurka, Sara Haden, Cora Witherspoon, Marjorie Gateson, Helen Westley, all of whom give to the screen authenticity, a spirit of gaiety, a touch of tragedy, a warmth of human sympathy and understanding."[9]

During the summer, Witherspoon played an uncredited role as Mrs. Sneddington, a book club spokeswoman, in *Honeymoon for Three*, starring Ann Sheridan and George Brent. It was her final film at Warner Bros. After starting the decade in two films that were mediocre at best and doing this uncredited role, she was cast in what today is one of her most highly ranked and popular films: *The Bank Dick*.[10] Unfortunately, her experience of working with W.C. Fields and his talented cast, including familiar faces like Jessie Ralph, Russell Hicks, and her friend Franklin Pangborn, would be entirely overshadowed by the catastrophe that engulfed her during the production.

In *The Bank Dick*, Fields famously plays yet another bemused and befuddled Everyman, Egbert Sousé ("accent grave over the 'e'"). The underemployed Mr. Sousé, who is spending more time than is good for him at the bar of the Black Pussy Cat Café, first embarks on a career as a film director, to no great effect, and then as a bank detective, which ultimately leads him to richly undeserved fame and fortune. Witherspoon portrays Fields' slatternly, lethargic, bovine, and termagant wife, Agatha Sousé, and the mother of Una Merkel and Evelyn Del Rio. To add to the charms of his all-female household, Fields also has to contend with his live-in mother-in-law, Mrs. Hermisillo Brunch, portrayed by Ralph. He finds himself under continuous attack from his womenfolk, including his physically abusive younger daughter Del Rio. The women munch, slurp, complain, and yell their way through the film. They treat Fields like a child. His mother-in-law is continuously threatening to "go on the county," if her daughter does not put her foot down and stop Fields from smoking, which Ralph claims has given her asthma. Merkel threatens to kill herself by starvation, because her father has been seen coming out of a saloon and smoking a pipe.

In these scenes of domestic discord and disorder, Witherspoon is no better than the rest. Indeed, it is a rare thing to see her so unkempt. The unreal effect is somewhat like watching Agnes Moorehead playing Velma Cruther in *Hush ... Hush, Sweet Charlotte*. By the last two minutes of the film, though, Fields has become the hero and patriarch of his now wealthy, genteel family, after capturing a bank robber and selling a story idea to Hollywood. The Sousé family has undergone an extreme makeover, and Witherspoon, in a filmy, flowing, chiffon dress, looks exactly as we are used to seeing her.

This delightful still is from the final scene of *The Bank Dick* (Universal, 1940), by which time the ne'er-do-well bumpkin Egbert Sousé, played by legendary comedian W.C. Fields, had won fame and fortune and his family's reluctant respect. Left to right, we see Evelyn del Rio and Una Merkel as daughters Elsie May and Myrtle, Witherspoon as wife Agatha, Fields himself, Jessie Ralph as mother-in-law Mrs. Hermisillo Brunch, and Grady Sutton as Myrtle's boyfriend Og Oggilby. Fields was probably more understanding than most when Witherspoon was arrested for a narcotics offense during production on the film. She moved back to the East coast as soon as she was done filming in October 1940, though she would return to Hollywood in the mid–1940s and sporadically in the 1950s (Photofest/Universal Pictures).

The trouble with Egbert Sousé, of course, is that he is exactly what his name alludes to: a souse. So Witherspoon found herself not just struggling with addiction but being publicly shamed as an addict while making a film about addiction. The irony was probably lost on her at the time. Production on the film began at Universal in early September 1940. According to Una Merkel, the last scene of the film, where the newly rich Sousé family is seen at the breakfast table enjoying their luxurious surroundings, was the first to be shot. This means Witherspoon would have been working from the beginning of the shoot and at the time she was arrested. The papers did not report that she had been cast until October 10, which was the same day as she pled guilty to the charge of possession of a hypodermic needle. The film wrapped October 22, 1940.[11]

Between mid–September and mid–November 1940, Witherspoon was embroiled in a highly publicized narcotics arrest and conviction in which she was publicly revealed to be a drug addict; though, technically, she only pleaded guilty to "possessing hypodermic equipment suitable for use in narcotic injections" and the charge of narcotics addiction was dropped. This public shaming constituted the low point of her life and was no doubt the main reason for her decision to leave Los Angeles and move back to the East. The headlines in the papers during these trying times were such as I can never recall having read in connection with any other character actress: "Cora Witherspoon Faces Dope Case" (*Hollywood Citizen-News*), "Actress Fights Morphine Charge" (*Los Angeles Daily News*), "Actress Denies Narcotic Charge" (*Denver Post*), "Former Actress Asks Mercy in Dope Case" (*Los Angeles Times*), "Cora Witherspoon Pleads Guilty to 'Needle' Ownership" (*Los Angeles Daily News*).[12] She was 50 years old at the time.

While the arrest in her apartment on N. Formosa Ave. in Hollywood took place on Saturday, September 13, she was not arraigned until September 19 and the story did not break until September 20. One of the most detailed accounts was found in the *Hollywood Citizen-News*, which opened its story as follows: "Cora Witherspoon, once a headliner as an actress, was under treatment today for drug addiction, following her arraignment late yesterday before Municipal Judge Arthur S. Guerin, where she pleaded not guilty to a formal charge." The charges were possession of a hypodermic needle and addiction to narcotics. According to the article, Witherspoon had admitted to state narcotics officer W.L. Yoakum, that she was "addicted to the use of narcotics." Following the arrest on Saturday in her home, she was taken to General Hospital, where Dr. H.J. Kirchner examined her and submitted a report confirming Yoakum's findings. The date for trial was set by Judge Guerin for October 10 and bail fixed at $500. The account in the *Hollywood Citizen-News* ended: "The actress, a veteran of the stage and screen, appeared in many leading roles and was at her height about 10 years ago when she was a member of the Wheeler and Woolsey cast in the production 'Peach-O-Reno.'" The International News Service (INS) sent out a bulletin on September 20.[13] There was also a UP news bulletin November 8, which would disseminate the story far beyond the Los Angeles area.

Witherspoon's case came up before Municipal Judge Leo Aggeler on the date fixed, October 10. Rather than go to trial, the actress pleaded guilty to the charge of possession of a hypodermic needle. The charge of addiction was dismissed. Witherspoon was granted a hearing on November 7 on a petition for leniency and released under $500 bond. The *Los Angeles Times*, who covered the case for the first time, described her as a "former film actress."[14]

The first preview of *The Bank Dick* was on November 3. On November 7, Witherspoon was sentenced to a 90-day suspended jail sentence on the basis of her good record, after her guilty plea to "a charge of possessing hypodermic equipment suitable for use in narcotic injections." Judge Aggeler said: "'Your excellent record makes you eligible for leniency.... The report shows that you have been cured of addiction. However you must pay a $75 fine and be certain to refrain from the use of narcotics for your probationary period. The fine may be paid when you are financially able.'" Witherspoon was placed on probation for a year. She said that she was "'between engagements' at the present time."[15] A California native, Judge Aggeler had just turned 40. He lived at 161 N. Fuller Ave. and died there of heart failure in 1976. A Catholic, Aggeler was married and had two daughters and a son.[16]

Unfortunately, Witherspoon had several members of her father's family living in Los Angeles with a front-row seat to the unfolding of this debacle. In 1940, no less than five of her Witherspoon cousins and their families were in the area; most of them had lived there much longer than her. Her 72-year-old cousin Thomas Casey Witherspoon II, the eminent surgeon now retired, and his second wife Rita, had lived in Los Angeles for ten years and occupied a pleasant bungalow just above San Vincente Boulevard and the Brentwood Country Club. Thomas's four-year younger brother, William Conner Witherspoon, and his second wife Lillian had been in the area since the early 1930s, having moved to Los Angeles from San Francisco, and now lived modestly in a small house on W. 60th St. in South Los Angeles. William was still working as a salesman. In addition, William's eldest son, J. Houston Witherspoon, a 40-year-old insurance broker, and his wife Carolin lived in an apartment on N. Orange Dr., near the Wilshire Country Club.[17]

Both Witherspoon's "double aunt" Caroline Bell Witherspoon and her son Leslie Witherspoon had lived in Los Angeles at the end of their lives. Leslie died there in 1922, when he was only 46, and Aunt Carrie in 1925 at age 84. This was long before Witherspoon moved to Los Angeles herself, but Carrie's unmarried daughter Grace Witherspoon and Leslie's widow Eleanor Howison Witherspoon still lived in Pasadena in 1940. Seventy-one-year-old Grace lived alone in a small apartment on Drexel Place, the current site of the Huntington Memorial Hospital; while her sister-in-law Eleanor, an heiress from Baltimore, lived in style with her maid only a few blocks away at 459 Bellefontaine St., in a large Shingle style house from 1907 worth $14,000. In comparison, Thomas Witherspoon's handsome home in Brentwood was worth $10,000. Eleanor died in 1944 and Grace in 1949.[18] I do not know if the proximity of so many Witherspoons at such a difficult time in her life was part of her decision to pull up stakes and return to the East. No doubt, she felt played out in the film business too. The signs of a decline in her screen career had been there before she got arrested.

After she had moved back East in late 1940, Witherspoon summed up her moviemaking experience in an interview with veteran drama critic Elliot Norton: "I would probably do it all again, if I should have a chance to go back to Hollywood.... It is very nice to be out there, with these big pay checks coming in every Saturday and people fussing for your autograph. I shouldn't have 'gone Hollywood' but I had a very good time doing it." By "going Hollywood," she meant that "she got a little lofty as a result of being rushed for autographs by shouting fans. She let the cheers affect her. She put on the dog ... just a bit." Witherspoon revealed to Norton, that "she went out and bought a huge, expensive car, hired a chauffeur and a special maid and behaved like a movie celebrity." The article related that she had spent five years in the movies, adding the interesting qualification: "during two of which she was ill."[19] This was true. Today, we recognize addiction as an illness, but for Witherspoon it was a way of casting a smoke screen over a difficult period in her life.

While Witherspoon was finding her feet in the East, she worked in radio. It was reported in April 1941, that she would "play an important character in support of Myrtle Vail and Helen Mack." Vail and Mack were the stars of *Myrt and Marge*, a popular 15-minute soap opera, that aired weekdays at 10:15 a.m. over CBS. It had debuted ten years earlier and was "one of the first important dramatic serials of radio." Produced in Chicago, it was originally sponsored by Wrigley's chewing gum and currently by Super Suds. The characters Myrtle Spear and Margie Minter were originally played by real-life mother and daughter Myrtle Vail and Donna Damerel.

The show had been struck by tragedy in mid–February 1941, when Damerel died in childbirth at age 29. Her child, a boy, survived. Mack replaced her in what would prove the serial's final year. It ended on March 27, 1942. Other of Witherspoon's radio credits included *Against the Town*, *Lux Theater of the Air*, *Campbell Soup Playhouse*, and *Radio Guild*.[20]

It was also about this time that Witherspoon had another accident. After rehearsing for an installment of *Armstrong's Theatre of Today* starring Madge Evans over CBS, she suffered a fractured arm when leaving the rehearsal. She tried to keep the arm with a cast hidden from director of the program, Frank Lindner, in fear that she would not be allowed to continue in the role. She was, and not only that, Lindner had one person to turn the pages of the script for her and another to hold her arm "in the straight position prescribed by the doctor." Witherspoon refers to the broken arm in an August 18 interview with the *Quincy Patriot Ledger*, so it happened before then.[21] She was busy in summer stock starting in early May, so I am guessing it happened before that too.

It was also at this time that she became acquainted with a young fellow Southerner, who would grow into one of the greatest of American dramatists. Tennessee Williams was about 30, had recently moved to New York, and was working as an elevator operator at night at a hotel called the San Jacinto, which he described in his 1975 *Memoirs* as "a sort of retirement home for dowagers of high degree but diminished fortune." A vivid presence at the hotel when Williams was working there was "a marvelous old character actress named Cora Witherspoon." Williams more than suggests that Witherspoon had fallen back into her bad habits and "was addicted to morphine." He and a fellow worker would fill her prescriptions at an all-night pharmacy. Then they would "rap" in the hotel lobby "till nearly daybreak," before they helped her back to her apartment and into bed. In addition to the newspaper reports from her arrest and trial in 1940, this is one of only two first-hand accounts we have of Witherspoon's problems with addiction. The San Jacinto Hotel, later known as the Versailles, was located at 18 E. 60th St. on the corner of Madison Ave. It was eight stories tall, had 210 rooms, and 65 baths. The building no longer exists.[22]

Despite her highly publicized troubles, the theater welcomed her back with open arms. It would have been reassuring to find that, after five years in Hollywood, she now had name recognition in a whole new way. The lifeline that that was thrown out to her was a role, a leading role in fact, in a post–Broadway production of George S. Kaufman and Moss Hart's recent play *George Washington Slept Here*. The papers noted that it was their record-breaking eighth collaboration and Kaufman's 32nd play to reach the stage.[23] Though a solid, workable comedy, *George Washington Slept Here* was not one of their most significant collaborations.

Brooks Atkinson had written in his review of the New York production in October the previous year, that, despite the actors being "off the top-shelf," the play was "a labored and empty enterprise." He added that "only good taste prevents this column from observing that George Washington could have slept there without missing amusement of any particular consequence." Burns Mantle noted in his annual review of the theatrical year, that "neither the authors nor their producing associates were ever very happy about it. Neither was audience-response what it should be": "Yet, when Summer came, this comedy was the first selection of 90 per cent of the barn theatre impresarios as an opening bill, and one of the most popular bills of the summer season."[24] Among actors, Witherspoon was the chief beneficiary of the play's unforeseen popularity in summer stock.

To the extent that it has a theme at all, *George Washington Slept Here* is about how the purchase of a ramshackle farmhouse in Bucks Co., Pennsylvania is the means of bringing a middle-aged, married couple closer together. Newton and Annabelle Fuller are solidly middle-class and live on the Upper West Side of Manhattan. Thus buying this home in the country is really more than they can afford, especially when the locals—represented by wily hired hand Mr. Kimber—take every opportunity to gouge them.

Created by Jean Dixon on Broadway, Annabelle Fuller is an interesting character, because she is the sensible, levelheaded, practical half of the Fuller marriage, while her husband Newton is the naïve, romantic, and impractical one, a "city man afflicted with rural rhapsody." Annabelle is more sympathetic, too, than most of Witherspoon's married women characters, being far from a termagant. She is described in the stage directions as "an attractive woman in the forties, and no fool, to say the least." She is forceful, but also indulgent. Like Witherspoon herself, Annabelle hates the country. She is a wry commentator on her husband's foibles, in the fast-talking dame tradition of the 1940s. Annabelle even gets "*a little high*" in the third act.[25] There the comedy develops in a carnivalesque way when the Fullers, their guests, and hired help—thinking they have lost the house to an unsympathetic neighbor—actively set out to return it to its "original condition." One of the better devices is the use of the Fullers' insufferable and irrepressible teenage nephew Raymond to say out loud what everyone else is thinking.

On May 6, 1941, Witherspoon made her triumphant return to the East coast stage after a five-year absence, at the Windsor Theatre in the Bronx, New York, with the veteran comic actor J.C. Nugent playing her husband Newton. After a week, the production moved to the Flatbush Theatre, followed by week-long engagements at the Capitol Theatre in New Britain, Connecticut; the Garden Pier Theatre in Atlantic City, New Jersey; the Glen Rock Playhouse in Glen Rock, New Jersey; the Spa Theatre in Saratoga Springs, New York; ending the summer season the week of August 18 with the South Shore Players at the Town Hall in Cohasset, Massachusetts.

George Ross noted in his column "Broadway," that Witherspoon, "who has spent too much time in Hollywood is making her way back to the Rialto via the subway circuit." One of the ads read: "The Famous Stage & Screen Comedienne Cora Witherspoon in the Smash Broadway Comedy Hit...." Having seen the play in Flatbush, Robert Francis was highly approving in his review for the *Brooklyn Daily Eagle*. He thought the "Summer 'road show' ... seemed superior to its original Broadway production." Francis reported that it "has had a face-lifting which makes it an exceedingly amusing evening's entertainment": "Miss Witherspoon gives the long-suffering wife a spontaneous and humorous warmth." All in all, Francis felt the show should return to Broadway. Another reviewer wrote: "Cora Witherspoon is magnificent as the long suffering wife ... a role that fits her like a glove." When she got to Cohasset, it must have been gratifying to find herself a "guest star" on par with stars she had previously supported, like Ruth Chatterton and Grace George. Here the critic for the *Boston Globe* wrote that Witherspoon, "clever comedian that she is, draws many a laugh. She delivers her lines of fine sarcasm as neatly as a flounder fisherman operating at high tide." There had been a "large audience."[26]

An interview that summer in the *Quincy Patriot Ledger* describes her as being "back in her element, the theater, after an absence of two years during which accidents dogged her heels. First she fractured her knee, then broke her arm.... But now Miss Witherspoon has fully recovered." Boston drama critic Elliot Norton wrote in the *Boston Post*, that she played her role "with comic effect and authority." He noted that "the playhouse audience seems not only to admire her but also to have considerable genuine affection for her."[27]

Witherspoon had one last hurrah as Annabelle Fuller in May the following year, when she did *George Washington Slept Here* with the Cambridge Summer Theatre, as the first production of their third summer season. Jack Sheehan played Newton Fuller this time. According to one review: "Last night in Brattle Hall, Cora Witherspoon romped her way through 'George Washington Slept Here' and an appreciative audience roared with mirth." It was, in the words of this critic, "an auspicious occasion." The *Boston Herald* found that her interpretation of the role was "rather less venomous than the character of Anabelle is customarily played, but it is a becoming benignity and lends the play a warmer, more human quality." A.E. Watts of the *Boston Traveler* recorded that Witherspoon "has lost none of her ability to sink home each fat line and situation and she also did very well last night with an entirely new situation." When she had fallen backward, she "just grazed the couch and it really became a plop. She built the situation up from the floor until the customers believed she meant to take the distance dive." She and Jack Sheehan "team wonderfully."[28]

At the end of the summer season, an article in the *Milwaukee Sentinel* pointed out that "those who occasionally wonder idly about the lost, strayed or forgotten in the world of theater and films, might find the old, familiar faces in the Eastern summer theaters." The writer mentioned Witherspoon in a list with "a few more troupers keeping alive the tradition of the stage": "Diana Barrymore, Violet Heming, Paul Robeson, Jane Cowl, Peggy Wood, Estelle Winwood, Henry Hull, Cora Witherspoon, Grace George, Irene Slezak and Irene Purcell."[29]

On September 4, 1941, Witherspoon was signed by British producer Lee Ephraim "for one of the important roles" in *All Men Are Alike*, a two-act farce by British beginner Vernon Sylvaine, which had been a success London. Rehearsals were already underway. When the play opened at the Hudson Theatre on October 6, postponed from September 22, Witherspoon had been away from Broadway for five and a half years. This was the longest break in her stage career, but it paled in comparison with her stage husband Reginald Denny, who was returning to Broadway after an absence of 21 years.[30] Witherspoon played Thelma Bandle and Denny her middle-aged Lothario husband Alfred J. Bandle. The star of the show was veteran comedian Bobby Clark.

Witherspoon should possibly have waited a little longer for her comeback. *All Men Are Alike* got the worst reviews of any of her plays. The New York critics had a field day, as some highly select, though representative, quotes will demonstrate. Brooks Atkinson: "Mr. Silvaine's farce is terrible, and some people left early last evening, looking as if they thought they had detected an odor somewhere." Burns Mantle: "a liability washed up by the war.... It includes pursuing wives, pursuing military, comic deserters, exposed lingerie, slamming doors, comic servants, strip-tease humor, bedroom humor, bathroom humor, and, as noted, Bobby Clark.... Reginald Denny, Lillian Bond, and Cora Witherspoon, Gawd help her, work like beavers." Edgar Price described it as "one of the most complicated plots we have ever listened to. We couldn't begin to tell you what it is all about, but we will say that is has to do with spies, British soldiers and an English business man [Denny] who still likes to have his fling with the ladies, despite the fact that he is supposed to be a respectable married man." The show closed November 1, after only 32 performances.[31] Without Bobby Clark, it would not have lasted even that long.

For Witherspoon, 1942 began with the announcement that she was to have a role in the new Irving Caesar show *My Dear Public*, only her second musical comedy. One of America's "leading song writers," Caesar was best known for "Tea for Two" and "Just a Gigolo." This was his first attempt at producing. The music to *My Dear Public* was by

Caesar, Gerald Marks, and Samuel Lerner, while the book was by Caesar and Charles Gottesfeld. The director was Joseph Pevney, the dance director was Carl Randall, the settings were by Albert Johnson, and the costumes by Lucinda Ballard. The cast included Mitzi Green, John Buckmaster, Tamara, Joe Smith and Charles Dale (of Smith & Dale), the Revuers, the Martins, April Ames, Rose Brown, Carl Malden, Kitty Mattern, and specialty dancer Miriam LaVelle. As for the plot, according to the *Boston Globe*: "What story there is concerns a Byronic genius of the theater named Byron Bach [Buckmaster], whose actress friend Jean [Green], persuades a harassed producer, Barney Short [Smith], to produce Byron's revue, an opus which promises to be a distinguished flop." Witherspoon was featured as Daphne Drew "the producer's actress wife."[32]

Rehearsals were underway by February 5. The world premiere took place at the Shubert Theatre in New Haven, Connecticut, a month later. Further tryouts followed at the Colonial Theatre in Boston and at the Forrest Theatre in Philadelphia. Originally slated to open at the Broadhurst Theatre on March 16, the New York opening was postponed till March 23 and then till April 2. On March 21, the *New York Daily News* reported that there was "a little financial trouble." A few days later, the show's Broadway opening was cancelled, after the "Philadelphia critics were unfavorably inclined." According to the *New York Times*, Caesar hoped to be able to reopen the show and recoup some of the $80,000 that had been invested, but it was "not a certainty." In fact, *My Dear Public did* finally open on Broadway, but not until September 9, 1943. By then Witherspoon was no longer part of it, nor was anyone else in the original cast. Daphne Drew now had three songs and was played by Ethel Shutta.[33]

The reviews of the pre–Broadway tour indicate that the show had a raft of problems at this stage. After the world premiere in New Haven on March 5, 1942, the *Hartford Courant* wrote that *My Dear Public* was "pretty good bit by bit, but pretty bad along its length and breadth, and it is very hard to say whether it adds up into anything at all, yet.": "A zany book, rather funny if you are at all acquainted with the backstage side of theater goings-on, some very excellent specialties, some production ideas that are good but awkwardly developed, a lot of noisy and generally poor music and an unfortunate cast, is about the way the credits lie." According to the *Courant*, "Mitzi Green goes prettily to waste in no part at all" and "by and large, the acting cast, and singing and dancing choruses are inept." The paper qualified this broad condemnation by adding: "To the principals, Joe Smith and Cora Witherspoon, go gentle forgiveness … for all being fish out of water."[34]

In Boston, where the show spent a week starting March 9, the *Globe* observed that Caesar "has hired some excellent people," including Green, Witherspoon, and Buckmaster. "He neglected, sad to tell, to obtain a book as good as the people who act it, and dialogue that is really witty. So 'My Dear Public' must be candidly described as an entertainment whose best parts do not make a consistently amusing whole." "Cora Witherspoon's fine comic talent makes as much as possible out of the part of the producer's actress wife." *My Dear Public* "can boast some excellent moments, but at present it does not jell." The *Boston Herald* felt that the show "never makes up its mind whether to be a book show or a revue." Before Broadway, they "will need to do away with most of his book or rewrite it. As it is now, it serves chiefly to get in the actors' way." The *Boston Traveler* observed that "Joe Smith, Charles Dale and Cora Witherspoon struggle with dialogue which falls completely flat."[35]

Things were no better in Philadelphia, where *My Dear Public* opened on March 16 and played two weeks. After a week, Joy Hodges took over for Mitzi Green in the leading role. The *Camden Courier-Post* agreed with the *Boston Herald*, that "the production never quite makes up its mind whether it's to be a play or a musical. The story keeps getting in the way of the musical, and vice versa." There was "some comedy by a couple of old hands, Cora Witherspoon and Joe Smith." The *Philadelphia Inquirer* felt that "Cora Witherspoon helps out quite a bit as the wise wife of the producer."[36] She played Daphne Drew for the last time the day the show closed in Philadelphia on March 28, 1942.

During the summer of 1942, Witherspoon was engaged by the Cape Playhouse in Dennis, Massachusetts, which is still in operation and can call itself "the longest running professional summer theater in the country." British-born Broadway star Gertrude Lawrence was running the theater, while her husband Richard Aldrich was in the army. The resident director was Arthur Sircom. Witherspoon had played at the Cape before, and it was Sircom who directed back in 1935 when she did *A Touch of Brimstone* (aka *All Bow Down*) with Roland Young and a revival of *The Constant Wife* with Ethel Barrymore there. The members of the company this summer included Harry Ellerbe, Gregory Peck, Murial Williams, Otto Hulett, Richard Kendrick, Rowland Hogue, Marcel Journet, and Margery Maude.[37]

The sixteenth season began on July 6, 1942, with Maugham's *The Circle* starring Fritzi Scheff and Karen Morley. This was followed by week-long productions of *Rebound* starring Ruth Chatterton and her ex-husband Ralph Forbes; Kaufman and Hart's *You Can't Take It with You* starring Fred Stone and his daughter Paula Stone, where Witherspoon was featured as Penelope Sycamore; *The Duenna* starring Jimmy Savo, Dorothy Sands, and Tamara; Noël Coward's *Fallen Angels* starring Gertrude Lawrence in her only summer stage appearance, where Witherspoon was featured ("a high point of the season"; "Delightfully satisfying was the work of Cora Witherspoon as the baffled maid, Saunders"); *Jane Eyre* starring Sylvia Sidney and her husband Luther Adler; *The Bat* in which Witherspoon starred as Lizzie Allen with Dorothy Sands as Cornelia Van Gorder; and finally, *Philadelphia Story* starring Muriel Williams and Lili Damita.[38] The summer season at the Cape ended on August 29.

The revival of *You Can't Take It with You* was such a success, that it generated week-long engagements at the Flatbush Theatre the week of September 7 and at the Emery Auditorium in Cincinnati the week of October 5. Fred and Paula Stone were still starring as Grandpa Martin Vanderhof and Essie, and Witherspoon reprised her role as Penelope. The critics found it "a first-rate professional job in all respects." Witherspoon described her role as "almost a low comedy part": "she is fun to play as she flits from one idea to another without any continuity, simply jumping a mental hurdle."[39] This was a busy time for her. In addition to these stage engagements, she was doing a film and rehearsing a new Broadway show.

Though one columnist observed generously in 1943, that "there isn't a producer in the film center who wouldn't let Miss Witherspoon write her own ticket to get her into his pictures," *Follies Girl*, produced on the East coast for William Rowland Productions and directed by William Rowland, was the only film Witherspoon lent her talents to between 1940 and 1945. Actually, "wasted her talents on" might be a more accurate description. Production began in New York on October 5, 1942.[40] The film was originally 74 minutes long, but the DVD version is only 56. No wonder it seems disjointed! In fact, *Follies Girl* is just about the oddest mish mash you have ever seen. It ostensibly deals with the tribulations of big-haired heroine Wendy Barrie as a designer at the White Way

Costume Co. and her slowly developing romance with a handsome young soldier, Jerry Hamlin (Gordon Oliver), who turns out to be the son of the owner of the company. This semblance of a plot is really only an excuse for recreating a burlesque show in all its nubile, undressed, and terpsichorean aspects. It is an integrated show, too, as one of the dance numbers is performed by African Americans. There are no persons of color in the audience, though.

The millionaire financier J.B. Hamlin, played by Witherspoon's *George Washington Slept Here* co-star J.C. Nugent, is a henpecked husband, who seeks relief in going to burlesque shows and in the lectures of "Professor Peabody," who turns out to be a bottle of beer. Predictably, Witherspoon plays his pixilated, domineering wife, and the mother of Jerry. Witherspoon's big scene is in the finale, which is a party at her palatial home. She gets drunk on spiked punch and imagines she can sing. The opera company that is supposed to entertain has been purposely rerouted to New Jersey. Hearing this, she is surprisingly pleased: "C'mon on gang, we're taking over!." We get a few seconds of her shockingly bad attempt to sing opera, before a clarinet breaks in and a saxophone and the party is saved by some of the era's biggest band leaders. Witherspoon is looking quite well in a little black dress and large pearls and her hair is no longer white. She towers over everyone, as usual.

Witherspoon was able to squeeze in *Follies Girl* between playing *You Can't Take It with You* in Cincinnati and her next Broadway show. By early November 1942, she had joined the cast of *The Willow and I* by John Patrick, who would have a huge hit with the stage version of *The Teahouse of the August Moon* in the mid–1950s. At the time of this play's premiere, he was "driving an ambulance in Libya." Rehearsals started the week of October 19 under the direction of Donald Blackwell, who was also co-producer with Raymond Curtis and David Merrick.[41] After being tried out in Wilmington, Philadelphia, and Boston, the play opened at the Windsor Theatre in New York on December 10, 1942.

The most interesting thing about *The Willow and I* was the cast, which included several familiar Hollywood faces and one that would soon become familiar. Katharine Locke withdrew from one of the two leading roles early in the rehearsal period and was replaced by Joanna Roos. Roos in turn was replaced by Barbara O'Neil, before the Broadway opening. O'Neil had had a modest role in *Forsaking All Others* in 1933 and had, of course, rocketed to fame in 1939 in *Gone with the Wind*. Since then, she had begun to specialize in playing "women on the edge" in films like *All This, and Heaven Too*. Martha Scott was returning from Hollywood, where she had been since her "spectacular success" in *Our Town*.[42] Character actor Edward Pawley was also returning to Broadway from Hollywood, where he had spent the past decade. Finally, this was 26-year-old Gregory Peck's second Broadway play and followed close on the heels of his first, *The Morning Star* by Emlyn Williams, which only ran for 24 performances and closed October 3.

The Willow and I was one of those plot-heavy, fateful, and tortured psychological melodramas, like *Ethan Frome* and *Kings Row*. The *Camden Courier-Post* described it as "a strange mixture of Victorian sentimentality, Chekhov and Ibsen, with some Hollywood overtones." When the *Wilmington Morning News* critic wrote that "it is not a pleasant play," it was one of the understatements of the year. In retrospect, it sounds like one of those full-throated, finely feathered, Thanksgiving-sized turkeys, which should have had producers and backers running for the hills. I am going to let the *Courier-Post* summarize the outlandish plot:

The play opens in a small Southern town at the turn of the century and introduces the sisters, Bessie Sutro, played by Miss Roos [and later O'Neil], and Mara, the part played by Miss Scott. Bessie, the younger, is the bold one, Mara, a Victorian carry-over, gentle and ladylike. The lavender and old lace romance of Mara and Robin Todd [Peck], the handsome doctor, ends with a gunshot which robs Mara of her mind and launches her into a mental darkness lasting 25 years. It was with this shot that Bessie meant to end her own life because of her love for the doctor. With Mara a mental invalid, Bessie marries the doctor and lives a life of bitterness and remorse. Losing her husband, she clings to her son [Peck in a dual role], now grown to a replica of his father. Mara is restored to her senses by a thunderstorm to find herself an aging woman, her groom-to-be now her nephew. Mara dies.

Pawley played the two women's father, Theodore Sutro. Witherspoon portrayed their aunt, Millie Sutro, "shepherdess of the household," whose "sense of decorum gives the household its stability."[43] Aunt Millie was not mentioned in any of the review plot summaries. She was only in the first act, set in around 1900.

Linton Martin opined after the Philadelphia premiere: "As a study in the morbid, the neurotic, and the psychopathic, 'The Willow and I' has its points. As entertainment it hasn't." The *Camden Courier-Post* found that Witherspoon "gives skillful support," but *The Willow and I* was "no great shakes as a play." The reception was better in Boston. The *Boston Globe* thought it "an absorbing and for these days unusual drama," with Witherspoon "acidly effective in a too small role." The *Boston Herald* was equally polite, calling it "an unusual and decidedly interesting play," where "a spinster aunt is briskly played by Cora Witherspoon." The *Boston Traveler* felt that "Cora Witherspoon makes the most of brief appearances in the first act."[44]

The all-important verdict of the *New York Times* was that "every one tried; the misfortune lies in the fact that it did not quite succeed." Burns Mantle described *The Willow and I* as "as plotty a melodrama as we have seen recently." He thought it might make "a first-class second grade picture": "As drama I fear it is much too complicated and too obviously strained in a plot sense to excite popular interest, for all it is attractively staged and exceptionally well acted." He gave it two plus stars. Arthur Pollock was terse in his verdict, concluding that "the play is plush melodrama" and "the actors are all right." UP drama critic Jack Gaver felt that it "somehow fails to achieve the impact that you feel the author intended it to have and which it should have to be a worthy play." In summing up the first half of the 1942–43 season, Dale Harrison observed: "'The Willow and I' had the advantage of fine actresses like Martha Scott, Barbara O'Neil and Cora Witherspoon, plus a sound production, but it couldn't hang on, perhaps because today's audiences have not the patience to relax and enjoy a psychological drama."[45] The reviews make it clear that Harrison is placing the blame for the play's rapid demise on the wrong shoulders.

The Willow and I closed on January 2, 1943, after only 28 performances. A month and a half later, Witherspoon was cast in producer Vinton Freedley's new musical comedy *Dancing in the Streets*, which was to star Mary Martin. Martin had burst into fame singing "My Heart Belongs to Daddy" in Freedley's show *Leave It to Me!* in 1938. Other notable names in the *Dancing in the Streets* cast were Dudley Digges, Ernest Cossart, Mary Wickes, and Helen Raymond. The book and lyrics were by Howard Dietz, John Cecil Holm, and Matt Taylor and the music by Vernon Duke. Martin, Kay Aldridge, and Lucille Bremer played three of the eleven "girl secretaries" who invade the Washington home of retired admiral and "likeable old fussbudget" Downey Windrip (Digges).

The admiral has invited a group of young naval officers to share his home, so that he can "exert some desirable influence on the tactics of the war" and gets the unexpected and unwanted Naval Dept. secretaries instead.[46] Witherspoon played the admiral's wife, Mabel Windrop.

The show opened at the Shubert Theatre in Boston on Tuesday, March 23 for a two-week, pre–Broadway run, which was extended to three weeks total when the show moved to the Boston Opera House on April 5. According to the *Boston Globe*, "At its best, 'Dancing in the Streets' is pleasant and relaxing, but the comic lines and the tunes are mostly undistinguished, and the book is thin." The reviewer also felt that "the acidulous comic talents of Mary Wickes, Cora Witherspoon and Helen Raymond are not sufficiently utilized in their sketchy roles." The *Boston Herald* concluded that the show "must be set down as a disappointment" and averred that "in its present state a Broadway visit would be hazardous." Witherspoon and Jack Smart "work dutifully in rather meagre assignments." Tom Chase, reviewing for the Associated Press, wrote that "uninspired is the only polite word for the proceedings." He thought that Witherspoon, Raymond, and Wickes "deserve more than passing mention for their valiant efforts in minor roles."[47] Due to the problems indicated by the reviews, and despite playing to capacity audiences, *Dancing in the Streets* was closed temporarily for overhauling after the Boston run. It was never seen again.

They say there are no small parts, only small actors. No better evidence of the truth of this well-worn adage need be sought, than Witherspoon's efforts during a massive eight-month, 26-city tour she did between June 1943 and January 1944, supporting Sylvia Sidney in a dramatization of *Jane Eyre*. Witherspoon played Hannah, and even if you are a *Jane Eyre* fan you may be forgiven for having forgotten who she is. Hannah is the Rivers family maid. In the play version, she only appeared in the third act, which was partially set in Moor House, the Rivers home. Incidentally, the stage setting for this scene was considered "one of the best of the play": "The color is skillful, the contrast of costume and furniture done with artistry." In her large cotton cap and white apron, Hannah looked a lot like Patty in *Quality Street*.[48] Hannah was a small role indeed for an actress of Witherspoon's stature and experience. She showed her dimensions by the talent and spirit she invested in a tiny part, and she proved the respect and affection critics and audiences alike held for her in the warm reception her efforts received.

The Theatre Guild had first presented Helen Jerome's dramatization of *Jane Eyre* seven years earlier on a tour including Boston, Chicago, Milwaukee, and ending in Baltimore, with Katharine Hepburn in the title role. Critics who had seen both productions, consistently deemed Sidney's interpretation of Jane Eyre to be superior. Jerome had also been responsible for a successful dramatization of *Pride and Prejudice* seen on Broadway in 1935–36. Sidney's husband Luther Adler directed and played Edward Rochester in the new production. In 1938, the couple had had a whirlwind romance aboard the Queen Mary, got engaged before the ship docked in London, and were married there on arrival.[49]

The two leading players surrounded themselves with the following cast (in order of appearance; forward slashes indicate a change of actor during the tour): Mrs. Fairfax (Ellen Hall/Teresa Dale/Margaret Arrow); Leah, the Thornfield maid (Vergel Cook); Adele Verens (Lorna Lynn/Jean Ashworth/Valentine Perkins), Grace Poole (Teresa Dale/Mary Perry), the Maniac (Katherine Allen), Blanche Ingram (Mary McCormack), Lady Ingram (Frederica Going/Mary Scott/Dorothy Scott), Lord Ingram (J.W. Austin),

Diana Rivers (Ruth Gregory), Hannah (Witherspoon), and St. John Rivers (John Bara-grey/Edward Hunt).

The tour started June 7, 1943, with two weeks at the Plymouth Theatre in Boston and then progressed to Camden, Philadelphia, Washington, Detroit, Chicago, Mil-waukee, Omaha, Salt Lake City, Los Angeles, Long Beach, San Diego, Pasadena, San Francisco, Oakland, Sacramento, Portland, and Seattle, closing out the year in Helena, Montana, before seeing in the new year in Butte, followed by Minneapolis, Cleveland, Rochester, Ithaca, and Hartford, and coming to an end with two days at the Playhouse in Wilmington, Delaware. The stopovers ranged from one-night stands to six weeks in Chicago. It was finally over on January 29, 1944.

When reading the many reviews of the *Jane Eyre* tour, it is touching to notice the high regard with which Witherspoon was being held. For the older critics beyond the northeastern United States, this would have been the first time they saw her on stage since she toured with *The Constant Wife* in 1927–28. Some reviewers in more remote places would have been seeing her live for the first time, maybe having admired her work on the screen. Things got off to a rough start, though, at the premiere in Boston. The *Boston Globe* noted that "the production last night was a mixture of very good and rather inferior acting." According to the paper, the third act was delayed by supporting actors forgetting their lines and "no prompter was on hand to aid the groping actresses." With-erspoon was not mentioned positively in this review, and she *was* in the third act.... By the time they got to Detroit, though, one gets the impression she was stealing the show; or at least the third act. We can read in the Detroit papers, that she "has a small part in the third act which she does brilliantly," "gives fresh evidence of her dependableness as a sharp tongued servant," and is "towering ... as a homely, hearty and boisterously amus-ing moorland servant."[50]

Witherspoon continued to be mentioned, sometimes at surprising length, in a number of reviews. I would have liked to have quoted all these accolades, which must have warmed her heart, but let me restrict myself to the most informative and laudatory ones: "One of the best things about 'Jane Eyre' ... is the brief appearance in the last act of Cora Witherspoon disguised as a serving maid of the moors" (*Chicago Times*); "Mem-orable was the performance of Cora Witherspoon, veteran Broadway character actress, who appeared as a housekeeper in one scene. She made a small part stand out because of her complete feeling for the part of a good humored, sharp-tongued household retainer" (*Salt Lake Telegram*); "As Hannah, Cora Witherspoon, veteran actress, turned in an unforgettable performance" (*Pasadena Post*); Witherspoon "makes one of the clearest characterizations of the supporting cast. Her crispness and comedy are delightful, even if she isn't seen until the third act" (*San Francisco Chronicle*); "Especially noteworthy ... Cora Witherspoon as a kindly housekeeper" (*San Francisco Examiner*); "A thoroughly profitable evening in the theater with competent work from a number of subordinate players topped by Cora Witherspoon, who got the only bit of comedy the script per-mits" (*Oakland Tribune*); "Cora Witherspoon created a droll character in Hannah, the housekeeper who numbers herself as one of the family" (*Sacramento Bee*); "Sharing hon-ors with the leads was another veteran actress, Cora Witherspoon, who was delightful in the role of the ancient but devoted Hannah. She, too, has been seen in motion pic-tures, where she gained great success for her presentation of grandiose dames" (*Helena Independent-Record*); "The salty portrayal of Hannah in the last act by Cora Wither-spoon provides one of the play's best acting bits" (*Minneapolis Star*); "Cora Witherspoon creates a sharp and effective character of the housekeeper in the briefly glimpsed Rivers home" (*Cleveland Plain Dealer*); "Cora Witherspoon gave a warm, lively interpretation of Hannah, as could be expected." (*Ithaca Journal*); "Cora Witherspoon's gusty Hannah brought forth both laughter and applause" (*Wilmington Morning News*). And finally this: "Miss Witherspoon, one of the best character actresses in America, makes a little gem of the character and she and Miss Sidney have the only authentic accents in the play."[51]

This production of *Jane Eyre* never made it to Broadway. A dramatization by Huntington Hartford had a brief run at the Belasco Theatre in the spring of 1958 and a musical version was presented at the Brooks Atkinson Theatre in 2000–2001. The film version starring Joan Fontaine and Orson Welles opened in New York on February 3, 1944, just days after the stage tour ended, and was in general release April 7. There was no Hannah in any of these stage and screen versions of Charlotte Brontë's classic novel.

If Witherspoon thought she was done with touring after sweeping the country in *Jane Eyre*, she was mistaken. The popular film comedienne ZaSu Pitts had finally found a workable stage vehicle. She had made her Broadway debut at the Royale Theatre on January 5, 1944, two days after her 50th birthday and, as it happened, on Witherspoon's 54th, in a "melodramatic farce" called *Ramshackle Inn*. It was the work of George Batson, who was currently serving as a sergeant in the Signal Corps, so he missed his Broadway debut as a playwright. The reception of his play had been lukewarm at best. The critic for the *New York Times* wrote that *Ramshackle Inn* "succeeds in being not very funny and not very exciting, which are two strikes against it in the Broadway league." He observed that "the carnage through murder and/or mayhem is enough for half a dozen plays." He felt forced to conclude that Pitts "cannot rescue the evening": "Miss Pitts has made her Broadway debut, but she will have better luck later."[52] As it happened, Pitts' only other Broadway show was nine years later playing Lizzie Allen in a revival of *The Bat* with Lucile Watson that flopped. In private life, Pitts was Mrs. John Woodall and had two grown children from her first marriage.

Pitts's Broadway bow, then, took place while Witherspoon was still doing *Jane Eyre* on tour, though the tour was over by the end of January. In mid–February, Ruth Gates left the cast of *Ramshackle Inn* and, for the second and final time, Witherspoon stepped in as a replacement, rather than originating the role on Broadway. She started February 15, and Margaret Callahan took over Ruth Holden's role the same day.[53]

Ramshackle Inn was "a melodramatic farce dealing with a spinsterish Vermont librarian who invests her savings in an old tavern near Gloucester." It was also described in one review as "a corny game of peek-a-boo and hide-and-seek in which a Vermont spinster plays 'Scotland Yard bloomer girl' and outsleuths a G woman assigned to clean up a black market liquor gang headed by 'the big boss.' There are two murders, the threat of a St. Valentine's Day Chicago massacre, and three sluggings in three acts." The setting was "Ye Olde Colonial Inn" (locally known as "Dracula's Gardens") at the Gloucester, Massachusetts, seaside on a stormy night. Pitts played Belinda Pryde, a high-strung ex-librarian of 20 years standing and a spinster from East Ipswich, Vermont. Tired of her eventless life, Belinda has bought the inn from Mame Phillips (Witherspoon) for $3,000, based on an ad in a magazine and after reading *Grand Hotel*. Belinda has a "life suitor" in the Commodore (played by Ralph Theodore). Unbeknownst both to Mame and Belinda, a gang of bootleggers in cahoots with a shady local banker are using the inn as a base for their illicit business activities. Belinda unravels the murder mystery, "aided no end by an F.B.I. glamour girl (Callahan), and in spite of a bonehead local constable (Harlan Briggs)," and reaps the $5,000 reward for capturing the crooks. In one of her best lines, she describes herself as "Scotland Yard in bloomers." The play had a running time of "scarcely two hours."[54]

There is some further clarification about Witherspoon's role in the reviews, where Mame is described as "the red-headed, ex-owner of 'Ramshackle Inn,' who likes her drinks and her memories." Claudia Cassidy of the *Chicago Tribune* wrote that Witherspoon played "a tippling landlady whose sole interest outside the bottle is clearing the name of her son, who is released from prison after a false conviction for theft just in time to be accused of murder." She also called her "a small time Texas Guinan."[55] The young actor playing Mame's son Bill kept changing. In Chicago, it was a 29-year-old Richard Basehart, who had not yet made his film debut. Off and on, the ingénue of the company was Mary Barthelmess, daughter of silent picture star Richard Barthelmess. Harlan Briggs had played Witherspoon's husband Virgil Miller in *Beg, Borrow or Steal* (1937), the coroner in *Charlie Chan's Murder Cruise* (1940), and Dr. Stall in *The Bank Dick* (1940). Witherspoon had no common film credits with Pitts.

It turns out Witherspoon needed the work. In a widely reprinted AP bulletin dated March 9, 1944, we can read: "Cora Witherspoon, stage and screen actress, has filed a voluntary petition in bankruptcy in Federal Court listing assets of $150 and liabilities of $14,639. She has appeared in 'Daddy Long Legs,' 'Jezebel' and 'Ramshackle Inn' on the stage and has had many movie roles." June 3 marked the 175th performance of the show, which closed in New York on July 8, after 216 performances. It was time for the tour, which Witherspoon went along with for nearly five months and 14 cities. It started in Washington, D.C., two days after the play closed in New York. From there it went to Chicago, St. Louis, Columbus, Newark, Zanesville, Cincinnati, Milwaukee, Davenport, Des Moines, Sioux City, St. Joseph, Wichita, and finally Los Angeles, where Witherspoon left the tour in early December; or, rather, the tour left her. If the touring schedule seems a little erratic, that may be because it was partially determined by astrology. In mid–July, the cast nearly had to go to Chicago without Witherspoon, after she discovered that the hotel they were staying in would not admit her dog "Lucky" and "forthwith refused to budge from New York." Press agent Lefty Miller "put on a crying act before the recalcitrant hotel manager—and Lucky got a place."[56]

Clearly, from a commercial standpoint the tour was a big success. Pitts packed them in. Sixteen hundred people attended the opening night in St. Louis; 2,700 people in Davenport, Iowa; 2,500 in Des Moines. The notices were no better than the play deserved. *Ramshackle Inn* was tellingly described as "the wildest potpourri of stock material I've ever seen lumped into play form" (*Washington Evening Star*); "very nearly a one-woman show in spite of the large and active cast" (*Chicago Sun*); "not the type of play that one would think of nominating for the Critics' Award, but it has lots of laughs, lots of suspense and lots of ZaSu Pitts" (*St. Louis Star and Times*); "a play that never remains poised long enough for anyone to absorb it" (*Los Angeles Times*); "an 'Arsenic and Old Lace' in baby pants" (*Los Angeles Evening Citizen News*); and "as pleasantly moronic as the customary expression of its star" (*Los Angeles Daily News*).[57]

Witherspoon received many flattering notices and could clearly hold her own, even against a comic veteran like Pitts. Witherspoon "as the retiring hotel owner and a mild dipsomaniac, adds to the merriment" (*Chicago Daily Times*). "Cora Witherspoon and Harlan Briggs are experienced comedians who could hold their own in a circus of clowns" (*St. Louis Star and Times*). "[A] lady with a none-too-flattering past, she lends a lot of comedy to the proceedings and wins her share of laughs" (*Davenport Daily Times*). Witherspoon, Downing, and Briggs "worked valiantly for laughs but the play's crippled dialog and trite situations defeated their best intentions" (*Rock Island Argus*). "You get the idea Cora Witherspoon knows the difference between Scotch and Bourbon the first time you see her" (*Quad-City Times*). "[T]here was another film veteran in 'Ramshackle Inn,' Miss Witherspoon, a character actress of much ability, renowned for raucous and undignified dowager roles" (*Des Moines Register*). "Most of the others in the cast were very good, especially Cora Witherspoon, who played the role of a battered hotel operator—a witty character not too lowbrow, but low enough" (*St. Joseph News-Press*).[58]

Finally, a self-professed fan of Pitts ended up devoting more space in her review to Witherspoon, who "came in for more than her share of laughs": "She gave an admirable performance as the rather rattle-brained ex-proprietress with a healthy 'yen' for a good drink any time and a desire to 'get away to a new start' with her son recently released from prison for taking the rap for something he didn't do, as she put it. The audience expected a laugh every time she came on the scene and they were not disappointed for she always came through, delivering her lines in a most amusing manner."[59]

On November 5, 1944, Maude Witherspoon's longtime companion Anna Venables Miller died of bronchopneumonia and myocardial failure in Hotel Dieu Hospital in El Paso, Texas, after being hospitalized for six days. She was 78. Witherspoon was on tour with *Ramshackle Inn* and played the Arcadia Theatre in Wichita, Kansas, the following day. Maude and Annie's son Warren V. Miller accompanied the body to New Orleans for burial in Metairie Cemetery. Maude and Annie had made a life together for more than 30 years.[60]

Ramshackle Inn may have been a ramshackle vehicle to tour the country in, especially after the relatively smooth ride of *Jane Eyre*, but it actually conveyed Witherspoon right back into the movie business. This happy result may also have been a cumulative effect of both her recent stage appearances in Los Angeles. In October 1943, she spent four weeks in *Jane Eyre* at the Biltmore Theatre in Los Angeles and was "noticed" by Edwin Schallert, who had reviewed so many of her films. Then, in mid–November 1944, she was back at the Biltmore in *Ramshackle Inn* and was mentioned positively by Schallert and several other local critics. Schallert wrote: "Cora Witherspoon is gratifyingly present, since she is a capable actress in almost any role."[61] These appearances would have reminded producers she was still working and available, after she had not been part of the movie colony for four years, an eternity in Hollywood. After *Ramshackle Inn* closed in Los Angeles, Witherspoon left the tour and was replaced by Helen MacKellar, no doubt to be able to accept the several film roles on offer.

The first of these was a part in *Colonel Effingham's Raid*, which started production at Twentieth Century–Fox immediately, in early December 1944. As we recall, Witherspoon had last worked at Fox in early 1940, when she did *I Was an Adventuress* and *Charlie Chan's Murder Cruise* there. Clearly, the studio was glad to have her back four years after her narcotics arrest and removal to the East.

Colonel Effingham's Raid stars Charles Coburn as a lifelong military man, who retires to his native Fredericksville, Georgia. He soon discovers that his hometown needs his powers of persuasion and civic zeal to unmask graft and corruption and to turn things around. The critic for the *New York Times* correctly pointed out that "this is Mr. Coburn's show." He also thought that "genial is the word for this film." Today we could probably think of some other, less benign descriptive terms for it, though. At the same time, it is giving this satirical comedy too much credit to suggest that it has any clear, unitary, or systematic ideological message—reactionary, racist, paternalist, conservative, or whatever—that makes it worse than a whole run of dramas and comedies set in the South during slavery, Reconstruction, or the Jim Crow era. Even on its release, *Colonel Effingham's Raid* was not taken seriously, even as a satire. Jay Carmody in the *Washington Evening Star* wrote of the film that "it clutches at meaning as a bobby-soxer for Van Johnson's necktie, but a cub reporter on PM would not be deceived by the result. After its last noble speech, 'Col. Effingham's Raid' represents not much more than a vehicle for Charles Coburn, who rides it comfortably, and an opportunity for producer-writer Lamar Trotti to get some angry words off his typewriter."[62]

In the midst of the small-town politicking and social maneuvering in the powerful and wealthy class of Fredericksville, we find Witherspoon's patrician character Clara Meigs (*née* Breckenbridge). Clara is one of Col. Effingham's childhood friends and current supporters, particularly in his crusade to save the historic old courthouse from being torn down and Confederate Monument Square being renamed after a carpetbagger. On meeting her again after many years, Effingham says she is "Still the finest figure in Georgia." She responds in kind: "I declare, I don't know how you ever escaped marriage." They used to be at dancing school together, as was her late husband, Charlie Meigs. According to Mrs. Meigs, the Colonel reminds her of General Lee, "if he had a beard" (Coburn, that is), which makes no sense at all. In other words, Mrs. Meigs is yet another upper-class flibbertigibbet in the Witherspoon repertoire; a modest part and one with no real function in the film, even as comic relief.

Producer Lamar Trotti believed that "every small part in a screen drama is of major importance and must be cast as carefully as are the principal roles." An article in a Los Angeles newspaper pointed out that in casting *Colonel Effingham's Raid* he had "drawn heavily on the ranks of the film city's top scene stealers to interpret the small town characters of the Barry Fleming story." More specifically: "Cora Witherspoon's authoritative versions of small town women of limited mental powers brought her into the 'Effingham' cast for the spot of the head of the United Daughters of the Confederacy." She had never worked for Trotti before. Though *Colonel Effingham's Raid* was the first of Witherspoon's new slate of films from the mid–1940s to be produced, it was the fourth to be released. The delay was due to an overproduction of movies at Twentieth Century–Fox.[63] Production wrapped in early February 1945, but the film was not released until a year later.

In the final, intermittent phase of her film career, Columbia was Witherspoon's most frequent employer. *Over 21* was her first film at that studio, where she did six of her 12 films between 1945 and 1953. Production started on January 9, 1945, under the direction of Charles Vidor. *Over 21* was based on "Ruth Gordon's featherweight comedy about an overage soldier and the little woman who prods him through Officer Candidate School while dealing with life in a Florida bungalow court."[64] Irene Dunne stars as Polly Wharton, a bestselling author and journalist determined to play the housewife and support her man when he goes into the army, while she clearly deserves to wear the pants in the family and should not be hiding her light under an army helmet. As her leading man, she had Alexander Knox. Alexander who? Sure, there was a war on, but they might as well have cast Gomer Pyle. Charles Coburn plays a wily newspaper editor hell-bent on luring Dunne away from dreary domestic life and back to where the real

Striking a characteristically coy and flirtatious pose, Witherspoon tries to feed a strawberry to a willing Charles Coburn in *Over 21* (Sidney Buchman Ent./Columbia, 1945), which starred Irene Dunne as a best-selling writer who decides to dedicate herself to army life when her husband, played by Alexander Knox, enlists in the army during World War II. Witherspoon plays the camp commander's mother-in-law, who is a fan of Dunne's books. Coburn plays a newspaper editor, trying to lure Dunne back to her desk in a Hildy Johnson–Walter Burns type situation. In addition to the strawberries, the fish has also been removed from Dunne's and Knox's over-filled refrigerator to enable the hosts to dislodge some ice for drinks. In the film, Witherspoon eats a strawberry herself, but does not offer one to Coburn.

action is. Static and stagey, this tedious and talkative film takes place almost entirely in one, very drab set: the living room of Dunne's and Knox's camp bungalow #26D at Palmetto Court in Tetley Field, Florida.

Witherspoon portrays yet another elegant, genteel dowager. This one is called Mrs. Gates, is the mother of Lee Patrick (who was only 11 years her junior), and the mother-in-law of the camp commander, Colonel Foley (Charles Evans). There is a running gag about people thinking Witherspoon is Evans's wife, rather than his mother-in-law. Mrs. Gates first appears at the grocery store 52 minutes into the film and recognizes Dunne, as they both reach for the same item on the shelf. She is a fan and so is her daughter, so she asks if they may call on Dunne at her home. Dunne says anytime. In her next and longest scene, Witherspoon shows up with Patrick and Evans, while Coburn is on his first surprise visit to the camp. It is all very convivial and adds a little life to this lifeless film. Mrs. Gates appears intermittently after that, usually with her daughter and son-in-law in tow. In one scene, Witherspoon is dressed in an incredible hat and matching muff, which look like an explosion of confetti.

The film was released July 25, 1945, so Edwin Schallert of the *Los Angeles Times* felt it was "belated" now that "peace hovers." Schallert, who had not reviewed a film with Witherspoon in it in five years, had a word for her "among the satisfactory, though more or less subsidiary company." Clearly, the critics were happy to see Witherspoon back in her element, and she received more mentions than the size of the part would normally warrant. Another *Los Angeles* critic thought "Lee Patrick and Cora Witherspoon are amusing as a couple of celebrity hounds." Harold V. Cohen felt the screen version was "a let-down." There were "a number of good minor performances here," though, including "Mr. Charles Evans as the pompous colonel and Miss Cora Witherspoon as his flibberti-gibbety mother-in-law." Edith Lindemann wrote: "The picture is keyed for laughs. Not the least are the contributions of Lee Patrick as the colonel's wife and Cora Witherspoon as her mother, who present sharply satirical portraits of army socialites." Bosley Crowther of the *New York Times* rightly dismissed the story as "a thin bit of artificial fluff."[65]

Production on *Colonel Effingham's Raid* at Fox was no sooner over in early February 1945, than shooting on a film called *Young Widow* started at Desilu Studios for Hunt Stromberg Productions. Witherspoon's role was limited to the early part of the film, though, so she may not have been needed from the start. To complicate matters, she was also working on *Over 21* at Columbia at this time. She had not been this busy in films since her first years as a contract player at MGM. Edwin Schallert commented in his column for April 23, 1945, that this was Witherspoon's "first role in the movies in months." His generous explanation was that she "has been appearing in the stage plays 'Jane Eyre' and 'Ramshackle Inn.'"[66] He must have known that Witherspoon had been gone from Hollywood for years, not months, and the reason why too.

Witherspoon and Connie Gilchrist only appear in the initial sequence of *Young Widow*, where the "young widow," bodacious Jane Russell, who also happens to be a journalist, returns to her ancestral Virginia manse, which looks very much like a famous Southern plantation, but which she refers to incongruously as a "farm." Russell is mourning the death of her husband in World War II and trying to get back on her feet. Witherspoon plays the snobbish, feminine, impractical, and orderly Aunt Emeline and Gilchrist is the folksy, masculine, practical, and untidy Aunt Cissie. On the mess in Cissie's room, Emeline comments that "our mother would turn in her grave." Cissie in turn refers to Emeline as "that bluenose sister of mine." Emeline has been married, while Cissie is a spinster.

Burying herself on the farm turns out not to be the solution. Russell leaves the farm 17 minutes into the film, and we do not see or hear from Witherspoon or Gilchrist again. Their efforts here received scant notice. Mildred Martin observed that "Connie Gilchrist and Cora Witherspoon fill in as Jane's aunties back in ol' Virginny." Mildred Stockard thought that "Connie Gilchrist and Cora Witherspoon, as Jane's aunts down in Virginia, are sheer caricatures." "All in all, it is a dreary picture," she opined.[67]

While *Over 21* was her first and best opportunity at Columbia, when she rebooted her film career in early 1945, Witherspoon also made a brief, uncredited appearance that year in Columbia's *She Wouldn't Say Yes*. Rosalind Russell plays a psychiatrist who faces the perennial choice for women of her day between marriage and a career and has to hold off the advances of a would-be mate with clear stalker tendencies for an interminable hour and a half. Witherspoon has a single scene at one hour and 15 minutes, as

Rosalind Russell, in her second film, *Young Widow* (Hunt Stromberg Prod., 1946), regards the pancakes with a melancholy air at the kitchen table with her two aunts, Witherspoon and Connie Gilchrist (far right), and their maid Louise Beavers. Never one to take herself too seriously, Russell rendered the best verdict on the film, when she quipped that "the young widow should have died with her husband." The two classic comediennes were wasted in this overlong home front film about a, you guessed it, young widow and her gradual return to life after her husband's death in World War II.

Mrs. Peterson, a dissatisfied, upper-middle-class wife on Russell's psychiatrist's couch, who has had a revelation that "I was more like a policeman than wife. It's all been my fault, hasn't it?" This sets off Russell's own dubious realization that she may have thrown away the man she loves forever. Naturally, Witherspoon's uncredited performance was not mentioned in the reviews. I do want to quote this observation, though, from the *New York Times*, about the film in general: "Columbia has provided Miss Russell with a sumptuous apartment, smart wardrobe, and all the rest—everything, in fact, except what was needed most, some really funny lines and situations."[68]

On August 6, Witherspoon was back at Republic Studios for her second and final film there. *I've Always Loved You* starred Philip Dorn and Catherine McLeod and was directed by Frank Borzage. Witherspoon played Edwina Blythe, the wealthy endower of a four-year scholarship for young pianists. She only appears in the opening scene of the film, which is set in her palatial Philadelphia home. Ms. Blythe is seen auditioning young potential recipients of her scholarship, with maestro Leopold Goronoff (Dorn) listening attentively. This brief, unremarkable dowager role is her usual mix of fawning and frowning. Witherspoon's hair is badly permed for such a rich woman and the Technicolor brings out its mousy brown color. Her lilac gown, though, is lovely. The only thing notable about "this silly, mawkish film" is that it was the first Technicolor film produced by Republic.

Its release was delayed due to hold-ups at the Technicolor plant.[69] Though production ended on October 25, the film did not hit the cinemas till late August the following year.

Nineteen forty-six was the last reasonably busy year of Witherspoon's acting career on stage and screen. Her first film role of the year was in a Universal comedy starring Joan Davis, *She Wrote the Book*, which was about as offbeat as its female star. Davis had been in *Just Around the Corner*, but she had no meaningful interaction with Witherspoon there. *She Wrote the Book* had the distinction of being Gloria Stuart's last film until 1982. She plays the wife of the dean of the college where Witherspoon and Joan Davis work and the author of the scandalous "tell all" autobiography *Always Lulu*. Witherspoon had played Stuart's mother in *The Lady Escapes*. Ten years later, Stuart is almost unrecognizable with long dark hair. Witherspoon is unrecognizable, too, in her few brief scenes, as a college teacher in conference with her colleagues at Croydon College, her thick, dark hair gathered in a quite elaborate bun at the nape of the neck.

Hedda Hopper reported in her column the first week of March, that Witherspoon had been tested for the role of Cousin Cora in *Life with Father* at War-

Witherspoon's role as a garrulous patient in *She Wouldn't Say Yes* (Columbia, 1945), starring Rosalind Russell as her psychiatrist, was little more than a cameo. Yet Witherspoon had thought her film career was over when she left Hollywood under a cloud in late 1940, and here she was back in the thick of things only five years later. Granted, Mrs. Peterson was an uncredited role, but Witherspoon got a better opportunity in *Over 21* in what appears to have been a three-picture deal at Columbia, that also included a modest mother role in *Dangerous Business*.

ner Bros. ZaSu Pitts and Billie Burke were among the many actresses who had a shot at the role.[70] It ultimately went to Witherspoon's *Ramshackle Inn* co-star.

In mid–August 1946, it was announced that Witherspoon was going into the revival of Ben Hecht and Charles MacArthur's classic crime reporter comedy *The Front Page*.[71] After a tryout at the Shubert Theatre in New Haven, the play opened at the Royale Theatre on September 4, directed by MacArthur himself. This was the first revival on Broadway since the original production back in 1928, but there had been two film versions in the interim: one under the original title from 1931 and *His Girl Friday* from 1940. Witherspoon was to play Mrs. Grant, a classic mother-in-law role that had been created on Broadway by Jessie Crommette, had been played by Effie Ellsler in the original film version, and most recently by Alma Kruger (as Mrs. Baldwin) in *His Girl Friday*.

The revival, which starred Lew Parker as Hildy and Arnold Moss as Walter Burns, was a moderate success. The reviews more mostly positive and affectionate towards the play and a little more mixed with regard to the current production. Brooks Atkinson noted in the

New York Times, that "the performance put on at the Royale last evening is a thoroughly uproarious piece of skullduggery and worth a lot of laughing at." He found "there are a lot of able actors making gutterish mischief throughout the evening." Witherspoon was recorded as "acting a blowsy mother of the bride with shrewish temper." Atkinson concluded that this classic pressroom play was "still a racy piece of sound theatrical fooling."[72]

The *Brooklyn Citizen* found *The Front Page* "still remains the best play about the Fourth Estate," though the current production was "not especially praiseworthy": "There is much to be desired of the cast; ditto of the direction, which is spotty and uneven." The tempo was "indecisive," "either too fast or too slow." One reviewer found Witherspoon "comically believable as Hildy's prospective mother-in-law." She was also singled out, because she, among others, did "fine work" and "kept the ball bouncing nicely," resulting in "an evening of moderately good fun." *The Front Page* was Witherspoon's 36th and final show on Broadway. It lasted 79 performances and closed on November 9, 1946.[73]

Witherspoon's only known professional activity in 1947 was five weeks working in summer stock between July 22 and August 31. The first two weeks, she supported the original Broadway "Mama" Mady Christians and "Papa" Richard Bishop, as Aunt Jenny in *I Remember Mama*, first at the Flatbush Theatre and then at the Windsor Theatre in the Bronx. Aunt Jenny was the jolly aunt and had been portrayed by Ruth Gates on Broadway and would be played by Hope Landin in the 1948 film version starring Irene Dunne. Only Robert Keith was featured, as Uncle Chris.[74]

Those two weeks in Brooklyn and the Bronx were followed by three weeks in a new comedy called *Profile* by the brothers Charles and Michael Robinson. *Profile* used the familiar device of the Connecticut house party to bring together a promising American interior decorator, her American lover, and the "other man," "a Soviet journalist over here with the U.N." Faye Emerson starred as the "shrewd young career girl," Edmond Ryan played "a bright and personable young writer from Maine," and Herbert Berghof the "typically smart, tough Muscovite."[75]

Profile had its world premiere at the Cape Playhouse in Dennis, Massachusetts, on August 11, 1947, and was directed by its resident director Arthur Sircom, whom Witherspoon had worked with at the Cape both in the summer of '35 and the summer of '42. A week in Dennis was followed by a week with the North Shore Players in Marblehead, Massachusetts, and a week at the Spa Summer Theatre in Saratoga Springs, New York. Emerson was currently married to Franklin Delano Roosevelt's son Elliott, though the relationship was on the rocks and would end in divorce in 1950. Roosevelt could not make it to the Dennis premiere but attended the one in Marblehead.[76]

Witherspoon played Fannie Clarke. Cyrus Durgin of the *Boston Globe* recorded after the Dennis premiere: "For comic lines delivered briskly and with the bite of lemon juice, there are Cora Witherspoon as a sharp-tongued hat designer and Morton L. Stevens as an equally heavy-dough comic strip creator." The third act was a disaster, though, according to Durgin: "That third act will have to be jacked up and extensively repaired if an attempt is made on Broadway." When Durgin returned to see the show at Marblehead, he found that it "runs considerably more smoothly than when it opened at the Cape Playhouse at Dennis last week. No major revisions have yet been made. The third act, though tighter in performance, still remains bad and in need of much rewriting." The critic found that leading man Ryan, Witherspoon "as the garrulous hat designer," and Berghof "are all deeper and smoother in their roles."[77] The play never made it to New York with or without a repaired third act.

After these brief stage outings in 1947, Witherspoon, who was only 57, went into unofficial retirement in Las Cruces, New Mexico. She would never act in the East again and would not be back on the screen until 1951. The year of 1948 would be the lost year in Witherspoon's biography, in which she was not engaged in any professional activities, nor was she mentioned in the press. She simply disappeared from public view. In 1949, there is evidence that she was living with her sister in Las Cruces, New Mexico. In late August, she was observed at a performance of John Van Druten's *There's Always Juliet* given by a local drama group called the Picacho Players and found it "most enjoyable." On October 9, 1949, there was a front-page feature article on Witherspoon in the *Las Cruces Sun-News* titled "Well Known Actress of Stage, Screen and Radio Resides Here." After a familiar run-down of her career, she is described as living "right here in Las Cruces" with her sister. Witherspoon expresses a predilection for fried chicken, watermelon, and fried bananas. The yellow rose is her favorite flower and honeysuckle her favorite scent. Her sister has lived in Las Cruces for 30 years and Witherspoon has visited her "often from time to time." "'Now I seem to be becoming a Las Crucen, too,'" she says. In December that year, she was described in the same paper as "visiting her sister Miss Maude Witherspoon."[78] So ended the turbulent 1940s.

7

Las Cruces Sunset

1950–57

"My dear, if I had to do it over again, I wouldn't change
a thing—I'd portray my silly society women, my second leads,
and my blue-stockinged matron parts just the same."[1]

For years prior to moving there permanently, Las Cruces, New Mexico, had been Witherspoon's safe harbor in the storm. By the time she found herself a permanent resident, I suspect that emotionally, physically, and probably also financially, she had come to the end of her rope. She sought shelter in the place that came closest to being home, the place where her sister Maude had lived for decades. She had said in an interview back in 1937: "It seems to me that of all fates, none is quite so bad as to be dependent on others in old age. I'm deathly afraid of insecurity." We do not know how needy or dependent Witherspoon was at this point. Clearly, though, Maude was in a position to help her sister towards the end of her life, in a way she had not supported her when she was a child. In an interview in 1968, Maude wanted to make it clear that her sister always had her own home in New York City or Hollywood, though she visited Las Cruces frequently: "When her health failed, she came here and died in my house."[2]

Maude was different from Cora; she kept her house literally and metaphorically in order. Maude had worked hard and supported herself all her life, even before her mother died. After moving to Los Cruces, she had embarked on a new career in real estate, buying and refurbishing old, run-down properties and selling them for a profit, long before "flipping" became a familiar term. She wanted something to do that would keep her outdoors. In the 1930s and into the '40s, she even owned and operated her own dairy. She owned her own home too (something her sister never did), which was estimated to be worth $5,500 in 1930, but only $3,500 in 1940, after the depreciation in property values during the depression. Maude was a capable bridge player and was committed to working for her local branch of the Humane Society. She also wrote poetry.[3]

Seeing her distinctive figure at the market two years before her death, a journalist charged over to the elderly woman to ask who she was. "And as I suspected," wrote "Lumarion" in her column "In Our Town" for the *Las Cruces Sun-Times*, "Miss Maude L. Witherspoon, 414 W. Las Cruces, was something else again." She paints a vivid picture of Witherspoon's sister at the end of her long life. "Tall and erect, her eyes look out clearly and levelly from behind great black horn-rimmed glasses. She dresses in the mode of the pre–1920s. Skirts down to shoetops. Fresh, neat shirtwaists with long sleeves and high neckline, and little bows under the collar." She drives an "old reddish-brown

Willis Overland Jeep wagon dating back to the '40s": "Its driver is in full control of the wagon and her own faculties. At 86, Miss Maude is a marvelous driver." At the end of her life, Maude lived alone on W. Las Cruces Ave. with her two German Shepherds. She commented that "our love of dogs was the only thing my sister and I had in common.... I am a businesswoman, she was an actress and a movie star. I never was interested in clothes, she always looked like a fashion plate. But both of us liked animals and always owned dogs."[4]

Even though Maude was eight years older, she survived Cora by 13 years, and died on June 6, 1970, at the age of 88. She was buried in the family plot in Metairie, though her name is not on the headstone. Maude was the last cousin to die on the Witherspoon side and the second to last on the Bell side. She left a trust fund for her dogs "Fritz" and "Hilda," and her will stipulated that they should go on living at 414 W. Las Cruces Ave. with a caretaker for the remainder of their lives.[5]

It was ironic that a city lover like Cora Witherspoon ended her days in Las Cruces. In 1950, it had a population of 12,325 and was as peaceful and quiet, spread out and wide open to the sky, as any fair-sized town could be. There would have been few of the city sounds she loved so well. The Witherspoon sisters lived in a quiet, established residential neighborhood just a few blocks west of Main Street and just east of Pioneer Women's Park. Maude had lived in her 1,400 square foot, two-bedroom Craftsman style home at 414 W. Las Cruces Ave. since she and Annie Miller moved to Las Cruces in around 1920. In fact, they may have built the house, as it dates from 1920. The property was a third of an acre. At the back, there was a Spanish Mission style bungalow, which I am guessing was built as a home for Witherspoon. Her obituary in a local newspaper mentions her "making her home alone in an apartment on the property of her sister, Miss Maude Witherspoon."[6]

Despite her retirement in 1947, Witherspoon kept on working intermittently in films and on the stage until 1955. She turned 60 on January 5, 1950. It was her last big birthday. Five months later, she found herself on the lot at Paramount, where she had never worked in her heyday. The job came about, once again, through the good offices of her longtime friend, the writer Charles Brackett, who was now working as a producer. According to the *Los Angeles Times*, which announced that she had been in cast in the film on May 28, she had been "spending time on a Texas ranch." One article claimed that Witherspoon was being brought out of retirement, after four years, by the same producer who had originally brought her to Hollywood in 1936. This was only partially true. Brackett had been a writer on *Piccadilly Jim*, not a producer, but he had suggested Witherspoon for the role of Nesta Pett. His new project at Paramount was called *The Mating Season*, based on an original screenplay by himself, Walter Reich, and Richard L. Breen, and was to be directed by Mitchell Leisen, whom Witherspoon had not worked with before. Production on the film began in mid–May 1950. According to the *Brooklyn Daily Eagle*, Witherspoon was "the last of the featured players to start work in the new Paramount comedy."[7] The film was in the can by early July, with some additional scenes being shot in August.

The Mating Season starred Gene Tierney and John Lund, both new to Witherspoon, as was Malcolm Keen, who played her beleaguered husband. Miriam Hopkins was a familiar face in the film, playing Tierney's cosmopolitan mother, though she and Witherspoon did not share any scenes. And then there was the sensational Thelma Ritter, the real star of the picture, who plays Lund's folksy mom and would be Oscar-nominated for her efforts. This was Ritter's ninth film to be released and followed her standout performance in *All About Eve*.

Mrs. Williamson in *The Mating Season* would have been an excellent opportunity for Witherspoon at any time. She made the most of it, giving one of her most chilling performances as the snobbish, overbearing wife of a wealthy industrialist, Lloyd Williamson (Keen) of Williamson, Maryland, whom Lund wants to involve in a major project at his company, Kalinger Machine Tools, in Meridian, Ohio. Mrs. Williamson was a Lucile Watson–Florence Bates kind of part, though Witherspoon made her more abrasive and vulpine than either of them would have played her. She brought a different physical presence to this type of dowager role, making particularly good use of her beady black eyes. One of her first good lines is when she interrupts a meeting at Lund's company to take her husband to lunch: "We're only just keeping an ulcer at bay." When the boss's son and Tierney's former beau, played by James Lorimer, asks Mrs. Williamson if he can get her anything, she responds: "I only want a cool breeze blowing off the Atlantic." In an unguarded moment, her husband says to Lund's boss Larry Keating: "My wife was born with rigor mortis."

Mrs. Williamson's plot function is to get involved in a spat with Tierney and to look down on Ritter, which tests Lund's loyalty to his wife and mother, as opposed to his

Gene Tierney (left) and Witherspoon enacted their own version of "The Beauty and the Beast" in a Mitchell Leisen comedy called *The Mating Season* (Paramount, 1951). Tierney played the wife of a young, ambitious executive, John Lund, and Witherspoon played Mrs. Williamson, just about the most unpleasant, overbearing, and insidious wife of an important client you could possibly imagine. Though the film came late in her career, Mrs. Williamson turned out to be one of Witherspoon's most indelible performances.

desire for advancement in his career. Sooner or later, someone needs to stand up to Mrs. Williamson. Lund turns out to be the one, but only after his wife has shown him the way, calling Mrs. Williamson "the rudest woman I've ever seen." By that point, Mrs. Williamson has practically accused Tierney of having an affair with Lorimer and cheating at the board game they are playing.

Mrs. Williamson is a sharp dresser. She wears big hats, including an amazing lace-trimmed picture hat and matching black suit in the final reception scene at the Meridian Plaza, where Lund introduces Mrs. Williamson to his mother Ellen McNulty (Ritter) and the latter tells the story of how she refused to serve a man with his murdered wife in a suitcase in her hamburger joint. Naturally, Mrs. Williamson is appalled ("What a horrible story"). Lund wants to prove to Tierney and to himself, that he is not ashamed of his mother. He tells Mrs. Williamson that they are a package; they must take both of them or not at all. "There is not the remotest possibility," says Mrs. Williamson. Lund loses the lucrative job offer at the Williamsons' company but regains the respect of his wife.

Despite being billed ninth, Witherspoon got some good notices for this one. The *Philadelphia Inquirer* described her as a "monstrously rude matron told off in no uncertain terms by Miss Tierney and later by Lund." John Rosenfield in the *Dallas Morning News* wrote: "Vastly amusing is Cora Witherspoon as a nervous, exacerbating grande dame." According to the *Seattle Daily Times*, she gave "valuable support." Annie Oakley in the *Windsor Star* took a more critical view, writing that "James Lorimer and Cora Witherspoon are travesties of folks from the upper crust. Such stock creatures out of social burlesque flutter and flit incongruously around a character that should be surrounded by equally believable and significant types."[8]

After *The Mating Season*, Witherspoon stayed on in Hollywood to see if she could get more work. In August 1950, she returned to the small screen. A lot had happened since she had played Mrs. Orcutt in a televised version of *Stage Door* in 1939. Drama anthology series were now a significant part of television programming. *The Fireside Theatre* was "one of the earliest filmed dramatic shows produced especially for television," and aired over NBC on Mondays on the East coast and on Tuesdays on the West Coast.[9] Witherspoon contributed to the two first episodes of the third season, which was the first season of the series in a 30-minute format. Both episodes were produced and directed by Frank Wisbar at the historic Hal Roach Studios in Culver City, built in 1920, which no longer exist.

Witherspoon's first episode aired August 28 and 29, 1950 and was often repeated in the coming years. It was called "Polly" and was variously described as "a murder thriller set in modern Hollywood" and "a thrilling melodrama about a girl and a parrot who betray a killer." More specifically, it dealt with "A young man, tied to his rich aunt's apron strings, [who] falls in love with a carhop." The young man was Kenneth Harvey, Ann Savage played the girl ("a meanie"), and Witherspoon, not surprisingly, played Harvey's wealthy Aunt Martha. Virginia Farner and Walter McGrail were also in the cast. "Stopover" was broadcast a week later and starred Warren Douglas as "an ex-GI [who] attempts to fulfill a vow of vengeance against his former top sergeant." Gertrude Michael was also in that one. After these experiences, Witherspoon referred to television as "the craziest business," but that did not deter her from returning to the medium several times in 1954.[10]

In March 1951, Witherspoon was fortunate to be cast in the Pacific coast production of *The Madwoman of Chaillot*, a black comedy by the experimental French dramatist

Jean Giraudoux, which had been a smash hit on Broadway with Martita Hunt in the title role and ran for 368 performances at the Belasco and Royale theaters. In the play, The Countess Aurelia, "The Madwoman of Chaillot," leads a plot against promoters who would drill for oil in Paris. "Aided by her crazy cronies, she schemes to decoy and destroy the greedy ones. After a trial in absentia, she sends them all packing to their doom through a trap door in her cellar." The lead role was now being played by veteran stage and film actress Aline MacMahon. Witherspoon was cast as Madame Constance, "The Madwoman of Passy," who had been created on Broadway by Estelle Winwood. Constance's big moment is when she brings an imaginary dog to the "wildly hilarious tea party at the beginning of the second act."[11] Mademoiselle Gabrielle, "The Madwoman of St. Sulpice," was played by Eve McVeagh.

Others in the cast were Barbara Rush (Irma), Robert Knapp (Pierre), Clarence Derwent (The President), Elfreda Derwent (Mme. Josephine), William Schallert (The Baron), Frank Fiumara, Peter Adams, Fay Roope, John E. Wengraf, Bill Sheidy, Jr., Barbara Hill, Allen Conner, Barbara Tabor, Duke Johnston, Michael Couzzi, and Al Shoenberg. Jeffrey Hunter later replaced Knapp as the male romantic lead. Clarence Derwent and Fay Roope were reprising their roles from the Broadway production. Besides being co-producer with Peter Adams and Frances Austin of the Actors' Album, which put on the show, Harold J. Kennedy played the Ragpicker and directed the play.[12]

The Madwoman of Chaillot opened at the Harout's Ivar Theatre in Hollywood on March 28, 1951, four days after The Mating Season was released. Four years after she ostensibly retired, Witherspoon was back both on stage and screen. The production was a critical and a popular success. Scheduled for a two-week run, but "twice held over," it did not close till May 5. The accolades chiefly went to MacMahon in the lead, but Witherspoon also came in for her share of the laurels. Edwin Schallert, who had reviewed so many of Witherspoon's films down through the years, wrote in the Los Angeles Times that "the production is the most interesting and significant yet given by the Actors' Album, and it yielded a special triumph to its leading feminine player." He added that "not only Miss MacMahon but also Cora Witherspoon and the very effective Eve McVeagh shone in their efforts." The Los Angeles Mirror News wrote that Witherspoon, MacMahon, and McVeagh: "played these parts as if they had all been transported four flights above drab reality." According to the Los Angeles Citizen-News: "There is so much that is absolutely enchanting about 'The Madwoman of Chaillot,' … one wishes the whole play was as wise and witty, as funny and fantastic as its best scenes": "Cora Witherspoon brilliantly maintains a mood of sheer idiocy as the emotional Constance." When the play was in its fourth week, the Los Angeles Times printed a tiny article headed "Cora Witherspoon Scores in Comedy Role." There we can read that she has "one of the most laugh-provoking roles" and that "the veteran comedienne's humorous scenes with an imaginary dog invariably bring laughter from audiences."[13]

Once thing led to another. Being back in Los Angeles and visibly active and capable not surprisingly led to offers of further roles. The First Time, a romantic comedy starring Robert Cummings and Barbara Hale, was not a first-rate production like The Mating Season, but the role of the eccentric and slightly eerie baby nurse, Miss Salisbury, was nothing to scoff at and would keep Witherspoon before the public. Under the direction of Frank Tashlin, the production period lasted from April 26 to May 22, thus overlapping with the last ten days of the run of The Madwoman of Chaillot. It was only her second film at Columbia, where she had made Over 21 in 1945.

Witherspoon's segment of this hour-and-a-half long film lasts only 11 minutes, but for those nearly a dozen minutes she dominates the action. Nurse Salisbury arrives in the midst of a grandmotherly fracas between Mona Barrie and Kathleen Comegys and immediately takes charge. She insists that she is *Miss* Salisbury and demands water for the mother. She notes that it has been a long time since she had a "case" with two grandmothers. Unusually one or the other has "passed on." The ominous significance Witherspoon is able to put into those two words is chilling. After inspecting baby Timothy, she asks for a hammer and literally nails the baby's schedule on the nursery door. "While I'm in charge, we'll all live according to the baby's schedule," she says. Nurse Salisbury is a bit of a martinet, who comes in at all hours and gives Hale the baby with the same words: "Your baby, Mrs. Bennet." There is a running gag where she is always sitting on things, such as Cummings's hat or his pajamas-clad leg in bed. She basically acts as if the father is not there and is totally focused on mother and child for her four weeks of work. Her parting words to Hale are: "If an emergency should arise, like the baby choking on a safety pin, feel absolutely free to call me." For some reason, she has a distinctly mid–Atlantic accent.

This still perfectly captures the mood of *The First Time* (Norma Prod./Halburt Prod., 1952), a comedy about first-time parents in which Witherspoon played a martinet baby nurse and Robert Cummings (right) her perpetually harried employer. Nurse Salisbury's focus is on the baby at all times, and she expects the budding parents to fall into line. Witherspoon looks very much worse for wear at age 61, as she meets her young charge for the first time, while Cummings, fear in his eyes, is still holding her hat and coat.

Witherspoon looks noticeably older here, in a way that was not so evident in *The Mating Season*. She arrives with a black hat pressed down on her head and a dark cloth coat over her nurse's uniform. She has a bad permanent and her hair is uncommonly messy. Nurse Salisbury dons a nurse's cap when she is working in the daytime and wears a funny dark robe with little pompons all over it at night.

The *San Francisco Chronicle* pointed out the obvious: "This isn't any Academy Award winner ... nor will the Venice Film Festival go crazy over it ... but it's grand fun for the most part." Similarly, the *Evansville Press* wrote: "Not an upper-level production, it's still no slouch." Witherspoon got her last notices for a film role: "once a stage stalwart, makes a positive and humorous figure out of a nurse"; "is perfect as the highly efficient and possessive nurse"; "makes a riotously funny baby nurse." A New Orleans paper thought that "the most amusing spots in the show are a pep meeting for the salesmen of a washing machine company for which Cummings works and Cora Witherspoon's antics as the baby's nurse."[14] They were right.

Opportunities kept coming, so Witherspoon stayed on in Los Angeles throughout the warm month of July, though she might have wished she had not. Harold J. Kennedy wanted her for a revival of *Peg o' My Heart*, one of the most "chestnutty" of old chestnuts of the American stage and a classic "Cinderella-Pygmalion" type story written by Hartley Manners in 1912 and a huge hit for his wife Laurette Taylor. The revival opened Thursday, July 5, 1951, at the Ivar Theatre, where they had done *The Madwoman of Chaillot*, and ran for three weeks. The opening had to be delayed two days, because "both Harold J. Kennedy, director-actor, and Cora Witherspoon are reported to have flu attacks."[15]

This production had "one of the most brilliant casts to be seen here in many months," which included Joan Evans in the title role and fellow film actor John Agar in his stage debut as the romantic lead Jerry, Craig Stevens as the villain of the piece, Witherspoon as Mrs. Chichester, "the straight-laced aunt who acts as Peg's supervisor during her remolding," Harold Kennedy as her "foppish son, Alaric," Eve McVeagh as Peg's cousin Ethel, Eve Halpern as the maid, John Tomecko as the footman, and Mervyn Williams as the family lawyer. Craig Stevens had been replaced by Michael Cozzi by July 16, because Stevens had a commitment at the La Jolla Playhouse. As the show started its second week July 12, the *Los Angeles Citizen News* wrote that "near-capacity audiences have been attracted to the hit." The paper also described how "signature hunters not only seek out the stars, but lie in wait for other motion picture names in the cast which includes Cora Witherspoon and Craig Stevens."[16]

Both the production and Witherspoon's individual efforts met with the critics' approval. Edwin Schallert yet again did the honors in the *Los Angeles Times*, writing that "though it creaks like an old wagon wheel today, it is made interesting by the company that Harold J. Kennedy has gathered together ... and particularly fascinating by the performance of Joan Evans in the title role." "Kennedy and Miss Witherspoon provide good enlivenment and laughs belatedly in the third act," he opined. Margaret Harford felt "the acting honors are handed over lock, stock and barrel to the women in the cast." Star Joan Evans's "best support last night came from Cora Witherspoon as the snobbish aunt, and Eve McVeagh who plays cousin Ethel, a frozen blonde, who proves a real trial to Peg's friendly disposition." Witherspoon also received praise from David Bongard: "Cora ('If you'd only do something with your hair') Witherspoon was excellent as Peg's impecunious aunt, who was granted 1000 pounds to make a lady of her niece under terms of a deceased brother's will." Tom Coffey wrote that "Cora Witherspoon reigns expertly in the role of Mrs. Chichester."[17] The next time Witherspoon's name appeared in the papers, it was in less happy circumstances.

"Walking Dog, Actress Jailed on Drunk Charge." "Drunk? No, Says Actress; Lands in Jail." "Actress Is Led to Jail by Dog." "Dog Wants Walk, Actress Runs into Cop Trouble." "Outraged Actress, 'Waiting for Dog,' Held as Drunk." "Burned Up: Police Jail Lady Comic Walking Dog." "Actress Arrested Walking Terrier." I am sure readers of these headlines the weekend of July 28–29, 1951, did not imagine that the actress in question was a 61-year-old character actress, since women of that background seldom, if ever, figured in news reports of this kind. Whether they were married or unmarried, rich or poor or in between, character actresses usually lived quiet, well-regulated lives and never made it into the papers unless one of their films was being released. Cora Witherspoon was the exception to the rule, which is part of the reason why her "case" is so interesting; it allows us to see how the media dealt with this anomaly. One interesting thing to notice right off is that, while she was identified by name in the articles, not one newspaper put her name in the headline.

Peg o' My Heart had closed on July 25, which was a Wednesday, and two days later disaster struck. Maybe the end of the play freed her to go on a bender. Maybe what was taken as drunkenness was actually a morphine-induced high. At any rate, Witherspoon decided late Friday night that she needed to walk her dog. Lucky had finally passed on to the big dog yard in the sky, and Witherspoon's current pooch was a West Highland terrier called "Mickey." Not bothering with her hair or dressing properly at this ungodly hour, she simply threw a cloth coat over her nightgown and ventured forth into the streets of Hollywood. She was living at the time in an apartment at 1800 Grace Avenue, in a part of town I call "Character Actress Central," since historically so many of her ilk have preferred to live near the intersection of Franklin Avenue and Whitley Avenue. The convenience of the location, close to the studios and to everything else, is readily apparent, especially if you do not drive or own a car, and there are plenty of apartment buildings of varying degrees of cost, charm, and prestige to choose from.

Witherspoon's fairly modest, two-story building stood on the corner of Yucca St., which she ventured down that fateful night with her dog in tow. While Mickey was doing his business, Witherspoon leaned up against the substantial, three-story apartment building at 6434 Yucca St., on the corner of Wilcox Ave., just one block west of her apartment. This was where a patrolling police car stopped to ask if she needed a drive home. Apparently, the aging actress took umbrage at the implication that she could not get home on her own. An exchange of words occurred, that escalated into a conflict. Before she knew it, Witherspoon was being transported to the Lincoln Heights police station at 421 N. Ave. 19, which was then also the site of the Los Angeles City Jail. Mickey was taken from her and had to spend the night in the Ann Street Animal Shelter, while his owner was booked, charged with public drunkenness, and forced to spend the night in jail.[18]

According to the *Los Angeles Daily News*, one of the first papers to carry the story, Witherspoon had been "booked on a drunk charge, an assertion she heatedly denied": "'I drank one cocktail on the way home from work,' she said. 'And now look—.'" To a reporter from the Associate Press, she pronounced: "'It's an outrage…. I'm just dying to get in court. It will be a real circus.'" She was less combative when she appeared before municipal judge Walter C. Allen the next day and was sentenced to a fine of $5 or to

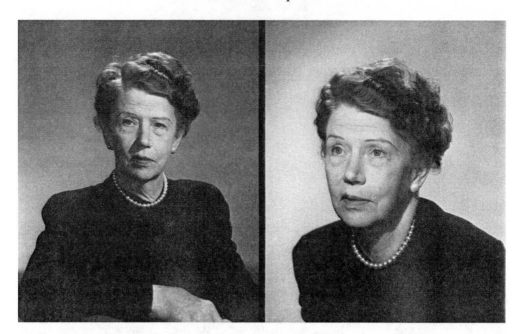

I find these two portraits from late in Witherspoon's life unsettling. There is a deadness about her eyes and a painful, tired resignation in her lop-sided face, which is such a sad contrast with the bright-eyed, sweet, hopeful expression of her younger years. Witherspoon's morphine addiction had clearly taken its toll and made her only a shadow of her former self (Billy Rose Theatre Division, The New York Public Library for the Performing Arts).

spend a day in jail. She accepted the sentence and was released, because she already spent a night in jail.[19] Judge Allen, a native of California and a former deputy city attorney and World War II veteran, was only 41 when Witherspoon came before him. He had been named to the Municipal Court by Governor Earl Warren in 1949. He was elevated to the Superior Court in 1957, retired in 1970, and died of cancer in St. Helena, California, in 1996. One of the more notorious cases to come before him was the wrongful death lawsuit filed by John Stompanato's ex-wife on behalf of their young son against Lana Turner and Cheryl Crane, which proceedings began in June 1958.[20]

By Sunday, July 29, the story of Witherspoon's arrest was all over the country, thanks to bulletins put out by the Associated Press and the International News Service. The INS bulletin was dated "Hollywood, July 28" and read in its entirety: "Film actress Cora Witherspoon, 61, was jailed on a drunk charge today after officers said that she appeared to be 'holding up a building, dressed only in negligee and coat.' She has portrayed society matrons on the screen." The AP bulletin was longer and described Witherspoon as "one of the movie's better known fluttery society woman types."[21]

The story did not appear in the *Los Angeles Times* until Sunday morning, when Witherspoon's many friends and colleagues in the city would have had plenty of time to take in the gory details with their morning coffee. Two photographs accompanied the article: a large one of a doleful Mickey and a smaller one of Witherspoon looking very much worse for wear and in the midst of saying something. Indeed, Mickey was very much part of the story and constituted its "non-human" interest. He even made it onto the front page of the tabloid *Los Angeles Mirror* in the form of a large photo of him behind bars with the caption "Actress, Dog in Jail."[22] The photo of Witherspoon, seated on a bench, her permed hair awry, and clearly trying to explain her absurd situation, was on page 3 of the *Mirror* with the rest of the story. So, to add insult to injury, the actress suffered the indignity of being upstaged by her dog....

Fortunately, when Witherspoon next appeared in the columns, it was good news. On November 6, 1951, veteran film writer Edwin Schallert reported in the *Los Angeles Times* that she would "really have a ball" in *Just for You* as "the alcoholic governess of Bing Crosby's daughter, Natalie Wood": "She will take part in a hilarious night court sequence in which she will sing 'I'll Si Si Ya in Bahia.'"[23] In view of recent events, some readers no doubt choked on their coffee.

As Schallert suggests, Witherspoon plays Wood's "dipso governess,"[24] Mrs. Angevine (AN-dju-vine), with hennaed hair with the roots showing and a general air of genteel decay. She has been hired on the strength of her pedigree and her connections, which are supposed to get young Barbara Blake (Wood) into the exclusive finishing school St. Hilary's. In the film, Barbara's mother has been dead ten years and Mrs. Angevine is only the most recent of a series of governesses. She does not last long, but this time due to her own bad behavior, not her charge's. Her big scene comes close to 30 minutes into the film, when Bing Crosby and his son, played by Robert Arthur, have to go down to the police station to pick her and Barbara up. Mrs. Angevine has been arrested after hitting a policeman with her purse, when he questioned her about leaving Barbara on the sidewalk while she was drinking in a bar. Mrs. Angevine gets fired on the spot and is dragged off by Crosby's lawyer Willis Bouchey, manically singing the lyrics from Crosby's latest hit "I'll Si-Si Ya in Bahia." On their way home in the car, Barbara explains Mrs. Angevine's drinking philosophy to her father: "Daddy, if a person is well-bred, she's never drunk. Ordinary people drink, because they can't measure up to life. But well-bred people drink, because life can't measure up to them. Mrs. Angevine explained it to me." Crosby refers to Mrs. Angevine as "A woman I wouldn't trust around my hair tonic" and a "boozy old babysitter."

While it was not uncommon for stars to play roles uncomfortably close to home, it was rare for art to imitate life in this way for a character actress. It is hard to imagine Witherspoon's recent, highly publicized arrest did not factor into her casting in this role. It is also hard to know what to think about this situation. On the one hand, for an actor working is better than not working and being cast in a high-profile film with major stars from a prestigious studio is never a bad thing. On the other hand, there was undoubtedly an element of cruelty in asking a woman with a serious addiction problem that had recently been splattered across the tabloids to play a woman who so closely resembled her darker side. Whether we like it or not, *Just for You* allows us to see what Witherspoon would have been like when she was high. One has to have a camp sensibility indeed to enjoy that spectacle.

Again, there are several sides to this issue. You might argue that no one was forcing Witherspoon to take this role. It might be seen as putting a brave face on things and acting as if there was no truth at all to those absurd reports. It was all a big misunderstanding. If there had been any truth to the stories, people would say, Witherspoon would never have dared to take this role. Her strategy, it seems, was the same as in 1940: to act as if nothing had happened and, if questioned directly—as she was by reporters at the police station—to deny adamantly that these ridiculous stories had any basis in fact. That was what women of her class and background would have been trained to do: *Ignore*, and, if that was not possible, *deny*, even in the face of strong evidence. There was no internet then, of course, which meant that sooner or later things would die down and the "facts" would no longer be readily available. Also, a woman of Witherspoon's age and background could depend on "the kindness of strangers," as Tennessee Williams so famously called it. This meant that few people were likely to have confronted her directly with the reports, though you can be sure there was a lot of talk behind her back.

Starting in late October at Paramount, *Just for You* (originally entitled *Famous*) was directed by Elliott Nugent, who had directed *Professor Beware* at the end of 1937. Ethel Barrymore was also in the film, though she and Witherspoon did not have any scenes together. It was 23 years since their long and successful collaboration on *The Constant Wife* ended in San Francisco, though they had one last hurrah as stage sisters when the play was revived at the Cape Playhouse in August 1935. Barrymore was now 72 and had been driven by financial need to seek her fortune in Hollywood, like so many aging actresses. She died in 1959.

Production on *Just for You* ended in mid–December 1951. With no further offers of work forthcoming, Witherspoon returned to Las Cruces. Just after Christmas, she starred as Judith Bliss in an amateur production of Noël Coward's *Hay Fever* in the Las Cruces Junior High School auditorium. It was sponsored by the Las Cruces Lions Club and the proceeds were to be used to purchase uniforms for the Junior High School band. According to the local newspaper: "The presence of Miss Cora Witherspoon in the leading role is keeping the rest of the cast on its toes in order to 'play up' to the professional."[25]

Ironically, Witherspoon's much publicized 1951 run-in with the police gave a kick to her career at a time when, according to Schallert, she had been planning to retire to her Texas ranch. This "ranch" was Hollywood hype for her modest home in Las Cruces. *Just for You* was treated as a comeback vehicle in the press. Strictly speaking, Witherspoon had already come back in *The Mating Season* and *The First Time*, both released in 1951, but maybe nobody noticed. Witherspoon was billed sixth in *Just for You*, which was not bad for such a limited role. The reviewers were generous, frequently going out of their way to point out that she was "a riot as the tipsy governess putting on dignity"; and that she had "a funny bit as a tipsy governess," "one priceless bit as the bottle-loving governess," "a funny bit … as a governess with 'a hollow leg,'" and "an amusing sequence, as a tipsy governess." Columnist Harold Heffernan was the only one who alluded to her fracas with the police, though strictly speaking he was describing her performance as Mrs. Angevine. According to Heffernan: "Previewers of Bing Crosby's new musical 'Just for You' are handing laurels to Cora Witherspoon…. The picture is sparked—damp though the source may be—by a scene in which Miss Witherspoon and young Natalie Wood end up behind bars simply because Cora gets tipsy, takes the child into a saloon, hits a cop on the head and calls the Mayor a Communist. Miss Witherspoon has been retired for four years, but her brief whirl at inebriation has ignited new interest in her among producers."[26]

Witherspoon's last sustained, substantial professional engagement was with the Sombrero Playhouse in Phoenix, Arizona, where she worked intermittently between 1952 and 1955. The Sombrero had been founded in 1948 "to bring the legitimate stage to Phoenix for the enjoyment of Valley of the Sun theater lovers." It was the brainchild of 30-year-old, Texas-born actress and rancher's daughter Ann Lee, who was already operating El Teatro El Santa Fe during the summer. The idea was that the Sombrero Playhouse would be her organization's winter home. With her co-producer Richard

Charlton, Lee purchased a plot of land at 4747 N. 7th St., half a block south of Camelback Rd., and a new $100,000, 550-seat theater was erected. While the stars were put up at the luxurious Paradise Inn in Scottsdale, members of the company were housed in 12 apartments on the grounds of the theater. Three meals a day were served in the "Backstage Club" adjoining the theater. The cast for the week would usually meet for the first time at rehearsals at 10 a.m. Tuesday morning. Unless you had done the play before, you were expected to attend rehearsals every day from 10 a.m. to 5 p.m. with a break for lunch between noon and 1 p.m. The dress rehearsal was held on stage on Sunday night. While all this was going on, members of the company would be doing performances of another play in the evening Monday to Saturday.[27] Nothing remains of the Sombrero Playhouse today. The Valley Commerce Center stands on the site.

The first half-season opened with Garson Kanin's *Born Yesterday* with William Bendix and Audrey Totter on March 29, 1949. In subsequent years, the theater presented a new play a week for 12 to 16 weeks each year, starting in January. By the time Witherspoon signed on, the theater was in its fourth season. She made her Sombrero debut playing the fortune teller in *The Skin of Our Teeth* by Thornton Wilder on February 5, 1952. The play had been a huge success on Broadway in 1942–43 starring Tallulah Bankhead, with Florence Reed playing the fortune teller. It even won the Pulitzer Prize for Drama. In Phoenix, Betty Field led the cast, which also included John O'Connor, Jacqueline Paige, and James Dobson in featured roles. The play was directed by Paul Guilfoyle, who had done it before in Hollywood. One genteel audience member pronounced: "It's too allegorical for me." The *Arizona Republic* praised the production and described it as "the maddest night of this Sombrero season." While the local reviewer failed to mention her, Witherspoon's billing was flattering. Just below the title in the ads stood: "with Cora Witherspoon."[28]

The following week, Witherspoon had a more modest role as the landlady Mae Jermyn in Wolcott Gibbs's "comedy of New York manners" *Season in the Sun*, set on Fire Island. Nancy Kelly had created the starring role of Emily Crane, faithful and supportive wife of an egotistical magazine "paragrapher" determined to turn himself into a serious writer, on Broadway during an epic run at the Cort and Booth theaters in 1950–51. She gave "the season's best performance" in her reprise at the Sombrero. Walter Coy played the husband, George Crane, played on Broadway by Richard Whorf and later Joseph Allen. O'Connor, Porter, and Paige were also in this one, as were Harris Brown and Peggy Converse. Guilfoyle directed again. Though she was not featured this time, the *Arizona Republic* noted: "Cora Witherspoon, who gave such a marvelous performance in her first dramatic role last week in 'The Skin of Our Teeth' goes back to a character role and literally tears it apart."[29]

Witherspoon reprised her role as "an antiquated landlady with youthful delusions" in *Season in the Sun* at the La Jolla Playhouse starting July 22, again in support of Nancy Kelly. This time Kelly's newspaperman husband was played by Howard Duff. James Neilson directed. According to the *San Diego Union*, Hollywood "turned out en masse" to attend the premiere. Among the luminaries were Duff's wife, Ida Lupino; Kirk Douglas, John Lund, and Robert Young. One reviewer noted her appearance as a "colorful landlady." He found "the players more intriguing than the vehicle": "a rather plotless resume of character sketches of the strange people he met at his favorite playground, the internationally famous sandbar of southern Long Island known as Fire Island."[30]

Witherspoon was back in La Jolla for the August 12 opening of its production of

The Corn Is Green, in which Ethel Barrymore had starred as the redoubtable school-teacher Lilly Moffat on Broadway and Bette Davis in the 1945 Warner Bros. film version. Witherspoon played the significant supporting role of Mrs. Watty, Miss Moffat's "psalm-singing, once wayward, Cockney housekeeper,"[31] created on the New York stage and on film by Rosalind Ivan. The lead role was played by Ann Harding this time and Douglas Dick played her talented pupil Morgan Evans. Ethel Barrymore's niece, Diana Barrymore, played Witherspoon's alluring daughter Bessie Watty, whose attractions threaten to derail Miss Moffat's dearly held plans for her protégé. Harry Ellerbe directed.

The *San Diego Union* noted that Witherspoon was "particularly good" as "the brat's tea-serving mother"; the *Los Angeles Times* that she was "her usual comic self" as "a thief who has found salvation." In what would prove her final stage appearance on the West coast, she went out with a bang. The day after the *Corn Is Green* opening, there was a gas explosion in a workshop at nearby La Jolla High School, as the audience was arriving for the matinee. The blast disrupted the electrical power in the area and the performance had to be called off.[32]

In February 1953, Witherspoon returned for the fifth season of the Sombrero Playhouse. Her first play of the season was *The Corn Is Green*, again playing Mrs. Watty to Ann Harding's Miss Moffat and Douglas Dick's Morgan Evans. Lewis Russell reprised the role of the Squire, that he had played 400 times on Broadway and on tour. The cast was directed by Lester Vail, who helmed all the Sombrero productions Witherspoon appeared in this season. The *Arizona Republic* found the production, which played the week of February 9, 1953, "truly impressive" and the supporting cast "distinguished." Harding's performance was "one for Phoenix to remember," Dick was "brilliant," and Witherspoon "no less good."[33]

Her Sombrero assignment the following week was playing the cook Clara in Noël Coward's comedy *Hay Fever*, about a weekend in the country gone awry. Who created Clara on Broadway, I wonder? Actually, it was an English character actress Alice Belmore Cliffe (1870–1943) with a string of Broadway credits to her name, starting in 1905. If you knew that, you are good. Miriam Hopkins starred as the dizzy dame and diva Judith Bliss, in Phoenix, that is. Both Hopkins and Harding had passed the zenith of their stardom by the time Witherspoon arrived in Hollywood; she had never worked with either of them in films in the 1930s. Co-producer Ann Lee took a part in this one, as one of the hapless guests; and former Miss America, Jacque Mercer, making her professional stage debut, played another. According to the *Arizona Republic*, Witherspoon was "making herself a Sombrero favorite" and filled her role "admirably." The *Los Angeles Times* film critic Edwin Schallert was in the audience at the *Hay Fever* premiere in order to "survey the activities" of the theater. He was impressed by the scope of Lee's and Charlton's "project" and credited Witherspoon with "importantly sustaining the [comic] effect" in this production.[34]

On February 23, the time had come for John Van Druten's fairly recent *Bell, Book and Candle*, a precursor of *Bewitched*, which had played on Broadway during the 1950–51 season, and starred Teresa Wright and Victory Jory in Phoenix. Witherspoon was given another good opportunity, as Miss Holroyd, played by Jean Adair of *Arsenic and Old Lace* fame on Broadway and by Elsa Lanchester in the 1958 film version. This is the only time I can think of when Witherspoon played a witch. The local reviewer could not resist observing that "the production weaves a strong spell during the first two acts," though he did not find the last act "as enchanting as the first two." "Miss Witherspoon as always is great fun," he added.[35]

Witherspoon appears to have been off for two weeks, but on March 16 she was back in Samson Raphaelson's *Jason*, starring Franchot Tone, Kenneth Tobey, and Anne Kimbell. It turned out to be the last play of the season, when plans for starring Joan Blondell in *Happy Birthday* the following week fell through.[36]

Production on what would prove Witherspoon's final film, *It Should Happen to You*, began at Columbia on May 23, 1953. Her role was so tiny this time, that she is unlikely to have been needed for more than a day or so. Like her part in *The Mating Season*, this opportunity came about through a personal connection. Witherspoon would end her film career as it had begun 22 years earlier: playing an uncredited role as a saleslady in a department store in a film directed by her friend George Cukor. Witherspoon was one of four "old-time stars" who had been given a part in *It Should Happen to You*, according to a widely reprinted news item. The other three were Mary Young, Donald Keith, and Hank Mann.[37] As we recall, Witherspoon had supported Young in *The Outrageous Mrs. Palmer* in Boston way back in 1920. They were in the same scene in *It Should Happen to You*.

Starring Judy Holliday and Jack Lemmon in his screen debut, *It Should Happen to You* is a highly intelligent and entertaining satire on celebrity culture, as a young woman through sheer force of will manages to make herself famous for no reason whatsoever. Witherspoon is in the film's best scene, where Holliday is beset by fans and autograph hounds, as Witherspoon is about to sell her some towels in Macy's linen department. Witherspoon had been playing various varieties of fawning, dizzy dames her entire career. The way she reacts when she recognizes Holliday as the girl from the billboard clearly visible through the store window—"It's *Gladys Glover!*"—is nothing short of brilliant. Witherspoon looks stylish in basic black and pearls, as she asks for an autograph for her niece. She draws in a gay colleague (Frank Nelson) and two old ladies (Margaret McWade and Mary Young), before all hell breaks loose.

It was a low-key finale to a film career, certainly, but then Witherspoon had always identified primarily as a stage actress. She got another stab at summer stock this year, when she reprised her role in support of Miriam Hopkins in *Hay Fever*. This time the venue was the Somerset Playhouse, on Route 138 in Somerset, Massachusetts, which closed out its summer season with the Coward comedy the week of September 7, 1953.[38]

In mid–January 1954, an article in the *Los Angeles Times* made it clear that Witherspoon was returning to the Sombrero Playhouse in Phoenix for her third season with the company. The season opened on January 18 with Noël Coward's *Design for Living*, starring Sylvia Sidney and Gene Raymond. Besides the stars, the cast included newcomer William Weaver, Thayer Roberts, John Stuart, and Witherspoon. According to the *Arizona Republic*, "it was Raymond's show all the way." Witherspoon's performance did not rate a mention in the review.[39]

The second week saw a revival of Clare Booth's *The Women*, starring Frances Dee as Mary Haines and Rose Hobart as Sylvia Fowler. Dorothy Patrick played Crystal Allen, Liz Slifer the Countess de Lage, and Witherspoon was relegated to the modest role of the cook, who has one scene in the second act with the maid, where they give us the servants' perspective on the demise of the Haines's marriage. This scene was singled out by the local reviewer: "some of [Dee's] fellow actresses were superb in their portrayals of character…. One cannot pass up the second scene of Act II, in which 'the help' go over the troubles of Mary and her husband as they decide upon a divorce. It is a dialogue between Jane, the maid, played by Jean Perkinson and Maggie, the cook, carried by Cora Witherspoon. You'll have to go far to find a better skit than they offered." Local women lent their fur coats "to add authenticity to the wardrobes." Dee's husband Joel McCrea was on hand to attend the premiere and spend the week with his wife at the Paradise Inn.[40]

Witherspoon's best opportunity this season came in the fourth week, when she supported veteran character actress Jane Darwell in *Suds in Your Eye*, together with Richard Jaeckel, Kasia Orzazewski, and Nancy Hale. This comedy by Jack Kirkland had had a brief run on Broadway ten years earlier with Darwell in the lead then too. Orzazewski also reprised her Broadway role, as Mrs. Rasmussen. Witherspoon played Miss Tinkham, the "third member of the trio of beer-drinking old women." Brenda Forbes had created this role in New York. The *Arizona Republic* began its review: "A comedy production badly in need of polishing still managed to keep the customers in good spirits last night." Merrill Windsor thought Darwell was "given excellent support in the grand manner by Cora Witherspoon who frequently stole the show."[41]

The fifth week saw a revival of the comedy *In Any Language*, which ran briefly on Broadway in 1952 with Uta Hagen, Walter Matthau, and Eileen Heckart. The Sombrero production starred Miriam Hopkins with George Givot, Robert Lowery, and Witherspoon in featured roles. Witherspoon gave her final performance in the sixth week, the half-way point of the Sombrero season, in Rosemary Casey's comedy *Late Love*, starring Mary Astor, with Ted Brenner, William Weaver, and Witherspoon in "important supporting roles." This play had ended its Broadway run of 95 performances as recently as January 2 that year. The legendary character actress Lucile Watson had created the role of Mrs. Colby on Broadway in what was her final appearance there. Merrill Windsor called this production "a new high mark for the season." He said further: "In the dryly humorous role of the writer's mother, Miss Witherspoon is even more fun than in the flighty roles she has played in other Sombrero productions this winter."[42]

Witherspoon's continued efforts at the Sombrero in the spring of 1954 may have alerted producers to her availability. She suddenly found herself in demand in television. The *Arizona Republic* noted that she was "turning up regularly all over the dial on the better drama shows": "Usually plays somebody's mother."[43] Apart from the two episodes of the *Fireside Theatre* I have already discussed, her remaining known output on the small screen was broadcast between May and August of 1954. During this brief period, she contributed to some of the finest dramatic anthology series of the 1950s, such as the *Kraft Television Theatre*, *Studio One*, and *Goodyear Television Playhouse*. Four of these five episodes were in a 60-minute format and were broadcast live from New York. The fifth was half an hour and was taped in New York. Thus Witherspoon's television work this summer had one further benefit: It gave her a final chance to live and work in the city where she had lived for so many years and where she last acted in *The Front Page* in 1946.

The *Kraft Television Theatre* was a classic NBC drama anthology series and "one of television's most prestigious showcases, winning top ratings and many awards, and becoming a Wednesday night institution." At this time, it was broadcast live from New York on Wednesdays at 9–10 p.m. and, as a result, nearly all the episodes have been lost. When Witherspoon came onboard in May 1954, the show was in its seventh season and was still in black and white. Her episode "A Touch of Summer" was based on an original teleplay by George Faulkner and was set in Brooklyn in 1895. The prolific character actor Jerome Cowan, who already had nearly two dozen television credits behind him, played

Witherspoon is almost unrecognizable in this snapshot taken outside the Sombrero Playhouse in Phoenix, Arizona in February 1954. The Sombrero had opened in 1948 in a purpose-built building at 4747 N. 7th St., which no longer exists. Witherspoon spent four consecutive seasons there, starting in 1952. Indeed, her work at the Sombrero in March 1955 would be her final professional engagement. The comedy *Suds in Your Eye* starred the ubiquitous Fox character actress Jane Darwell, whom Witherspoon had never worked with in films (Billy Rose Theatre Division, The New York Public Library for the Performing Arts).

a former Shakespearean actor, whose domestic life is troubled by "his wife's inability to appreciate the glory that was his when he trod the boards of the finest theaters in the English-speaking world": "His talent for quotation and rhetoric causes him only trouble and leaves him an actor without applause in his own home." The wife, played by Witherspoon, "thinks the theater is an unsavoury institution and all connected with it are frivolous wastrels." She cautions her daughter, Ruth Matteson, to shun actors, but the daughter nevertheless falls in love with an actor, and the father "accepts the challenge to prove to his wife the importance of the theater in the culture of a country." He plays the title role in *Henry V*, which apparently is a revelation to the wife.[44] Kenneth Nelson and Rita Vaughn were also in the cast. The episode was broadcast May 19.

During the summer of 1954, Witherspoon also lent her talents to two episodes of *Studio One*, which was produced by CBS in New York and broadcast live on Mondays at 10–11 p.m. The episode "A Guest at the Embassy" aired as part of *Studio One Summer Theater* on July 12, 1954, and starred Nina Foch, a *Studio One* regular, with support from Leslie Nielsen, Betsy Palmer, Madeline Clive, Paul McGrath, and Witherspoon. The story was a modern-day adaptation by Jerome Ross of the "celebrated La Ronciere Case" from 1835. In this psychological melodrama set in Paris, "Young attractive misfit— Nina Foch—attempts novel, but complicated, method of breaking up impending marriage of former school girl friend," according to a summary in the *Pittsburgh Press*. The episode was directed by Allen Reisner, as was "The House of Gair," which was also part of *Studio One*'s sixth season and aired August 16. This drama was adapted by Michael Dyne from a work by Eric Linklater. Besides Witherspoon, the cast included Basil Rathbone, Hurd Hatfield, Wesley Addy, Iola Lynn, and Eva Condon. Described as a "taught melodrama set in the Scottish moors," it was "An odd but fascinating story with lively dialogue about a flamboyant blackmailer and chisler and nephew with a talent for murder, who combine to sell fake paintings to rich old ladies."[45] Witherspoon played Aunt Fanny, one of the rich old ladies, in what would prove her final appearance in an audio-visual medium. These episodes were also an hour long and were broadcast live in black and white.

Goodyear Television Playhouse was another highly successful NBC drama anthology series, which ran between 1951 and 1960 and at this point aired on Sundays at 9–10 p.m. "Dear Harriet Heart-Throb" was an episode from the third season of the series. This "unusual love story" by Robert Alan Arthur dealt with "40 year old, cynical, unmarried male journalist stuck with unpleasant task of writing an advice column. Struck by letter from 39-year-old widow. He engineers a ruse to meet her, they fall in love, while she keeps writing to him as advice columnist without knowing it." The journalist was Elliott Reid and the widow Leora Dana; Betsy Palmer and Witherspoon were featured, and Pat O'Malley, Jane Moultrie, and Raymond Bramley were also in the cast.[46] This episode, which aired live from New York on July 18, was directed by Delbert Mann, whose Oscar-winning feature film *Marty* had originated as an episode of *Goodyear Television Playhouse* in 1953.

Only 11 days later, Witherspoon was seen in an episode of *The Telltale Clue* called "The Case of the Dying Accusation." *The Telltale Clue* was a short-lived, half-hour CBS police drama, which "enabled home viewers to become familiar with modern police technology," making it "a variation on the Ellery Queen–style whodunit." Anthony Ross played Capt. Richard Hale, head of criminology in the police department of an unnamed major city. Besides Witherspoon, the major cast in this episode were Hurd Hatfield, Leslie Nielsen, and Marian Seldes. Witherspoon plays Mrs. Jordan, an upper-class dowager and the mother of Hatfield. The episode opens with the visually arresting image of young Jordan's dying wife Yvonne being thrown out of a passing car. Jordan and Yvonne have been married five years, but "led separate lives," and Jordan imagines that his wife runs around with other men. Seldes plays Yvonne's intense sister from Hartford, a buyer in a department store, who is visiting at the time of the murder. Things look pretty bad for Jordan, eliciting a lot of handkerchief-wringing and worried looks from his mother, but naturally things are not as simple as all that. Yvonne was a bigamist, it turns out, and her hoodlum first husband James Duval (Nielsen) "dunnit." Despite her emotional turmoil, Witherspoon is looking slim and trim in a dark dress with a shawl collar, regulation pearls, and a diamond brooch. "The Case of the Dying Accusation" has the added interest of having been written by Gore Vidal, under the pseudonym "Edgar Box," and constituted his debut as a writer for television. Beautifully restored in 2018, this is Witherspoon's only television performance that is readily available; indeed, it is probably the only one that exists.[47]

Through some miracle, on August 17, the day after the Monday-night live broadcast of *Studio One*'s "The House of Gair" over CBS, Witherspoon opened in *The Happiest Years* with the Shady Lane Players, who offered dining and theater at Shady Lane Farm at 24803 W. Grant Highway (U.S. Highway 20) near the hamlet of Marengo, Illinois.

She must have caught an early flight to Chicago. *The Happiest Years* was a comedy by Thomas Coley and William Roerick, which had flopped at the Lyceum Theatre in New York in April 1949. The play focused on "an endearing, albeit suspicious, mother-in-law, who gets a notion that her son-in-law, an ex-G.I. and college student, is straying from the straight and narrow." *New York Daily News* critic John Chapman had thought *The Happiest Years* "dandy for Summer stock, but it is hardly important enough to exercise the talents of Miss Walker and Miss Wood." The Shady Lane Players had taken Chapman at his word and here were Peggy Wood and June Walker reprising their Broadway roles in summer stock. Witherspoon probably played Alida Wentworth, the role created by Jessie Busley. Moultrie Patten, Teena Starr, and Louis Tanne were also in the cast.[48] After fires in 2009 and 2014, nothing now remains of the Shady Lane playhouse and the restaurant save the sign.

Witherspoon was on a roll. *The Happiest Years* closed August 22, after a week's run, and on August 30, 1954, she opened in a new play called *The Other Devil* at the Pocono Playhouse in Mountainhome, Pennsylvania. Written by Louis Pelletier and Jack Finke, this was "a delightfully refreshing comedy about a young librarian in a small community who has the courage of her convictions in the selection of books for the reading public." Patricia Benoit starred as the young librarian with Witherspoon, Joe Maross, Addison Richards, Lois Holmes, Jackie Kelk, Perry Fiske, and others in supporting roles.[49] John O'Shaughnessy, from this year's season at the Sombrero, directed.

In March 1955, Witherspoon returned to the Sombrero Playhouse for what turned out to be the last engagement of her career. In William Inge's *Picnic*, which starred Scott Brady as Hal Carter, she played Helen Potts, the sympathetic old lady Hal encounters when he drifts into her small Kansas town on Labor Day, looking for an old college friend. Mrs. Potts had been created on Broadway by Ruth McDevitt in 1953 and would be portrayed on the screen by Verna Felton the following year. The cast, directed by Charles K. Freeman, also included Georgianna Carter (Madge Owens), Elinor Donahue (Millie Owens), Alice Drake (Flo Owens), Carol Hill (Rosemary Sydney), Robert Patten (Alan Seymour), Gerald Masterton (Bomber), and Lynne Gray and Joan Chapman as Irma Kronkite and Christine Schoenwalder. *Picnic* played the week of March 21 and was the penultimate play of the Sombrero season. Anson B. Cutts of the *Arizona Republic* wrote: "Cora Witherspoon as the kind-hearted neighbor Mrs. Potts, who befriends Hal, contributed another of her memorable characterizations, being always believable and lovable."[50]

Witherspoon was also on hand for the Sombrero Playhouse's eleventh and final production of the 1955 season, *Liliom* by the Hungarian dramatist Ferenc Molnár, which is best known today for forming the basis for the musical *Carousel*. Husband and wife movie stars Fernando Lamas and Arlene Dahl starred as the carnival worker and cad Liliom and his long-suffering wife Julie. The cast also included Benay Venuta as Mrs. Muskat, owner of the carousel and Liliom's erstwhile employer and lover, and Jay Novello as his villainous crony Ficzur. Though they were all film folk, Witherspoon had not worked with them before. They were directed by Benno Schneider, who had helmed the most recent Broadway revival starring Burgess Meredith and Ingrid Bergman.

In her final show on any stage, Witherspoon was cast as Mother Hollunder, Julie's aunt, who gives her a home and a job in her photographer's studio, where part of the play is set. The role had been created by Lilian Kingsbury on Broadway in 1921 and played in revivals by Leona Roberts in 1932 and Margaret Wycherly in 1940. This time *Arizona*

Republic drama critic Anson B. Cutts felt Witherspoon "over-projected her portrayal.... Something she has not done before in all of her splendid characterizations this season."[51] Though Cutts seems to suggest she played more roles than Mrs. Potts and Mother Hollunder at the Sombrero this season, I have found no evidence of this. The season had begun on January 17, 1955, with Edward Chodorov's *Oh, Men! Oh, Women!* starring Terry Moore.

By the time she died in November 1957, nothing had been heard of Witherspoon in the press since her final engagement at the Sombrero Playhouse in March 1955. We must assume she was living quietly on her sister's property on Las Cruces Ave.

We all die alone in some sense of the word, but Witherspoon died more alone than most. Around four o'clock in the afternoon of Sunday, November 17, 1957, a female friend stopped by her home to invite her to dinner and found her dead, "wedged between her bed and the wall of her bedroom." According to the newspaper accounts, her death had taken place "a considerable time earlier." Witherspoon was last seen alive on Tuesday, November 12. In her death notice in the *New Orleans Times-Picayune*, her time of death was given as 8 a.m. on Wednesday, November 13. She died of a heart attack. Thus ended a fabled life in a small bedroom in a modest bungalow facing an alley in Las Cruces, New Mexico.[52]

Witherspoon's death was front-page news in her local newspaper and was widely covered in the press. Nearly all of her obituaries were based on the bulletin written by the Associated Press, including her obituary in the *New York Times*. The AP obituary mentioned the many stars she had supported and gave a run-down of several of her stage and screen credits. It noted that she had last performed in 1955 and had been a resident of Las Cruces "for the past three years."[53] Most papers chose to omit the specific, grotesque detail of the state in which her body was found. Some included a wistful portrait of her from *Ramshackle Inn*, with her hair badly permed and three strings of pearls.

When first considering how to describe Witherspoon's funeral, I found it hard to imagine who would have been there, besides her sister Maude. Surely, Witherspoon could not have had many friends left in New Orleans, when she had not lived there in 50 years and rarely visited after her uncle's death in 1923. That was before I discovered the extensive extended family she had in the city, the descendants of Samuel and Carrie Bell, her maternal grandparents, who would have come out in force to pay a final tribute to their clan's most famous and, at times, infamous member. There were no Bell cousins still alive in 1957, but the "esprit de corps" of her married aunts' descendants—the Wisdoms, the Denises, the Mortimers, and the Renshaws, would have impelled them to attend the funeral, in addition to their affection for their lively and endearing cousin.

At her death, only four of Witherspoon's first cousins were still alive: Henry Edgeworth Frick (1875–1960), who had been named for Witherspoon's father; the siblings Louise Denis (1878–1960) and Edmund Derbigny Denis (1887–1960), and Lea McLean Renshaw (1887–1973). Eighty-two-year-old cousin Henry was the only surviving first cousin on her father's side and lived in Montclair, New Jersey. Louise, Edmund, and Lea, on the other hand, all lived in New Orleans. Louise Denis never married and never worked, like her older sister Bella, who died just five months before Witherspoon. Louise's younger brother Edmund had married when he was 44 and would have been accompanied to the funeral by his wife Marie (*née* McCann). Lea Renshaw was unmarried and was the last of Witherspoon's cousins to die, in 1973, three years after her sister Maude.

Beyond her few surviving first cousins, Witherspoon had several first cousins once removed, that is, her cousins' children, living in New Orleans. Most prominent among them was John Minor Wisdom (1905–99); indeed, he was the only member of the extended Witherspoon-Bell clan with a claim to fame to rival Witherspoon's own, though in a completely different field. Only months before her death, he was nominated by President Eisenhower to a seat on the United States Court of Appeals for the Fifth Circuit, where he was part of several landmark legal decisions that have been credited with dismantling segregation. If his schedule allowed and he attended the funeral, cousin John would no doubt have brought his charming wife Bonnie (*née* Mathews). Among her many accomplishments was teaching future senator Lamar Alexander how to eat an artichoke. Among other New Orleans cousins of this younger generation who may have been at the funeral, we find John's older half-sister Jessie Wisdom (1884–1975), who was married to retired Vice-Admiral Roland Munroe Brainard. John's older brother William Bell Wisdom (1900–77), who owned an advertising company and was a "noted collector of rare books and manuscripts,"[54] may have been there with his wife Mary (*née* Freeman); and their younger brother Norton Labatt Wisdom (1907–81), special attorney for the U.S. Department of Justice, and his wife Peggy (*née* McGehee).

Witherspoon's cousin Eliza Johnston Wisdom is almost sure to have been there. Like cousin Cora, who was three years her senior, Eliza had been orphaned at an early age, though the circumstances were more dramatic. In 1906, a couple of years after Eliza's mother Mamie died of septic pneumonia and kidney failure at the age of 37, her father, another William Bell Wisdom, killed himself with a shot to the head. An only child, Eliza lived off her substantial inheritance until her death in 1967. Other potential attendees were cousin Frank Hastings Mortimer, Jr. (1902–70), and his wife Lucille Minor Mortimer, and cousin Dorothy Shepard Crutcher (1910–98), whose 19-year-old twin brother Edward T. Shepard, Jr., had died so tragically in 1929 by taking carbolic acid in a Memphis hotel room.[55]

Among New Orleans friends from her childhood and youth, Alice Graveley was still alive and may have attended the funeral. Graveley, who was one month older than Witherspoon, never married and worked as a high school teacher. She did not die until 1981, when she was 91. Witherspoon's now 78-year-old acting teacher and friend Jessie Tharp was also still going strong in their native city 13 years after her retirement from the New Orleans public school system, where she had worked for 37 years. Maybe she came to celebrate her most famous pupil's life and work. Tharp died in 1961.[56]

According to custom, the services were held only three days after Witherspoon's body was found in Las Cruces and sent for burial in the city of her birth. I imagine, then, there was a fair-sized gathering at eleven in the morning on Wednesday, November 20, 1957. The funeral was held in one of the elegant parlors of Jacob Schoen and Son, a funeral home that still operates out of an imposing French Chateau style edifice at 3827 Canal St. in the Mid–City section of New Orleans.

As the funeral was public and was announced both in the *Times-Picayune* and the *New Orleans States*,[57] I like to think there were also some old fans and admirers present as well, like Albert Michell, a 75-year-old widower who worked at one time as a night watchman in a factory. Michell wrote a brief letter to the editor of the *Times-Picayune* published on November 25 to remind his fellow New Orleanians that they should be "proud of this fine and gracious lady of the theater." Michell recalled that he "had the privilege of meeting Miss Witherspoon when we talked of our beloved New Orleans."[58]

The Screen Actors Guild sent a wreath. Curiously, the card accompanying the flowers from Frank J. Reyes & Co., "New Orleans' Leading Florist," with the handwritten message "with sympathy Screen Actors Guild" is to be found in the Witherspoon clipping file at the New York Public Library for the Performing Arts. On the back, we find written in pencil: "Spray R. glads R. carna."[59]

Witherspoon was laid to rest with her parents, Aunt Sophie, and Uncle Samuel Bell and his partner Ernest Cucullu, in the rectangular, stone-edged, grass-covered plot Samuel had selected for himself many years earlier, when he was the guiding spirit and first manager of Metairie Cemetery. Her name appears on the bottom of the simple yet solid, rectangular headstone on a plinth: "Cora Bell Witherspoon 1890–1957."[60] After half a century, she had finally come home.

Chapter Notes

Preface

1. "Veteran Actress Recalls Visit to Cousin Here 27 Years Ago," *Quincy Patriot Ledger* (August 18, 1941), p. 9.

2. Alex Barris, *Hollywood's Other Women* (South Brunswick and New York: A.S. Barnes, 1975), p. 111; David Ragan, *Who's Who in Hollywood 1900–1976* (New Rochelle, NY: Arlington House, 1977), p. 836; Walter Winchell, "Walter Winchell on Broadway," *Burlington Daily News* (January 27, 1937), p. 6.

3. Nina Vecchi, "They Judge You by Your Roles," *Brooklyn Daily Eagle* (September 29, 1935), p. 2C; H.H. Niemeyer, "Any Role, Any Studio," *St. Louis Post-Dispatch* (April 2, 1937), p. 3F.

4. George McKinnon, "Marquee: Rep Homecoming a Theater Event," *Boston Globe* (October 22, 1976), p. 30.

Chapter 1

1. "Miss Cora Witherspoon," *New Orleans Times-Picayune* (May 19, 1907), p. 4.

2. Niemeyer, "Any Role, Any Studio," p. 3F.

3. "United States Census, 1850," database with images, *Family Search* (https://www.familysearch.org/ark:/61903/1:1:MH5C-26R: 12 July 2021), H C Witherspoon in household of H M Witherspoon, Mobile, Mobile, Alabama, United States; citing family, NARA microfilm publication (Washington, D.C.: National Archives and Records Administration, n.d.); "United States Census, 1860," database with images, *Family Search* (https://familysearch.org/ark:/61903/1:1:MHDN-CGS: 18 February 2021), Henry E Witherspoon in entry for Mary J Witherspoon, 1860; Daniel McCalla Witherspoon, findagrave.com.

4. "United States Census (Slave Schedule), 1860," database with images, *Family Search* (https://familysearch.org/ark:/61903/1:1:WKNR-L5ZM: 16 October 2019), Mary J Witherspoon, 1860.

5. Thomas M. Owen, "No. 31. Generals, Aides-de-Camp, Colonels of Infantry and Cavalry Regiments, with Battalion and Artillery Commanders from Alabama in the War Between the States," *Montgomery Advertiser* (April 13, 1902), p. 21.

6. In a voter registration record from 1891, he is registered as having lived in the parish for 26 years. See "Louisiana, Orleans and St. Tammany Parish, Voter Registration Records, 1867–1905," database, *Family Search* (https://www.familysearch.org/ark:/61903/1:1:WX69-8DW2: 30 April 2020), H. E. Witherspoon, 1891. A later record from 1896 gives the year 1865. See "Louisiana, Orleans and St. Tammany Parish, Voter Registration Records, 1867–1905," database, *Family Search* (https://www.familysearch.org/ark:/61903/1:1:WVV4-ZRW2: 30 April 2020), Hy E Witherspoon, 1896.

7. "Alabama, Church Records, 1831–1994," database, *Family Search* (https://familysearch.org/ark:/61903/1:1:QGPT-MFPK: 11 October 2019), Henry E Witherspoon and Sylla Withers, 16 Dec 1868; citing Marriage, Mobile, Alabama, United States, Library of Congress, Washington, D.C.; Trinity Episcopal Church, Mobile; Government Street Presbyterian Church, Mobile. See also "United States Census, 1850," database with images, *Family Search* (https://www.familysearch.org/ark:/61903/1:1:MH5Z-W8S: 20 December 2020), Pricilla Withers in household of Jay M Withers, Mobile, Mobile, Alabama, United States; citing family, NARA microfilm publication (Washington, D.C.: National Archives and Records Administration, n.d.); "United States Census, 1860," database with images, *Family Search* (https://familysearch.org/ark:/61903/1:1:MHDN-HQ6: 18 February 2021), Priscilla Mc D Withers in entry for Jones M Withers, 1860.

8. "Grand Entertainment," *New Orleans Times-Picayune* (June 22, 1869), p. 1; *New Orleans Times-Picayune* (July 2, 1869), p. 1; "The Regatta Yesterday," *New Orleans Republican* (July 17, 1869), p. 1; *New Orleans Times-Picayune* (April 3, 1869), p. 8.

9. Priscilla McDowell "Sylla" Withers Wither-spoon, findagrave.com.

10. "United States Census, 1880," database with images, *Family Search* (https://familysearch.org/ark:/61903/1:1:MNQH-XZN: 19 February 2021), H E Witherspoon in household of Leslie Frick, Baltimore, Baltimore, Maryland, United States; citing enumeration district ED 109, sheet 104C, NARA microfilm publication T9 (Washington, D.C.: National Archives and Records Administration, n.d.), FHL microfilm 1,254,501.

11. "Illinois, Cook County Marriages, 1871–1968," database, *Family Search* (https://familysearch.org/ark:/61903/1:1:N76S-Z5Y: 10 March 2018), Henry E. Witherspoon and Cora S. Bell, 24 Aug 1880; "Marriages," *Chicago Daily Tribune* (August 29, 1880), p. 8. See also "Married," *Chicago Inter Ocean* (August 30, 1880), p. 8; and "Married," *New Orleans Times-Picayune* (September 19, 1880), p. 2.

12. "United States Census, 1850," database with images, *Family Search* (https://www.familysearch.org/ark:/61903/1:1:MCJ4-TYC: 22 December 2020), Cora Bell in household of C A Kellogg, Orleans, Louisiana, United States; citing family, NARA microfilm publication (Washington, D.C.: National Archives and Records Administration, n.d.); "United States Census, 1860," database with images, *Family Search* (https://familysearch.org/ark:/61903/1:1:MFP4-223: 18 February 2021), Cora Bell in entry for Sam Bell, 1860. The month of Cora Bell's birth is given in the U.S. census for 1900: "United States Census, 1900," database with images, *Family Search* (https://familysearch.org/ark:/61903/1:1:MS5V-6SP: 17 July 2021), Cora Witherspoon, 3rd Precinct New Orleans city Ward 6, Orleans, Louisiana, United States; citing enumeration district (ED) 57, sheet 1A, family 5, NARA microfilm publication T623 (Washington, D.C.: National Archives and Records Administration, 1972.); FHL microfilm 1,240,572.

13. Marjory Adams, "Cora Witherspoon's Life Gives Homely Girls Hope," *Boston Globe* (March 9, 1942), p. 4.

14. "Mrs. Brown-Potter Dies in France, 76," *New York Times* (February 13, 1936), p. 19.

15. "Louisiana Parish Marriages, 1837–1957," database with images, *Family Search* (https://familysearch.org/ark:/61903/1:1:QKJC-9389: 18 February 2021), J M Witherspoon and Carry M Bell, 18 Mar 1867; citing Orleans, Louisiana, United States, various parish courthouses, Louisiana; FHL microfilm 903,920.

16. "United States Census, 1880," database with images, *Family Search* (https://familysearch.org/ark:/61903/1:1:MXJQ-KQL: 19 February 2021), Cora S Bell in household of J M Witherspoon, Chicago, Cook, Illinois, United States; citing enumeration district ED 190, sheet 469D, NARA microfilm publication T9 (Washington, D.C.: National Archives and Records Administration, n.d.), FHL microfilm 1,254,199.

17. "Vincent vs. Vincent," *Memphis Daily Appeal* (September 28, 1883), p. 2.

18. "Louisiana Parish Marriages, 1837–1957," database with images, *Family Search* (https://familysearch.org/ark:/61903/1:1:QKJC-SFTN: 18 February 2021), Charles Vincent and Cora L Bell, 02 Aug 1865; citing Orleans, Louisiana, United States, various parish courthouses, Louisiana; FHL microfilm 903,932; "Married," *New Orleans Times-Picayune* (August 5, 1865), p. 4.

19. "Illinois, Cook County Deaths, 1871–1998," database, *Family Search* (https://familysearch.

org/ark:/61903/1:1:Q2M3-13B6: 8 March 2018), Carrie Vincent, 15 May 1881; citing Chicago, Cook, Illinois, United States, source reference 4712, record number, Cook County Courthouse, Chicago; FHL microfilm 1,031,433.

20. "United States Census, 1870," database with images, *Family Search* (https://www.familysearch.org/ark:/61903/1:1:M87H-GR8: 29 May 2021), C Vincent in entry for Samuel Bell, 1870; "United States Census, 1880," Cora S Bell in household of J M Witherspoon; "She Would Not Remain: Why Did She Leave Him Alone and Forsaken," *National Republican* (January 18, 1877), p. 1.

21. "She Would Not Remain," p. 1.

22. "Letter from Washington," *Baltimore Sun* (June 8, 1877), p. 4.

23. "District of Columbia Marriages, 1830–1921," database, *Family Search* (https://familysearch.org/ark:/61903/1:1:F718-ZLH: 11 January 2020), Charles Vincent, 1877; *Daily Memphis Avalanche* (June 29, 1877), p. 4.

24. "The Vincent Divorce Case: Family Troubles Ventilated," *Washington Evening Star* (September 27, 1883), p. 3; "The Vincent Divorce Decree Sustained," *Washington Evening Star* (October 27, 1884), p. 1.

25. "District of Columbia Deaths and Burials, 1840–1964," database, *Family Search* (https://familysearch.org/ark:/61903/1:1:F7YR-CTG: 16 January 2020), Charles Vincent, 1897; "Mortality Record," *Washington Evening Times* (December 24, 1897), p. 2.

26. "Illinois, Cook County, Birth Certificates, 1871–1949," database, *Family Search* (https://familysearch.org/ark:/61903/1:1:Q23M-85GD: 18 May 2016), Maude Lillian Witherspoon, 16 Mar 1882; Chicago, Cook, Illinois, United States, reference/certificate 100044, Cook County Clerk, Cook County Courthouse, Chicago; FHL microfilm.

27. "The Railroads: The Convalescents," *New Orleans Times-Picayune* (June 10, 1884), p. 6; "The Railroads: The Washington Through Line Office," *New Orleans Times-Picayune* (August 7, 1884), p. 6; "Witherspoon Final Rites Set Tuesday," *Las Cruces Sun-News* (June 8, 1970), p. 2.

28. See, for example, the 1900 U.S. census and Witherspoon's 1924 passport application: "United States Census, 1900," database with images, *Family Search* (https://familysearch.org/ark:/61903/1:1:MS5V-6SR: 28 March 2021), Cora Witherspoon in household of Cora Witherspoon, 3rd Precinct New Orleans city Ward 6, Orleans, Louisiana, United States; citing enumeration district (ED) 57, sheet 1A, family 5, NARA microfilm publication T623 (Washington, D.C.: National Archives and Records Administration, 1972.); FHL microfilm 1,240,572; "United States Passport Applications, 1795–1925," database with images, *Family Search* (https://familysearch.org/ark:/61903/1:1:QV5Y-WZWR : 16 March 2018), Cora Witherspoon, 1924; citing Passport Application, New York, United States, source certificate #436567, Passport Applications, January 2, 1906—March 31, 1925, 2558, NARA

microfilm publications M1490 and M1372 (Washington D.C.: National Archives and Records Administration, n.d.).

29. "Actress Hates Men: Girlish Vow Not to Marry Until 28 Leads Miss Witherspoon to Scorn the Opposite Sex," *Milwaukee Journal* (December 31, 1909), p. 5.

30. "Kentucky, County Marriages, 1797–1954," database with images, *Family Search* (https://familysearch.org/ark:/61903/1:1:Q2QD-DFLB: 9 March 2021), Samuel Bell and Caroline Matilda Headington, 1834; citing Marriage, Jefferson, Kentucky, United States, various county clerks and county courts, Kentucky; FHL microfilm 482,706; "United States Census, 1840," database with images, *Family Search* (https://www.familysearch.org/ark:/61903/1:1:XHTD-VG7: 8 December 2020), Saml Bell, New Orleans, Orleans, Louisiana, United States; citing p. 64, NARA microfilm publication (Washington D.C.: National Archives and Records Administration, n.d.), roll; FHL microfilm; "Louisiana, Orleans Parish Death Records and Certificates, 1835–1954," database, *Family Search* (https://www.familysearch.org/ark:/61903/1:1:ZWNJ-WJW2: 29 April 2020), Samuel Bell, 1876; "Died," *New Orleans Times-Picayune* (January 16, 1874), p. 4; "Samuel Bell," *New Orleans Times-Picayune* (August 3, 1876), p. 1.

31. "T.C. Witherspoon Dies in West," *St. Louis Post-Dispatch* (February 19, 1917), p. 3.

32. "John M. Witherspoon," *New Orleans Times-Picayune* (February 13, 1888), p. 4.

33. "Alabama County Marriages, 1809–1950," database with images, *Family Search* (https://familysearch.org/ark:/61903/1:1:VRJ5-6BF: 19 February 2021), William Frick and Leslie Witherspoon, 26 Dec 1864; citing Mobile, Alabama, United States, County Probate Courts, Alabama; FHL microfilm 1,294,423.

34. "United States Census, 1850," C L Witherspoon in household of H M Witherspoon, Mobile, Mobile, Alabama, United States; "United States Census, 1860," Leslie Witherspoon in entry for Mary J Witherspoon, 1860; "United States Census, 1910," database with images, *Family Search* (https://familysearch.org/ark:/61903/1:1:M2FQ-9CF: 20 July 2021), Leslie Witherspoon Frick in household of Robert S Downs, Baltimore Ward 11, Baltimore (Independent City), Maryland, United States; citing enumeration district (ED) ED 161, sheet 14B, family 278, NARA microfilm publication T624 (Washington D.C.: National Archives and Records Administration, 1982), roll 556; FHL microfilm 1,374,569.

35. "Died," *Baltimore Sun* (February 1, 1917), p. 6; "T.C. Witherspoon Dies in West," p. 3; "California, County Birth and Death Records, 1800–1994," database with images, *Family Search* (https://familysearch.org/ark:/61903/1:1:QP39-91LR: 1 March 2021), Thos K C Witherspoon, 1917.

36. "Died," *New Orleans Crescent* (January 23, 1849), p. 2.

37. "Samuel H. Bell, One of Metairie's Founders, Dies," *New Orleans Item* (December 15, 1923), p. 6; "Samuel H. Bell, 79 Years, Is Dead of Heart Attack: Metairie Cemetery Founder, Confederate Veteran Is Called," *New Orleans Times-Picayune* (December 15, 1923), p. 5.

38. "United States Census, 1900," database with images, *Family Search* (https://familysearch.org/ark:/61903/1:1:MS5V-5S7: 20 July 2021), Samuel H Bell, 2nd Precinct New Orleans city Ward 7, Orleans, Louisiana, United States; citing enumeration district (ED) 63, sheet 1B, family 13, NARA microfilm publication T623 (Washington, D.C.: National Archives and Records Administration, 1972.); FHL microfilm 1,240,572; "United States Census, 1910," database with images, *Family Search* (https://familysearch.org/ark:/61903/1:1:MPYN-F5D: 20 July 2021), Samuel H Bell, New Orleans Ward 7, Orleans, Louisiana, United States; citing enumeration district (ED) ED 105, sheet 10A, family 169, NARA microfilm publication T624 (Washington D.C.: National Archives and Records Administration, 1982), roll 521; FHL microfilm 1,374,534; "United States Census, 1920," database with images, *Family Search* (https://www.familysearch.org/ark:/61903/1:1:MV78-5LT: 1 February 2021), Samuel H Bell, 1920; Herman J. Seiferth, "The Last Confederate Tells His Story: Dashing Rebel Officer Laid Down Sword Two Months After Lee's Army Surrendered," *New Orleans Times-Picayune* (April 15, 1923), p. 1.

39. "Stage Star's Sister Here for Opening," *Hollywood Citizen-News* (August 12, 1939), p. 14.

40. The voter registration record for August 22, 1891 gives this address and also indicates that Henry Witherspoon had lived in the same ward for seven years. That does not mean that he lived in the same house. See "Louisiana, Orleans and St. Tammany Parish, Voter Registration Records, 1867–1905," H. E. Witherspoon, 1891; "Louisiana, Orleans and St. Tammany Parish, Voter Registration Records, 1867–1905," Hy E Witherspoon, 1896.

41. "Died," *New Orleans Times-Picayune* (February 27, 1898), p. 4. There was also a death announcement in the *Semi-Weekly Times Democrat* (March 4, 1898), p. 3. "Louisiana, New Orleans, Interment Registers, 1836–1972," database, *Family Search* (https://familysearch.org/ark:/61903/1:1:44RS-823Z: 19 November 2019), H E Witherspoon, 1898; Henry Edgeworth Witherspoon, findagrave.com.

42. "Award to Women at the Fair," *New Orleans Times-Picayune* (May 27, 1899), p. 3.

43. "Necrological: Mrs. M.O.H. Norton," *New Orleans Times-Democrat* (May 13, 1899), p. 4; "Died," *New Orleans Times-Democrat* (May 13, 1899), p. 2; "Death of Mrs. M.O.H. Norton," *New Orleans Times-Democrat* (May 14, 1899), p. 3; Maria Winn Bell Norton, findagrave.com.

44. "United States Census, 1900," database with images, *Family Search* (https://familysearch.org/ark:/61903/1:1:MS5V-6SP: 29 May 2021),

Cora Witherspoon, 3rd Precinct New Orleans city Ward 6, Orleans, Louisiana, United States; citing enumeration district (ED) 57, sheet 1A, family 5, NARA microfilm publication T623 (Washington, D.C.: National Archives and Records Administration, 1972.); FHL microfilm 1,240,572.

45. "Louisiana, Orleans Parish Death Records and Certificates, 1835–1954," database, *Family Search* (https://www.familysearch.org/ark:/61903/1:1:83XC-LT3Z: 30 June 2020), Cora S Bell Witherspoon, 1900; "Deaths," *New Orleans Times-Picayune* (July 19, 1900), p. 3; "Mrs. H.E. Witherspoon," *New Orleans Times-Picayune* (July 19, 1900), p. 12. See also the interment register for New Orleans, where Cora Slocomb Witherspoon's name is given as H.E. Witherspoon: "Louisiana, New Orleans, Interment Registers, 1836–1972," database, *Family Search* (https://familysearch.org/ark:/61903/1:1:4H3R-VQN2: 19 November 2019), H E Witherspoon, 1900.

46. Niemeyer, "Any Role, Any Studio," p. 3F.

47. Advertisement, *New Orleans Times-Democrat* (September 26, 1897), p. 6; advertisement, *New Orleans Times-Democrat* (September 28, 1897), p. 5; advertisement, *New Orleans Times-Democrat* (October 1, 1901), p. 5.

48. "Pursell-Shields Graded School Sends Forth Four Bright Graduates at the Sessions End," *New Orleans Times-Picayune* (June 17, 1902), p. 12.

49. "Social and Personal," *New Orleans Item* (February 8, 1902), p. 3.

50. "Society Notes," *New Orleans Times-Democrat* (March 1, 1903), p. 2.

51. Niemeyer, "Any Role, Any Studio," p. 3F; "Cora Witherspoon to Play the Lady from Louisville," unidentified, undated clipping [March 1936] (NYPL); "Veteran Actress Recalls Visit," p. 9; "Her Accent's a Natural," *Chicago Sun* (August 29, 1943), p. 18.

52. "St. Anna's Festival Show," *New Orleans Item* (November 6, 1904), p. 16.

53. "Maison Hospitalière," *New Orleans Times-Picayune* (February 3, 1905), p. 7; "New Dramatic Club: To Revive the Glories of the Old Days," *New Orleans Times-Picayune* (July 16, 1905), p. 11.

54. Jean Walrath, "'Pug-Nosed' Girl to Stage Modiste, That's Cora Witherspoon's Story," *Rochester Democrat and Chronicle* (October 22, 1932), p. 15.

55. "Stage Star's Sister Here for Opening," p. 14; Adams, "Cora Witherspoon's Life Gives Homely Girls Hope," p. 4.

56. John Hobart, "On the Stage and Screen: The Hound of the Witherspoon," *San Francisco Chronicle* (July 30, 1939), p. 15.

57. "Well Known Actress of Stage, Screen and Radio Resides Here," *Las Cruces Sun-News* (October 9, 1949), p. 6.

58. "Getting Laughs from Audience Old Stuff to Cora Witherspoon," *New York Herald Tribune* (February 27, 1944) (NYPL).

59. "Louisiana, Orleans Parish Death Records and Certificates, 1835–1954," database, *Family Search* (https://familysearch.org/ark:/61903/1:1:-Z7H5-G5MM: 25 April 2020), Michel Variol, 1896; "Died," *New Orleans Times-Picayune* (December 6, 1896), p. 4.

60. "Veteran Actress Recalls Visit," p. 9; Hobart, "On the Stage and Screen," p. 15; "Stage Star's Sister Here for Opening," p. 14; Lulah Ragsdale, "Orleanians Who Have Made Good on the Stage," *New Orleans Times-Picayune* (September 14, 1913), p. 1; Adams, "Cora Witherspoon's Life Gives Homely Girls Hope," p. 4. The article mistakenly gives the manager's name as "Baldwin Melville."

61. "Miss Witherspoon's Debut," *New Orleans Times-Democrat* (September 24, 1905), p. 5; "Music and Drama," *New Orleans Times-Democrat* (September 24, 1905), p. 8; "Emilie Melville Dead; Doyenne of Our Stage," *New York Times* (May 21, 1932), p. 15.

62. "Lady Gwendolyn's Society Chat," *New Orleans Item* (September 24, 1905), p. 4.

63. "Mary Mannering at Wallack's," *New-York Tribune* (December 11, 1900), p. 8; *Janice Meredith* advertisement, *New Orleans Item* (September 24, 1905), p. 5.

64. "Grand Opera House," *New Orleans Item* (September 24, 1905), p. 5; "Grand Opera House Gives 'Janice Meredith,'" *New Orleans Times-Democrat* (September 25, 1905), p. 10.

65. "Getting Laughs from Audience Old Stuff to Cora Witherspoon" (NYPL).

66. "'Mrs. Dane's Defense' Presented at Grand Opera," *New Orleans Times-Democrat* (November 6, 1905), p. 4; "At the Theatres: 'Mrs. Dane's Defence' and Some Other New Plays," *New York Times* (January 6, 1901), p. 22; "New Play at the Empire: 'Mrs. Dane's Defence,'" *New York Tribune* (January 1, 1901), p. 9; "'Mrs. Dane's Defence' at the Grand Opera House," *New Orleans Times-Picayune* (November 6, 1905), p. 2; "Grand Opera House," *New Orleans Item* (November 6, 1905), p. 2.

67. Madeleine Lucette Ryley, *An American Citizen* (New York and London: Samuel French, 1895), p. 15; "'An American Citizen' at the Grand Opera House," *New Orleans Times-Picayune* (November 27, 1905), p. 2; "Grand Opera House," *New Orleans Item* (November 27, 1905), p. 2; "Grand Opera House," *New Orleans Times-Democrat* (November 27, 1905), p. 4.

68. "'Hearts Aflame' at the Grand Opera House," *New Orleans Times-Picayune* (December 11, 1905), p. 11; "The Theatres Last Night: 'Hearts Aflame' Brought Out at the Garrick," *New York Times* (May 13, 1902), p. 9; "Grand Opera House," *New Orleans Times-Democrat* (December 25, 1905), p. 4; "'Cinderella' and 'Scaramouche,' at the Grand Opera House," *New Orleans Times-Picayune* (December 25, 1905), p. 10; "Amusements: Grand Opera House," *New Orleans Item* (December 25, 1905), p. 2.

69. "Player Folk in a Delightful City: Tell the Thoughts Nearest to Their Happy Hearts," *New Orleans Times-Picayune* (December 26, 1905), p. 8.

70. "'The Gay Lord Quex' at the Grand Opera House," *New Orleans Times-Picayune* (January 1, 1906), p. 10.

71. "'The School for Scandal' at the Grand Opera House," *New Orleans Times-Picayune* (January 8, 1906), p. 12; "'Sowing the Wind' at the Grand Opera House," *New Orleans Times-Picayune* (January 29, 1906), p. 13; "'Romeo and Juliet' at the Grand Opera House," *New Orleans Times-Picayune* (February 5, 1906), p. 7; "'Mistress Nell' at the Grand Opera House," *New Orleans Times-Picayune* (February 19, 1906), p. 16.

72. "Veteran Actress Recalls Visit," p. 9.

73. "Findlay's Benefit at Lyric Theatre," *New Orleans Item* (May 15, 1906), p. 7; "Cora Witherspoon," *New Orleans Times-Democrat* (December 16, 1906), p. 5; "'At Piney Ridge' at Baldwin Theatre," *New Orleans Times-Picayune* (December 17, 1906), p. 2; "Amusements: Baldwin Theater," *New Orleans Item* (December 17, 1906), p. 2.

74. "Women's Edition," *New Orleans Times-Picayune* (May 15, 1907), p. 15; "Society Girls to Sell Woman's Item: They Will Handle Papers Where the Street Stands End," *New Orleans Item* (May 15, 1907), p. 15; "Woman's Edition," *New Orleans Times-Picayune* (May 21, 1907), p. 5; "Reporters for Woman's Item Getting Ready," *New Orleans Item* (May 18, 1907), p. 1.

75. "Women's Edition," p. 15.

76. Helen Pitkin, "Women at Home and Abroad," *New Orleans Times-Democrat* (May 19, 1907), p. 4.

77. "Green Room Gossip: Cora Witherspoon," *New Orleans Times-Picayune* (May 19, 1907), p. 3; "Testimonial Benefit to New Orleans Actress," *New Orleans Item* (May 26, 1907), p. 3; "Miss Witherspoon a Clever Actress," *New Orleans Item* (June 2, 1907), p. 2.

78. "A Night of New Plays: 'Zaza' Imported from Paris and Adapted by David Belasco," *New York Times* (January 10, 1899), p. 7.

79. "Miss Witherspoon a Clever Actress," p. 2; "Miss Witherspoon's Benefit: A Fine Farewell Tribute to the Fair Orleanian," *New Orleans Times-Picayune* (June 3, 1907), p. 5.

80. "Miss Witherspoon's Benefit," p. 5.

81. "The Thespians," *New Orleans Times-Picayune* (June 3, 1907), p. 5; "Amusements: A New Play, 'The Charity Ball,' Made and Acted at the Lyceum Theatre," *New York Sun* (November 20, 1889), p. 2; "Charity Ball at Tulane Theatre," *New Orleans Item* (June 7, 1907), p. 9; "'Charity Ball' Presented to Crowded House by Local Organization," *New Orleans Item* (June 8, 1907), p. 2.

82. "Biloxi: Miss Sophie Bell and Miss Cora Witherspoon Hurt in Car Accident," *New Orleans Times-Picayune* (July 6, 1907), p. 14.

83. "Lyric Theater Reopens Monday," *Buffalo Evening News* (October 23, 1907), p. 1.

84. "Lyric Theater Reopens Monday," p. 1; "'The Dairy Farm' at Lyric Theater," *Buffalo Times* (October 29, 1907), p. 4; "Lyric Opens with Fine Old Play," *Buffalo Commercial* (October 29, 1907), p. 12; "Lyric—'The Diary Farm," *Buffalo Courier* (October 29, 1907), p. 7; "Developments in the Lyric Fight," *Buffalo Enquirer* (October 29, 1907), p. 6.

85. "Lyric Theater Opens Next Monday," *Buffalo Enquirer* (October 23, 1907), p. 3; "Lyric Notes," *Buffalo Sunday Morning News* (October 27, 1907), p. 10; *Illustrated Buffalo Express* (November 3, 1907), p. 4.

86. "Prodigal Daughter," *Buffalo Express* (November 5, 1907), p. 5.

87. "Bijoy: Stock Company Scores a Big Success in 'Turned Up,'" *New Haven Morning Journal-Courier* (December 17, 1907), p. 3.

88. "Amusements: Blaney's Lyric Theatre," *New Orleans Times-Democrat* (February 10, 1908), p. 4; "Society," *New Orleans Item* (March 21, 1908), p. 3.

89. "Green Room Gossip: Miss Cora Witherspoon in St. Louis," *New Orleans Times-Picayune* (June 7, 1908), p. 11; Marguerite Martin, "Would You Have Tears Without a Red Nose? See Miss Harned Weep," *St. Louis Post-Dispatch* (June 1, 1908), p. 3.

90. "Green Room Gossip: Miss Cora Witherspoon in St. Louis," p. 11.

91. "United States Census, 1910," database with images, *Family Search* (https://familysearch.org/ark:/61903/1:1:M21B-D7K: 25 July 2021), William C Witherspoon in household of James M Houston, St Louis Ward 25, St Louis (Independent City), Missouri, United States; citing enumeration district (ED) ED 400, sheet 8A, family 138, NARA microfilm publication T624 (Washington D.C.: National Archives and Records Administration, 1982), roll 822; FHL microfilm 1,374,835; "Missouri, County Marriage, Naturalization, and Court Records, 1800–1991," database with images, *Family Search* (https://familysearch.org/ark:/61903/1:1:-WGP4-JX3Z: 1 October 2019), W C Witherspoon, 3 Jul 1913; citing Marriage, St. Charles, Missouri, United States, Missouri State Archives, Jefferson City; FHL microfilm 007514123.

92. "At the Summer Gardens," *St. Louis Globe-Democrat* (June 29, 1908), p. 5.

93. "News of the Gardens: Henrietta Crosman Presents Mistress Nell at Suburban," *St. Louis Globe-Democrat* (August 3, 1908), p. 5.

94. "'The Crisis' at Suburban," *St. Louis Post-Dispatch* (August 16, 1908), p. 16.

95. "Society," *New Orleans Item* (September 1, 1908), p. 3; "Society," *New Orleans Item* (September 17, 1908), p. 5.

96. "One Who Lost His Voice and Dramatized the Loss," *New York Times* (November 28, 1915), p. 9; "Leo Ditrichstein an American from Hungary," *Buffalo Evening News* (March 16, 1917), p. 12; "Leo Ditrichstein Dies in Austria," *New York Times* (June 30, 1928), p. 17.

97. "New Orleans Has America's Best Little Theater," *New Orleans Times-Picayune* (August 13, 1922), p. 6; "Actor Should Seek Parts He Plays Best: Leo Ditrichstein Favors 'Type' Idea in Drama," *Boston Globe* (January 1, 1917), p. 8.

98. "Cora Witherspoon Likes Both Stage and Film Acting," *Philadelphia Inquirer* (July 4, 1943), p. 6.

99. "Members of Ditrichstein's Co.," *Cleveland Plain Dealer* (November 1, 1908), p. 2; Malcolm MacDonald, "Leo Ditrichstein Pleases Greatly: Begins Season at Colonial with Fine Dramatic Offering," *Cleveland Plain Dealer* (November 10, 1908), p. 8.

100. Malcolm MacDonald, "Leo Ditrichstein Offers His Funniest Play at Colonial," *Cleveland Plain Dealer* (November 24, 1908), p. 5; Malcolm MacDonald, "Keith Opens Hip to Great Crowd," *Cleveland Plain Dealer* (December 29, 1908), p. 3.

101. "Seen at the Local Playhouses," *Pittsburgh Press* (January 3, 1909), p. 1; "Theatrical Attractions This Week," *Pittsburgh Daily Post* (January 3, 1909), p. 3.

102. "In the Theaters Last Evening," *Pittsburgh Daily Post* (January 5, 1909), p. 6; "In the Spotlight: News and Gossip of the Stage," *Pittsburgh Press* (January 5, 1909), p. 4; Amy Leslie, "Big Vaudeville Week," *Chicago Daily News* (January 27, 1909), p. 14.

103. "Green Room Gossip: Miss Cora Witherspoon Engaged for St. Louis," *New Orleans Times-Picayune* (June 13, 1909), p. 9; "At the Summer Gardens," *St. Louis Globe-Democrat* (June 7, 1909), p. 7.

104. "News of the Gardens," *St. Louis Globe-Democrat* (June 21, 1909), p. 5; Ripley D. Saunders, "Dipsomania, as Girl's Heritage, Gives New Plot," *St. Louis Post-Dispatch* (June 21, 1909), p. 6; "News of the Gardens," *St. Louis Globe-Democrat* (June 28, 1909), p. 7.

105. "News of the Gardens," *St. Louis Globe-Democrat* (July 19, 1909), p. 7; Ripley D. Saunders, "'New Lamps and Old' Has Great Tragic Figure," *St. Louis Post-Dispatch* (July 19, 1909), p. 4.

106. Ripley D. Saunders, "'Peter Pan' Is Finely Put on Suburban Stage," *St. Louis Post-Dispatch* (July 26, 1909), p. 4; "News of the Gardens," *St. Louis Globe-Democrat* (July 26, 1909), p. 7; "'Peter Pan,' Suburban," *St. Louis Post-Dispatch* (July 28, 1909), p. 4.

107. "Talented Actress Will Appear Here," *Wilmington Morning News* (October 17, 1927), p. 10.

108. "Stageland: Holmes on the Job," *Milwaukee Journal* (October 19, 1909), p. 6; "Stageland, St. Elmo as a Play," *Milwaukee Journal* (October 23, 1909), p. 11; "Stageland: Mr. Sherman Dictates," *Milwaukee Journal* (November 9, 1909), p. 4; "Stageland: Carmen with Music," *Milwaukee Journal* (November 2, 1909), p. 7; "Doings in Stageland: The Pit at the Shubert," *Milwaukee Journal* (November 13, 1909), p. 8.

109. "Actress Hates Men," p. 5.

Chapter 2

1. Vecchi, "They Judge You by Your Roles," p. 2C.

2. "Cora Is 'Catty' Only on Stage," *Philadelphia Inquirer* (March 1, 1925), p. 29; "A New Effie from Louisville," *Brooklyn Times Union* (April 15, 1936), 17.

3. Adams, "Cora Witherspoon's Life Gives Homely Girls Hope," p. 4.

4. "Topics of the Day," *Providence Evening Bulletin* (January 21, 1911), p. 4; "At the Theaters," *Sioux City Journal* (November 11, 1911), p. 11; Hobart, "On the Stage and Screen," p. 15.

5. Ragsdale, "Orleanians Who Have Made Good on the Stage," p. 1.

6. J. Willis Sayre, "Best of Season's Comedies Now Here," *Seattle Daily Times* (April 15, 1913), p. 11.

7. "Theatrical Attractions," *Pittsburgh Daily Post* (September 13, 1910), p. 4; Elmer K. Rupp, "Theatrical: The Nixon," *Pittsburgh Press* (September 20, 1910), p. 9; "Belasco's Play and Rural Drama More Popular Than 'The Blue Bird,'" *Washington Post* (October 9, 1910), p. 2.

8. Rupp, p. 9; "Review of the Week's Plays," *Baltimore Evening Sun* (September 27, 1910), p. 9.

9. "Musical and Dramatic: 'The Concert,'" *Burlington Free Press* (September 28, 1910). p. 4; "'The Concert': New Play at the Belasco Theatre Scores," *Brooklyn Citizen* (October 5, 1910), p. 5; *Brooklyn Daily Eagle* (April 23, 1911), p. 36; "Theater Topics," *Brooklyn Daily Eagle* (May 26, 1911), p. 4; *The Concert* advertisement, *New York Evening World* (May 27, 1911), p. 9.

10. "Personal Notes," *New Orleans Item* (June 29, 1911), p. 9; "Social Events," *New Orleans Times-Democrat* (July 13, 1911), p. 14.

11. "Qualified Pharmacists: Fifteen Applicants Pass Examinations Before State Board," *New Orleans Times-Picayune* (February 16, 1910), p. 5; "Pharmacy Winners," *New Orleans Times-Picayune* (November 12, 1911), p. 6.

12. "United States Census, 1910," database with images, *Family Search* (https://familysearch.org/ark:/61903/1:1:MPYL-C8L: 24 July 2021), Mandwe Wetherspoon in household of Annie Miller, New Orleans Ward 13, Orleans, Louisiana, United States; citing enumeration district (ED) ED 214, sheet 12B, family 279, NARA microfilm publication T624 (Washington D.C.: National Archives and Records Administration, 1982), roll 524; FHL microfilm 1,374,537; "Louisiana, Orleans Parish, Birth Records, 1819–1906," database, *Family Search* (https://familysearch.org/ark:/61903/1:1:-W1J2-XMPZ: 5 November 2019), Anna Mathilda Venables, 1866; "United States Census, 1870," database with images, *Family Search* (https://www.familysearch.org/ark:/61903/1:1:M87L-QTZ: 29 May 2021), Annie Venalles in entry for Richard Venalles, 1870; "United States Census, 1880," database with images, *Family Search* (https://familysearch.org/ark:/61903/1:1:MDXJ-TBQ: 19 February 2021), Annie Venables in household of Richard S Venables, Amite City, Tangipahoa, Louisiana, United States; citing enumeration district ED 180, sheet 469B, NARA microfilm publication T9 (Washington, D.C.: National Archives

and Records Administration, n.d.), FHL microfilm 1,254,471; "United States Census, 1880," database with images, *Family Search* (https://familysearch. org/ark:/61903/1:1:MDXJ-TBQ: 19 February 2021), Annie Venables in household of Richard S Venables, Amite City, Tangipahoa, Louisiana, United States; citing enumeration district ED 180, sheet 469B, NARA microfilm publication T9 (Washington, D.C.: National Archives and Records Administration, n.d.), FHL microfilm 1,254,471; "Louisiana Parish Marriages, 1837–1957," database with images, *Family Search* (https://familysearch. org/ark:/61903/1:1:QKJ4-841T: 17 February 2021), Warren H Miller and Annie Venables, 25 Apr 1887; citing Orleans, Louisiana, United States, various parish courthouses, Louisiana; FHL microfilm 907,775; "Louisiana, Orleans Parish Death Records and Certificates, 1835–1954," database, *Family Search* (https://www.familysearch.org/ ark:/61903/1:1:ZLHB-Z46Z: 6 June 2020), Warren H. Miller, 1889; "United States Census, 1900," database with images, *Family Search* (https:// familysearch.org/ark:/61903/1:1:MS5R-Q31: 24 July 2021), V Anna Miller in household of E Mary Venables, 5th Precinct New Orleans city (incl. Jewish Widows and Orphans Home) Ward 13, Orleans, Louisiana, United States; citing enumeration district (ED) 128, sheet 6A, family 55, NARA microfilm publication T623 (Washington, D.C.: National Archives and Records Administration, 1972.); FHL microfilm 1,240,575.

13. "Social Events," *New Orleans Times-Democrat* (August 3, 1911), p. 14; "Society," *New Orleans Item* (August 30, 1911), p. 7; "Nautical Notes: Travelers by Sea," *New Orleans Times-Picayune* (September 2, 1911), p. 11; "Society," *New Orleans Times-Democrat* (September 3, 1911), p. 3; "United States Census, 1910," database with images, *Family Search* (https://familysearch. org/ark:/61903/1:1:MPYK-B8F: 21 July 2021), Belle Norton, New Orleans Ward 11, Orleans, Louisiana, United States; citing enumeration district (ED) ED 182, sheet 11A, family 224, NARA microfilm publication T624. (Washington D.C.: National Archives and Records Administration, 1982), roll 523; FHL microfilm 1,374,536.

14. "Society," *New Orleans Times-Picayune* (August 18, 1912), p. 1; "Society," *New Orleans Item* (August 31, 1912), p. 7; "Society," *New Orleans Times-Picayune* (September 1, 1917), p. 1.

15. "News of Plays and Players," *New York Sun* (May 27, 1911), p. 4; *The Concert* advertisement, *Brooklyn Daily Eagle* (September 14, 1911), p. 4; *The Concert* advertisement, *Brooklyn Daily Eagle* (October 14, 1911), p. 4.

16. See, for example, J.D.H., "In the Theaters Last Evening," *Pittsburgh Daily Post* (September 20, 1910), p. 3; "Brilliant Comedy Beautifully Acted: Leo Ditrichstein Superb in the Concert at Belasco's Theatre," *New York Times* (October 5, 1910), p. 11.

17. "'Concert' Is Long Laughfest at Columbia: Playwright Brings Fine Comedy and Cast," *San Francisco Examiner* (March 11, 1913), p. 9; Hale, "'The Concert' at the Hollis," p. 5; "'The Concert' Returns," *Brooklyn Daily Eagle* (March 12, 1912), p. 7; "'The Concert' at Ford's," *Baltimore Sun* (March 19, 1912), p. 9; "'The Concert': Domestic Satire Ably Presented at the Court Square Theatre," *Springfield Union* (November 30, 1912), p. 6; "'The Concert,' Play of Laughs, Is Given Premiere in Fresno, Casts Spell Upon Audience," *Fresno Morning Republican* (March 9, 1913), p. 16; H.W., "Amusements," *Sacramento Star* (March 31, 1913), p. 8; F.H.C., "Pleasing Comedy by Dietrichstein in 'The Concert,'" *Los Angeles Evening Express* (February 25, 1913), p. 4; Hector Alliot, "Placidly Platonic: The Artistic Temperament," *Los Angeles Times* (February 25, 1913), p. II:7; Caryl B. Storrs, "At the Playhouses," *Minneapolis Star Tribune* (May 9, 1913), p. 8.

18. *The Concert* advertisement, *Boston Herald* (January 12, 1912), p. 16; Hale, "'The Concert' at the Hollis," p. 5.

19. "Ditrichstein Play Well Worth While and Very Amusing," *Washington Times* (January 30, 1912), p. 9; *The Concert* advertisement, *Philadelphia Inquirer* (February 4, 1912), p. III:8; "Plays and Players," *Dayton Herald* (August 17, 1912), p. 6; "New Plays by Shaw and Arnold Bennett at Hand," *New York Evening World* (September 14, 1912), p. 5; "'The Concert' Is Harmonious," *Elmira Star-Gazette* (October 3, 1912), p. 11; "'The Concert' at the Hollis," *Boston Globe* (November 5, 1912), p. 11; F.H.C., "Pleasing Comedy by Dietrichstein in 'The Concert,'" p. 4; "'Concert' Is Long Laughfest at Columbia," p. 9.

20. Hale, "'The Concert' at the Hollis," p. 5; "'The Concert' Is a Real Comedy Gem," *Springfield Daily News* (January 17, 1912), p. 5; "Ditrichstein Play Well Worth While and Very Amusing," p. 9; "Shows," *Dayton Herald* (April 20, 1912), p. A22; "The Concert Wonderful," *St. Louis Globe-Democrat* (January 28, 1913), p. 4; Alice Rohe, "Ditrichstein Presents Subtle Masterpiece," *Denver Rocky Mountain News* (February 11, 1913), p. 14; "'The Concert' at Ford's," *Baltimore Sun* (September 27, 1910), p. 10; "The Musical Temperament," *Brooklyn Daily Eagle* (October 5, 1910), p. 4; Percy Hammond, "'Rebellion' and Some of the Other Plays of the Week," *Chicago Tribune* (October 22, 1911), p. 13; "'The Concert' Is Remarkable," *Buffalo Commercial* (April 9, 1912), p. 12; Sayre, "Best of Season's Comedies Now Here," p. 11.

21. Rupp, "Theatrical: The Nixon," p. 9; Charles M. Bregg, "Belasco Presents a German Comedy," *Pittsburgh Post-Gazette* (September 20, 1910), p. 12; J.D.H., "In the Theaters Last Evening," p. 3; The *New York Tribune*'s review quoted in "'The Concert' at Belasco Theatre," *Hartford Courant* (October 7, 1910), p. 7.

22. "'The Concert' Is a Real Comedy Gem," p. 5; "At the Theaters," *Brooklyn Standard Union* (January 23, 1912), p. 11; "Drama," *Buffalo Times* (April 9, 1912), p. 7; "Leo Ditrichstein in 'The Concert,'" *Buffalo Enquirer* (December 13, 1912), p. 5; "At the Theaters," *Louisville Courier-Journal* (January 7,

1913), p. 4; "Amusements," *Washington Evening Star* (January 30, 1912), p. 4; L.G.S., "The Stage," *Detroit Free Press* (April 16, 1912), p. 4; "Amusements," *Salt Lake Telegram* (February 21, 1913), p. 5; "'Concert' Is Long Laughfest at Columbia," p. 9.

23. Gladys Jane Canter, "At Grand Last Night," *Salem Statesman Journal* (April 1, 1913), p. 7.

24. E.S. Carroll, "The Theater," *Sacramento Bee* (March 31, 1913), p. 4; H.W., "Amusements," p. 8.

25. "Green Room Gossip: Brilliant Engagement for Miss Cora Witherspoon," *New Orleans Times-Picayune* (April 6, 1913), p. 4.

26. Waldemar Young, "Unique San Francisco! The Theatrical Center of the Good Old Summertime," *San Francisco Chronicle* (June 8, 1913), p. 21. See, for example, the advertisement in the *San Francisco Chronicle* (June 5, 1913), p. 3.

27. "Ditrichstein at Alcazar," *San Francisco Chronicle* (June 5, 1913), p. 10; J. Willis Sayre, "Ditrichstein Will Try Out New Play," *Seattle Daily Times* (April 16, 1913), p. 9; "Ditrichstein in His Play at the Alcazar," *San Francisco Examiner* (May 31, 1913), p. 7; "Ditrichstein Will Appear at Alcazar in His Own Plays," *San Francisco Chronicle* (June 1, 1913), p. 23; Young, "Unique San Francisco!," p. 21; "This Week's Attractions at the Theatres," *San Francisco Examiner* (June 8, 1913), p. 31; "At the Alcazar," *San Francisco Examiner* (June 10, 1913), p. 9; "Engagement of 'The Concert' at the Alcazar Theater to Be Extended," *San Francisco Call* (June 12, 1913), p. 7.

28. "'Such Is Life' to Have San Francisco Premiere," *San Francisco Chronicle* (June 8, 1913), p. 28; Neill Wilson, "Morning at the Alcazar Behind Asbestos: Ditrichstein Discourses, Isabel Irving Glimpses Stock Troubles," *San Francisco Chronicle* (June 8, 1913), p. 32; "Alcazar," *San Francisco Chronicle* (June 22, 1913), p. 22.

29. "Ditrichstein Wins Plaudits in Farce," *San Francisco Call* (June 24, 1913), p. 8; Neill Wilson, "Leo Ditrichstein Is Whole Show in Himself: 'Such Is Life' Has Gaiety, Many Chuckles," *San Francisco Examiner* (June 25, 1913), p. 9.

30. "Alcazar," *San Francisco Call* (June 29, 1913), p. 32; Arthur L. Price, "'Are You a Mason?' Daisy Blooms Once More," *San Francisco Call* (July 8, 1913), p. 5; "'Are You a Mason?' Repeats Success," *San Francisco Chronicle* (July 8, 1913), p. 10.

31. "Nautical Notes: Travelers by Sea," *New Orleans Times-Picayune* (July 23, 1913), p. 11; "Society," *New Orleans Times-Picayune* (July 24, 1913), p. 14.

32. "Belasco Theatre: 'The Temperamental Journey' an Ingenious Comedy," *New York Tribune* (September 5, 1913), p. 9; "Ditrichstein Play Unreal, But Amusing," *Brooklyn Daily Eagle* (September 5, 1913), p. 8; Dixie Hines, "Police Stop Two New York Shows: Theatrical News Notes and Gossip of Gotham Plays and Players," *Montgomery Advertiser* (September 14, 1913), p. 7.

33. "'Temperamental Journey' at the Republic Theater," *Brooklyn Standard Union* (September 30, 1913), p. 10; *The Temperamental Journey*

advertisement, *New York Tribune* (December 20, 1913), p. 18; "Big Belasco Triumph," *Brooklyn Times Union* (December 20, 1913), p. 4; *The Temperamental Journey* advertisement, *Brooklyn Daily Eagle* (December 20, 1913), p. 15; ibdb.com.

34. "Behind the Footlights," *Rochester Democrat and Chronicle* (March 1, 1914), p. 23.

35. "The Week's Amusements," *Washington Evening Star* (February 22, 1914), p. 8; Julia Chandler Manz, "At the Theaters Last Night," *Washington Herald* (February 24, 1914), p. 7; "Charm and Humor in 'Daddy Long Legs,'" *New York Times* (September 29, 1914), p. 11.

36. "Cora is 'Catty' Only on Stage," p. 29.

37. *Daddy Long Legs* advertisement, *Chicago Tribune* (August 28, 1914), p. 8; Manz, "At the Theaters Last Night," p. 7; "In the Theaters," *Rochester Democrat and Chronicle* (March 6, 1914), p. 25; "Plays and Players: A New Star of Charm and Distinction in an Old-Fashioned Love Story," *Indianapolis News* (March 10, 1914), p. 14; "Charm and Humor in 'Daddy Long Legs,'" *New York Times* (September 29, 1914), p. 11; Hector Turnbull, "Affairs of the Week in the Playhouses," *New York Tribune* (September 27, 1914), p. III:6; *Daddy Long Legs* advertisement, *New York Tribune* (May 15, 1915), p. 16.

38. "Society," *New Orleans Item* (July 15, 1915), p. 4; "Society," *New Orleans Item* (August 13, 1915), p. 7; "Announcements," *New Orleans Item* (August 22, 1915), p. 3; "Social Events," *New Orleans Times-Picayune* (August 25, 1915), p. 6.

39. "Louisiana, Orleans Parish Death Records and Certificates, 1835–1954," database, *Family Search* (https://www.familysearch.org/ark:/61903/1:1:ZKR7-TPPZ: 4 June 2020), Sophie J Bell, 1915; "Louisiana, New Orleans, Interment Registers, 1836–1972," database, *Family Search* (https://familysearch.org/ark:/61903/1:1:4L1B-9LT2: 16 December 2019), Sophie J Bell, 1915; "Death Notices," *New Orleans Item* (September 7, 1915), p. 11; Sophie J. Bell, findagrave.com.

40. "Society," *New Orleans Times-Picayune* (September 11, 1913), p. 14.

41. Ella Mae Hawthorne, "The Theaters: Detroit Opera House," *Detroit Times* (October 26, 1915), p. 3.

42. "Ditrichstein in 'The Great Lover,'" *New York Times* (November 11, 1915), p. 13; "Four Years to Write 'The Great Lover,'" *Washington Times* (January 23, 1917), p. 8; "Comedy Drama at Ford's: 'The Great Lover,' Given for First Time Here, Pleases," *Baltimore Sun* (November 2, 1915), p. 5.

43. "Ditrichstein in 'The Great Lover,'" p. 13; "Miss Cora Witherspoon," *New Orleans Times-Picayune* (July 16, 1916), p. 5.

44. "Ditrichstein in 'The Great Lover,'" p. 13.

45. "News of Society," *Baltimore Sun* (November 2, 1915), p. 4.

46. *The Great Lover* advertisement, *New York Tribune* (June 10, 1916), p. 9; Pixie Hines, "Gossip of the Stage," *Meridien Journal* (June 14, 1916), p. 14; *The Great Lover* advertisement, *Brooklyn Times*

Union (September 4, 1916), p. 4; "Detroit: Leo Ditrichstein Returns in 'The Great Lover,'" *Detroit
Free Press* (September 24, 1916), p. 1.

47. "Ditrichstein Acts 'The Great Lover,'" *New
York Sun* (November 11, 1915), p. 5; "Amusements:
New National," *Washington Evening Star* (January
30, 1917), p. 4; Carlos F. Hurd, "'The Great Lover' a
Play of Splendid Balance," *St. Louis Post-Dispatch*
(March 5, 1917), p. 9.

48. *Shirley Kaye* advertisement, *Detroit Free
Press* (May 6, 1917), p. IV:10; Ella Mae Hawthorn,
"The Stage," *Detroit Times* (May 15, 1917), p. 2;
G.P.G., "The Theater," *Detroit Free Press* (May 15,
1917), p. 4; "Coming," *Detroit Free Press* (April 29,
1917), p. 13.

49. "Theaters," *Detroit Times* (May 22, 1917), p. 6.

50. G.P.G., "The Theater," *Detroit Free Press*
(June 12, 1917), p. 4; "Society," *Detroit Times* (June
12, 1917), p. 4; G.P.G., "The Theater," *Detroit Free
Press* (June 19, 1917), p. 4.

51. G.P.G., "The Theater," *Detroit Free Press*
(June 26, 1917), p. 4; G.P.G., "The Theater," *Detroit
Free Press* (July 10, 1917), p. 4; Ella Mae Hawthorn,
"The Stage," *Detroit Times* (July 10, 1917), p. 4.

52. "Bonstelle Company to Open Season July
26," *Buffalo Evening News* (July 13, 1917), p. 13;
"Miss Bonstelle and Company at Star July 30,"
Buffalo Times (July 15, 1917), p. 57; "Bonstelle
Company Opens Here Monday," *Buffalo Evening
News* (July 25, 1917), p. 3; "At the Theaters and
Summer Resorts," *Buffalo Enquirer* (July 31, 1917),
p. 3; "This Week at the Theaters," *Buffalo Courier*
(July 31, 1917), p. 6; "'His Majesty Bunker Bean' at
the Star Theatre," *Buffalo Times* (August 5, 1917),
p. 50; "Bonstelle Stock Company Present 'His
Majesty, Bunker Bean," *Buffalo Times* (August 7,
1917), p. 4; "At the Playhouses," *Buffalo Evening
News* (August 7, 1917), p. 7; "At the Theaters and
Summer Resorts," *Buffalo Enquirer* (August 7,
1917), p. 2.

53. "This Week at the Theaters," *Buffalo Courier*
(August 12, 1917), p. 42; "The Local Theaters Next
Week," *Buffalo Evening News* (August 11, 1917),
p. 4; "This Week at the Theaters," *Buffalo Courier*
(August 21, 1917), p. 6; "At the Playhouses," *Buffalo
Evening News* (August 21, 1917), p. 13.

54. *The King* advertisement, *Chicago Tribune*
(May 18, 1918), p. 14.

55. Percy Hammond, "Scolded by Mr.
Ditrichstein," *Chicago Tribune* (November 18,
1917), p. VII:2.

56. "Mrs. Fiske and Leo Ditrichstein Re-Enter,"
New York Times (November 18, 1917), p. 8; "'The
King' Is Produced: Leo Ditrichstein in New Play
Speaks French with German Accent," *Brooklyn
Daily Eagle* (November 21, 1917), p. 7.

57. "Ditrichstein Seen in French Comedy,"
New York Sun (November 21, 1917), p. 7; "Leo
Ditrichstein a Hit in 'The King,'" *New York Times*
(November 21, 1917), p. 11; Philip Hale, "Tremont
Play Lively Satire," *Boston Herald* (April 2, 1918), p.
11; "Theatrical Notes," *New York Times* (February
25, 1918), p. 10; "Theaters: Broad Street Theatre,

Newark," *Passaic Daily News* (March 9, 1918), p. 5;
ibdb.com.

58. "Leo Ditrichstein a Hit in 'The King,'" *New
York Times* (November 21, 1917), p. 11; Ralph
Block, "Drama: 'The King' Presents Ditrichstein
in an Uproarious Burlesque," *New York Tribune*
(November 21, 1917), p. 9; "Theatrical Notes:
Ditrichstein in 'The King,'" *Brooklyn Times Union*
(November 21, 1917), p. 4; "'The King' Is Produced:
Leo Ditrichstein in New Play Speaks French with
German Accent," *Brooklyn Daily Eagle* (November
21, 1917), p. 7; "Ditrichstein Seen in French
Comedy," *New York Sun* (November 21, 1917), p. 7.

59. "'The King' Opens at Tremont: Leo
Ditrichstein Wins Success in French Comedy,"
Boston Globe (April 2, 1918), p. 10; Hale, "Tremont
Play Lively Satire," p. 11; *Boston Globe* (April 7,
1918), p. 47.

60. "All Is Quiet Along the Rialto These Days,"
Brooklyn Daily Eagle (June 30, 1918), p. 7; "Plays
and Players," *New York Tribune* (July 2, 1918), p.
9; "The Call Boy's Seashore Chat," *Philadelphia
Inquirer* (July 14, 1918), p. 10.

61. "National," *Washington Evening Star*
(August 4, 1918), p. 4; "Amusements: National,"
Washington Evening Star (August 6, 1918), p. 10;
"Mystery Plays," *Cincinnati Enquirer* (August 25,
1918), p. 2.

62. "'Matinee Idol' [sic] Is Well Received,"
Hartford Courant (September 13, 1918), p. 7.

63. "'The Matinee Hero' Powerful Play,"
Poughkeepsie Eagle-News (October 7, 1918), p. 2.

64. "'The Matinee Hero' Has Great Cast," *Central New Jersey Home News* (October 18, 1918), p. 7;
"Up-to-the-Minute News of Stage and Screen Players," *Reading Times* (October 24, 1918), p. 4.

65. "'Matinee Idol' [sic] Is Well Received," p.
7; "Drama: Leo Ditrichstein Opens in 'The Matinee Hero,'" *New York Tribune* (October 8, 1918),
p. 13; "Leo Ditrichstein as Matinee Idol," *Brooklyn
Daily Eagle* (October 8, 1918), p. 8; Charles Darnton, "The New Plays: Ditrichstein Better Than 'The
Matinee Hero,'" *New York Evening World* (October
8, 1918), p. 22.

66. "'Matinee Idol' [sic] Is Well Received," p. 7;
Philip Hale, "Ditrichstein as a Matinee Hero," *Boston Herald* (September 17, 1918), p. 12; "Leo Ditrichstein in 'The Matinee Hero,'" *Boston Globe*
(September 17, 1918), p. 5; "Ditrichstein Acts in an
Actor's Play," *New York Herald* (October 8, 1918),
p. 9; "Plays and Players," *Brooklyn Life* (October 19,
1918), p. 14.

67. "'Daddy Long Legs' Is Back Again," *New
York Times* (November 18, 1918), p. 13; "A Popular
Revival," *Brooklyn Life* (November 30, 1918), p. 20.

68. "Plays and Players," *Stamford Daily Advocate*
(December 12, 1918), p. 11; "Grace George Com-
ing," *Springfield Republican* (December 15, 1918),
p. 3A; "Grace George and Her New Play," *Stamford
Daily Advocate* (December 17, 1918), p. 7; "Grace
George Seen in New Play," *Hartford Courant*
(December 22, 1918), p. 8; "Last Night at Theaters,"
Washington Herald (December 25, 1918), p. 3.

69. "Amusements: Shubert-Belasco," *Washington Evening Star* (December 25, 1918), p. 18.

70. "In the Local Playhouses," *Detroit Times* (March 9, 1919), p. 4; Harlowe R. Hoyt, "Varied Career Experienced by New Playwright," *Cleveland Plain Dealer* (March 17, 1919), p. 12.

71. Alexander Woollcott, "The Play," *New York Times* (September 12, 1919), p. 18.

72. "Grace George Seen in Comedy of Gold," *New York Herald* (September 12, 1919), p. 11; L.G.S., "The Theater," *Detroit Free Press* (March 11, 1919), p. 4; "McElliott," "He 'Learned About Women' Somewhere," *New York Daily News* (September 12, 1919), p. 12.

73. Harlowe R. Hoyt, "Varied Career Experienced by New Playwright," *Cleveland Plain Dealer* (March 17, 1919), p. 12; L.G.S., "The Theater," p. 4; "The Stage," *Detroit Times* (March 11, 1919), p. 2.

74. L.G.S., "The Theater," p. 4; "The Stage," p. 2.

75. "New Plays Rounded Up by Grace George," *New York Herald* (April 7, 1919), p. 10.

76. Alexander Woollcott, "The Play," *New York Times* (September 12, 1919), p. 18.

77. "Grace George Seen in Comedy of Gold," p. 11; "Grace George in New Comedy," *Brooklyn Citizen* (September 13, 1919), p. 10; *Brooklyn Life* (September 27, 1919), p. 22; "Grace George Appears in a Fragile Comedy," *Springfield Republican* (September 28, 1919), p. 11A; "'Scandal' Forfeits Bit of Real Art," *New York Herald* (October 9, 1919), p. 12; Cynthia St. Charles, "Cynthia St. Charles' Letter," *New Orleans States* (December 7, 1919), p. 26; ibdb.com.

78. "United States Census, 1920," database with images, *Family Search* (https://www.familysearch.org/ark:/61903/1:1:MV72-WYQ: 1 February 2021), Maude Witherspoon, 1920; "Miss Witherspoon Here," *New Orleans States* (November 16, 1919), p. 31; "Witherspoon Final Rites Set Tuesday," p. 2; "Mrs. Anna Miller," *El Paso Times* (November 6, 1944), p. 2; "Miller-Doan Nuptials," *Rice Belt Journal* (September 21, 1917), p. 4; "Personal—But Not Too Personal and Local Items of Interest," *Rice Belt Journal* (September 21, 1917), p. 4; "Sports Official Dies at Age of 59: Ailing Leader in Sugar Bowl Organization Succumbs," *New Orleans Times-Picayune* (June 23, 1947), p. 1; "W.V. Miller Last Rites Set Today," *New Orleans Item* (June 23, 1947), p. 7.

79. "Society News Notes," *New Orleans Item* (November 18, 1919), p. 7; St. Charles, "Cynthia St. Charles' Letter," p. 26.

Chapter 3

1. Unidentified, undated clipping [1942] (NYPL).

2. "Lumarion," "In Our Town," *Las Cruces Sun-News* (September 4, 1968), p. 9.

3. "United States Census, 1920," database with images, *Family Search* (https://www.familysearch. org/ark:/61903/1:1:MJBL-JD4: 2 February 2021), Cora B Witherspoon, 1920; "New York Passenger Arrival Lists (Ellis Island), 1892–1924," database with images, *Family Search* (https://familysearch. org/ark:/61903/1:1:JNHT-KMD: 2 March 2021), Cora Witherspoon, 1924; "Mimi Carte Blanche Peggy Passe Partout," *New Orleans States* (January 4, 1925), p. 5; "Peggy Passe Partout's Letter," *New Orleans States* (September 5, 1926), p. 3.

4. "Cordially Received: Players in 'Why Marry?' Show High Dramatic Quality," *Springfield Republican* (May 22, 1919), p. 17.

5. "Illinois, Cook County, Birth Certificates, 1871–1949," database, *Family Search* (https://familysearch.org/ark:/61903/1:1:N7M6-SMG: 18 May 2016), Myra Doyle, 17 Feb 1894; Chicago, Cook, Illinois, United States, reference/certificate cn 5468, Cook County Clerk, Cook County Courthouse, Chicago; FHL microfilm 1,287,794; "Illinois, Chicago, Catholic Church Records, 1833–1925," database with images, *Family Search* (https://familysearch.org/ark:/61903/1:1:Q2Y9-Z4FT: 17 February 2021), Miriam Adele Doyle, Baptism 22 Feb 1894; citing Catholic Church parishes, Chicago Diocese, Chicago; FHL microfilm 1,685,790; "United States Census, 1900," database with images, *Family Search* (https://familysearch.org/ark:/61903/1:1:MS3D-J93: 22 July 2021), Merriam Doyle in household of Austin J Doyle, Precinct 12 Chicago city Ward 12, Cook, Illinois, United States; citing enumeration district (ED) 340, sheet 6B, family 123, NARA microfilm publication T623 (Washington, D.C.: National Archives and Records Administration, 1972.); FHL microfilm 1,240,258; "United States Census, 1910," database with images, *Family Search* (https://familysearch.org/ark:/61903/1:1:MK88-JY3: 22 July 2021), Miriam A Doyle in household of Austin J Doyle, Chicago Ward 32, Cook, Illinois, United States; citing enumeration district (ED) ED 1381, sheet 2A, family 26, NARA microfilm publication T624 (Washington D.C.: National Archives and Records Administration, 1982), roll 278; FHL microfilm 1,374,291; "Miriam Doyle, Ex-Actress and Producer on Broadway," *New York Times* (September 19, 1962), p. 39; ibdb.com.

6. "New Orleans Has America's Best Little Theater," p. 6; "New York, New York Passenger and Crew Lists, 1909, 1925–1957," database with images, *Family Search* (https://familysearch.org/ark:/61903/1:1:24XN-9B1: 2 March 2021), Miriam Doyle, 1929; citing Immigration, New York, New York, United States, NARA microfilm publication T715 (Washington, D.C.: National Archives and Records Administration, n.d.); "United States Census, 1930," database with images, *Family Search* (https://familysearch.org/ark:/61903/1:1:X42F-PGN: 22 July 2021), Miriam Doyle, Manhattan (Districts 0501–0750), New York, New York, United States; citing enumeration district (ED) ED 651, sheet 7B, line 65, family 157, NARA microfilm publication T626 (Washington D.C.: National Archives and Records Administration, 2002), roll

1564; FHL microfilm 2,341,299; Amanda Woolard to Axel Nissen, 4 July 2020; Miriam Adele Doyle, findagrave.com.

7. "Craig Returns with New Play," *Boston Herald* (February 3, 1920), p. 8; "Craig to Produce an Unusual Play," *Boston Herald* (January 18, 1920), p. 7.

8. "In the Spotlight," *Washington Evening Star* (January 11, 1920), p. III:12; *The Outrageous Mrs. Palmer* advertisement, *Boston Globe* (April 24, 1920), p. 3; "Play of Stage Life at the Arlington," *Boston Globe* (February 3, 1920), p. 4; "Craig Returns with New Play," p. 8; "Stage and Screen," *Boston Herald* (February 9, 1920), p. 1D.

9. "A Designer of Fashionable Clothes Becomes a Capable Actress," *Brooklyn Times Union* (July 10, 1927), p. 1B; Walrath, "'Pug-Nosed' Girl to Stage Modiste," p. 15; "Cora Witherspoon Has Role in 'Frankie and Johnny,'" *Springfield Republican* (February 25, 1934), p. 4C; "Cora Witherspoon to Play the Lady from Louisville" (NYPL).

10. Daniel Blum, *Great Stars of the American Stage: A Pictorial Record* (New York: Grosset and Dunlap, 1952), profile 48; "Marie Doro, 74, Retired Actress," *New York Times* (October 10, 1956), p. 39.

11. Charles Darnton, "The New Plays: 'Lilies of the Field' Off Color but Amusing," *New York Evening World* (October 5, 1921), p. 28; H.F.L., "Marie Doro Scores Hit in New Play," *Bridgeport Evening Farmer* (September 27, 1921), p. 8; "In the Theatres: Park," *Bridgeport Evening Farmer* (September 26, 1921), p. 8; "Plays and Players," *Stamford Daily Advocate* (September 28, 1921), p. 8; "Shows a Side of New York Life," *Stamford Daily Advocate* (September 30, 1921), p. 11.

12. Alexander Woollcott, "The Play," *New York Times* (October 5, 1921), p. 20.

13. "Another Play on the Golddiggers and a Vulgar One," *New York Herald* (October 5, 1921), p. 11.

14. "Not a Moral Woman in 'Lilies of Field,'" *St. Louis Post-Dispatch* (October 5, 1921), p. 11; James Whittaker, "Feminine Mob at Its Best in 'Lilies of Field,'" *New York Daily News* (October 5, 1921), p. 17; "Shows a Side of New York Life," p. 11; B.F., "'Lilies of the Field' Is Neither Real Nor Gilded," *New York Tribune* (October 6, 1921), p. 10; "New Orleans Has America's Best Little Theatre," p. 6.

15. "Gossip," *New York Evening World* (February 13, 1922), p. 22. See also "Notes of Plays and Players," *Denver Post* (February 26, 1922), p. 13. *Lilies of the Field* advertisement, *New York Herald* (February 25, 1922), p. 9; "Passed On," *New York Daily News* (February 26, 1922), p. 22; Burns Mantle, ed., *The Best Plays of 1921–22* (New York: Dodd, Mead, 1955), p. 558; Sheppard Butler, "Something Like 'The Golddiggers,'" *Chicago Tribune* (May 1, 1922), p. 21; "Henry Miller to Play on the Coast," *Richmond Times Dispatch* (April 23, 1922), p. 12.

16. Thomas Nunan, "Henry Miller Triumphs in U.S. Premiere of 'La Tendresse': Ruth Chatterton Wins Praise at Columbia," *San Francisco Examiner* (May 30, 1922), p. 11; Thomas Nunan, "Richman Comedy Back After New York Run," *San Francisco Examiner* (May 1, 1923), p. 15.

17. Heywood Broun, "'The Awful Truth' Is First Smart Play," *St. Louis Post-Dispatch* (September 19, 1922), p. 10.

18. "The New Play: 'The Awful Truth' Bright and Clever Comedy," *Brooklyn Times Union* (September 19, 1922), p. 3; Alexander Woollcott, "The Play: The New Richman Comedy," *New York Times* (September 20, 1922), p. 14. See also Brett Page, "Broadway Fans Are Rushed to Keep Up with New Shows," *Great Falls Tribune* (October 1, 1922), p. 8; Buford Gordon Bennett, "Richman's New Play Is a Triumph," *San Francisco Examiner* (May 16, 1922), p. 13; and George C. Warren, "'Awful Truth' Crackles with Excellent Wit," *San Francisco Chronicle* (May 16, 1922), p. 9.

19. Pearl Rall, "Ruth Chatterton to Open New Miller Season," *Los Angeles Evening News* (August 2, 1922), p. 16; "In the Spotlight," *Washington Evening Star* (August 20, 1922), p. III:3; "'Laughing Lady' Next Vehicle for Miss Barrymore," *New York Daily News* (January 15, 1923), p. 16; Burns Mantle, ed., *The Best Plays of 1922–23* (New York: Dodd, Mead, 1938), p. 583; "Dramatic: West Sees Play First," *Seattle Daily Times* (May 25, 1923), p. 11.

20. "Amusements: Belasco—'The Alarm Clock,'" *Washington Evening Star* (July 23, 1923), p. 4; Burns Mantle, ed., *The Best Plays of 1923–24* (Boston: Small, Maynard, 1924), p. 374; "Current Attractions: Belasco—'The Alarm Clock,'" *Washington Evening Star* (July 29, 1923), p. III:1.

21. Woollcott, "The Play: The New Richman Comedy," p. 14; "In the Theaters This Week," *Pittsburgh Daily Post* (October 30, 1923), p. 9; Robert Benchley's review in *Life* (October 5, 1922) quoted in Anthony Slide, ed., *Selected Theatre Criticism, Volume 2: 1920–1930* (Metuchen, NJ: Scarecrow Press, 1985), p. 6.

22. Warren, "'Awful Truth' Crackles with Excellent Wit," p. 9; George C. Warren, "'Awful Truth' Great Success at Columbia," *San Francisco Chronicle* (May 18, 1922), p. 12.

23. B., "Ford's: 'The Awful Truth,'" *Baltimore Sun* (September 12, 1922), p. 5; "The New Play: 'The Awful Truth' Bright and Clever Comedy," p. 3.

24. Arthur Pollock, "The New Plays," *Brooklyn Daily Eagle* (September 19, 1922), p. 8; "'The Awful Truth' Pleases First Nighters," *Brooklyn Standard Union* (September 19, 1922), p. 11; Robert Garland, "Ina Claire Opens Season with Appealing Comedy," *Baltimore American* (September 12, 1922), p. 7; Page, "Broadway Fans Are Rushed to Keep Up with New Shows," p. 8; "In the Brooklyn Theaters: 'The Awful Truth' Mildly Amusing," *Brooklyn Daily Eagle* (January 23, 1923), p. 12; Sheppard Butler, "Ina Claire Is Delightful in Airy Comedy," *Chicago Tribune* (February 20, 1923), p. 21.

25. Warren, "'Awful Truth' Crackles with Excellent Wit," p. 9; Garland, "Ina Claire Opens Season with Appealing Comedy," p. 7; J.O.L., "Ina

Claire Opens Season at Ford's," *Baltimore Evening Sun* (September 12, 1922), p. 8; Lawrence Reamer, "'The Awful Truth' a Comedy Success with Ina Claire," *New York Herald* (September 19, 1922), p. 10; Broun, "'The Awful Truth' Is First Smart Play," p. 10; "Ina Claire Aids Comedy Success," *Spokane Spokesman-Review* (May 30, 1923), p. 5; "'The Awful Truth' Pleases Audience," *Salt Lake Telegram* (April 21, 1923), p. 4; "Amusements: National—'The Awful Truth,'" *Washington Evening Star* (October 23, 1923), p. 10.

26. "Louisiana, Orleans Parish Death Records and Certificates, 1835–1954," database, *Family Search* (https://familysearch.org/ark:/61903/1:1:ZMM7-2T2M: 17 April 2020), Samuel H. Bell, 1923; "Samuel H. Bell, One of Metairie's Founders, Dies," p. 6; "Louisiana, Orleans Parish Death Records and Certificates, 1835–1954," database, *Family Search* (https://familysearch.org/ark:/61903/1:1:ZMMM-RKW2: 17 April 2020), Ernest D. Cucullu, 1923; "Died," *New Orleans Times-Picayune* (August 19, 1923), p. 4; Meigs O. Frost, "Pals Not Divided in Death," *New Orleans States* (December 23, 1923), p. 1, 3; Samuel H. Bell, findagrave.com; Ernest Cucullu, findagrave.com.

27. "Two New Plays on Theatrical Menu," *Philadelphia Inquirer* (March 1, 1925), p. 30.

28. "Notes About the Players," *Boston Globe* (February 17, 1924), p. 52.

29. Burns Mantle, ed., *The Best Plays of 1924–25* (Boston: Small, Maynard, 1925), pp. 457–58; "Amusements: Ina Claire in 'Grounds for Divorce,'" *Washington Evening Star* (March 4, 1924), p. 16.

30. "On the Pittsburgh Stage," *Pittsburgh Daily Post* (March 11, 1924), p. 8; "Cora Witherspoon Is Without Usual Temperament, She Says," *Denver Post* (June 27, 1926), p. 44.

31. "Belasco—Ina Claire, 'Grounds for Divorce,'" *Washington Evening Star* (March 2, 1924), p. 3:14; Frederick Donaghey, "Miss Claire Once More a Severed Wife," *Chicago Tribune* (March 25, 1924), p. 21.

32. "Stage and Screen Bits," *Philadelphia Inquirer* (February 24, 1924), p. 35; "'Judith' Given U.S. Premiere at Baltimore," *New York Daily News* (February 26, 1924), p. 22.

33. "United States Passport Applications, 1795–1925," database with images, *Family Search* (https://familysearch.org/ark:/61903/1:1:QV5Y-WZWR: 16 March 2018), Cora Witherspoon, 1924; citing Passport Application, New York, United States, source certificate #436567, Passport Applications, January 2, 1906—March 31, 1925, 2558, NARA microfilm publications M1490 and M1372 (Washington D.C.: National Archives and Records Administration, n.d.).

34. "New York Passenger Arrival Lists (Ellis Island), 1892–1924," database with images, *Family Search* (https://familysearch.org/ark:/61903/1:1:JNHT-KMD: 2 March 2021), Cora Witherspoon, 1924.

35. Nanette Kutner, "When Hubby Takes Joy Out of Dancing," *New York Graphic* (October 30, 1924) (NYPL).

36. *Grounds for Divorce* advertisement, *New York Daily News* (January 10, 1925), p. 20; Mantle, ed., *The Best Plays of 1924–25*, p. 606; V.A., "From the Second Balcony," *Daily Northwestern* (April 4, 1924), p. 2; "Ina Claire in Gay Play," *Cincinnati Post* (March 26, 1924), p. 14; T.M.C., "Ina Claire Plays Leading Role in New Vajda Comedy," *Baltimore Sun* (September 17, 1924), p. 11.

37. Frederick Donaghey, "Miss Claire Once More a Severed Wife," *Chicago Tribune* (March 25, 1924), p. 21; Burns Mantle, "'Grounds for Divorce' an Amusing Trifle," *New York Daily News* (September 24, 1924), p. 24; Arthur Pollock, "The New Play: 'Grounds for Divorce,'" *Brooklyn Daily Eagle* (September 24, 1924), p. 9; "At the Theaters," *Brooklyn Standard Union* (September 24, 1924), p. 8.

38. R.H., "Bright Comedy at Garrick," *Detroit Times* (March 17, 1924), p. 9; William Smith Goldenburg, "Grounds for Divorce," *Cincinnati Enquirer* (March 26, 1924), p. 6; Philip Hale, "New Comedy at the Plymouth," *Boston Herald* (January 27, 1925), p. 28; "The Theater," *Detroit Free Press* (March 17, 1924), p. 6; Mantle, "'Grounds for Divorce' an Amusing Trifle," p. 24; "Ina Claire at the Plymouth," *Boston Globe* (January 27, 1925), p. 15; Charles A. Collins, "Play-Days," *Columbus Dispatch* (October 5, 1924), p. 94.

39. "Amusements: Belasco—'The Fall of Eve,'" *Washington Evening Post* (May 12, 1925), p. 18.

40. "The Fall of Eve in Modern Eden," *Stamford Daily Advocate* (May 9, 1925), p. 8; "Amusements: Belasco—'The Fall of Eve,'" p. 18; "'The Fall of Eve' Snappy and Lively Tale of Wedlock," *Stamford Advocate* (August 22, 1925), p. 7; "The Play: 'The Fall of Eve,'" *Asbury Park Press* (August 25, 1925), p. 11.

41. "The Play: Ruth Gordon Runs Through a Play," *New York Times* (September 1, 1925), p. 18.

42. A.J.B., "The New Play: Ruth Gordon's Hour," *Brooklyn Times Union* (September 1, 1925), p. 6; R.W.H., "The Premiere: 'The Fall of Eve,'" *Brooklyn Citizen* (September 1, 1925), p. 5; "'The Fall of Eve' at the Booth," *Brooklyn Standard Union* (September 1, 1925), p. 6; Arthur Pollock, "Plays and Things," *Brooklyn Daily Eagle* (September 1, 1925), p. 7; Brett Page, "Along Old Broadway!," *Buffalo Times* (September 6, 1925), p. 60; Burns Mantle, ed., *The Best Plays of 1925–26* (New York: Dodd, Mead, 1926), p. 607; "An Actress's Avocation," *New York Sun* (September 30, 1925) (NYPL).

43. Ruth Gordon, *Myself Among Others* (New York: Atheneum, 1971), p. 251.

44. "'Al' Jackson's New Play at Park Today," *Bridgeport Telegram* (February 22, 1926), p. 13; "Hush Money," *Bridgeport Telegram* (February 23, 1926), p. 20; *Hush Money* advertisement, *Bridgeport Telegram* (February 20, 1926), p. 10; "Amusements: Park Theatre," *Bridgeport Telegram* (February 20, 1926), p. 10.

45. "'Hush Money' Crooks of Familiar Sort,"

New York Times (March 16, 1926), p. 22; "'Hush Money' at the 49th Street Theatre," *Brooklyn Standard Union* (March 16, 1926), p. 10; "'Hush Money' Has Its Premiere," *Brooklyn Times Union* (March 16, 1926), p. 1A; *Hush Money* advertisement, *New York Daily News* (May 1, 1926), p. 22; Mantle, ed., *The Best Plays of 1925–26*, p. 608.

46. "Florence Eldridge Will Head New Elitch Gardens Company," *Denver Post* (April 27, 1926), p. 18; "Elitch Recruits Talented Players for Coming Season," *Denver Post* (May 2, 1926), p. 55; *The Swan* advertisement, *Denver Post* (June 8, 1926), p. 23.

47. "Florence Eldridge Will Head," p. 18; "Elitch Recruits Talented Players for Coming Season," *Denver Post*, p. 55; "Cora Witherspoon Is Without Usual Temperament," p. 44; A. De Bernardi, Jr., "Elitch Theater Season Opens with Brilliant Presentation of Ferenc Molnar's 'The Swan,'" *Denver Post* (June 14, 1926), p. 23; A. De Bernardi, Jr., "Wise-Crack Comedy Is Show at Elitch Theater for Week," *Denver Post* (June 21, 1926), p. 17.

48. A. De Bernardi, Jr., "'Dancing Mothers' at Elitch Is Drama of Modern Jazz Age," *Denver Post* (June 28, 1926), p. 15; A. De Bernardi, Jr., "'The Music Master Delights Initial Audiences at Elitch," *Denver Post* (July 5, 1926), p. 23.

49. *Craig's Wife* advertisement, *Denver Post* (July 10, 1926), p. 9; *Craig's Wife* advertisement, *Denver Post* (July 16, 1926), p. 15; "'Craig's Wife' Is New Elitch Play," *Denver Post* (July 11, 1926), p. 11; A. De Bernardi, Jr., "Pulitzer Prize Winning Play Is Offering at the Elitch," *Denver Post* (July 12, 1926), p. 15.

50. Burns Mantle, "Denver Recalls Old Days of the Theater," *Denver Post* (July 25, 1926), p. 61; "Asides," *Denver Post* (September 19, 1930), p. 22; unidentified, undated clipping [1942] (NYPL).

51. "Players at Elitch Gardens Master Southern Dialect," *Denver Post* (August 26, 1926), p. 29; Betty Craig, "Heard in Theater Lobbies," *Denver Post* (August 28, 1926), p. 9; A. De Bernardi, Jr., "'Liliom,' Imaginative Molnar Play, Is Offering at Elitch," *Denver Post* (August 9, 1926), p. 19.

52. A. De Bernardi, Jr., "'Icebound' Is a Real Drama of Cheerless New England Life," *Denver Post* (July 26, 1926), p. 17; A. De Bernardi, Jr., "'Not Herbert,' Mystery Comedy Is Entertaining Elitch Play," *Denver Post* (August 2, 1926), p. 17; A. De Bernardi, Jr., "'Easy Come, Easy Go' Is Best Comedy Seen Here in a Year," *Denver Post* (August 16, 1926), p. 13; "Michael Arlen Comedy at Elitch Gardens Clever and Entertaining," *Denver Post* (August 30, 1926), p. 12.

53. "Talented Actress Will Appear Here," *Wilmington Morning News* (October 27, 1927), p. 10; Betty Craig, "Heard in Theater Lobbies," *Denver Post* (November 6, 1926), p. 9.

54. "Ethel Barrymore's Play: She Is to Return to Frohman Management in 'The Constant Wife,'" *New York Times* (September 17, 1926), p. 19; "New Barrymore Play," *Brooklyn Times Union* (November 18, 1926), p. 6A.

55. W. Somerset Maugham, *The Collected Plays of W. Somerset Maugham, Vol. II* (London: William Heinemann, 1952), p. 95, 96, 102, 118.

56. Maugham, p. 160, 180, 188, 197; Richard S. Davis, "Quite the Thing for Miss Ethel: 'The Constant Wife' Is Found the Wittiest of Comedies," *Milwaukee Journal* (April 10, 1928), p. 15.

57. R.L.F., "The Constant Wife," *Brooklyn Times Union* (November 30, 1926), p. 9; "Ethel Barrymore Charming in Role Designed for Her," *St. Louis Star and Times* (April 17, 1928), p. 10; "'Constant Wife Makes Hit Here," *Wilmington New Journal* (October 18, 1927), p. 10; L.L., "A Real Star Returns," *Kansas City Star* (April 24, 1928), p. 11; "Great Actress and Fine Play at Parson's," *Hartford Courant* (October 28, 1927), p. 4; Eleanor Clarage, "Main Street Meditations," *Cleveland Plain Dealer* (November 4, 1926), p. 18.

58. Clarage, p. 18.

59. Ralph Holmes, "New Comedy Is Very Clever," *Detroit Times* (November 9, 1926), p. 17; Len G. Shaw, "The Theater," *Detroit Free Press* (November 9, 1926), p. 6; "In the Pittsburgh Theaters," *Pittsburgh Daily Post* (November 16, 1926), p. 15; "Nixon: 'The Constant Wife," *Pittsburgh Press* (November 16, 1926), p. 32; "In the Theaters Last Night," *Pittsburgh Post-Gazette* (November 16, 1926), p. 17; Ph. J., "Opening Attractions in Washington Theaters," *Washington Evening Star* (November 23, 1926), p. 20.

60. Brooks Atkinson, "'The Constant Wife' Deft and Sparkling," *New York Times* (November 30, 1926), p. 26; R.L.F., "The Constant Wife," *Brooklyn Times Union* (November 30, 1926), p. 9; Arthur Pollock, "Plays and Things," *Brooklyn Daily Eagle* (November 30, 1926), p. 10A.

61. Barrett H. Clark in *The Drama* (January 1927) quoted in Slide, ed., *Selected Theatre Criticism*, p. 32; Davis, "Quite the Thing for Miss Ethel," p. 15.

62. Pierre de Rohan, "Comedy Almost Talks Self to Death: Only Ethel Barrymore's Artistry Saves 'The Constant Wife' from Boredom," *Camden Courier-Post* (September 27, 1927), p. 19.

63. "The Golden Dozen," *New York Daily News* (August 6, 1927), p. 19; Burns Mantle, ed., *The Best Plays of 1927–28* (New York: Dodd, Mead, 1937), p. 562.

64. Emanuel Levy, *George Cukor, Master of Elegance: Hollywood's Legendary Director and His Stars* (New York: William Morrow, 1994), pp. 37–38.

65. Louise Mace, "Notes of the Theaters: Author and Star Form Expert Combination," *Springfield Republican* (October 25, 1927), p. 9; "'Constant Wife' Is Fine Comedy," *Chicago Daily News* (December 28, 1927), p. 17; Davis, "Quite the Thing for Miss Ethel," p. 15; "Plays in Brooklyn," *Brooklyn Times Union* (September 20, 1927), p. 8; "Great Actress and Fine Play at Parson's," p. 4; "'Constant Wife' Is Charming," *Wilmington Evening Journal* (October 18, 1927), p. 21; "'Constant Wife Makes Hit Here," *Wilmington New Journal* (October 18, 1927), p. 10;

H.H. Niemeyer, "Miss Barrymore as 'The Constant Wife,'" *St. Louis Post-Dispatch* (April 17, 1928), p. 21; "Famous Artist Triumphant in 'Constant Wife,'" *Salt Like City Tribune* (May 11, 1928), p. 14; "Ethel Barrymore in Charming Role at S.L. Theatre," *Salt Lake City Telegram* (May 11, 1928), p. 5; "Denver Papers Enthusiastic About Barrymore's Play," *Grand Junction Daily Sentinel* (May 3, 1928), p. 9; Helen Eastom, "Another 'Celebrity' Party in Offing," *Denver Post* (May 1, 1928), p. 14; Helen Eastom, "Miss Whitehead to Entertain," *Denver Post* (May 2, 1928), p. 18; George C. Warren, "Ethel Barrymore at Curran: Maugham Has Brilliant Love Comedy," *San Francisco Chronicle* (May 29, 1928), p. 9; George C. Warren, "Last Week of Barrymore at Curran: Star Superb in Comedy by Maugham," *San Francisco Chronicle* (June 16, 1928), p. 15.

66. "Leo Ditrichstein Dies in Austria," p. 17.

67. Rowland Field, "The New Play," *Brooklyn Times Union* (October 17, 1928), p. 5A; "Fay Compton to Act Here," *New York Times* (August 24, 1928), p. 23.

68. J. Brooks Atkinson, "The Play: Among Molnar's Well-Born," *New York Times* (October 17, 1928), p. 26; Rowland Field, "The New Play," *Brooklyn Times Union* (October 17, 1928), p. 5A; Burns Mantle, "'Olympia' a Lover's Vengeance: New Molnar Comedy Tells One on Haughty Princess," *New York Daily News* (October 17, 1928), p. 35; Donald Mulhern, "The New Play: Ferenc Molnar Supplies in 'Olympia' a Fable in One-Syllable Words," *Brooklyn Standard Union* (October 17, 1928), p. 11; Arthur Pollock, "The Theaters," *Brooklyn Daily Eagle* (October 17, 1928), p. 12A; Robert F. Sisk, "Molnar's Play a Flop," *Baltimore Sun* (October 21, 1928), p. II:1.

69. Atkinson, "The Play: Among Molnar's Well-Born," p. 26; Field, "The New Play," p. 5A; Mulhern, "The New Play," p. 11; Pollock, "The Theaters," p. 12A; Mantle, "'Olympia' a Lover's Vengeance," p. 35.

70. *Olympia* advertisement, *Brooklyn Times Union* (November 16, 1928), p. 5A, Burns Mantle, ed., *The Best Plays of 1928–29* (New York: Dodd, Mead, 1929), p. 398; *Brooklyn Life* (January 5, 1929), p. 17.

71. "Theatre Notes," *New York Daily News* (December 24, 1928), p. 19; "Playhouse News," *Brooklyn Times Union* (December 30, 1928), p. 27; Mantle, ed., *The Best Plays of 1928–29*, p. 455.

72. *Brooklyn Life* (January 5, 1929), p. 17; R.M., "Flatbush Sees Forbes' Comedy," *Brooklyn Standard Union* (January 6, 1929), p. 15; "Precious," *Brooklyn Daily Eagle* (January 8, 1929), p. 10A; Burns Mantle, "'Precious' Featherbrain Comedy," *New York Daily News* (January 15, 1929), p. 33; Rowland Field, "The New Play," *Brooklyn Times Union* (January 15, 1929), p. 3A; "'Precious' a Comedy Full of Innuendo," *New York Times* (January 15, 1929), p. 22.

73. "Stars of the Theatre Are Turning to Radio," *Allentown Morning Call* (July 7, 1929), p. 20.

74. "Plays and Players," *Brooklyn Daily Eagle* (September 5, 1929), p. 23; "'Nancy's Private Affair' to Start," *New York Times* (September 6, 1929), p. 23.

Chapter 4

1. Unidentified, undated clipping [1942] (NYPL).

2. "June Walker and Glenn Hunter in Sherwood Play," *New York Daily News* (November 2, 1929), p. 23.

3. "Tremont Theater: 'Waterloo Bridge,'" *Boston Herald* (November 17, 1929), p. 44; Louise Mace, "Here and There in the Theater: Young Woodley Goes to War," *Springfield Republican* (November 15, 1929), p. 6E.

4. Robert E. Sherwood, *Waterloo Bridge* (New York: Charles Scribner's, 1930), pp. 7–8.

5. Sherwood, p. 113, 116–121.

6. Sherwood, p. 156.

7. "'Waterloo Bridge' Winsome War Play," *Boston Globe* (November 22, 1929), p. 34; Walter Brown, "Glenn Hunter, June Walker, in New Play," *Hartford Courant* (November 13, 1929), p. 17; J. Brooks Atkinson, "The Play: Love Will Tell," *New York Times* (January 7, 1930), p. 29; Burns Mantle, "'Waterloo Bridge' About Love, War," *New York Daily News* (January 7, 1930), p. 29; Arthur Pollock, "The Theater," *Brooklyn Daily Eagle* (January 7, 1930), p. 21; Rowland Field, "The New Play," *Brooklyn Times Union* (January 7, 1930), p. 3A.

8. "'Waterloo Bridge' Winsome War Play," p. 34; Philip Hale, "The Theaters," *Boston Herald* (November 22, 1929), p. 25; Brown, "Glenn Hunter, June Walker, in New Play," p. 17; Atkinson, "The Play: Love Will Tell," p. 29; Mantle, "'Waterloo Bridge' About Love, War," p. 29; "Stage Styles Change to Fit New Roles," *Brooklyn Times* (July 13, 1930) (NYPL).

9. *Waterloo Bridge* advertisement, *New York Daily News* (March 1, 1930), p. 21; Burns Mantle, ed., *The Best Plays of 1929–30* (New York: Dodd, Mead, 1969), p. 474.

10. "United States Census, 1930," database with images, *Family Search* (https://familysearch.org/ark:/61903/1:1:X42G-YNM: 22 July 2021), Cora Witherspoon, Manhattan (Districts 1001–1249), New York, New York, United States; citing enumeration district (ED) ED 1215, sheet 34A, line 28, family 21, NARA microfilm publication T626 (Washington D.C.: National Archives and Records Administration, 2002), roll 1567; FHL microfilm 2,341,302.

11. "'Reunion' in Rehearsal," *Brooklyn Standard Union* (July 2, 1930), p. 13.

12. Roland Holt, "The Living Stage: Bright Beach Group Stages Hot 'Reunion,'" *Springfield Republican* (August 3, 1930), p. 6F; W.M.F., "'Reunion' Opens at the Brighton," *Brooklyn Standard Union* (July 15, 1930), p. 7.

13. "Rehearsals Start on 'Reunion' and Russian Comedy," *New York Daily News* (July 1, 1930), p. 33; "'Reunion' in Rehearsal," *Brooklyn Standard Union* (July 2, 1930), p. 13.

14. W.M.F., "'Reunion' Opens at the Brighton," p. 7; Arthur Pollock, "The Theater: 'Reunion' Opens at the Brighton," *Brooklyn Daily Eagle*

(July 15, 1930), p. 19; Charles Hastings, "Theatres: 'Reunion' Marked at the Brighton, by Splendid Acting," *Brooklyn Times Union* (July 15, 1930), p. 3A; Max D. Davidson, "The Play: Dear Old Alma Mater," *Asbury Park Press* (July 22, 1930), p. 17.

15. W.M.F., "'Reunion' Opens at the Brighton," p. 7; Holt, "The Living Stage," p. 6F; Hastings, "Theatres," p. 3A.

16. George C. Warren, "Behind the Back Row," *San Francisco Chronicle* (July 8, 1930), p. 9; "Plays, Pictures and Players," *Los Angeles Evening Express* (July 16, 1930), p. 20.

17. A.D.M., "That's the Woman," *Jersey Journal* (August 26, 1930), p. 17.

18. "Theatre Notes," *New York Daily News* (September 12, 1930), p. 61; "The Stage: At the Broad," *Jewish Chronicle* (October 3, 1930), p. 8.

19. "Breezy Farce Comedy, 'Oh Promise Me,' Provides Hilarious Entertainment," *Newark Ledger* (October 7, 1930) (NYPL); C.F.F., "Sam Harris Presents 'Oh Promise Me' at the Boulevard," *Brooklyn Times Union* (October 14, 1930), p. 6A; "Row G, Two Seats on the Aisle," *Jersey Journal* (October 7, 1930), p. 11; Richard Murray, "Oh Promise Me," *Brooklyn Standard Union* (October 14, 1930), p. 13.

20. "'Oh, Promise Me' Premiere Soon," *New York Times* (November 6, 1930), p. 22; "Row G, Two Seats on the Aisle," p. 11; "Breezy Farce Comedy, 'Oh Promise Me,' Provides Hilarious Entertainment," *Newark Ledger* (October 7, 1930) (NYPL); Murray, "Oh Promise Me," p. 13.

21. "'Philip Goes Forth,' New Kelly Play," *Denton Journal* (December 27, 1930), p. 6; D.K., "Philip Goes Forth, New Comedy, at Ford's Theater," *Baltimore Sun* (December 30, 1930), p. 5; M.W.R., "Here and There About Town," *Barnard Bulletin* (February 10, 1931), p. 2; Burns Mantle, "On Broadway," *Boston Herald* (January 25, 1931), p. 40.

22. Rowland Field, "Both Sides of the Curtain," *Brooklyn Times Union* (January 18, 1931), p. 12; George Kelly, *Philip Goes Forth: A Play in Three Acts* (New York: Samuel French, 1931), p. 15, 67.

23. Kelly, *Philip Goes Forth*, p. 26; "Theatre Fashions," *Paducah Sun-Democrat* (February 27, 1931), p. 6. See also Ruth Stuyvesant, "Fashions from Paris," *San Francisco Chronicle* (March 4, 1931), p. 8.

24. Kelly, pp. 32–33, 42.

25. Norman Clark, "Baltimore Critic Praises Comedy Here Next Week," *Lancaster Intelligencer Journal* (January 1, 1931), p. 4, reprinted from the *Baltimore News*; L.McC., "New George Kelly Comedy at Ford's," *Baltimore Evening Sun* (December 30, 1930), p. 8; J.P.R., "'Philip Goes Forth' Is Brilliant Comedy," *Camden Courier-Post* (April 7, 1931), p. 12; Field, "Both Sides of the Curtain," p. 12; "New Kelly Play Proves Success in Try Out Here," *Lancaster Intelligencer Journal* (January 6, 1931), p. 16.

26. D.K., "Philip Goes Forth," p. 5; Arthur Pollock, "The Theaters," *Brooklyn Daily Eagle* (January 13, 1931), p. 19; Mantle, "On Broadway," p. 40; J.

Brooks Atkinson, "The Play," *New York Times* (January 13, 1931), p. 35.

27. L.McC., "New George Kelly Comedy at Ford's," p. 8; D.K., "Philip Goes Forth," p. 5; Burns Mantle, "Kelly Comedy Tells Human Adventure of Eager Youth," *New York Daily News* (January 13, 1931), p. 39; "'Philip Goes Forth' Season's High Spot," *Lancaster New Era* (January 6, 1931), p. 4; M.W.R., "Here and There About Town," p. 2.

28. Clark, "Baltimore Critic Praises Comedy Here Next Week," p. 4, reprinted from the *Baltimore News*; "New Kelly Play Is Good Comedy," *Philadelphia Inquirer* (April 7, 1931), p. 10; Atkinson, "The Play," p. 35; Percy Hammond, "Two Important New Plays," *Washington Evening Star* (January 18, 1931), p. IV:2; Mantle, "On Broadway," p. 40; Edwin C. Stein, "Philip Goes Forth," *Brooklyn Standard Union* (January 13, 1931), p. 8; Pollock, "The Theaters," p. 19; "New Kelly Play Proves Success in Try Out Here," p. 16; *Philip Goes Forth* advertisement, *New York Daily News* (April 4, 1931), p. 27; Burns Mantle, ed., *The Best Plays of 1930–31* (New York: Dodd, Mead, 1931), p. 478.

29. Tallulah Bankhead, *Tallulah: My Autobiography* (New York: Harper, 1952), p. 190; Brendan Gill, *Tallulah* (New York: Holt, Rinehart & Winston, 1972), p. 49; aficatalog.afi.com.

30. Bankhead, p. 190.

31. Edwin Schallert, "Bankhead Feature Is a Misfit," *Los Angeles Times* (June 4, 1931), p. I:11; Bankhead, p. 191.

32. Hobart, "On the Stage and Screen," p. 15; Niemeyer, "Any Role, Any Studio," p. 3F.

33. Hobart, p. 15; "'Lucky' Famous on Stage, Screen," *Lansing State Journal* (November 15, 1937), p. 13.

34. Mel Washburn, "The Spotlight," *New Orleans Item* (July 18, 1937), p. 78.

35. Hobart, "On the Stage and Screen," p. 15; "'Lucky' Famous on Stage, Screen," p. 13.

36. Hobart, p. 15.

37. Mildred Brown Robbins, "The Adventures of Millie-the-Pooh," *San Francisco Chronicle* (July 27, 1939), p. 6; "Veteran Actress Recalls Visit," p. 9; "Room for Dog Delays Actress," *Chicago Sun* (July 17, 1944), p. 16.

38. J. Brooks Atkinson, "The Play," *New York Times* (June 2, 1931), p. 34; Burns Mantle, "Players Club Annual Classic Is Fairly Heavy Going," *New York Daily News* (June 2, 1931), p. 41.

39. "'Way of the World': Players Club Revives Congreve Comedy," *Brooklyn Daily Eagle* (June 2, 1931), p. 21; Irene Vail, "Speaking of Style," *Napa Journal* (June 13, 1931), p. 5; Mantle, ed., *The Best Plays of 1930–31*, p. 16.

40. Harry Green, "Gaige Preparing 'Poor Shyster,'" *New York Daily News* (June 26, 1931), p. 43; "Mrs. Phillips Giving Tea Before Dramatic Season," *Boston Herald* (July 5, 1931), p. 2; "Polly Frederick for Pasadena," *Los Angeles Daily News* (March 12, 1930), p. 21.

41. "Offerings at the Summer Playhouses: At Magnolia," *Boston Herald* (August 9, 1931), p. 4;

J.T., "The Theatres," *Boston Herald* (August 12, 1931), p. 22.

42. "Fire Levels Magnolia Hotel," *Boston Globe* (December 11, 1958), p. 15.

43. "R.K.O. Offers New Bill That's Full of Laughs," *Oregonian* (December 25, 1931), p. 20.

44. Dan Thomas, "Hollywood Film Shop," *Pittsburgh Press* (November 17, 1931), p. 26; Irene Thirer, "Peach O'Reno Mayfair Film," *New York Daily News* (December 24, 1931), p. 24.

45. Lecta Rider, "Amusement News," *Houston Chronicle* (December 25, 1931), p. 16; G.C.W., "Orpheum Has Wheeler and Woolsey," *San Francisco Chronicle* (December 26, 1931), p. 7; "'Peach O'Reno New Laugh Hit," *Altoona Tribune* (January 1, 1932), p. 10; Pearl E. Thibos, "Hilarious Film Fun at Palace," *South Bend Tribune* (December 27, 1931), p. 5; Albert Armitage, "Matinee & Evening," *Knoxville Journal* (January 14, 1932), p. 2.

46. Irene Thirer, "'Ladies of Jury' Mayfair Comic Hit," *New York Daily News* (April 1, 1932), p. 52.

47. "New Films Reviewed," *Boston Globe* (February 15, 1932), p. 20; E. de S.M., "Edna May Oliver Scores in 'Ladies of the Jury,'" *Washington Evening Star* (January 17, 1932), p. B2; Q.E.D., "For Film Fans," *Baltimore Evening Sun* (March 28, 1932), p. 28; "On Local Screens," *Brooklyn Daily Eagle* (June 1, 1932), p. 7; *Ladies of the Jury* review, *Cleveland Plain Dealer* (February 21, 1932), p. 7.

48. "Finish 'Ladies of Jury,'" *Worcester Evening Gazette* (November 23, 1931), p. 21; "Play by Old Master," *Chicago Tribune* (November 22, 1931), p. VII:12; "'The Tadpole' Premiere on Dec. 29," *New York Times* (November 21, 1931), p. 21; "Tadpole's First Wiggle Set for Jackson Heights," *New York Daily News* (November 22, 1931), p. 48B; "Winchell Smith's Play, 'Tadpole,' at Boulevard," *New York Daily News* (November 29, 1931), p. 50B; "'The Tadpole' Opening at Parsons's Theatre Dec. 7 for Week's Run," *Hartford Courant* (December 6, 1931), p. D3; "'The Tadpole' Begins Week at Parsons's," *Hartford Courant* (December 8, 1931), p. 8; Louise Mace, "Here and There in the Theatre: Just an Amoeba," *Springfield Republican* (December 17, 1931), p. 11; Walter Brown, "When a Playwright Is Right He is Dubbed a 'Satirist,'" *Hartford Courant* (December 27, 1931), p. 2B.

49. "'The Tadpole': New Play at the Boulevard Is Sadly Sweet," *Brooklyn Daily Eagle* (December 1, 1931), p. 21; "'The Tadpole' Begins Week at Parsons's," p. 8; Louise Mace, "Here and There in the Theatre," p. 11.

50. "Theatre Notes," *New York Daily News* (December 5, 1931), p. 27.

51. "'Jewel Robbery' with Famous Stars, Comes to Newark," *Paterson News* (January 2, 1932), p. 12; "Jewel Robbery," *Jersey Journal* (January 5, 1932), p. 3; Arthur Pollock, "The Theaters," *Brooklyn Daily Eagle* (January 14, 1932), p. 19; E. de S. Melcher, "From the Front Row," *Washington Evening Star* (December 29, 1931), p. B7.

52. J. Brooks Atkinson, "The Play: Robber's Romance," *New York Times* (January 14, 1932), p. 17; E. de S. Melcher, "From the Front Row," p. B7; Burns Mantle, "'Jewel Robbery' Under Suspicion," *New York Daily News* (January 14, 1932), p. 33; Edwin C. Stein, "The Stage," *Brooklyn Standard Union* (January 14, 1932), p. 12; *Jewel Robbery* advertisement, *New York Daily News* (February 27, 1932), p. 23; Burns Mantle, ed. *The Best Plays of 1931-32* (New York: Dodd, Mead, 1932), p. 464.

53. "Old Opera House at Central City Is Opened Again," *Helena Independent-Record* (July 17, 1932), p. 7; W.J.S., "Camille," *Jersey Journal* (October 25, 1932), p. 9.

54. "Glories of Gold Rush Revived as Central City Sees 'Camille,'" *Denver Post* (July 17, 1932), p. 1, 5; "Plays and Players: Old Chairs Held as Memorials to Pioneer," *Springfield Republican* (October 10, 1934), p. 5C; "Lillian Gish Returns," *New York Times* (September 24, 1932), p. 18; Charles Affron, *Lillian Gish: Her Legend and Life* (Berkeley: University of California Press, 2002), p. 267; E.P., "The Premiere," *Brooklyn Citizen* (November 2, 1932), p. 14; Burns Mantle, ed., *The Best Plays of 1932-33* (New York: Dodd, Mead, 1933), p. 9, 414.

55. Brooks Atkinson, "The Play," *New York Times* (November 2, 1932), p. 23; "'Camille' as a Pastel," *New York Daily News* (November 2, 1932), p. 43; E.P., "The Premiere," p. 14.

56. George L. David, "Theater Reviews," *Rochester Democrat and Chronicle* (October 22, 1932), p. 11; "Lillian Gish in 'Camille' at Parsons's," *Hartford Courant* (October 15, 1932), p. 2; "'Camille' as a Pastel," p. 43; "Lillian Gish Scores Hit as 'Camille,'" *Albany Times-Union* (October 20, 1932), p. 20; E.P., "The Premiere," p. 14; Mantle, ed., *The Best Plays of 1932-33*, p. 9.

57. Walter Winchell, "Walter Winchell on Broadway," *Reading Times* (November 29, 1932), p. 2; Mark Barron, "In New York," *Minneapolis Star Tribune* (December 10, 1932), p. 6.

58. "Role for Miss Bankhead," *New York Times* (January 6, 1933), p. 22; Bankhead, *Tallulah*, p. 204; Rowland Field, "The New Play," *Brooklyn Times Union* (March 2, 1933), p. 6A; Joel Lobenthal, *Tallulah! The Life and Times of a Leading Lady* (New York: HarperCollins/Regan Books, 2004), p. 215.

59. Lee Israel, *Miss Tallulah Bankhead* (New York: G.P. Putnam, 1972), pp. 149-150.

60. Brendan Gill, *Tallulah* (New York: Holt, Rinehart & Winston, 1972), p. 55; Lobenthal, *Tallulah!*, p. 216.

61. Bankhead, *Tallulah*, p. 205; "Theatre Notes," *New York Daily News* (January 11, 1933), p. 39; Len G. Shaw, "Detroit to See Pulitzer Prize Attraction," *Detroit Free Press* (January 8, 1933), p. 10; Philip Hale, "The Theatres," *Boston Herald* (February 14, 1933), p. 14; Brook Atkinson, "The Play," *New York Times* (March 2, 1933), p. 21.

62. Mark Barron, "A Faithful Spouse Gets a Bad Idea," *Detroit Free Press* (January 15, 1933), p. 12;

Israel, *Miss Tallulah Bankhead*, p. 150; Lobenthal, *Tallulah!*, p. 215; *Brooklyn Times Union* (February 14, 1933), p. 6A; Carlton Miles, "Miss Bankhead Wins Triumph on the Stage," *Minneapolis Star* (March 13, 1933), p. 6.

63. Israel, *Miss Tallulah Bankhead*, p. 149; Mantle, ed., *The Best Plays of 1932–33*, p. 470; Bankhead, *Tallulah*, p. 208; Hale, "The Theatres," p. 14; Lobenthal, *Tallulah!*, p. 217.

64. Bankhead, p. 205; Gill, *Tallulah*, p. 55; Israel, pp. 149–151, 152.

65. E. de S. Melcher, "From the Front Row," *Washington Evening Star* (February 7, 1933), p. A-5; Hale, "The Theatres," p. 14; Field, "The New Play," p. 6A; Arthur Pollock, "The Theaters," *Brooklyn Daily Eagle* (March 2, 1933), p. 18; Richard Lockridge, "The New Play," reproduced in Gill, *Tallulah*, p. 161.

66. Atkinson, "The Play," p. 21; C.L.J., "New Play Given Popular Acclaim," *Wilmington Morning News* (February 4, 1933), p. 9; "Plays and Films of the Week," *Boston Globe* (February 14, 1933), p. 19; Burns Mantle, "'Forsaking All Others' and 'Run Little Chillun' New Plays," *New York Daily News* (March 2, 1933), p. 35.

67. *Forsaking All Others* advertisement, *New York Daily News* (June 3, 1933), p. 21; Mantle, ed., *The Best Plays of 1932–33*, p. 470; Bankhead, *Tallulah*, p. 209.

68. Wanda Hale, *Midnight* review, *New York Daily News* (March 10, 1934), p. 24; B.W.J., "New Shows in Town," *New Orleans Times-Picayune* (February 19, 1934), p. 10; J.W., "The Screen," *Brooklyn Daily Eagle* (March 12, 1934), p. 13; F.A.M., "Around the Theatres," *Regina Leader-Post* (November 1, 1934), p. II:11.

69. "Behind the Back Row," *San Francisco Chronicle* (May 30, 1933), p. 8; L.N., "The Play," *New York Times* (June 13, 1933), p. 22.

70. L.N., p. 22; Burns Mantle, "'Shooting Star at the Selwyn," *New York Daily News* (June 13, 1933), p. 41; Martin Dickstein, "The Screen: 'Shooting Star' Joins Broadway's Summer Play List," *Brooklyn Daily Eagle* (June 13, 1933), p. 11; "Francine Larrimore in 'Shooting Star' at Selwyn Theatre," *Brooklyn Times Union* (June 13, 1933), p. 6A; "The Premiere," *Brooklyn Citizen* (June 13, 1933), p. 14; Dorothy Roe, "Broadwayfare," *New Orleans States* (June 20, 1933), p. 9; Edgar Price, "This Side of the Footlights," *Brooklyn Citizen* (June 24, 1933), p. 8; "The Premiere," p. 14; Burns Mantle, "Plays and Players: Jeanne Eagels's Life Subject of New Drama," *Springfield Republican* (June 29, 1933), p. 11; "To Close," *New York Daily News* (June 24, 1933), p. 21; Mantle, ed., *The Best Plays of 1932–33*, p. 501. Mantle is mistaken in indicating that the play only lasted eight performances.

71. "On the Stage: Country Playhouse," *Stamford Daily Advocate* (July 31, 1933), p. 4; "Brackett's Comedy Has Premiere at Country Playhouse," *Stamford Daily Advocate* (August 1, 1933), p. 4. In addition to the sources already cited, information in this paragraph was taken from "On the Stage," *Stamford Daily Advocate* (July 27, 1933), p. 15;

Present Laughter advertisement, *Stamford Daily Advocate* (July 29, 1933), p. 4; and Charles Brackett, *"It's the Pictures That Got Small": Charles Brackett on Billy Wilder and Hollywood's Golden Age*, ed. Anthony Slide (New York: Columbia University Press, 2015), p. 52.

72. "Theatre Notes," *New York Daily News* (August 17, 1933), p. 33; "Gives Up 'Jezebel' Role: Miss Bankhead Not to Appear in New Play Because of Illness," *New York Times* (September 14, 1933), p. 26; Bankhead, *Tallulah*, p. 211; Lobenthal, *Tallulah!*, p. 221.

73. "'Jezebel' Is Suspended: Proposed Tallulah Bankhead Play Definitely Withdrawn," *New York Times* (September 18, 1933), p. 26.

74. Bankhead, *Tallulah*, p. 212; Israel, *Miss Tallulah Bankhead*, p. 154.

75. "Miriam Hopkins Is Summoned for Role in 'Jezebel,'" *New York Daily News* (November 13, 1933), p. 47; "'Jezebel' to Open December 19," *New York Times* (November 30, 1933), p. 38; "Theatrical Notes," *New York Times* (December 12, 1933), p. 30; Allan R. Ellenberger, *Miriam Hopkins: Life and Films of a Hollywood Rebel* (Lexington: University Press of Kentucky, 2018), p. 92.

76. Bankhead, *Tallulah*, pp. 209–210.

77. Edgar Price, "The Premiere," *Brooklyn Citizen* (December 20, 1933), p. 14; Brooks Atkinson, "The Play," *New York Times* (December 20, 1933), p. 26; Rowland Field, "The New Play," *Brooklyn Times Union* (December 20, 1933), p. 6A; Arthur Pollock, "The Theaters," *Brooklyn Daily Eagle* (December 20, 1933), p. 13; Bushnell Dimond, "Broadway as Seen by the Critic," *Wilkes-Barre Evening News* (January 3, 1934), p. 2; Jack Gaver, "'Jezebel' Featured by Beautiful Sets," *Miami Herald* (January 28, 1934), p. 1; *Jezebel* advertisement, *Brooklyn Daily Eagle* (January 13, 1934), p. 5; "Seven Plays Close," *Brooklyn Citizen* (January 16, 1934), p. 14; Burns Mantle, ed., *The Best Plays of 1933–34* (New York: Dodd, Mead, 1935), p. 468; Dramatic Notes," *Brooklyn Times Union* (January 5, 1934), p. 6; "Leaves Cast of 'Jezebel,'" *New York World-Telegram* (January 9, 1934) (NYPL).

78. "Theatre Notes," *New York Daily News* (January 9, 1934), p. 35; C.F.F., "'Mackerel Skies' Is Presented at the Playhouse," *Brooklyn Times Union* (January 24, 1934), p. 6A; "'Mackerel Skies': New Piece at the Playhouse Is About a Young Singer," *Brooklyn Daily Eagle* (January 24, 1934), p. 23; "'No More Ladies' and 'Mackerel Skies' New Plays: A Drama of Jealousy, Genius and the Opera in the Playhouse," *New York Daily News* (January 24, 1934), p. 41; Michael March, "The Premiere: 'Mackerel Skies,' Story of a Cardboard Diva, Comes to the Playhouse," *Brooklyn Citizen* (January 24, 1934), p. 14.

79. L.N., "Stormy Weather," *New York Times* (January 24, 1934), p. 20; "'Mackerel Skies,'" p. 23; March, "The Premiere," p. 14; C.F.F., "'Mackerel Skies' Is Presented at the Playhouse," p. 6A; *Mackerel Skies* advertisement, *New York Daily News* (February 10, 1934), p. 23; Mantle, ed., *The Best Plays of 1933–34*, p. 484.

80. E.S., "Helen Morgan Well Cast at Playhouse," *Dayton Daily News* (July 18, 1936), p. J20; Irene Kuhn, "Old Biograph Plant Filming 'Frankie and Johnnie,'" *Pittsburgh Press* (March 4, 1934), p. 6; aficatalog.afi.com.

81. "'Frankie, Johnnie' Work of Kirkland: 'Tobacco Road' Author Wrote Picture Coming to Casino," *Pittsburgh Post-Gazette* (April 29, 1936), p. 8; L.L., "'Frankie and Johnnie,' the Old, Old Song, Lives Anew in Motion Pictures at the Tower," *Kansas City Star* (May 3, 1936), p. 1D; Kuhn, "Old Biograph Plant Filming," p. 6; Sigmund Spaeth, "Music for Everybody," *Knoxville Journal* (June 2, 1957), p. 16D; aficatalog.afi.com.

82. F.S.N., "'Frankie and Johnnie' at Globe," *New York Times* (May 25, 1936), p. 23; Wanda Hale, "Films Do Wrong by 'Frankie and Johnnie," *New York Daily News* (May 25, 1936), p. 34.

83. "How Feminine Stars of Broadway and Hollywood Dive into the 'Bankruptcy Bath' to Dodge Huge Debts of Folly and Extravagance," *San Francisco Chronicle* (March 18, 1934), p. 12.

84. Mantle, ed., *The Best Plays of 1933-34*, p. 5.

85. Burns Mantle, "'Jig Saw,' or Sex in a Penthouse: Theatre Guild Winds Up Season with a Little Something About Free Livers," *New York Daily News* (May 1, 1934), p. 41; "This Side of the Footlights," *Brooklyn Citizen* (May 8, 1934), p. 8.

86. E. de S. Melcher, "Perfect Comedy Machine Slows Up in Last Scenes," *Washington Evening Star* (April 24, 1934), p. C8; Arthur Pollock, "The Theaters: The Theater Guild Present a Not Unpleasant Trifle Called 'Jig Saw' at the Ethel Barrymore Theater," *Brooklyn Daily Eagle* (May 1, 1934), p. 9.

87. Charles Whitacre Forbes, "Footlights of Broadway," *Dayton Daily News* (May 6, 1934), p. 5; Melcher, "Perfect Comedy Machine Slows Up in Last Scenes," p. C8; E., "'Jig-Saw' Pleasant Summer Diversion," *Springfield Republican* (June 10, 1934), p. 7C.

88. "Grace George to Play Barrie Role at Cape Cod," *New York Daily News* (June 8, 1934), p. 55; "Truex Takes Guild's 'Jig Saw' for a Week at His Own Summer Theatre," *New York Daily News* (June 14, 1934), p. 51; E. de S. Melcher, "Why a Reviewer of Plays Worries in Spare Moments," *Washington Evening Star* (May 6, 1934), p. F4.

89. "Delightful Comedy at Casino Theatre: 'Her Master's Voice' Scores Decided Hit," *Newport Mercury* (July 20, 1934), p. 1.

90. Mildred Martin, "George M. Cohan Star of Fox Film," *Philadelphia Inquirer* (November 3, 1934), p. 11; aficatalog.afi.com.

91. "New Films Reviewed," *Boston Globe* (November 17, 1934), p. 12; Andre Sennwald, "The Screen," *New York Times* (December 4, 1934), p. 22; Martin Dickstein, "The Screen," *Brooklyn Daily Eagle* (December 5, 1934), p. 21; Mae Tinée, "Cohan Scores in Drama with Heart Pull," *Chicago Tribune* (January 12, 1935), p. 11.

92. "Cora Witherspoon in a New Role," *New York Herald Tribune* (August 26, 1934) (NYPL); Rowland Field, "Both Sides of the Curtain," *Brooklyn Times Union* (August 29, 1934), p. 11; "Stage and Screen," *Pittsburgh Post-Gazette* (October 12, 1934), p. 19; "3 Legitimate Players in First Musical, 'Say When,'" *Boston Herald* (October 28, 1934), p. 26.

93. "3 Legitimate Players," p. 26.

94. "'Say When' to Open at Shubert Oct. 22," *Boston Herald* (October 10, 1934), p. 21; "Rehearsals Starting on Two New Broadway Shows," *Los Angeles Times* (September 25, 1934), p. 1:19.

95. Burns Mantle, ed., *The Best Plays of 1934-35* (New York: Dodd, Mead, 1935), p. 406; "The Stage: Shubert Theatre 'Say When,'" *Boston Globe* (October 24, 1934), p. 23.

96. "The Stage," p. 23; Arthur Pollock, "The Theater," *Brooklyn Daily Eagle* (November 9, 1934), p. 23; Burns Mantle, "'Say When' a Show Broadway Ordered," *New York Daily News* (November 9, 1934), p. 61.

97. Brooks Atkinson, "The Play," *New York Times* (November 9, 1934), p. 24; Rowland Field, "The New Play: 'Say When' Wins Comedy Honors at the Imperial," *Brooklyn Times Union* (November 9, 1934), p. 4A; Bushnell Dimond, "Broadway Nights," *Birmingham News* (November 18, 1934), p. 12.

98. Rowland Field, "Both Sides of the Curtain," *Brooklyn Times Union* (November 25, 1934), p. 11; Carlton Miles, "Musical Comedies Start Descent Upon Broadway, Carlton Miles Reports," *Minneapolis Star* (November 13, 1934), p. 13; Paul Harrison, "Old Home Week on Broadway; Stars Shine in Own Right in New Shows: 'Say When' Greeted on Rialto as Tuneful Comedy," *Madison Capital Times* (November 18, 1934), p. 10; Mantle, ed., *The Best Plays of 1934-35*, p. 406. *Life Begins at 8:40* ran till March 16, 1935 (237 performances) at the Winter Garden Theatre, i.e., longer than *Say When*. It probably did not help matters that the immortal *Anything Goes* opened November 21, 1934 at the Alvin. It ran for a year.

99. Annie Oakley, "The Theatre and Its People," *Windsor Star* (January 5, 1935), p. 2; "Rival Producers in Move to Cut Plays to $2 Top," *New York Daily News* (January 6, 1935), p. 74; "This Side of the Footlights," *Brooklyn Citizen* (January 12, 1935), p 8; Mantle, ed., *The Best Plays of 1934-35*, p. 448.

100. Michael March, "The Premiere," *Brooklyn Citizen* (February 6, 1935), p. 14; Burns Mantle, "'It's You I Want' from the Boulevards," *New York Daily News* (February 6, 1935), p. 47.

101. Arthur Pollock, "The Theater," *Brooklyn Daily Eagle* (February 6, 1935), p. 23; Brooks Atkinson, "The Play: On an Old Last," *New York Times* (February 6, 1935), p. 23; Rowland Field, "The New Play," *Brooklyn Times Union* (February 6, 1935), p. 8.

102. "The Stage," *Boston Globe* (February 20, 1935), p. 21.

103. Brooks Atkinson, "The Play," *New York Times* (March 6, 1935), p. 22; Rowland Field, "The New Play," *Brooklyn Times Union* (March 6, 1935), p. 7; Arthur Pollock, "The Theater," *Brooklyn Daily Eagle* (March 6, 1935), p. 21.

104. Atkinson, p. 22; Field, p. 7.

105. Burns Mantle, "'De Luxe' Crowded with Actors," *New York Daily News* (March 7, 1935), p. 43; Field, "The New Play," p. 7; Paul Harrison, "Silly Season of Shows Heralds Advent of Spring Along Broadway," *Charleston Daily Mail* (March 17, 1935), p. 8.

106. "Trouper Elsa Celebrates," *New York Daily News* (March 12, 1935), p. 26.

107. capeplayhouse.com.

108. "Drama News," *Brooklyn Times Union* (August 5, 1935), p. 7; "Drama News," *Brooklyn Times Union* (July 24, 1935), p. 7; "Stage News," *Brooklyn Daily Eagle* (August 1, 1935), p. 11.

109. "Stage News," *Brooklyn Daily Eagle* (August 14, 1935), p. 7; "Mary Rogers Playing in 'Ceiling Zero' as Father's Plane Crashes," *New York Daily News* (August 17, 1935), p. 21; "The Stage," *Boston Globe* (August 20, 1935), p. 18; Elinor Hughes, "Ethel Barrymore Scores in 'Constant Wife,'" *Boston Herald* (August 20, 1935), p. 20; "Barrymore to Tour; Cantor in December," *New York Daily News* (August 24, 1935), p. 23; "New John Golden Show Opens Sunday, Sept. 22," *Brooklyn Citizen* (September 8, 1935), p. 9.

110. "Boulevard to Offer John Golden Comedy," *New York Daily News* (September 8, 1935), p. 40B; "First Sunday Play Likely to Be Last," *New York Times* (September 23, 1935), p. 20; Brooks Atkinson, "The Play," *New York Times* (September 23, 1935), p. 20.

111. Atkinson, "The Play," p. 20; Arthur Pollock, "The Theater," *Brooklyn Daily Eagle* (September 23, 1935), p. 7.

112. Burns Mantle, "'A Touch of Brimstone' Explosive," *New York Daily News* (September 23, 1935), p. 37; "Cameragraphs," *Boise City News* (December 5, 1935), p. 6.

113. Elinor Hughes, "The Theatre: 'All Bow Down' at Cape Theatre," *Boston Herald* (August 6, 1935), p. 18; "700 or More See World Premiere, 'All Bow Down,'" *Rutland Daily Herald* (August 6, 1935), p. 3; Rowland Field, "The New Play," *Brooklyn Times Union* (September 23, 1935), p. 5A; Burns Mantle, ed., *The Best Plays of 1935–36* (New York: Dodd, Mead), p. 6.

114. "Broadway: A Rough Appraisal," *New York Daily News* (October 1, 1935), p. 42; "News of the Stage," *New York Times* (December 5, 1935), p. 31; *A Touch of Brimstone* advertisement, *New York Daily News* (December 16, 1935), p. 47; Mantle, ed., *The Best Plays of 1935–36*, p. 407; "Roland Young Coming Here in His Comedy," *Springfield Republican* (December 9, 1935), p. 2; "Plays Current and Coming," *Philadelphia Inquirer* (December 15, 1935), p. 9.

Chapter 5

1. "Golden Gate Has Singing Cowboy, Kibbee Comedy," *San Francisco Examiner* (August 27, 1937), p. 8.

2. "Cora Witherspoon to Play the Lady from Louisville" (NYPL).

3. "A New Effie from Louisville," p. 17; Rowland Field, "Both Sides of the Curtain," *Brooklyn Times Union* (March 20, 1936), p. 9; "Drama News," *Brooklyn Times Union* (March 31, 1936), p. 5A.

4. "Theatre Notes," *New York Daily News* (January 28, 1936), p. 37; Harold W. Cohen, "The Drama Desk," *Pittsburgh Post-Gazette* (January 28, 1936), p. 14; "Drama: News of the Theatrical World," *Hanover Evening Sun* (February 1, 1936), p. 4.

5. Brooks Atkinson, "The Play," *New York Times* (January 17, 1936), p. 15.

6. Mantle, ed., *The Best Plays of 1935–36*, p. 461.

7. Lynn Riggs, *Russet Mantle and The Cherokee Night: Two Plays by Lynn Riggs* (New York: Samuel French, 1936), p. 12.

8. "Cora Witherspoon to Play the Lady from Louisville" (NYPL).

9. Brooks Atkinson, "The Play," *New York Times* (January 17, 1936), p. 15; Willard Keefe, "Choice Bits Stand Out as Broadway Season Nears Its End," *New Orleans Times-Picayune* (March 29, 1936), p. 21; Rowland Field, "Both Sides of the Curtain," *Brooklyn Times Union* (April 12, 1936), p. 10; Mantle, ed., *The Best Plays of 1935–36*, p. 11; "'Russet Mantle' Enters Last Week," *Brooklyn Citizen* (April 20, 1936), p. 16; Mantle, ed., *The Best Plays of 1935–36*, p. 460.

10. Brackett, *"It's the Pictures That Got Small,"* p. 78, 83; Edwin Schallert, "Madge Evans in 'Piccadilly Jim,'" *Los Angeles Times* (June 2, 1936), p. I:13; "M-G-M Signs Three," *Brooklyn Times Union* (June 6, 1936), p. 9.

11. "Bob Leonard Celebrates His 30th Year in Films," *Brooklyn Times Union* (June 20, 1936), p. 4.

12. "Passes First Test," *Pittsburgh Sun-Telegraph* (July 19, 1936), p. IV:4; Henry Sutherland, "Actor Tracy Admirer of Track Stars," *Pittsburgh Press* (June 30, 1936), p. 14.

13. "Piccadilly Jim," *Detroit Free Press* (August 16, 1936), p. 13; A.L.B., "New Shows in Town: Author's Funniest Story Is Told in Brightest, Merriest Film," *New Orleans Times-Picayune* (August 22, 1936), p. II:11; Frank S. Nugent, "The Screen," *New York Times* (August 31, 1936), p. 19; Rowland Field, "The Current Cinema," *Brooklyn Times Union* (September 1, 1936), p. 4; Edna B. Lawson, "At the Theatres," *Honolulu Advertiser* (September 14, 1936), p. 4; *Piccadilly Jim* review, *Schenectady Daily Gazette* (September 25, 1936), p. 26; Philip K. Scheuer, "'Piccadilly Jim' Amusing Fare at Loew's, Chinese," *Los Angeles Times* (October 1, 1936), p. I.10.

14. "News of the Theaters," *Beaumont Enterprise* (August 17, 1936), p. 14; *Piccadilly Jim* review, *Great Falls Tribune* (August 16, 1936), p. 5; R.B.C., "For Film Fans," *Baltimore Evening Sun* (August 22, 1936), p. 5; "Fine Week Booked in All Theatres," *Decatur Daily Review* (October 11, 1936), p. 26; Mollie Merrick, "Autograph Seekers Keep Michael Whalen Signing," *Detroit Free Press* (August 8, 1936), p. 11; "Gay Romance Scores

Hit at Paramount," *Salt Lake Tribune* (August 14, 1936), p. 11; *Piccadilly Jim* review, *Indianapolis News* (August 15, 1936), p. 8; Ralph Holmes, "Merry 'Piccadilly Jim' and Ziegfeld Girls at Michigan," *Detroit Times* (August 15, 1936), p. 11; "On Screen and Stage," Grand Rapids Press (August 24, 1936), p. 14; Keith Wilson, "Sly Comedy Ranks High," *Omaha World-Herald* (August 29, 1936), p. 11; "Stage, Screen and Air," *Hackensack Record* (October 1, 1936), p. 29; Mae Tinée, "'Piccadilly Jim' Is Jolly Movie by Wodehouse," *Chicago Tribune* (October 3, 1936), p. 19.

15. "Varied Fare for Christmas Week in Films," *Decatur Daily Review* (December 20, 1936), p. 26; "New Orleans Actress," *New Orleans Item* (August 21, 1936), p. 4.

16. Nugent, "The Screen," p. 19; Field, "The Current Cinema," p. 4; "Gay Romance Scores Hit at Paramount," p. 11; *Piccadilly Jim* review, *Indianapolis News*, p. 8; "Paramount Film Offers Pleasing Fair," *Deseret News* (August 14, 1936), p. 6; Rob Nixon, "Piccadilly Jim," tcm.com.

17. "Flies Across Continent for 5 Hours in New York," *Boston Globe* (August 31, 1936), p. 7; Rowland Field, "Both Sides of the Curtain," *Brooklyn Times Union* (July 29, 1936), p. 4; "High School Youngsters Can Show Professional Dancers Few Things," *Hackensack Record* (August 18, 1936), p. 13; Brackett, "*It's the Pictures That Got Small*," p. 86.

18. R.B.C., "For Film Fans," *Baltimore Evening Sun* (August 22, 1936), p. 5; James Kotsilibas-Davis and Myrna Loy, *Myrna Loy: Being and Becoming* (New York: Primus/Donald I. Fine, 1988), p. 141.

19. "Some of the New Movie Bills Due Friday Seem Quite Lively," *Louisville Courier-Journal* (October 15, 1936), p. 2:5; Mollie Merrick, "Hollywood in Person!," *Tampa Times* (November 11, 1936), p. 4; "For Stars Head Cast in Film, 'Libeled Lady,'" *Grand Rapids Press* (November 6, 1936), p. 33; "Quartet of Star Appear in Merry Film Comedy," *Los Angeles Times* (October 18, 1936), p. II:17; Kate Cameron, "'Libeled Lady' Excellent Farce, *New York Daily News* (November 8, 1936), p. 39; Seymour Roman, "The Current Cinema," *Brooklyn Times Union* (October 31, 1936), p. 8; "Four Star Comedy Film at Warfield," *San Francisco Chronicle* (November 2, 1936), p. 10; aficatalog.afi.com.

20. "Cora Witherspoon in 'Quality Street,'" *Los Angeles Times* (September 23, 1936), p. 14; Niemeyer, "Any Role, Any Studio," p. 3F.

21. Eddie Cohen, "For Your Amusement," *Miami News* (March 20, 1937), p. 5.

22. *Quality Street* review, *Boston Globe* (March 27, 1937), p. 17; Karl Krug, "Penn Shows Hepburn Talkie," *Pittsburgh Sun-Telegraph* (March 20, 1937), p. 9; Clarke Wales, "Reviews of the New Films," *Detroit Free Press* (March 21, 1937), p. 13; Gilbert Kanour, "For Film Fans," *Baltimore Evening Sun* (March 26, 1937), p. 26; "New Shows in Town," *New Orleans Times-Picayune* (March 26, 1937), p. 30; Donald Kirkley, "Katharine Hepburn in 'Quality Street,'" *Baltimore Sun* (March 27,

1937), p. 6; Mae Tinée, "Finds Hepburn is Tired in Historic Film," *Chicago Tribune* (March 29, 1937), p. 17; Kate Cameron, "Charm Marks New Music Hall Picture," *New York Daily News* (April 9, 1937), p. 60; C.P.J., "New Shows in Town," *New Orleans Times-Picayune* (April 10, 1937), p. 6.

23. *Quality Street* advertisement, *Chillicothe Constitution-Tribune* (April 17, 1937), p. 8; *Quality Street* advertisement, *Simpson County News* (June 17, 1937), p. 4.

24. Cohen, "For Your Amusement," p. 5; aficatalog.afi.com.

25. Edna B. Lawson, "Avenue Comedy Well Dressed but Is Miscast," *Honolulu Advertiser* (March 6, 1937), p. 5.

26. "Starts Monday," *Brooklyn Times Union* (November 6, 1936), p. 82; "Announce New Contracts," *Brooklyn Times Union* (November 13, 1936), p. 5A; "Character Star Signed," *Pittsburgh Post-Gazette* (November 30, 1936), p. 16.

27. Kate Cameron, "'On the Avenue' Full of Fun, Lively Music," *New York Daily News* (February 5, 1937), p. 48; Mildred Martin, "Camera Angles on Film Folk," *Philadelphia Inquirer* (February 6, 1937), p. 13; Edith Lindeman, "The Virginia Reel," *Richmond Times Dispatch* (February 12, 1937), p. 4; Diggory Venn, "'On the Avenue' Offers New Kind of Musical Production," *San Francisco Chronicle* (February 12, 1937), p. 12; Louise Mace, "'On the Avenue' Tinkles with Berlin Melodies," *Springfield Republican* (February 13, 1937), p. 9; "Keith-Memorial: 'On the Avenue,'" *Boston Globe* (February 20, 1937), p. 12; "Delightful Filmusical at Keith's," *Dayton Daily News* (February 20, 1937), p. F22; "For Your Entertainment," *New Orleans States* (March 5, 1937), p. 12; Murray E. Wyche, "The Front Row," *Chattanooga News* (March 22, 1937), p. 8.

28. "Best Performances in Current Pictures," *Los Angeles Times* (February 14, 1937), p. III:1; Kaspar Monahan, "The Show Shops: Fulton's New Movie Gay and Melodious," *Pittsburgh Press* (February 15, 1937), p. 14; "'On the Avenue' Good Film Fare," *St. Joseph Gazette* (February 15, 1937), p. 3.

29. "Dangerous Number," *Baltimore Sun* (February 13, 1937), p. 6; "At the Theaters," *Baton Rouge Advocate* (January 28, 1937), p. 18.

30. Bess Stephenson, "'Dangerous Number' Merriest Kind of Romantic Nonsense," *Fort Worth Star-Telegram* (February 4, 1937), p. 11; "New Films," *Boston Globe* (March 13, 1937), p. 12; A.C.S., "New Shows in Town: Robert Young and Ann Sothern Offer and Amusing Comedy," *New Orleans Times-Picayune* (February 6, 1937), p. 25; B.R.C., "The Screen: At Loew's State," *New York Times* (March 12, 1937), p. 19.

31. "Stage Revue Draws Crowd to Paramount," *Salt Lake Tribune* (March 1, 1937), p. 9; Charles P. Jones, "Post-View," *New Orleans Times-Picayune* (February 7, 1937), p. 12; Walter Whitworth, "The New Films," *Indianapolis News* (February 13, 1937), p. 10; S.L.S., *Dangerous Number* review, *Philadelphia Inquirer* (February 27, 1937), p. 14;

Dangerous Number review, *New York Daily News* (March 13, 1937), p. 65; "Dangerous Number," *Jersey Journal* (June 11, 1937), p. 12.

32. Walter Winchell, "Walter Winchell on Broadway," *Burlington Daily News* (January 27, 1937), p. 6; Guy Fowler, "Veteran Troupers Learning to Call Hollywood 'Home,'" *Seattle Daily Times* (July 4, 1937), p. 6; Alexander Kahn, "Hollywood Film Shop," Marietta Journal (August 10, 1937), p. 2; Vecchi, "They Judge You by Your Roles," p. 2C.

33. Read Kendall, "Around and About in Hollywood," *Los Angeles Times* (October 13, 1937), p. I:16; Henry Sutherland, "Hollywood," *Ventura Morning Free Press* (October 14, 1937), p. 4.

34. Grace Wilcox, "The Hollywood Reporter," *Detroit Free Press* (May 30, 1937), p. 2; Diggory Venn, "New Gate Show: Singing Cowboy Pleases," *San Francisco Chronicle* (August 26, 1937), p. 8.

35. Niemeyer, "Any Role, Any Studio," p. 3F.

36. Harold W. Cohen, "The Drama Desk," *Pittsburgh Post-Gazette* (February 10, 1937), p. 12; Hubbard Keavy, "$3,000-a-Week Star Once—Now Works as a Stand-In," *Hazleton Standard-Speaker* (March 1, 1937), p. 4; Henry Sutherland, "American's Film, Made in Europe, Strikes Big Snag," *Nevada State Journal* (June 2, 1937), p. 4; "Witherspoon Writes Stage Reminiscences," *San Diego Union* (June 20, 1937), p. 3; "Hollywood Film Flashes," *New York Journal American* (June 30, 1937), p. 18.

37. B.R.C., "The Screen," *New York Times* (April 16, 1937), p. 27.

38. "Harlow Shows Unknown Arts," *Coshocton Tribune* (January 31, 1935), p. 4; "Theaters: Strand," *Stamford Daily Advocate* (April 22, 1937), p. 34.

39. "Carole to Carol for First Time in New Film," *Mansfield News-Journal* (March 22, 1937), p. 5; John Hobart, "Harlow Versus Taylor," *San Francisco Chronicle* (April 3, 1937), p. 8; Sterling Sorenson, "Drama in Madison," *Madison Capital Times* (April 25, 1937), p. 11; Ida Hermann, "The Screen," *Camden Courier-Post* (May 15, 1937), p. 4.

40. "Comedienne Signs for Second Film," *Indianapolis Star* (March 21, 1937), p. 18; Sara Day, "Spring Romance: Fashion Is Very Careful to Match the Moment," *Atlanta Constitution* (May 2, 1937), p. 11; "The Lady Escapes," *Detroit Free Press* (June 13, 1937), p. 13.

41. One contemporary source suggests Kibbee was freelance at this point and another that this was the first film of his new RKO contract. See Louella O. Parsons, "Strike Forces Actors to Do Own Makeup," *Cedars Rapid Gazette* (May 3, 1937), p. 7; and Perez, "Picture Parade," *Miami Tribune* (September 6, 1937), p. 17; aficatalog.afi.com.

42. Diggory Venn, "New Gate Show," *San Francisco Chronicle* (August 26, 1937), p. 8; *The Big Shot* review, *New York Daily News* (August 12, 1937), p. 49.

43. "Guy Kibbee Scores as 'The Big Shot' Now at Richmond," *North Adams Transcript* (August 20, 1937), p. 7; H.M. Levy, "Guy Kibbee Farce Plays at Orpheum," *Oakland Tribune* (September 1, 1937),

p. 8B; Perez, "Picture Parade," p. 17; Jerry Fox, "Guy Kibbee's Best: Beginning Slow, but, Oh, the End," *Dayton Herald* (September 15, 1937), p. 19; *The Big Shot* review, *Montreal Gazette* (September 25, 1937), p. 11; "'The Big Shot' Is Film Showing at the Rialto," *Missoulian* (October 3, 1937), p. 3.

44. "The Pageant of the Film World," *Los Angeles Times* (July 29, 1937), p. 8; "Comedienne in First Hard-Boiled Role," *Pittsburgh Press* (August 2, 1937), p. 13.

45. "New Metro Contract for Cora Witherspoon," *Dallas Morning News* (August 22, 1937), p. III:10; "McHugh Star of 'Larger Than Life,'" *Los Angeles Times* (August 11, 1937), p. I:8; Harriet Parsons, "An Ace 'Scene Stealer' But Star Like Frank McHugh," *San Francisco Examiner* (December 5, 1937), p. B5; Dorothy Masters, "Frank M'Hugh Stars in Film Full of Fun," *New York Daily News* (March 31, 1938), p. 45.

46. Edna B. Lawson, "Amusing Comedy Opens at Princess," *Honolulu Advertiser* (January 7, 1938), p. 7.

47. Hedda Hopper, "Hedda Hopper's Hollywood," *Los Angeles Times* (January 20, 1939), p. 11.

48. "Rainer Assigned New Part in 'Madelon,'" *Louisville Courier-Journal* (December 5, 1937), p. 3; A.D. Mackie, "Our Reel News," *Jersey Journal* (December 31, 1937), p. 6; James Curtis, *James Whale: A New World of Gods and Monsters* (Minneapolis: University of Minnesota Press, 2003), p. 319.

49. Louella O. Parsons, "Jack Haley Wins New Contract," *Philadelphia Inquirer* (December 17, 1937), p. 21.

50. "Glamor Aplenty in Movie Film," *Spokane Chronicle* (January 27, 1938), p. 10.

51. Hobart, "On the Stage and Screen," p. 15.

52. "It's Vacation Time in Hollywood," *San Diego Union* (April 3, 1938), p. 4.

53. "News of the Stage and Screen," *Pittsburgh Post-Gazette* (May 7, 1938), p. 8.

54. Karl Krug, "New Temple Musical in Alvin," *Pittsburgh Sun-Telegraph* (November 25, 1938), p. 22; Kate Cameron, "Shirley Only Bright Spot in Her New Film," *New York Daily News* (December 3, 1938), p. 28; Frank S. Nugent, "The Screen," *New York Times* (December 3, 1938), p. 11.

55. See, for example, *Three Loves Has Nancy* advertisement, *Jasper County News* (January 12, 1939), p. 4.

56. "Pageant of the Film World," *Los Angeles Times* (July 21, 1938), p. 8; Erskine Johnson, "Behind the Makeup," *San Francisco Examiner* (July 25, 1938), p. 14; "Beery Paired with Cora Witherspoon," *Los Angeles Times* (July 22, 1938), p. 15.

57. Anita Mary Tipping, "California Trip," *New Orleans States* (August 10, 1938), p. 11; Hedda Hopper, "Hedda Hopper's Hollywood," *Chicago Daily News* (September 2, 1938), p. 23.

58. Hobart, "On the Stage and Screen," p. 15.

59. Elizabeth Hemphill, "For the Younger Generation Only," *Miami Herald* (April 23, 1939), p.

7B; "Star Portrays Thrilling Role," *Arizona Republic* (May 14, 1939), p. III:10; Edith Lindeman, "'Dark Victory' Is Bette Davis to Perfection," *Richmond Times Dispatch* (April 29, 1939), p. 7; Mildred Stockard, "'Dark Victory,' Tragedy Play, Tops Week's Movie Offering," *Houston Chronicle* (May 7, 1939), p. 6F.

60. "Pageant of the Film World," *Los Angeles Times* (October 29, 1938), p. II:7.

61. "'Woman Doctor' Wins Favor for Human Quality," *Los Angeles Times* (January 26, 1939), p. I:11; B.R.C., "The Screen," *New York Times* (March 24, 1939), p. 27.

62. Hobart, "On the Stage and Screen," p. 15.

63. *New York Daily News* (July 21, 1939), p. 37, "Noted Play Will Open at Curran," *San Francisco Examiner* (July 24, 1939), p. 28; "Tubbs' Play to Make Debut," *Oakland Tribune* (July 24, 1939), p. B7; Ada Hanifin, "'Outward Bound' Is Presented," *San Francisco Examiner* (July 25, 1939), p. 16; "Mystical Ship to Sail," *Los Angeles Times* (August 6, 1939), p. 2; "Stage League Revival of 'Outward Bound' Due at the Biltmore Tonight," *Hollywood Citizen-News* (August 14, 1939), p. 4; "'Outward Bound' Ends Run," *Los Angeles Daily News* (August 24, 1939), p. 21.

64. Sutton Vane, "Outward Bound," *The Best Plays of 1923–1924*, ed. Burns Mantle (Boston: Small Maynard, 1924), p. 105.

65. Vane, p. 106.

66. "California, San Francisco County Records, 1824–1997," database with images, *Family Search* (https://familysearch.org/ark:/61903/1:1:QKD4-TV3Z: 13 May 2016), Max D Hamburger, 24 Jul 1939; citing Death, San Francisco, San Francisco, California, United States, San Francisco Public Library, California; FamilySearch digital folder 004879178; Herb Caen, "It's News to Me," *San Francisco Chronicle* (July 28, 1939), p. 13.

67. Hanifin, "'Outward Bound' Is Presented," p. 16; Wood Soanes, "'Outward Bound' Given in Revival," *Oakland Tribune* (July 25, 1939), p. C23.

68. Philip K. Scheuer, "Haunting Play Given New Life," *Los Angeles Times* (August 15, 1939), p. 9; Carl Combs, "Death Drama Revived at Biltmore," *Hollywood Citizen-News* (August 15, 1939), p. 9; Larry Mines, "Group Sails into Afterlife," *Los Angeles Daily News* (August 15, 1939), p. 18.

69. "Actress Wins Battle of Foxes… The Fur Kind," *Los Angeles Times* (August 17, 1939), p. 8; Soanes, "'Outward Bound' Given in Revival," p. C23.

70. "Dog's Leash Trips Actress; Leg Broken," *Spokane Chronicle* (August 25, 1939), p. 2.

71. *Los Angeles Daily News* (August 25, 1939), p. 26; Read Kendall, "Gala Screen Event Attracts 15,000," *Los Angeles Times* (September 1, 1939), p. 10.

72. Hobart, "On the Stage and Screen," p. 15.

73. "Stage Star's Sister Here for Opening," p. 14.

74. *Las Cruces Sun-News* (October 12, 1939), p. 4; Brackett, *It's the Pictures That Got Small*," p. 137, 142.

75. "Barrymore Drunk," *New York Daily News*

(December 10, 1939), p. 79. See also "Barrymore's Skill at Ad Libbing," *Chicago Daily News* (November 11, 1939), p. 18.

76. *Brooklyn Daily Eagle* (December 16, 1939), p. 18; ibdb.com.

77. George S. Kaufman et al., *Kaufman & Co.: Broadway Comedies* (New York: Library of America, 2004), p. 597; Ben Gross, "Listening In," *New York Daily News* (December 18, 1939), p. 46.

Chapter 6

1. "Cora Witherspoon Is Without Usual Temperament," p. 44.

2. Harrison Carroll, "Behind the Scenes in Hollywood," *New Orleans Times-Picayune* (February 2, 1940), p. 29.

3. "Ameche Paired with Alice Faye: Witherspoon, Grapewin, Field in New Roles," *Brooklyn Daily Eagle* (January 10, 1940), p. 8.

4. "Notes" to *I Was an Adventuress*, tcm.com.

5. John L. Scott, "Zorina Wins Favor as Adventuress," *Los Angeles Times* (May 9, 1940), p. II.10; T.S., "The Screen," *New York Times* (May 20, 1940), p. 19; C.J. Bulliet, "Zorina Superb in an Adult Crime Film," *Chicago Daily News* (June 19, 1940), p. 13; Ada Hanifin, "'I Was an Adventures' Makes Hit at Paramount," *San Francisco Examiner* (June 27, 1940), p. 16.

6. "'Brooklyn Bridge' Is Scheduled as New Fox Feature," *New Orleans Times-Picayune* (February 25, 1940), p. 14.

7. B.C., "The Screen in Review," *New York Times* (May 3, 1940), p. 17; Kate Cameron, "Good Charlie Chan Mystery at Palace," *New York Daily News* (May 3, 1940), p. 52; M.B., "Chan Feature Previewed," *Los Angeles Times* (May 4, 1940), p. I:12; C.S., "New Shows in Town," *New Orleans Times-Picayune* (October 10, 1940), p. 11; James L. Neibaur, *The Charlie Chan Films* (Albany, GA: Bear-Manor Media, 2018), pp. 151–52.

8. "United States Census, 1940," database with images, *Family Search* (https://www.familysearch.org/ark:/61903/1:1:K9C6-5ZL: 6 January 2021), Cora Witherspoon, Los Angeles, Los Angeles, California, United States; citing enumeration district (ED) 60–144, sheet 62A, line 31, family 274, Sixteenth Census of the United States, 1940, NARA digital publication T627. Records of the Bureau of the Census, 1790–2007, RG 29. Washington, D.C.: National Archives and Records Administration, 2012, roll 399.

9. Grace Wilcox, "Hollywood's Most Interesting Women," *Milwaukee Journal* (June 16, 1940), p. 3.

10. This according to the Internet Movie Database (imdb.com), where *The Bank Dick* receives a score of 7.2 and is placed fourth in votes after *The Women*, *Dark Victory*, and *Libeled Lady*.

11. Edwin Schallert, "Maureen O'Sullivan to Return for Film Lead," *Los Angeles Times* (October

10, 1940), p. I:15; James Curtis, *W.C. Fields: A Biography* (New York: Alfred A. Knopf, 2003), p. 421, 422, 424.

12. "Cora Witherspoon Pleads Guilty to 'Needle' Ownership," *Los Angeles Daily News* (October 11, 1940), p. 6. Sources of the other headlines in the notes below.

13. "Cora Witherspoon Faces Dope Case," *Hollywood Citizen-News* (September 20, 1940), p. 8; "Denies Drug Count," *Salt Lake Tribune* (September 20, 1940), p. 18; "Actress Denies Narcotic Charge," *Denver Post* (September 20, 1940), p. 22.

- 14. "Former Actress Asks Mercy in Dope Case," *Los Angeles Times* (October 11, 1940), p. II:2.

15. "Actress Wins Lighter Penalty: Cora Witherspoon Gets Suspended Jail Sentence and Extension on Fine," *Los Angeles Times* (November 8, 1940), p. II:2.

16. "United States Census, 1940," database with images, *Family Search* (https://www.familysearch.org/ark:/61903/1:1:K9CL-CM6: 6 January 2021), Leo Aggeler, Los Angeles, Los Angeles, California, United States; citing enumeration district (ED) 60-202, sheet 7B, line 41, family 266, Sixteenth Census of the United States, 1940, NARA digital publication T627. Records of the Bureau of the Census, 1790-2007, RG 29. Washington, D.C.: National Archives and Records Administration, 2012, roll 405; "California, County Birth and Death Records, 1800-1994," database with images, *Family Search* (https://www.familysearch.org/ark:/61903/1:1:8LVV-2SZM: 9 December 2020), Leo Ignatius Aggeler, 1976.

17. "United States Census, 1940," database with images, *Family Search* (https://www.familysearch.org/ark:/61903/1:1:K9C5-8MD: 6 January 2021), Thomas Witherspoon, Los Angeles, Los Angeles, California, United States; citing enumeration district (ED) 60-230, sheet 9A, line 1, family 248, Sixteenth Census of the United States, 1940, NARA digital publication T627. Records of the Bureau of the Census, 1790-2007, RG 29. Washington, D.C.: National Archives and Records Administration, 2012, roll 408; "United States Census, 1930," database with images, *Family Search* (https://familysearch.org/ark:/61903/1:1:XCDN-QMC: 26 July 2021), William C Witherspoon, San Francisco (Districts 1-250), San Francisco, California, United States; citing enumeration district (ED) ED 94, sheet 12B, line 52, family 19, NARA microfilm publication T626 (Washington D.C.: National Archives and Records Administration, 2002), roll 198; FHL microfilm 2,339,933; "United States Census, 1940," database with images, *Family Search* (https://www.familysearch.org/ark:/61903/1:1:K9ZD-Q4J: 6 January 2021), William Witherspoon, Los Angeles, Los Angeles, California, United States; citing enumeration district (ED) 60-440, sheet 63B, line 61, family 193, Sixteenth Census of the United States, 1940, NARA digital publication T627. Records of the Bureau of the Census, 1790-2007, RG 29. Washington, D.C.: National Archives and Records Administration,

2012, roll 425; *Los Angeles City Directory 1932* (Los Angeles: Los Angeles Directory Co., 1932), p. 2296; "W.C. Witherspoon," *Santa Rosa Press Democrat* (March 30, 1951), p. 11; "United States Census, 1940," database with images, *Family Search* (https://www.familysearch.org/ark:/61903/1:1:-K9CL-185: 6 January 2021), J Houston Witherspoon, Los Angeles, Los Angeles, California, United States; citing enumeration district (ED) 60-313, sheet 5B, line 41, family 114, Sixteenth Census of the United States, 1940, NARA digital publication T627. Records of the Bureau of the Census, 1790-2007, RG 29. Washington, D.C.: National Archives and Records Administration, 2012, roll 406.

18. "California Death Index, 1905-1939," database with images, *Family Search* (https://familysearch.org/ark:/61903/1:1:QKSM-VBMP: 23 February 2021), Leslie Witherspoon, 29 Apr 1922; citing 17954, Department of Health Services, Vital Statistics Department, Sacramento; FHL microfilm 1,686,047; "California, County Birth and Death Records, 1800-1994," database with images, *Family Search* (https://familysearch.org/ark:/61903/1:1:QGNV-66XD: 1 March 2021), Carrie M Witherspoon, 1925; "United States Census, 1940," database with images, *Family Search* (https://www.familysearch.org/ark:/61903/1:1:-K9WW-3DR: 5 January 2021), Grace Witherspoon, Pasadena Judicial Township, Los Angeles, California, United States; citing enumeration district (ED) 19-501, sheet 1A, line 30, family 12, Sixteenth Census of the United States, 1940, NARA digital publication T627. Records of the Bureau of the Census, 1790-2007, RG 29. Washington, D.C.: National Archives and Records Administration, 2012, roll 242; "United States Census, 1940," database with images, *Family Search* (https://www.familysearch.org/ark:/61903/1:1:K9WW-MQL: 5 January 2021), Elenor Witherspoon, Pasadena Judicial Township, Los Angeles, California, United States; citing enumeration district (ED) 19-503, sheet 6B, line 49, family 139, Sixteenth Census of the United States, 1940, NARA digital publication T627. Records of the Bureau of the Census, 1790-2007, RG 29. Washington, D.C.: National Archives and Records Administration, 2012, roll 242; "United States Census, 1940," Thomas Witherspoon; "California, County Birth and Death Records, 1800-1994," database with images, *Family Search* (https://familysearch.org/ark:/61903/1:1:QG2W-J3J7: 1 March 2021), Eleanor Howison Witherspoon, 1944; "California Death Index, 1940-1997," database, *Family Search* (https://familysearch.org/ark:/61903/1:1:VPDW-WZY: 26 November 2014), Grace Witherspoon, 09 Jan 1949; Department of Public Health Services, Sacramento.

19. Elliot Norton, "Went High Hat in Hollywood," *Boston Post* (August 22, 1941) (NYPL).

20. "Major Bowes Will Salute Home Town of San Francisco on WDAE Tonight," *Tampa Times* (April 10, 1941), p. 24; "Marge of Air Show Dies in New Jersey," *Canton Repository* (February

16, 1941), p. 28; "Well Known Actress of Stage, Screen," p. 1; John Dunning, *On the Air: The Encyclopedia of Old-Time Radio* (New York and Oxford: Oxford University Press, 1998), pp. 474–475.

21. "Radio Player Breaks Arm But Show Goes On: Broadway Actress Proves to Be Real Trouper, Acts with Injury," *Atlanta Constitution* (October 27, 1941), p. 15; "Veteran Actress Recalls Visit," p. 9.

22. Tennessee Williams, *Memoirs* (Garden City, NY: Anchor Press/Doubleday, 1983), pp. 69–70; information on the San Jacinto Hotel from Ron Bowers, June 28, 2020.

23. "'George Washington Slept Here' is No. 8 for Hart and Kaufman," *Brooklyn Daily Eagle* (May 11, 1941), p. 44.

24. Brooks Atkinson, "The Play," *New York Times* (October 19, 1940), p. 20; Burns Mantle, ed., *The Best Plays of 1940–41* (New York: Dodd, Mead, 1949), p. 6.

25. Atkinson, "The Play," p. 20; George S. Kaufman and Moss Hart, *Six Plays by Kaufman and Hart* (New York: Modern Library, 1942), p. 512, 574.

26. George Ross, "Broadway," *Pittsburgh Press* (April 30, 1941), p. 31; *George Washington Slept Here* advertisement, *Hartford Courant* (May 30, 1941), p. 14; Robert Francis, "Kaufman-Hart Comedy Comes to Flatbush," *Brooklyn Daily Eagle* (May 14, 1941), p. 11; "Glen Rock Theatre Has Premiere," *Ridgewood Herald-News* (July 17, 1941), p. 11; "Stage and Screen News: South Shore Players," *Boston Globe* (June 6, 1941), p. 20; "South Shore Players," *Boston Globe* (August 19, 1941), p. 9; "Kaufman and Hart Comedy Given in Cohasset Town Hall," *Boston Herald* (August 19, 1941), p. 9.

27. "Veteran Actress Recalls Visit," p. 9; Norton, "Went High Hat in Hollywood" (NYPL).

28. M.L.A., "Brattle Hall," *Boston Globe* (May 12, 1942), p. 10; "The Theater," *Boston Herald* (May 12, 1942), p. 22; A.E. Watts, "Season Opens in Cambridge," *Boston Traveler* (May 12, 1942), p. 30.

29. "The 'Missing' Turn Up on Summer Circuit," *Milwaukee Sentinel* (September 7, 1941), p. 47.

30. "Theatre Wins Fight Against New Taxes in Senate Victory," *New York Daily News* (September 5, 1941), p. 51M; "Eric Brotherson Gets Featured Billing in 'Lady in the Dark,'" *Brooklyn Daily Eagle* (September 5, 1941), p. 12; Edgar Price, "The Premiere," *Brooklyn Citizen* (October 7, 1941), p. 14.

31. Brooks Atkinson, "The Play: Bobby Clark Whirls 'All Men Are Alike' Around the Stage of the Hudson Theatre," *New York Times* (October 7, 1941), p. 27; Burns Mantle, "'All Men Are Alike,' Except Bobby Clark, and He Is Unlucky," *New York Daily News* (October 7, 1941), p. 39B; Price, "The Premiere," p. 14; *All Men Are Alike* advertisement, *New York Daily News* (November 1, 1941), p. 21M; ibdb.com.

32. Elinor Hughes, "Theater and Screen: Song Writer Irving Caesar to Produce 'My Dear Public,'" *Boston Herald* (February 14, 1942), p. 13;

Harold V. Cohen, "The Drama Desk," *Pittsburgh Post-Gazette* (January 27, 1942), p. 23; "Saroyan Drama Is Threatened with a Busy Spring Season," *New York Daily News* (February 5, 1942), p. 40; "Seats Now on Sale at Shubert Theater for New Musical," *Hartford Courant* (February 21, 1942), p. 8; "'My Dear Public' Comes to Shubert Next Thursday," *Hartford Courant* (March 1, 1942), p. 6A; *My Dear Public* advertisement, *Boston Herald* (March 1, 1942), p. 10A; C.W.D., "On the Boston Stage," *Boston Globe* (March 10, 1942), p. 19.

33. "Saroyan Drama," *New York Daily News*, p. 40; "News of the Stage," *New York Times* (February 19, 1942), p. 22; "News of the Stage," *New York Times* (March 7, 1942), p. 12; "'My Dear Public' Gets Joy Hodges," *New York Times* (March 20, 1942), p. 25; "Three Openings Here Next Week," *New York Times* (March 23, 1942), p. 18; "'Nathan' and 'V We Sing' to Broadway," *New York Daily News* (March 21, 1942), p. 23; "'My Dear Public' Cancels Broadway Debut," *New York Times* (March 25, 1942), p. 27; ibdb.com.

34. T.H.P., "New Musical Comedy Has Good Innings," *Hartford Courant* (March 6, 1942), p. 8.

35. C.W.D., "On the Boston Stage," *Boston Globe* (March 10, 1942), p. 19; Elinor Hughes, "The Theater," *Boston Herald* (March 10, 1942), p. 11; Helen Eager, "'My Dear Public,' New Musical at Colonial for One Week," *Boston Traveler* (March 10, 1942), p. 16.

36. "Katharine Hepburn Due in New Play on Monday; Two Shows Held Over," *Camden Courier-Post* (March 21, 1942), p. 8; "'My Dear Public' Gets Joy Hodges," *New York Times* (March 20, 1942), p. 25; J.O'N., "'My Dear Public' Gets Fine Welcome," *Camden Courier-Post* (March 17, 1942), p. 17; Samuel L. Singer, "'My Dear Public' Opens at the Forrest," *Philadelphia Inquirer* (March 17, 1942), p. 15.

37. "Gertrude Lawrence Running Playhouse While on Vacation," *Chicago Tribune* (July 26, 1942), p. VI:2; "Chatterton, Forbes at Dennis July 13," *Boston Herald* (June 10, 1942), p. 19; https://www.capeplayhouse.com/about-us/.

38. "Summer Theaters Enter Second Week," *Boston Herald* (July 5, 1942), p. 19; *You Can't Take It with You* advertisement, *Boston Herald* (July 19, 1942), p. 11; "Lawrence to Star in New Coward Play," *New York Daily News* (August 1, 1942), p. 17; "Gertrude Lawrence at Cape Playhouse," *Boston Traveler* (August 3, 1942), p. 30; "Summer Stage," *Boston Globe* (August 7, 1942), p. 23; *The Bat* advertisement, *Boston Herald* (August 16, 1942), p. 35.

39. "Fred Stone Plays in Comedy Revival on Flatbush Stage," *Brooklyn Daily Eagle* (September 8, 1942), p. 7; "Fred Stone Opens Emery," *Cincinnati Enquirer* (September 27, 1942), p. III:3; E.B. Radcliffe, "Out in Front," *Cincinnati Enquirer* (October 6, 1942), p. 15; "Tickets Now on Sale for Fred Stone at Emery," *Cincinnati Enquirer* (October 2, 1942), p. 15; unidentified, undated clipping [October 1942] (NYPL).

40. "Grand Has Fun Film on Today," *Huntsville*

Times (December 26, 1943), p. 6; Philip K. Scheuer, "R.K.O. Arranging to 'Save' Lorentz Picture," *Los Angeles Times* (October 6, 1942), p. I:15.

41. "Rialto Ramblings: Joanna Roos Joins Cast," *Brooklyn Citizen* (November 3, 1942), p. 10; "Martha Scott Stars in 'The Willow and I,'" *Wilmington News Journal* (November 19, 1942), p. 31; "News of the Stage," *New York Times* (October 17, 1942), p. 10.

42. "Rialto Ramblings," *Brooklyn Citizen*, p. 10; "'The Willow and I' Opens at Playhouse Next Friday," *Wilmington News Journal* (November 14, 1942), p. 15; "'The Willow and I' Is Opening Tonight," *New York Times* (December 10, 1942), p. 33.

43. "'The Willow and I' Opens at Walnut," *Camden Courier-Post* (November 24, 1942), p. 26; C.L.J., "Outstanding Cast in 'Willow and I,'" *Wilmington Morning News* (November 21, 1942), p. 21; "'The Willow and I' Opens at Playhouse Next Friday," p. 15; "Play Makes Bow Monday at Walnut," *Camden Courier-Post* (November 14, 1942), p. 10; "Joanna Roos is Featured in 'The Willow and I' Here Tomorrow for 2 Days," *Wilmington Morning News* (November 19, 1942), p. 19.

44. Linton Martin, "Morbid New Play Opens at the Walnut," *Philadelphia Inquirer* (November 24, 1942), p. 26; "'The Willow and I' Opens at Walnut," p. 26; C.W.D., "The Stage," *Boston Globe* (December 1, 1942), p. 23; Elinor Hughes: "The Theater: 'The Willow and I' Opens at the Shubert," *Boston Herald* (December 1, 1942), p. 26; Helen Eager, "Amusements: Martha Scott Starred in 'The Willow and I,'" *Boston Traveler* (December 1, 1942), p. 36.

45. Lewis Nichols, "The Play," *New York Times* (December 11, 1942), p. 32; Burns Mantle, "'The Willow and I' Drama About Good and Bad Sisters," *New York Daily News* (December 11, 1942), p. 65B; Arthur Pollack, "'The Willow and I' Goes Way, Way Back," *Brooklyn Daily Eagle* (December 11, 1942), p. 19; Jack Gaver, "'Willow and I' Meaty Drama but Lacks Impact," *Austin American-Statesman* (December 27, 1942), p. 6; Dale Harrison, "Theatergoers on Season's Casualty List: Box Office Happy, Customers Sad," *Chicago Sun* (January 31, 1943), p. III:23.

46. "Pack Musical with Names," *New York Daily News* (February 17, 1943), p. 51B; Elinor Hughes, "The Theater: 'Dancing in the Streets' Opens," *Boston Herald* (March 24, 1943), p. 18; ibdb.com.

47. "Mary Martin Show for Opera House," *Boston Traveler* (March 31, 1943), p. 11; C.W.D., "The Stage," *Boston Globe* (March 24, 1943), p. 14; *Dancing in the Streets* advertisement, *Boston Herald* (April 4, 1943), p. 10; Hughes, "The Theater," p. 18; Tom Chase, "Mary Martin Has New Daddy in Musical Now Running in Hub," *Burlington Daily News* (March 31, 1943), p. 2.

48. Hazel Bruce, "'Jane Eyre' Lives Again at the Geary," *San Francisco Chronicle* (November 10, 1943), p. 8; "Charlotte Brontë Love Story Due on Stage Here," *Long Beach Independent* (October 24, 1943), p. 33.

49. M.L.A., *Jane Eyre* review, *Boston Globe* (June 8, 1943), p. 16; "Locust Books 'Jane Eyre,'" *Camden Courier-Post* (June 12, 1943), p. 8; Jay Carmody, "'Jane Eyre' a Fiery Spirit in Sylvia Sidney's Version," *Washington Evening Star* (July 13, 1943), p. B7; "Stars of Jane Eyre Met Aboard Ship," *Sacramento Bee* (December 10, 1943), p. 2.

50. M.L.A., *Jane Eyre* review, p. 16; Charles Gentry, "'Jane Eyre' Is Superb at Cass," *Detroit Evening Times* (July 20, 1943), p. 21; Len G. Shaw, "Sidney, Adler Score in 'Jane Eyre,'" *Detroit Free Press* (July 20, 1943), p. 18; Annie Oakley, "The Theatre and Its People," *Windsor Star* (July 20, 1943), p. 13.

51. "Drama Notes," *Chicago Times* (September 12, 1943), p. 4; "Players Win Acclaim in 'Jane Eyre,'" *Salt Lake Telegram* (October 5, 1943), p. 15; "'Jane Eyre' Brings Ominous Atmosphere to Civic Stage," *Pasadena Post* (November 4, 1943), p. 9; Bruce, "'Jane Eyre' Lives Again at the Geary," p. 8; Alexander Fried, "'Jane Eyre' at Geary Theatre Is Notable Stage Production," *San Francisco Examiner* (November 10, 1943), p. 11; Wood Soanes, "'Jane Eyre' Rescued by Good Acting," *Oakland Tribune* (November 9, 1943), p. 19; Mila Landis, "Local Audience Is Pleased with Jane Eyre Play," *Sacramento Bee* (December 11, 1943), p. 2; A.G., "Superb Cast Puts 'Jane Eyre' in Highest Rank," *Helena Independent-Record* (December 31, 1943), p. 5; John K. Sherman, "Drama," *Minneapolis Star* (January 7, 1943), p. 14; W. Ward Marsh, "Adler and Sylvia Sidney Play 'Jane Eyre' in Hanna for all the Show Is Worth," *Cleveland Plaindealer* (January 11, 1944), p. 11; E.B.R., "Stage: 'Jane Eyre,'" *Ithaca Journal* (January 20, 1943), p. 4; C.L.J., "'Jane Eyre' Hailed as Delightful Play," *Wilmington Morning News* (January 29, 1943), p. 13; Russell McLaughlin, "Theatre Bills Both Continue," unidentified, undated clipping [July 1943] (NYPL).

52. E.B. Radcliffe, "Out in Front," *Cincinnati Enquirer* (October 14, 1944), p. 16; Lewis Nichols, "The Play: Grin and Kill," *New York Times* (January 6, 1944), p. 17.

53. David Quirk, "Gene Fowler Is Sought to Write Musical's Book," *New York Daily News* (February 4, 1944), p. 38; "'Hayride' Cast in Garden Benefit; 'Svoboda' to Hub," *New York Daily News* (February 15, 1944), p. 27.

54. "ZaSu Pitts Opens in Farce Tonight: Screen Comedienne to Make Broadway Stage Debut in 'Ramshackle Inn,'" *New York Times* (January 5, 1944), p. 14; E.B. Radcliffe, "Out in Front," *Cincinnati Enquirer* (October 16, 1944), p. 10; Edwin Schallert, "ZaSu Pitts Arrives in Hectic Comedy," *Los Angeles Times* (November 15, 1944), p. I:11.

55. Bill Hill, "Zasu Pitts Makes Like Crazy in a Zany 'Ramshackle Inn,'" *Washington Evening Star* (July 11, 1944), p. A12; Claudia Cassidy, "Plot Is Leaky, but Miss Pitts' Play is Creepy," *Chicago Tribune* (July 18, 1944), p. 13.

56. "Actress Is Broke," *Chicago Daily News* (March 9, 1944), p. 23; "Cora Witherspoon," *Brooklyn Daily Eagle* (June 3, 1944), p. 8; Sam Zolotow, "Three More Shows to Close Saturday," *New*

York Times (July 4, 1944), p. 25; Virginia Wright, "Drama Editor," *Los Angeles Daily News* (November 3, 1944), p. 29; "Room for Dog Delays Actress," *Chicago Sun* (July 17, 1944), p. 16.

57. Jack Balch, "'Ramshackle Inn' Opens Season Here," *St. Louis Post-Dispatch* (October 2, 1944), p. 3B; Belle Ayer, "Play Attracts 2,700: ZaSu Pitts Stars in Dubious Orpheum Offering," *Rock Island Argus* (October 31, 1944), p. 18; O.G.D., "Play Weak, but Zasu Triumphs," *Des Moines Register* (November 1, 1944), p. 16; Bill Hill, "Zasu Pitts Makes Like Crazy in a Zany 'Ramshackle Inn,'" *Washington Evening Star* (July 11, 1944), p. A12; Henry T. Murdock, "ZaSu Pitts Adds Laughs to Murder and Mayhem," *Chicago Sun* (July 19, 1944), p. 22; William Inge, "ZaSu Pitts Play Spells Good Time," *St. Louis Star and Times* (October 2, 1944), p. 16; Edwin Schallert, "ZaSu Pitts Arrives in Hectic Comedy," *Los Angeles Times* (November 15, 1944), p. I:11; Lowell E. Redelings, "ZaSu Pitts Brightens 'Ramshackle Inn,'" *Los Angeles Evening Citizen News* (November 15, 1944), p. 7; Virginia Wright, "Stage Review," *Los Angeles Daily News* (November 15, 1944), p. 35.

58. Robert Pollak, "Zasu a Hit in Farcical Melodrama," *Chicago Daily Times* (July 18, 1944), p. 24; Inge, "ZaSu Pitts Play Spells Good Time," p. 16; "Zasu Pitts Plays to Capacity House in Dramatic Fare," *Davenport Daily Times* (October 31, 1944), p. 15; Ayer, "Play Attracts 2,700," p. 18; John O'Donnell, "Zasu Pitts and Co., Manage to Survive Murders," *Quad-City Times* (October 31, 1944), p. 8; O.G.D., "Play Weak, but Zasu Triumphs," p. 16; "ZaSu," *St. Joseph News-Press* (November 3, 1944), p. 6.

59. Sophia Kondos, "One Fan's Opinion," *Moline Dispatch* (October 31, 1944), p. 11.

60. "Texas Deaths, 1890–1976," database with images, *Family Search* (https://familysearch.org/ark:/61903/1:1:KS13-4W8: 20 February 2021), Anna Venables Miller, 05 Nov 1944; citing certificate number 51190, State Registrar Office, Austin; FHL microfilm 2,137,819; "Mrs. Anna Miller," *El Paso Times* (November 6, 1944), p. 2; Annie Venables Miller, findagrave.com.

61. Schallert, "ZaSu Pitts Arrives in Hectic Comedy," p. I:11.

62. T.M.P., "The Screen," *New York Times* (April 5, 1946), p. 21; Jay Carmody, "Coburn Plays Comic Reformer in 'Colonel Effingham' Role," *Washington Evening Star* (February 22, 1946), p. B12.

63. David Hanna, "Film Employs Scene-Stealers," *Los Angeles Daily News* (February 1, 1945), p. 10; Frank Miller, "Colonel Effingham's Raid (1946)," tcm.com.

64. M.M., "Boyd Screen Present 'Over 21,' a Comedy," *Philadelphia Inquirer* (October 11, 1945), p. 14.

65. Edwin Schallert, "War-Linked Humor Feature Engaging," *Los Angeles Times* (August 11, 1945), p. II:5; Virginia Wright, "Film Review: 'Over 21,'" *Los Angeles Daily News* (August 11, 1945), p. 7; Harold V. Cohen, "The New Films," *Pittsburgh Post-Gazette* (September 17, 1945), p. 21; Edith

Lindeman, "Irene Dunne Scores Hit at Byrd, State: Broadway Comedy Loaded with Laughs," *Richmond Times Dispatch* (September 20, 1945), p. 11; Bosley Crowther, "The Screen," *New York Times* (August 17, 1945), p. 20.

66. Edwin Schallert, "Willy-Nilly, Barry's Bound to Be Starred," *Los Angeles Times* (April 23, 1945), p. II:2.

67. Mildred Martin, "Jane Russell in Debut Here in Stanton Film," *Philadelphia Inquirer* (July 25, 1946), p. 24; Mildred Stockard, "Odds Favor 'Kid from Brooklyn' for Laughs," *Houston Chronicle* (September 20, 1946), p. 13.

68. T.M.P., "The Screen," *New York Times* (January 12, 1946), p. 12.

69. Bosley Crowther, "The Screen," *New York Times* (September 7, 1946), p. 11; tcm.com.

70. Hedda Hopper, "Hedda Hopper Looking at Hollywood," *Los Angeles Times* (March 8, 1946), p. II:3.

71. Harold V. Cohen, "Drama Desk," *Pittsburgh Post-Gazette* (August 12, 1946), p. 14.

72. Brooks Atkinson, "The Play," *New York Times* (September 5, 1946), p. 22.

73. Edgar Price, "The Premiere," *Brooklyn Citizen* (September 5, 1949), p. 10; Arlene Wolf, "Hildy Isn't News Anymore, Doesn't Make 'Front Page,'" *Fort Worth Star-Telegram* (September 8, 1946), p. 9; Dorothy Quick, "'Front Page' Reviewed by Dorothy Quick," *Central New Jersey Home News* (September 29, 1946), p. 8; Jack O'Brian, "New York Review: 'Front Page' Still Good—Revival of Old Rowdy Play Liked," *Omaha World-Herald* (September 8, 1946), p. 10E; ibdb.com.

74. "Richard Bishop Due at Flatbush," *Brooklyn Daily Eagle* (July 19, 1947), p. 12; Jane Corby, "Theater," *Brooklyn Daily Eagle* (July 23, 1947), p. 6; "'I Remember Mama' Back for Second Week at the Flatbush," *Brooklyn Daily Eagle* (August 13, 1947), p. 13.

75. Doris Sperber, "Cape Playhouse 'Profile,'" *Boston Herald* (August 13, 1947), p. 19; Cyrus Durgin, "Summer Stage: Cape Playhouse 'Profile,'" *Boston Globe* (August 12, 1947), p. 9.

76. Durgin, "Summer Stage,'" p. 9; John W. Riley, "No Politics in 'Rustic' Interview with Faye Emerson (Roosevelt)," *Boston Globe* (August 17, 1947), p. A13; "Faye Emerson at Marblehead," *Boston Herald* (August 19, 1947), p. 11. Unlike in Dennis and Marblehead, Witherspoon was not featured in the ads for *Profile* in Saratoga Springs. Only Berghof was featured there. I have not identified any reviews or other positive evidence that Witherspoon was in the production in upstate New York, but it seems likely. She had nothing else going on at the time. See *Profile* advertisement, *Troy Times Record* (August 26, 1947), p. 8.

77. Durgin, "Summer Stage," p. 9; C.W.D., "North Shore Players 'Profile,'" *Boston Globe* (August 19, 1947), p. 12.

78. "Picacho Players Production Is Big Success," *Las Cruces Sun-News* (August 28, 1949), p. 5; "Well Known Actress of Stage, Screen," p. 1, 7; "Guest

Artists to Take Part in New El Teatro Chico Play," *Las Cruces Sun-News* (December 12, 1949), p. 3.

Chapter 7

1. Maggie Wilson, "Neon Patrol: Actress Finds Stock Most Fun," *Arizona Republic* (February 11, 1953), p. 20.

2. Niemeyer, "Any Role, Any Studio," p. 3F; "Lumarion," "In Our Town," p. 9.

3. "United States Census, 1930," database with images, *Family Search* (https://familysearch.org/ark:/61903/1:1:XCMM-RY9: 24 July 2021), Maude Witherspoon, Las Cruces, Dona Ana, New Mexico, United States; citing enumeration district (ED) ED 5, sheet 5B, line 62, family 138, NARA microfilm publication T626 (Washington D.C.: National Archives and Records Administration, 2002), roll 1394; FHL microfilm 2,341,129; "United States Census, 1940," database with images, *Family Search* (https://www.familysearch.org/ark:/61903/1:1:-KMRW-J8V: 6 January 2021), Maude L Witherspoon, Las Cruces, Doña Ana, New Mexico, United States; citing enumeration district (ED) 7-6, sheet 12B, line 58, family 299, Sixteenth Census of the United States, 1940, NARA digital publication T627. Records of the Bureau of the Census, 1790–2007, RG 29. Washington, D.C.: National Archives and Records Administration, 2012, roll 2443; "LasCruces, State College and Mesilla Social Events," *El Paso Times* (September 10, 1933), p. 20; "Protested Dairy Four Years Old," *Las Cruces Sun-News* (November 29, 1940), p. 1; "Lumarion," p. 9; Cal Traylor, "Humane Society Reaches Its Goal: An Animal Shelter," *Las Cruces Sun-News* (May 10, 1970), p. 25; Maude Witherspoon, "Prayer for Peace," *McKinney Courier-Gazette* (June 7, 1970), p. 9.

4. "Lumarion," p. 9.

5. "United States Social Security Death Index," database, *Family Search* (https://familysearch.org/ark:/61903/1:1:JG8V-JZ6: 11 January 2021), Maude Witherspoon, Jun 1970; citing U.S. Social Security Administration, *Death Master File*, database (Alexandria, Virginia: National Technical Information Service, ongoing); "Louisiana, New Orleans, Interment Registers, 1836–1972," database, *Family Search* (https://familysearch.org/ark:/61903/1:1:4VX8-GK6Z: 6 December 2019), Maud Witherspoon, 1970; "Witherspoon Final Rites Set Tuesday," p. 2; "Dogs Inherit Full Facilities of Residence," *Las Cruces Sun-News* (July 24, 1970), p. 2. See also "Lumarion," "In Out Town," *Las Cruces Sun-News* (October 28, 1970), p. 3.

6. "Cora Witherspoon, Actress, Dies Here," unidentified, undated clipping (NYPL); zillow.com.

7. "Cora Witherspoon Cast," *Los Angeles Times* (May 28, 1950), p. IV:3; "Veteran Player Back in Films," *Oregonian* (June 18, 1950), p. 13; "Gets Comedy Role," *Brooklyn Daily Eagle* (June 25, 1950), p. 34.

8. M.M., "'The Mating Season' Shown at Randolph," *Philadelphia Inquirer* (March 26, 1951), p. 13; John Rosenfield, "Screen in Review: Thelma Ritter Continues Her Amusing Course Even Beating Fast Company," *Dallas Morning News* (May 5, 1951), p. II:4; Richard E. Hays, "Fine Comedy Opens Today at 5th Ave.," *Seattle Daily Times* (March 24, 1951), p. 3; Annie Oakley, "The Theatre and Its People: 'The Mating Season,'" *Windsor Star* (April 16, 1951), p. 16.

9. "Cora Witherspoon Is on Hollywood Television Show," *Las Cruces Sun-News* (August 27, 1950), p. 1; Tim Brooks and Earle Marsh, *The Complete Directory to Prime Time Network and Cable TV Shows 1946-Present* (New York: Ballantine, 2003), p. 411.

10. "Television This Week," *Kansas City Star* (August 19, 1951), p. 7D; "Television and Radio," *Rock Island Argus* (August 11, 1952), p. 16; "Television Programs," *Los Angeles Times* (December 12, 1950), p. 20; "Television This Week," *Kansas City Star* (August 19, 1951), p. 7D; Maggie Wilson, "Neon Patrol: Actress Finds Stock Most Fun," *Arizona Republic* (February 11, 1953), p. 20; imdb.com.

11. Edwin Schallert, "Aline MacMahon Triumphs in Madwoman of Chaillot," *Los Angeles Times* (March 29, 1951), p. I:16; Margaret Harford, "MacMahon Stand Out in Chaillot," *Los Angeles Evening Citizen News* (March 29, 1951), p. 18.

12. Edwin Schallert, "Louis Hayward Sets Producing Deal," *Los Angeles Times* (March 19, 1951), p. III:9; "Seats on Sale for Broadway Comedy," *North Hollywood Valley Times* (March 20, 1951), p. 13; John Scott, "Local Stage Horizon Brightened by Plans," *Los Angeles Times* (March 25, 1951), p. IV:3; Schallert, "Aline MacMahon Triumphs in Madwoman of Chaillot," p. I:16; "'Madwoman' Draws Many Repeaters," *North Hollywood Valley Times* (April 20, 1951), p. 17; "Two Cast Replacements in Madwoman at Ivar," *Los Angeles Evening Citizen News* (April 26, 1951), p. 20.

13. "'Madwoman' Draws Many Repeaters," p. 17; "'Madwoman' Stirs Interest," *Los Angeles Times* (April 22, 1951), p. VI:2; "'The Madwoman' in Fifth Week," *North Hollywood Valley Times* (April 25, 1951), p. 17; "Moliere Satire Booked for Ivar," *Los Angeles Times* (April 30, 1951), p. III:7; Schallert, "Aline MacMahon Triumphs in Madwoman of Chaillot," p. I:16; Tom Coffey, "'Mad' Ladies in Fragile French Comedy at Ivar," *Los Angeles Mirror* (March 29, 1951), p. 47; Harford, "MacMahon Stand Out in Chaillot," p. 18; "Cora Witherspoon Scores in Comedy Role," *Los Angeles Times* (April 19, 1951), p. III:10.

14. Hortense Morton, "'First Time' Is Gay Comedy of Newlyweds," *San Francisco Examiner* (February 16, 1952), p. 12 (ellipses in original); "The Stork Plays in This One," *Evansville Press* (March 20, 1952), p. 40; Louise Mace, "Theater News and Views: 'The First Time' Pleasant Comedy on Bijou's Bill," *Springfield Union* (March 21, 1952), p. 8; E.W.C., "'The First Time' Draws Big Laughs in First Showing," *Spokane Chronicle* (March 28, 1952), p. 7;

V.Q., "Pictures in Passing," *Brooklyn Tablet* (April 5, 1952), p. 29; F.J., "First Baby Upsets House Like Cyclone," *New Orleans States* (May 26, 1952), p. 6.

15. "'Peg' Opening Postponed," *Los Angeles Times* (June 30, 1951), p. I:8.

16. "Film Celebrities to Attend Opening of Peg o' My Heart," *North Hollywood Valley Times* (July 2, 1951), p. 5; Fred Broomfield, "Joan Evans Sparkles in 'Peg o' My Heart,'" *North Hollywood Valley Times* (July 6, 1951), p. 12; Tom Coffey, "Joan Evans Shows Great Talent as 'Peg' at Ivar," *Los Angeles Mirror* (July 6, 1951), p. 35; "Cora Witherspoon Cast in Ivar Comedy," *Los Angeles Times* (June 25, 1951), p. III:6; "Movieland Briefs," *Los Angeles Times* (June 27, 1951), p. I:14; "Agar to Star in 'Peg' Drama," *Los Angeles Evening Citizen News* (June 29, 1951), p. 17; "'Peg' Begins Run Tonight," *Los Angeles Times* (July 5, 1951), p. III:9; Margaret Harford, "'Peg o' My Heart': Joan Evans Scores Well," *Los Angeles Evening Citizen News* (July 6, 1951), p. 17; "Michael Cozzi Will Replace Heart Actor," *Los Angeles Times* (July 16, 1951), p. III:8; "'Peg' Play Opens Second Big Week," *Los Angeles Evening Citizen News* (July 12, 1951), p. 17; "Autograph Hunters Have Field Day at Ivar's 'Peg,'" *Los Angeles Evening Citizen News* (July 11, 1951), p. 15.

17. Edwin Schallert, "Joan Evans Brightens Dated 'Peg o' My Heart," *Los Angeles Times* (July 6, 1951), p. III:7; Margaret Harford, "'Peg o' My Heart': Joan Evans Scores Well," *Los Angeles Evening Citizen News* (July 6, 1951), p. 17; David Bongard, "Stage Review: 'Peg o' My Heart," *Los Angeles Daily News* (July 6, 1951), p. 27; Tom Coffey, "Joan Evans Shows Great Talent as 'Peg' at Ivar," *Los Angeles Mirror News* (July 6, 1951), p. 35.

18. *Peg o' My Heart* advertisement, *Los Angeles Daily News* (July 25, 1951), p. 18; "Drunk? No, Says Actress; Lands in Jail," *Los Angeles Mirror* (July 28, 1951), p. 3.

19. "Actress Walks Dog, Land in Jail on Drunk Charge," *Los Angeles Daily News* (July 28, 1951), p. 2; "Walking Dog, Actress Jailed on Drunk Charge," *Los Angeles Times* (July 29, 1951), p. I:2; "Actress Is Led to Jail by Dog," *Raleigh News and Observer* (July 29, 1951), p. II:8.

20. "California Death Index, 1940–1997," database, *Family Search* (https://familysearch.org/ark:/61903/1:1:VP8G-G6K: 26 November 2014), Walter Clark Allen, 10 Jun 1996; Department of Public Health Services, Sacramento; "Walter C. Allen; Retired Judge," *Los Angeles Times* (June 12, 1996), p. B11.

21. "Jailed as Drunk," *Scrantonian* (July 29, 1951), p. 16; "Burned Up: Police Jail Lady Comic Walking Dog," *Miami Herald* (July 29, 1951), p. 1.

22. "Walking Dog, Actress Jailed on Drunk Charge," p. I:2; "Actress, Dog in Jail," *Los Angeles Mirror* (July 28, 1951), p. 1, 3.

23. Edwin Schallert, "Jack Carson Will Star as TV Jockey," *Los Angeles Times* (November 5, 1951), p. II:7.

24. Helen Bower, "Jane and Bing Sing with Zing," *Detroit Free Press* (September 19, 1952), p. 27.

25. "Lions Club to Raise Curtain on 'Hay Fever,'" *Las Cruces Sun-News* (December 26, 1951), p. 1; "Light Rehearsals Set This Week for 'Hay Fever,'" *Las Cruces Sun-News* (December 17, 1951), p. 3.

26. Edwin Schallert, "Jack Carson Will Star as TV Jockey," *Los Angeles Times* (November 5, 1951), p. II:7; Edwin Martin, "Songs of a City: Spectacle Numbers in 'Just for You,'" *San Diego Union* (September 19, 1952), p. A15; William Hogan, "Songs, Ballet, Gentle Laughs: 'Just for You'—Bing, Jane, Young Love," *San Francisco Chronicle* (September 13, 1952), p. 5; Edith Lindeman, "'Just for You' Opens Here at Colonial: Film Stars Crosby and Jane Wyman," *Richmond Times-Dispatch* (October 2, 1952), p. 10; Bill Barton, "Amusements by Bill Barton: A Spruce Cosby Sparkles Musical," *Dayton Daily News* (October 3, 1944), p. 44; Kate Cameron, "Bing's New Picture Fine Entertainment," *New York Daily News* (October 10, 1952), p. 76; Harold Heffernan, "Film Topers Put Accent on Comedy," *Washington Evening Star* (September 7, 1952), p. E1.

27. This account of life at the Sombrero is mainly based on "Sombrero Rehearsals Continue All Week," *Arizona Republic* (February 8, 1953), p. 4. See also "Legitimate Theater Venture Is Started," *Arizona Republic* (December 19, 1948), p. 2:11.

28. Legitimate Theater Venture Is Started," p. 2:11; "Actor to Start Play Rehearsals," *Arizona Republic* (March March 21, 1949), p. 2; "Audrey Totter to Costar in Sombrero Theater Play," *Arizona Republic* (March 23, 1949), p. 13; C.M., "Sombrero Has Maddest Night with 'The Skin of Our Teeth,'" *Arizona Republic* (February 6, 1952), p. 13.

29. C.M., "'Season in the Sun Brilliant with Shining Nancy Kelly," *Arizona Republic* (February 13, 1952), p. 9.

30. "Gibbs' Play Wins Praise," *Los Angeles Times* (July 25, 1952), p. III: 6; E.M., "Film Group Attends Comedy at La Jolla," *San Diego Union* (July 23, 1952), p. A6; E.M., "Players Overshadow Vehicle at La Jolla," *San Diego Union* (July 24, 1952), p. A8.

31. J.L., "Entire Cast Pleases: Harding Gives Phoenix Treat in 'The Corn Is Green' Revival," *Arizona Republic* (February 10, 1953), p. 11.

32. Don Freeman, "'Corn Is Green' Hailed as Fine La Jolla Play," *San Diego Union* (August 13, 1952), p. A4; "Ann Harding Stars in 'The Corn Is Green,'" *Los Angeles Times* (August 14, 1952), p. III:7; Jeannette White, "Ann Harding Stars in 'Corn Is Green' Play at La Jolla Playhouse," *Escondido Times-Advocate* (August 13, 1952), p. 3; "School Blast Stops La Jolla Play Matinee," *Los Angeles Times* (August 14, 1952), p. I:23.

33. J.L., "Entire Cast Pleases," p. 11.

34. J.L., "At the Sombrero: 'Hay Fever' Provides Hilarious Evening," *Arizona Republic* (February 17, 1953), p. 13; Edwin Schallert, "Sombrero Maintaining High Quality Theater," *Los Angeles Times* (February 20, 1953), p. II:7.

35. J.L., "It's About a Witch: Sombrero Players Please in 'Bell, Book and Candle," *Arizona Republic* (February 24, 1953), p. 9.

36. J.L., "End of Sombrero Season: 'Jason' Has Comedy, Drama and Message," *Arizona Republic* (March 17, 1953), p. 4.

37. "Old Stars Return," *Allentown Morning Call* (July 19, 1953), p. 17.

38. "Miriam Hopkins Is Somerset Star," *Providence Journal* (September 6, 1953), p. 2; *Hay Fever* advertisement, *Providence Journal* (September 6, 1953), p. 5.

39. Edwin Schallert, "Mason, Boyer Soon May Join 2,000 Leagues; New Process Lures Ryan," *Los Angeles Times* (January 13, 1954), p. III:5; M.W., "Season Opener at Sombrero's All Raymond's," *Arizona Republic* (January 19, 1954), p. 8.

40. H.F., "Sombrero Playhouse: 'The Women' Shows Superb Acting Here," *Arizona Republic* (January 26, 1954), p. 8; Janet Sanford, "Have You Heard?," *Arizona Republic* (January 26, 1954), p. 12; "Star's Star," *Arizona Republic* (January 26, 1954), p. 19.

41. "'Suds' to Fill Sombrero Eye," *Arizona Republic* (February 8, 1954), p. 15; Merrill Windsor, "'Suds' Brings Laughs to Sombrero Audience," *Arizona Republic* (February 9, 1954), p. 8.

42. "Hopkins in Phoenix," *Valley Times* (February 16, 1954), p. 8; "Mary Astor Here in Comedy," *Arizona Republic* (February 22, 1954), p. 16; Merrill Windsor, "Mary Astor Top Notch Star in Sombrero's 'Late Love,'" *Arizona Republic* (February 23, 1954), p. 7.

43. Maggie Wilson, "Tune In: TV Coat, Tie Battle Comfort," *Arizona Republic* (August 10, 1954), p. 16.

44. Brooks and Marsh, *The Complete Directory to Prime Time Network and Cable TV Shows*, p. 649; "Victorian Era Comedy to Star Jerome Cowan on TV Theater," *Dallas Morning News* (May 19, 1954), p. II:5; "An Actor Wins Out in TV Comedy," *Atlanta Constitution* (May 19, 1954), p. 27.

45. "What's on the Air," *Los Angeles Daily News* (July 12, 1954), p. 39; "Nina Foch Stars in 'Studio One,'" *Cleveland Plain Dealer* (July 10, 1954), p. 14; "TV Previews: Studio One Presents Nina Foch," *Pittsburgh Press* (July 12, 1954), p. 27; "Television Show Will Star Basil Rathbone," *Sacramento Bee* (August 14, 1954), p. F27; "TVKey Previews," *Hackensack Record* (August 16, 1954), p. 22.

46. "Playhouse," *Charlotte News* (July 17, 1954), p. 7A; "Lovelorn Columnist Play Hero," *Dallas Morning News* (July 18, 1954), p. VII:5; "Norway Music Festival Will Be Aired," *Richmond Times Dispatch* (July 18, 1954), p. L5.

47. "TV Previews," *Baltimore Evening Sun* (July 29, 1954), p. 34; Brooks and Marsh, *The Complete Directory to Prime Time Network and Cable TV Shows*, p. 1179. This episode is available at youtube.com.

48. Sam Zolotow, "Comedy Will Begin Run Here Tonight," *New York Times* (April 25, 1949), p. 19; John Chapman, "'Happiest Years' Frail Comedy

with Peggy Wood, June Walker," *New York Daily News* (April 26, 1949), p. 55; "6 New Plays Open Tuesday in Summer Theaters," *Chicago Daily News* (August 14, 1954), p. 12.

49. "'Miss Peepers' to Be Starred at Playhouse," *Scranton Tribune* (August 25, 1954), p. 5; *The Other Devil* advertisement, *Scranton Tribune* (August 26, 1954), p. 9.

50. Anson B. Cutts, "First Performance: Intense Drama Sombrero Fare," *Arizona Republic* (March 22, 1955), p. 14. See also "Sombrero to Give Critic Award Play," *Arizona Republic* (March 20, 1955), p. 10.

51. Anson B. Cutts, "Wife Shares Honors: New Star Shines in Final Production at Sombrero," *Arizona Republic* (March 29, 1955), p. 14; "'Liliom' to Ring Down Curtain on Sombrero Playhouse's Season," *Arizona Republic* (March 27, 1955), p. 7.

52. This account of Witherspoon's death is based on "Long-time Film and Stage Actress Succumbs at Her Residence in Las Cruces," *Las Cruces Sun-News* (November 18, 1957), p. 1; "Veteran Film Actress Dies," *San Bernardino Telegram* (November 18, 1957) (NYPL); "Deaths," *New Orleans Times-Picayune* (November 20, 1957), p. 2; "Cora Witherspoon, Actress, Dies Here" (NYPL).

53. Cora Witherspoon, Actress, 67, Is Dead; Performer 50 Years Made Bow at 15," *New York Times* (November 19, 1957), p. 33.

54. Susan Finch, "Bonnie M. Wisdom, Widow of N.O. Judge," *New Orleans Times-Picayune* (February 9, 2002), p. B4; "William B. Wisdom Funeral Services Announced," *New Orleans Times-Picayune* (March 20, 1977), p. 4.

55. "Louisiana, Orleans Parish Death Records and Certificates, 1835–1954," database, *Family Search* (https://familysearch.org/ark:/61903/1:1:-CY8Z-Q5N2: 10 April 2020), Mary H Johnston Wisdom, 1904; "Louisiana, Orleans Parish Death Records and Certificates, 1835–1954," database, *Family Search* (https://familysearch.org/ark:/61903/1:1:ZQYN-1X3Z: 23 April 2020), William Bell Wisdom, 1906; "Tennessee Deaths, 1914–1966," database with images, *Family Search* (https://familysearch.org/ark:/61903/1:1:NSF4-22B: 1 March 2021), Edward T. Shepard Jr., 27 Aug 1929; Death, Memphis, Shelby, Tennessee, United States, Tennessee State Library and Archives, Nashville.

56. "Deaths," *New Orleans Times-Picayune* (February 22, 1981), p. 24; "Death Claims Miss Tharp, 82: Retired Orleans School Teacher Succumbs," *New Orleans Times-Picayune* (October 16, 1961), p. 8.

57. "Deaths," *New Orleans Times-Picayune*, p. 2; "Deaths," *New Orleans States* (November 20, 1957), p. 4.

58. "United States Census, 1940," database with images, *Family Search* (https://www.familysearch.org/ark:/61903/1:1:VY5M-GMC: 4 January 2021), Albert Michell in household of David Pond, New Orleans, Orleans, Louisiana, United States; citing enumeration district (ED) 36–450, sheet 15A, line 39, family 302, Sixteenth Census of the

United States, 1940, NARA digital publication T627. Records of the Bureau of the Census, 1790–2007, RG 29. Washington, D.C.: National Archives and Records Administration, 2012, roll 1436; Albert Michell, "Cora Witherspoon," *New Orleans Times-Picayune* (November 25, 1957) (NYPL).

59. Business card, Frank J. Reyes & Co. (NYPL).

60. "Louisiana, New Orleans, Interment Registers, 1836–1972," database, *Family Search* (https://familysearch.org/ark:/61903/1:1:4JYP-PNN2: 4 December 2019), Cora Witherspoon, 1957; Cora Witherspoon, findagrave.com.

Bibliography

Affron, Charles. *Lillian Gish: Her Legend and Life*. Berkeley: University of California Press, 2002.

Bankhead, Tallulah. *Tallulah: My Autobiography*. New York: Harper, 1952.

Barris, Alex. *Hollywood's Other Women*. South Brunswick and New York: A.S. Barnes, 1975.

Blum, Daniel. *Great Stars of the American Stage: A Pictorial Record*. New York: Grosset and Dunlap, 1952.

Brackett, Charles. *"It's the Pictures That Got Small": Charles Brackett on Billy Wilder and Hollywood's Golden Age*. Ed. Anthony Slide. New York: Columbia University Press, 2015.

Brooks, Tim, and Earle Marsh. *The Complete Directory to Prime Time Network and Cable TV Shows 1946-Present*. New York: Ballantine, 2003.

Curtis, James. *James Whale: A New World of Gods and Monsters*. Minneapolis: University of Minnesota Press, 2003.

_____. *W.C. Fields: A Biography*. New York: Alfred A. Knopf, 2003.

Dunning, John. *On the Air: The Encyclopedia of Old-Time Radio*. New York and Oxford: Oxford University Press, 1998.

Ellenberger, Allan R. *Miriam Hopkins: Life and Films of a Hollywood Rebel*. Lexington: University Press of Kentucky, 2018.

Gill, Brendan. *Tallulah*. New York: Holt, Rinehart & Winston, 1972.

Israel, Lee. *Miss Tallulah Bankhead*. New York: G.P. Putnam, 1972.

Kaufman, George S., and Moss Hart. *Six Plays by Kaufman and Hart*. New York: Modern Library, 1942.

Kaufman, George S., et al. *Kaufman & Co.: Broadway Comedies*. New York: Library of America, 2004.

Kelly, George. *Philip Goes Forth: A Play in Three Acts*. New York: Samuel French, 1931.

Kotsilibas-Davis, James, and Myrna Loy. *Myrna Loy: Being and Becoming*. New York: Primus/Donald I. Fine, 1988.

Levy, Emanuel. *George Cukor, Master of Elegance: Hollywood's Legendary Director and His Stars*. New York: William Morrow, 1994.

Lobenthal, Joel. *Tallulah! The Life and Times of a Leading Lady*. New York: HarperCollins/Regan Books, 2004.

Los Angeles City Directory 1932. Los Angeles: Los Angeles Directory Co., 1932.

Mantle, Burns, ed. *The Best Plays of 1921-22*. New York: Dodd, Mead, 1955.

_____, ed. *The Best Plays of 1922-23*. New York: Dodd, Mead, 1938.

_____, ed. *The Best Plays of 1923-24*. Boston: Small, Maynard, 1924.

_____, ed. *The Best Plays of 1924-25*. Boston: Small, Maynard, 1925.

_____, ed. *The Best Plays of 1925-26*. New York: Dodd, Mead, 1926.

_____, ed. *The Best Plays of 1927-28*. New York: Dodd, Mead, 1937.

_____, ed. *The Best Plays of 1928-29*. New York: Dodd, Mead, 1929.

_____, ed. *The Best Plays of 1929-30*. New York: Dodd, Mead, 1969.

_____, ed. *The Best Plays of 1930-31*. New York: Dodd, Mead, 1931.

_____, ed. *The Best Plays of 1931-32*. New York: Dodd, Mead, 1932.

_____, ed. *The Best Plays of 1932-33*. New York: Dodd, Mead, 1933.

_____, ed. *The Best Plays of 1933-34*. New York: Dodd, Mead, 1935.

_____, ed. *The Best Plays of 1934-35*. New York: Dodd, Mead, 1935.

_____, ed. *The Best Plays of 1935-36*. New York: Dodd, Mead, 1936.

_____, ed. *The Best Plays of 1940-41*. New York: Dodd, Mead, 1949.

Maugham, W. Somerset. *The Collected Plays of W. Somerset Maugham, Vol. II*. London: William Heinemann, 1952.

Neibaur, James L. *The Charlie Chan Films*. Albany, GA: BearManor Media, 2018.

Ragan, David. *Who's Who in Hollywood 1900-1976*. New Rochelle, NY: Arlington House, 1977.

Riggs, Lynn. *Russet Mantle and The Cherokee Night: Two Plays by Lynn Riggs*. New York: Samuel French, 1936.

Ryley, Madeleine Lucette. *An American Citizen*. New York and London: Samuel French, 1895.

Sherwood, Robert E. *Waterloo Bridge*. New York: Charles Scribner's, 1930.

Slide, Anthony, ed. *Selected Theatre Criticism, Volume 2: 1920–1930*. Metuchen, NJ: Scarecrow Press, 1985.

Vane, Sutton. "Outward Bound." *The Best Plays of 1923–1924*. Ed. Burns Mantle. Boston: Small Maynard, 1924. 105–131.

Williams, Tennessee. *Memoirs*. Garden City, NY: Anchor Press/Doubleday, 1983.

Index

Page numbers in **bold italics** indicate pages with illustrations